Karl Polanyi

Key Contemporary Thinkers series

Karl Polanyi

The Limits of the Market

Gareth Dale

polity

First published in 2010 by Polity Press

Polity Press
65 Bridge Street
Cambridge CB2 1UR, UK

Polity Press
350 Main Street
Malden, MA 02148, USA

ISBN-13: 978-0-7456-4071-6 (hardback)
ISBN-13: 978-0-7456-4072-3 (paperback)

A catalogue record for this book is available from the British Library.

Typeset in 10.5 on 12 pt Palatino
by Toppan Best-set Premedia Limited
Printed and bound in Great Britain by MPG Books Group Limited, Bodmin, Cornwall

The publisher has used its best endeavours to ensure that the URLs for external websites referred to in this book are correct and active at the time of going to press. However, the publisher has no responsibility for the websites and can make no guarantee that a site will remain live or that the content is or will remain appropriate.

Every effort has been made to trace all copyright holders, but if any have been inadvertently overlooked the publisher will be pleased to include any necessary credits in any subsequent reprint or edition.

For further information on Polity, visit our website: www.politybooks.com

Contents

Preface

This book is a critical introduction to the work of Karl Polanyi. It
provides an exposition of his key texts and presents a range of criticisms of his principal theses. Its origins lie in my interest in Polanyi's
method. He meshes concepts from a variety of sociological and
political-economic traditions to produce his own distinctive
approach, but which ones was he appropriating and to what uses
was he putting them? As I engaged more intensively with his works
that sense of puzzlement began to recede. In its place there arose
an admiration for the depth, breadth and originality of his intellectual engagement, albeit coupled with a greater awareness of its
shortcomings in a number of areas, both empirical and theoretical.
This book, then, is written from a broadly sympathetic yet critical
standpoint.

During the first stages of my research it was at once apparent
that no full-length general introduction to Polanyi's work yet
existed. There is one useful and well-researched monograph, Ron
Stanfield's *The Economic Thought of Karl Polanyi* (1986), but as the
title indicates its focus is upon economic thought, and this, although
indubitably the centre of Polanyi's attention, was not his sole
concern. Rather than giving a critical exposition of Polanyi's ideas,
moreover, Stanfield tends to bend them towards his own neo-
Veblenian framework. In addition, his book has by now become
dated. In the intervening decades a profusion of new primary materials and secondary literature has been published, the world has
turned, and Polanyi has gained new and wider audiences. Apart
from Stanfield's, the only other monographs that even partially

occupy the terrain of this book are Allen Sievers' *Critique of Karl Polanyi's New Economics* (1949) and Gregory Baum's *Karl Polanyi on Ethics and Economics* (1996), but neither is similar in purpose or character to this book. The former is a polemical critique, not a critical introduction, and anteceded the publication of all but one of its subject's own books. The latter is an extended essay containing Polanyian meditations on theology and ethics.

In *Karl Polanyi: The Limits of the Market* I aspire to a comprehensive treatment of Polanyi's work, but for reasons of space have omitted a number of topics. These I discuss elsewhere. They include, first and foremost, his political and intellectual formation in Hungary[1] and his biography (the subject of my next book).[2] They also include certain aspects of the 'embeddedness' theorem[3] and of the research propaedeutic to the writing of *The Great Transformation* (in particular with respect to his understanding of 'regulated capitalism' and of the contradictions between democracy and capitalism),[4] as well as his sometimes ambivalent and controversial comments on welfare states, the Bretton Woods system and the social democratic tradition.[5]

In addition to Polanyi's published works, interviews with his daughter Kari Polanyi-Levitt, and the secondary literature – of which a trio of volumes from the early 1990s, edited by Polanyi-Levitt (1990), by Marguerite Mendell and Daniel Salée (1991) and by Kenneth McRobbie (1994), are the most valuable – I have relied heavily upon texts archived at the Karl Polanyi Institute of Political Economy at Concordia University. It is thanks above all to my research there that I came to recognize the inadequacies of prevailing interpretations of Polanyi's oeuvre, given that they rely for the most part upon such a limited range of his published (and mainly English-language) works. In what follows, citations that begin with numerals in the form '1-11' are of folders and files in the Polanyi archive. Wherever possible I have included the dates of documents, and where I have made repeated use of a major text from the archive I have included it in the references. Translations from German sources, published and unpublished, are my own.

Karl Polanyi was an institutionalist, and it is perhaps fitting that, when turning to thank those who have helped this book on its way, I begin with an institution. The archive of the Karl Polanyi Institute was, as already mentioned, the source of all of the unpublished materials cited as well as a good many published ones. Containing draft manuscripts, correspondence with colleagues and friends, outlines of projected books, notes, memorabilia, part of Polanyi's own library, and a cornucopia of other treasures, it is an indispensable resource – and one, moreover, that is well organized and welcoming. It is, then, to its co-founder, its administrator and its director – respectively, Kari Polanyi-Levitt, Ana Gomez and Margie Mendell – that I have incurred the greatest debts. I have also had the pleasure of attending two of the international Karl Polanyi conferences that the Institute has organized in recent years, in Istanbul and Montréal. To Kari, in addition, I express my gratitude for her willingness to sit unflaggingly through interview after interview, in Montréal and by telephone, over the course of nearly three years. Thanks are also due to Mathieu and Frédérique Denis, who helped to make my sojourns in Montréal so welcoming and enjoyable, and to Brunel University's Business School and School of Social Sciences, which financed my conference and research trips.

As regards preparation of the manuscript, my greatest debt is to three individuals who read a penultimate draft in its entirety. Chris Hann meticulously combed through chapter after chapter, commenting eruditely and with humour upon my errors, and nudging me towards improvements. Georgi Derluguian was tremendously encouraging. His remarks were incisive and useful – and provide much food for thought for my next book too. Keith Hart offered penetrating criticisms and constructive suggestions. In addition, I would like to express thanks to Costas Lapavitsas, who read and provided insightful advice on several chapters of an early draft. (Our inconclusive debate on the origins of money convinced me to leave that topic to sink beneath the Mesopotamian sands.) Margie Mendell's assiduous reading of one chapter helpfully uncovered a tangle of ambiguities while David Tandy and Mohammad Nafissi provided thoughtful comments on another. I am grateful to Dan Tompkins both for his observations on a chapter and for sharing his primary materials. In addition, Michael Hudson, Michele Cangiani, Kari Polanyi-Levitt, Tim Ingold, Johannes Renger and Keir Martin read and commented on one draft chapter each, Derek Wall checked part of the final manuscript, and Emma Hutchinson at Polity provided all the advice and support that one could possibly hope for. I wish to express my sincere thanks to them all.

Abbreviations

DST   Karl Polanyi (1966) *Dahomey and the Slave Trade: An Analysis of an Archaic Economy*, Seattle: University of Washington Press.

LOM   Karl Polanyi (1977) *The Livelihood of Man*, New York: Academic Press.

PAME   Karl Polanyi (1968) *Primitive, Archaic, and Modern Economies*, ed. George Dalton, New York: Anchor Books.

TGT   Karl Polanyi (2001) *The Great Transformation: The Political and Economic Origins of Our Time*, Boston: Beacon Press.

TMEE   Karl Polanyi, Conrad M. Arensberg and Harry W. Pearson, eds (1957) *Trade and Market in the Early Empires: Economies in History and Theory*, New York: Free Press.

To the memory of
Chris Harman
(1942–2009)

Introduction

> History has not been kind to Polanyi's prognostications. Free market capitalism is a resilient and stable system in much of the world – particularly in English-speaking countries. The gold standard is gone, but has been replaced by floating exchange rates, set by market forces. Better monetary management has greatly reduced business cycle severity. The great puzzle of Polanyi's book is thus its enduring allure, given the disconnect between his predictions and modern realities.
>
> Gregory Clark, *New York Sun*, June 2008

Stock markets are in meltdown. Trade, investment, output and employment graphs all point south. Protectionist stirrings are in the air. The prescriptions of free market liberalism are revealed as recipes for chaos. The 'smooth-tongued wizards' of 'the Market' (Kipling) – of whom the just-quoted economics professor is a fine example – lost confidence in their spells. This was the outlook as I wrote these lines in early 2009. It was also the world of the early 1930s, over which the Hungarian economic journalist Karl Polanyi was casting his critical eye.

Polanyi was a child of late nineteenth-century liberalism. It was a civilization that, his friend G. D. H. Cole recalled, seemed to rest upon strong foundations, in contrast to the inter-war order, which 'threatens to tumble at any moment in ruins about our ears'.[1] Over the course of the turbulent 1930s Polanyi grappled with the causes of the crisis, developing a distinctive position that was presented in his masterwork, *The Great Transformation* (hereafter, TGT). It was a crisis, he argued, that should not be construed as occurring in disconnected stages – world war, Great Depression, world war – for these were all symptoms of a deeper malaise, a civilizational breakdown, no less. Tracing the genesis of the collapse, he located its origin in the rise of free market capitalism; in this sense liberal civilization had sown the seeds of its own destruction. Market society had generated two sorts of pathologies that could not be remedied by its own mechanisms. One may be described as 'social diremption', by which I refer to the separation of state and market that, in the age of universal suffrage, becomes converted into an irreconcilable antagonism between political democracy and business oligarchy. The other may be dubbed 'ethical fragmentation'. Liberalism had created an ethically impoverished society, thanks to its creation of an environment in which human beings can only act effectively if they are rational egotists – the *Homo oeconomicus* model of man.

It is a critical diagnosis but the prognosis is not gloomy. Economic liberalism, Polanyi shows, was a utopian experiment and as such was bound to founder. Unlike any previous economic system the market economy, as it emerged in nineteenth-century Britain, stood out in that its functioning depended upon the commodification of land, labour and money. Turning such crucial components of the substance of life and nature over to the calculus of purchase and sale produced such corrosive tendencies that spontaneous reactions of 'social protection' were inevitable. Polanyi traces the 'disruptive strains' that ensue, which culminated in fascism and two world wars – during the last of which he wrote TGT. Yet despite being written at this darkest of times there is an implicit optimism: that a 'protective' society will win through in the end.

Karl Polanyi for the neoliberal age

For many years it has been apparent that Polanyi's ideas resonate. They speak to the condition of neoliberal globalization in an idiom that for the most part sounds remarkably familiar today – as in his proposition, within a discussion of the nineteenth-century world economy, that 'with free trade the new and tremendous hazards of planetary interdependence sprang into being'.[2] There is no shortage of literature that draws on his work to warn that 'market fundamentalism', in the words of his compatriot and fellow émigré George Soros, poses an existential threat to the 'open society',[3] or, in the more urgent idiom of William Greider, that so long as neoliberal dogma reigns unchallenged the 'manic logic' of globalization 'will continue to hurtle forward, fatefully out of control'.[4] The notion of a countermovement by society in response to the effects of the unregulated market system, one recent contribution avers,

> is an inspired perspective to focus on globalisation, its discontents and the counter-movements it generates. . . . Neo-liberal globalisation – as Polanyi showed so eloquently for a previous wave – dissolves social bonds and society resists.[5]

Neoliberals and the far right apart, Polanyi attracts interest from all points of the political compass, with particular appeal to critics of globalization (for whom he has become 'a kind of patron saint', in the words of a senior fellow at the Cato Institute).[6] 'It often seems as if Polanyi is speaking directly to present-day issues', remarks Joseph Stiglitz in the Foreword to the most recent edition of TGT, adding that Polanyi's arguments and concerns are consonant in particular 'with the issues raised by the rioters and marchers who took to the streets in Seattle and Prague in 1999 and 2000 to oppose the international financial institutions'.[7] Those arguments include first and foremost a radical critique of the neoliberal utopia. 'To allow the market mechanism to be sole director of the fate of human beings and their natural environment', Polanyi blazes,

> would result in the demolition of society. For the alleged commodity 'labour power' cannot be shoved about, used indiscriminately, or even left unused, without affecting also the human individual who happens to be the bearer of this peculiar commodity. . . . Robbed of the protective covering of cultural institutions, human beings would perish from the effects of social exposure; they would die as the victims of acute social dislocation. . . . Nature would be reduced to its elements, neighbourhoods and landscapes defiled, rivers polluted, military safety jeopardized, the power to produce food and raw materials destroyed.[8]

On some 'alterglobalization' protests placards insisting 'We live in a Society, not an Economy' have appeared – a message that Polanyi would have endorsed wholeheartedly. The various segments of the alterglobalization (a.k.a. 'global justice') movement may identify different structures as the underlying evil (globalization, capitalism or industrialism) but they unite in opposition to neoliberalism, the updated edition of Polanyi's nemesis, which was the classical liberalism of Ricardo, Spencer and Hayek. More speculatively, I would venture that Polanyi's 'double movement' thesis, which I elucidate in chapter 2, may exert an appeal to the collective unconscious of the left as a whole, inverting as it does the familiar right-wing indictment against socialism: that it represents a utopian exercise in social engineering, inhuman in its suppression of catallactic spontaneity. With Polanyi the tables are turned. In his schema economic liberals are the utopian extremists while their opponents express a 'spontaneous reaction of social protection'. After the publication of TGT any university course on 'political extremism' that failed to include neoliberalism in its curriculum would be sadly lacking in credibility.

Polanyi's work evidently appeals to alterglobalization activists and socialists, but its appeal extends also to greens, social democrats and social conservatives. Within the latter group, one of his greatest admirers is the former Margaret Thatcher advisor John Gray, whose *False Dawn: The Delusions of Global Capitalism* settles accounts with her programme, in a blast against the economic dislocation, social chaos and political instability that it has spawned. Also deserving of mention are Jonathon Porritt, former co-chair of the Green Party and advisor to the governments of Tony Blair and Gordon Brown,[9] and David Marquand, a founder member of Britain's Social Democratic Party. In the 1990s Marquand suggested that Polanyi's work spoke 'even more loudly' to that decade than it had to the 1940s, both in terms of the potential for a progressive response to neoliberalism and in the form of a reactionary countermovement – which for Marquand would be likely to take the form of a 'fundamentalist tribalism', as exemplified by Bosnian Serbs, Tory MP Michael Portillo, Jean-Marie Le Pen, Chechen separatists, Silvio Berlusconi and Pat Buchanan.[10]

Alongside the appeal of his ideas to activists and the wider penumbra of critics of neoliberalism, Polanyi's influence is most strongly felt within the academy. Although in the first two decades after his death in 1964 he was known primarily to anthropologists, since then his influence has branched out across the social sciences. In social theory, for example, one may note that Jürgen Habermas' thesis of the 'uncoupling of system and lifeworld', as expounded in his *Theory of Communicative Action*, owes a good deal to Polanyi, while economic sociologists and moral philosophers have acknowledged their debts to his research into the 'embedding' of economic life in social systems. From the field of political ecology has flowed a steady stream of texts that take their cue from Polanyi in developing a critique of how industrial society came 'to understand nature in economic categories and subordinated the surface of the planet to the needs of accumulation'.[11] Arguably the most prominent of this group is the Christian environmental economist Herman Daly, who cites Polanyi in support of his case that a sustainable 'economics for community', while allowing markets a significant role, could not tolerate the commodification of labour and land in the model of 'One Big Market'.[12]

In economics 'proper', Polanyi's name, where known at all, is often reviled. Many heterodox economists, however, would agree with Joseph Stiglitz when he opines that 'Economic science and economic history have come to recognize the validity of Polanyi's key contentions' (although one wonders whether Polanyi himself would recognize this accolade; he did after all wish his magnum opus to be entitled combatively *Freedom From Economics*).[13] Institutionalist economists, moreover, tend to look more kindly upon Polanyi, not least in the burgeoning literatures on 'varieties of capitalism' and comparative social policy,[14] while in international political economy his work is renowned. John Ruggie's notion of 'embedded liberalism', referring to the postwar compromise whereby a liberal international trade regime was constructed to include a normative commitment to interventionist governmental action at the domestic level, owes much to Polanyi.[15] In addition, one could point to the Régulation School, at least two of the founders of which are avowedly Polanyian,[16] as well as the world-systems school, established by his friends Terry Hopkins and Immanuel Wallerstein. (Polanyi has even been described as 'the most influential forerunner of "world-system" analysis' – although Braudel and Marx would have legitimate grounds to dispute that crown.[17])

Individual responsibility and the quest for community

As we shall see in the pages to come, there are a great many paradoxes and debates concerning the intellectual and political currents for which Polanyi is claimed, as well as over the meaning and applicability of his concepts and theses. Key terms such as 'market economy' have been interpreted in wildly divergent ways. The discussion in TGT of the role played by states in capitalist society has been taken as an argument for their potential to rescue capitalism from itself and to usher in its destruction, while its axial concept, the 'double movement', can be viewed as a metaphor both for class struggle and for class reconciliation.

There are several reasons why Polanyi's writings are subject to such varying interpretations. In part it is the normal consequence of representing a thinker in the singular, when his political views and social-scientific postulates alter over time. Although fairly consistent in his views over his lifetime, his approach to some issues did alter – there is, for example, no certified Polanyian position on questions of economic determinism or social evolution. Another factor, as we shall see, consists in his proclivity to balance between quite different, even antithetical traditions. He has, for example, been categorized as a Marxist, a liberal and a Romantic, and within anthropology alone he has attracted the labels empiricist, institutionalist and functionalist.[18] These difficulties in comprehending his *Weltanschauung* are compounded by the fact that his views were formed in a political and intellectual environment, early twentieth-century Central Europe, that is *terra incognita* to many of those who cite his work.

In conceiving this book I encountered a dilemma. A fully developed account of Karl Polanyi's work requires a close look at his life, including the socioeconomic environment and the political and geopolitical conflicts that impacted upon him, not to mention the intellectual traditions that excited his interest and the 'context of refutation' that he encountered – the prevailing theories that provoked his critical inquiry, the arguments he rebutted and the positions he sought to challenge. So turbulent were the times that he lived through, however, and so extraordinary that 'Great Generation' of Jewish Budapest intellectuals to which he belonged, that these cannot possibly be given the space they deserve within the confines of this book. I have therefore engaged in detail with his life and times in separate studies.[19] That said, a brief conspectus of his life and times, with particular focus upon his political, spiritual and intellectual formation, is indispensable.

The basic facts are well known. Born in 1886 into a bourgeois Jewish family, Polanyi passed his childhood and youth in Hungary during a tumultuous era, one that included rapid industrialization in the 1890s, political polarization in the 1900s, and war, followed by the 'Aster Revolution' of October 1918 and the Soviet Republic of early 1919. When a teenager, he joined a Socialist Students society, and was active at Budapest University in resisting a movement of anti-Semitic conservatives, a physical clash with whom led to his expulsion. Rather than allow the energy of their campaign to dissipate, Polanyi and his friends took the opportunity to found the 'Galilei Circle', an organization dedicated to moral regeneration and education – 'To learn and to teach' was its motto. From 1913 he was co-editor of the Galileists' fortnightly periodical *Szabadgon-dolat* ('Free Thought'), and in 1914 was elected general secretary of the newly founded National Radical Bourgeois Party. Injured in war, he was unable to play an active part either in the Aster Revolution, which he supported wholeheartedly, or in the Soviet Republic, which he regarded with ambivalence.

Following a brief flirtation with Second International Marxism, in the later 1900s Polanyi had gravitated towards a political current known as Liberal Socialism, associated with the Fabians, 'revisionist' Marxists such as Eduard Bernstein, and the sociologist Franz Oppenheimer. By socialism these thinkers understood a movement with an idealistic logic centred upon the ethic of solidarity, coupled to a deterministic drive: the tendency to socialization of the major means of production. The collectivist society that was coming into being, Polanyi firmly believed, would render liberal individualism antiquated. No longer concentrated in the hands of individual owners, capital was becoming ever less personal, management ever more bureaucratic, and in society at large personality was losing its centrality: in future, people would be valued less for their individuality than for their sociality. As a result of these trends, he ventured in 1909, '*in the coming period of a stable capitalism the ruling ideology will be socialist*'.[20]

Despite his own socialist mores, Polanyi was uncomfortable with this forecast, for reasons of substance and of method. Substantively, his concern was that the shift towards socialism involved a deception: the middle classes were wresting the movement back from the working classes – rather as the Roman Empire, by adopting Christianity, had taken over and defanged the religion of the rebellious slaves. In order to guide their struggle against 'a capitalist society which [was] becoming more and more socialist itself', some of pre-war Europe's rebellious slaves were turning instead to syndicalism – a movement with which he had more than a little sympathy. The methodological question concerned the scientific reasoning behind the prognosis. The model of human behaviour offered by deterministic positivism posed problems for Polanyi's most cherished tenet, individual responsibility. Could developments of such *ethical* import really be attributed to *socioeconomic* developments? This problem reflects a conflict with which he wrestled throughout his life, that between the ethic of individual responsibility and 'the reality of society'. It is a familiar dilemma, an impressively sophisticated and simplifying account of which has been given by Martin

Hollis, in his *Models of Man*. Are human beings best conceived of as 'Plastic Man': life-forms that develop through adaptive responses to their environment? If so, they are subject to scrutiny by scientific method, but where then lies the space for the exercise of individual ethical choice? Or are they better conceived as 'Autonomous Man': sovereign possessors of free will who are in themselves the explanation of their own actions? This model acknowledges ethical freedom but treats the individual as a black box, its actions amenable to hermeneutic interpretation but not to scientific analysis.[21]

It was a conflict with both intellectual and political aspects, and throughout his life Polanyi's philosophical and political reflections revolved around puzzles concerning the role of the individual in 'complex society', and how to steer political engagement between the rocks of determinism and voluntarism. Rational scientific analysis, he believed, demonstrated that society was destined to become more collectivist, yet ethically he was an individualist, championing the notion of individual responsibility and aspiring to live virtuously. The essence of moral life, he maintained, is the acceptance of individual responsibility; in Gregory Baum's description, he 'greatly treasured the emergence of the "bourgeois" or "civil" conscience, that is, the autonomous conscience of the person who recognizes himself or herself as a responsible agent'.[22]

The paradox involved in ethical individualists espousing positivist determinism was gleefully seized upon by clerical conservatives. Not only did they advance the stock argument that the denial of traditional religious beliefs begets moral degeneration, they also accused the Budapest radicals of inconsistency. How could they see ethical principles as merely the reflex of economic conditions, yet simultaneously demand that society prioritize a particular set of ethics centred on social justice and, moreover, that social movements rally behind liberal and/or socialist platforms?

To the charge of the Christian conservatives that the radicals and socialists were undermining what Hungarians called 'religious ethics' Polanyi replied in kind. It was *their* belief system that undermined morality. Centred upon supernatural intervention in the natural order, it lessened our sense of responsibility for our own actions – and it is the acceptance of responsibility, of 'man's self-determination', that constitutes the essence of true belief.[23] Moreover, 'religious ethics' destroys the bases of a truly ethical life: moral community and moral freedom. It undermines the former by sanctifying and exacerbating the antagonisms between nationalities and classes, and it repudiates moral freedom by permitting men to choose between good and evil without allowing them to decide *what* is good and *what* is evil – the issue is simply referred to authority or tradition. 'The trouble with religious ethics', Polanyi concluded, 'is not that it is religious, but that it is not ethical.'[24]

Yet his attitude to Christianity *per se* was far from hostile. Even when writing those words (in 1911), Tolstoy was an intellectual enthusiasm, and Polanyi had come to appreciate the 'socialist flavour' of New Testament revelation.[25] Like Tolstoy, he neither became an observant Christian, nor believed in the divinity or the resurrection of Jesus, but did perceive religion to be an indispensable social construction. Defined broadly as a total conception of the universe and man's place within it such as to warrant the belief that life itself has meaning, religion furnishes a framework essential to the individual's sense of moral purpose.

Polanyi's understanding of Christianity was decidedly unorthodox. It is a religion that, it is conventionally assumed, departed from the Hellenic view of man as citizen, adapted to life in the polis, in favour of a concentration upon living in communion with God. If the Greeks emphasized the polis as the arena in which virtue was practised, Christians see virtue as submission to divine will. Put in these terms, Polanyi reads Christianity through a Hellenic prism. For him, its vital function is to unify individuality and sociality, creating a community of morally responsible persons; using Tönniesian terms he describes it as a movement devoted to converting *Gesellschaft* into *Gemeinschaft*.[26] Although the weight placed upon Christian themes varied greatly throughout his life, Polanyi's conception of man, although fundamentally Aristotelian, never lost its theological bent. With Aristotle and Marx he defines man as a social creature, but whereas for Marx man's sociality evolves out of human interaction with nature through social labour, Polanyi privileges the creation of moral community, a human capacity that achieves its highest form in religious myth. The importance of religion lies not in its supernatural cosmology but in the broaching of eschatological questions and above all in the creation of spiritual connectedness and ethical community.

Some systemically satanic features of capitalism

In 1919 Polanyi moved to Vienna, in whose radical political culture he felt thoroughly at home. The city was, as has often been noted, a laboratory of modernity in which the question of the nature of democracy and its interaction with capitalism took centre stage. 'There was a real sense of the trade unions, the working class, being involved in political decision making', as Kari Polanyi-Levitt describes it. 'When you think of my father with his bourgeois background, theories of the working class as vanguard had only seemed hot air, until that living reality of Vienna, with its May Day parades – a demonstration of pride which saw the whole city draped in red.'[27] Polanyi developed an admiration for the achievements of Social Democracy in Vienna that was unreserved. In the process, he drew closer to the Marxism of its leading intellectuals, notably Otto Bauer, and engaged in a thoroughgoing re-evaluation of Marxism, which – together with academic sociology – he had previously castigated as positivist and deterministic.

In the following two decades he wrote a series of essays that drew heavily upon Marx's philosophy and anthropology, exploring the ethical implications of Marx's theories of alienation and commodity fetishism in a manner not unlike that of his childhood friend Georg Lukacs in *History and Class Consciousness*. One of these essays, 'Community and Society', advances the argument that the market economy negates authentic individual responsibility, undermines community, and systematically obstructs moral behaviour. Where for Bernard Mandeville the market system mischievously but magically converts private vice into public virtue, for Polanyi the alchemy is demonic, transmuting private virtue into public vice. The essay is a powerful tract, and characteristic of his output in the inter-war period; as such, an excerpt warrants reproduction.

The market acts like an invisible boundary isolating all individuals in their day-to-day activities, as producers and consumers. They produce for the market, they are supplied from the market. Beyond it they cannot reach, however eagerly they may wish to serve their fellows. Any attempt to be helpful on their part is instantly frustrated by the market mechanism. Giving your goods away at less than the market price will benefit somebody for a short time, but it would also drive your neighbour out of business, and finally ruin your own, with consequent losses of employment for those dependent on your factory or enterprise. Doing more than your due as a working man will make the conditions of work for your comrades worse. By refusing to spend on luxuries you will be throwing some people out of work, by refusing to save you will be doing the same to others. As long as you follow the rules of the market, buying at the lowest and selling at the highest price whatever you happen to be dealing in, you are comparatively safe. The damage you are doing to your fellows in order to serve your own interest is, then, unavoidable. The more completely, therefore, one discards the idea of serving one's fellows, the more successfully one can reduce one's responsibility for harm done to others. Under such a system, human beings are not allowed to be good, even though they may wish to be so.[28]

Another essay from the inter-war period, 'On Liberty', identifies and attempts to resolve the dilemmas of liberal moral philosophy, as well as presenting Marxian reflections on the domination of society by market forces. In a market society, Polanyi argues,

> it is not human will but prices that determine the purposes of labour, and not human will but the interest rate that commands capital. . . . Capitalists, workers, and indeed people in general, appear as mere extras on the economic stage. The only real and functioning objective facts of society are competition, capital, interest, prices and so forth; here, human free will is but a mirage, a fantasy. . . . Like bedazzled slaves we read our fate from market prices which are, ultimately, nothing but an emanation of our own selves, alienated from our consciousness.[29]

In chapter 1 I discuss this essay in detail, as well as Polanyi's other writings dealing with the theme of individual morality in an alienated social system.

Although Polanyi's critique of capitalism was trenchant, rarely in his life did he engage in organized political activity. However, in Vienna, and later in Britain, he did attach himself to the Christian socialist movement. Christianity and socialism, he believed, were not only complementary movements but positively required symbiosis. The similarities between the economic and social form of early Christian and communist societies are well known, he pointed out, but his specific interest lay in the congruence between the moral and spiritual questions that the two traditions pose.[30] Common to both was a belief in the unique worth of each individual as it is realized through communal life. Only socialism could secure for the human personality its unique, God-given value.[31] Conversely, something greater was required for human liberation than simply a classless society: new cultures and new forms of social behaviour, which, he proposed, should follow the contours 'of a Christian-spirited guild life'.[32] This theme is explored in greater detail in chapter 1, which also provides an overview of a selection of Polanyi's economic and philosophical writings from the inter-war period.

Turning to the practical question of how alienation could be overcome and social unity established, the simple and abstract answer was socialism, but what would this entail in practice? Criticizing the market economy was one thing, but what could be offered in its place? Capitalism patently lacked an adequate economic mechanism for enabling the needs of people qua conscious members of society (as opposed to individual consumers) to be expressed, but how could such a system be designed? These are rarely pressing practical questions for socialists, but with the Bolsheviks in charge in Russia and Social Democracy in Vienna this was no ordinary historical conjuncture.

It was in Vienna that many of the contributions to the famous 'accounting debate' over the feasibility of socialist economy were written, including two by Polanyi himself. His was a unique approach, offering a critique both of central planning and of classical liberalism, and sympathetic to the 'socialist practitioners' Otto Bauer, Lenin and G. D. H. Cole but not to the 'dogmaticians' Karl Kautsky, Trotsky and Otto Neurath.[33] It was based, he later summarized, upon:

> functional premises (which I borrowed from G. D. H. Cole's *Guild Socialism*); equilibrium economics (mainly from Schumpeter, *Das Wesen und der Hauptinhalt der theoretischen Nationalökonomie*); ethical and humanitarian socialism (which was my main postulate).[34]

Polanyi reworks these three elements around a pivotal concept, *Übersicht*. Normally translated as 'overview' or 'oversight',[35] in his usage it means the taking stock of, or insight into, human needs and the availability of resources, and the possibility of making economic decisions which take both into consideration.[36] It is not entirely unrelated to, but is far from being a synonym of, the present-day use of the term 'oversight', with its sense of the regulation of business combined with greater transparency.[37] Because the fundamental premise of socialism is the conscious and responsible control of the economic process by the workers themselves, Polanyi argues, its viability depends upon the creation of oversight within economic relations.[38] In chapter 1 I present a précis of his case.

At first sight it may appear strange that Polanyi was strongly influenced by Marxism even while his schema for a socialist economy drew heavily upon an antithetical current: Schumpeterian marginalism. This raises the question of how best to characterize his economic thought. Was it Marxist, or marginalist? The short answer is 'neither' (or 'both'), but there is more to it than that. Let me explain, by way of a brief excursus on the landscape of economic theory that obtained in Central Europe at the time.

There were three major schools of thought. One, marginalism, embodied a benign set of assumptions concerning market behaviour: that the system functions in a way that is beneficent, even if the motives underlying individual actions may not be; that capitalist institutions are practical devices that enable individuals to pursue their interests as perfectly as is possible in a flawed world; that free markets enable the formation of efficient distribution equilibria, with market clearing taken as a given; and that profits derive from property ownership and entrepreneurial skill. The second, Marxism, had no truck with marginalism's equilibrium assumption. Behind that, the economist Henryk Grossman argued, lay 'the need to justify the existing social order as a "reasonable," "self-regulating" mechanism'. Indeed, the term 'self-regulating market' itself was explicitly intended to direct attention away from 'the actually prevailing chaos' thrown up by capitalism's recurrent crises, and the injustice and arbitrariness of the distribution of wealth.[39] For Marxists, in contrast, the market system is based upon a class relationship, and generates tendencies both towards polarization between property owners and the proletariat and towards economic crisis. At their root is the contradiction between the use value and exchange value of commodities, which translates in Marx's crisis theory into a contradiction between the tendency towards the absolute development of the productive forces without regard to exchange value and the imperative of preserving existing exchange value. The revolutionizing of the productive forces thus generates conditions that are inconsistent with the further self-expansion of capital, a tension that is manifested in overaccumulation crises. Crises, in this perspective, are conceived of not as an abnormal disequilibrium irrupting into a normal state of equilibrium; rather, they 'are always but momentary forcible solutions of the existing contradictions, violent eruptions which act to restore the disrupted equilibrium'.[40] Such a system can emphatically not be described in terms of social harmony or economic stability.

The third branch of economic theory in Polanyi's youth, Germany's 'Historical School', is less well known today. Its pioneering figures were Friedrich List and Gustav Schmoller, with followers that included Eugen Dühring, and sociological outriders such as

Ferdinand Tönnies. Whereas for Marxism socioeconomic harmony is impossible in capitalism, and for marginalism it derives from the operation of the 'self-regulating market', for the historicists it may be fashioned under any mode of production, but this requires the conscious design of economic and social institutions. Against the marginalist perception of the growth of markets as a natural phenomenon, List, Schmoller and company stressed their historical specificity, and insisted upon the centrality of the state in organizing markets. Unlike marginalists, they were troubled by the threat to social cohesion that free markets posed, warned of the 'casino speculation mentality' that it spawned, and advocated welfare measures, state regulation of the economy and a humanistic educational policy.[41] In this way the state would be able to translate the normative premises of social justice into a new institutional framework in order to recreate community, resolving the conflict between the 'fourth estate' (workers) and the other classes such that the former can be 'reintegrated harmoniously into the social and political organism'.[42]

Needless to say, the three schools of thought were not exclusive; there existed numerous individuals who combined elements from two or more. Max Weber, famously, carved out a space between marginalism and historicism, coupling the methodological individualism of the former with the latter's critique of universal economic laws. Some historicists adopted marginalism's subjective-psychological theory of value. There were also the 'neo-harmonist' Marxists, such as Karl Kautsky, Otto Bauer and Rudolf Hilferding, so called because they believed that state action could potentially eliminate economic crises, given that these were understood to be the outcome of disproportions between economic sectors.[43] Some thinkers were able to pitch their tent in all three camps. Werner Sombart was one such, Eduard Bernstein another – he was heavily influenced both by Marx and by Dühring, but preferred marginalist value theory to either Ricardo's 'natural' labour value theory or Marx's 'social' emendation thereof. This was Polanyi's position too. Despite espousing the marginalist theory of value he shared much of the Marxist and historicist critique of marginalism: that the quest for a formal, rule-governed economic theory was a futile enterprise, that the economy is determined not by given and unchanging natural laws but by social norms and conventions that are malleable over time, and that economic analysis begins with institutions and must be grounded in empirical inquiries that draw upon anthropology, statistics or history.

From civilizational breakdown to neoliberalism

If Polanyi had ceased writing in 1933, when he was forced into exile for a second time – this time to Britain – his work would be remembered as little more than a footnote to the socialist accounting debate. But in the 1930s he found his metier, and the tools he required to master it. The subject was the collapse of nineteenth-century liberal civilization and the 'great transformation' to a new social order. The tools arrived through his engagement, while an instructor with the Workers' Educational Association, with economic and social history.

With hindsight, he himself was aware that a sharp change had occurred. 'From 1909 to 1935 I achieved nothing' was his (characteristically hyperbolic) assessment. 'I strained my powers in the futile directions of stark idealism, its soarings lost in the void.'[44] 'What can he possibly have meant by this?', I asked Kari Polanyi-Levitt. By 'stark idealism', she replied,

> I think he is referring to his work on the socialist accountancy debate – it involved building an ideal model. He never seemed to resolve the problem that he was working on, but slithered around between neoclassical ideas and Keynesian theory, never quite getting to the bottom of it all. But then in England he turned to economic and social history. In this he discovered a more positive way of addressing the problem of the market, and one that he, with his skills as a historian and his ability to open the scope of economic history to include anthropology, was well adapted to. This no longer involved imagining a model of an ideal economy but actual concrete research.[45]

The breakthrough work was *The Great Transformation*, which I discuss in detail in chapter 2. It is in TGT that Polanyi introduces the concepts for which he became known: the 'double movement' of marketization and societal countermovement, 'fictitious commodities', and 'embeddedness', a metaphor (denoting a state of dependence upon or subordination to) that refers to the relationship between 'economy' and 'society'. In essence, its argument is that the pathological developments through which Polanyi's generation was living – the First World War, the rise of fascism, the Great Depression, world-market implosion, and an arms race that pointed towards renewed world war – were not disconnected events but manifestations of an underlying problem, the disruption of social unity, which was rooted in the rise of 'market society'. The origins of the 'cataclysm', as Polanyi put it, 'lay in the utopian endeavor of economic liberalism to set up a self-regulating market system'.[46] Such is the destructive impact upon human beings and the environment that a reaction against the market economy is inevitable, giving rise to state economic intervention, but this undermines the vitality of the market itself. As a result, regulated capitalism is an unstable formation that was doomed to collapse.

Polanyi scholars have been unable to agree on whether or not the prediction that resulted from this diagnosis, that the great transformation away from market liberalism was set to continue, was borne out by subsequent events. A literal reading of TGT reveals the prediction that because regulated capitalism is inherently unstable its replacement by socialism or fascism was inevitable. That this did not come to pass has stimulated debate upon how to interpret the postwar epoch in Polanyian terms. For some, it was characterized not by a self-regulating market system but by 'embedded liberalism', with governments able to play a muscular role in mediating between the national and international economy. This, some maintain, lies within the bounds of Polanyi's forecast. Still others maintain that the civilizational crisis with which Polanyi was concerned was of capitalism, and not merely of its liberal form, and even the regulated capitalism of the postwar 'golden age' could not succeed in overcoming the cultural contradictions between habitat and improvement, society and economy.

It is perhaps unfortunate that Polanyi himself did not tackle this subject head on during the years between the end of the war and his death in 1964. He remained, however, as intellectually active as ever, and prolific too, producing a string of essays, a monograph and a book manuscript. He devoted his energies to developing a universal, comparative and non-ethnocentric 'general economic history': a framework capable of making sense of modes of economic organization even where systems of interconnected price-making markets are absent. At Columbia University, where he was based from 1947, Polanyi and his collaborators designed a research programme in comparative economic history, examining the nature of markets, trade and money in 'primitive' and archaic societies. In the process they invented a range of new concepts, including the 'substantive economy' and 'forms of integration', that would enable the various species of economy that have existed throughout history to be classified, analysed and understood. I introduce these concepts, as well as the debates within economic anthropology that they stimulated, in chapter 3.

In following the argument of Polanyi and his co-thinkers it is vital to distinguish between the various meanings of 'market'. The term can mean simply the process of agreeing a commercial contract, or a market *place* – the location where people meet for the purpose of transferring goods. It is sometimes used broadly to indicate economic exchange motivated by individual gain or, at the limit, any situation in which people compete over scarce resources. But its other meanings also include: an aggregation of such sites into a system, involving repeated exchanges of commodities; a mechanism that determines the production and distribution of resources through supply–demand feedback (which Polanyi refers to as 'a price-making market system'); and an institution that co-ordinates *ex post* the strategies of multiple traders whereby each is independent, but all are interrelated through their contributions to the process of price formation upon which the behaviour of each depends.[47] Polanyi is careful to avoid mistaking the presence of a market place for the existence of a competitive mechanism of the supply–demand type; to assume so, he argues, is to make a category error. Whereas the former is in the reach of the archaeologist,

> a market mechanism is beyond the most nimble spade. While it may be comparatively easy to locate an open space where, sometime in the past, crowds were wont to meet and exchange goods, it is much less easy to ascertain whether, as a result of their behaviour, exchange rates were fluctuating and, if so, whether the supply of goods offered was changing in response to the . . . up or down movement of those rates.[48]

Economic historians, he adds, should beware of surmising the presence of markets from cultural traits such as gambling, meticulous accountancy, display of gainful motives or vigorous competition. These may play a vital part in the social life of many 'primitive' and archaic communities but their presence is no proof of the existence of functioning markets.[49]

In developing this case, Polanyi researched the economic history of a variety of 'archaic' empires, taking as his paradigm examples Mesopotamia, ancient Greece and Dahomey. In each case, the focus is upon the institutionalization of trade, markets and money. The thrust of his argument is that although many archaic empires were characterized by a complex division of labour (at least in the towns), developed trading networks, money dealing, as well as forms of banking, discounting and arbitrage, money, markets and trade were institutionalized separately from each other, and this explains the fundamental rift between them and the modern market system. In chapter 4 I chart the course of his research in this area and evaluate the criticisms that have been levelled against it.

If the focus of the first four chapters is on Polanyi's output, with only limited discussion of subsequent interpretations, in chapters 5 and 6 that ratio is reversed. These closing chapters survey the ways in which his work has been used since his death, taking as their themes the two concepts for which he is best known: embeddedness and the double movement. The first of these has been used primarily within sociology. (Indeed, one survey of recent literature in economic sociology finds Polanyi to be the most frequently cited author after Weber, Marx and Durkheim.[50]) What exactly, I ask in chapter 5, does embeddedness mean? How should it be used? And how does it relate to previous conceptualizations of the relationship between economy and society? The chapter explores these questions, as well as the term's family resemblances to concepts developed by Marx, Tönnies and Weber, and the rather different interpretations offered by late twentieth-century sociologists.

Bringing the narrative up to the present day, the final chapter inquires into the origins and nature of the neoliberal ascendancy and the potential for its demise. The chapter reviews Polanyian accounts of the rise of neoliberalism, and surveys the uses to which the double movement concept has been put over the last two decades. Following an analysis of the strengths and weaknesses of the 'pendular' refunctioning of Polanyi's thesis, the chapter closes by asking whether the current global economic crisis signals a swing of the pendulum from the market-fundamentalist extreme back towards a form of socially co-ordinated capitalism.

1

The economics and ethics of socialism

Every form of Socialism is based on the hope of mankind to attain to a form of social being in which people would normally, in their everyday existence, realize their responsibilities to their fellows, because they would know how their commissions and omissions affect them and they would be able to act accordingly.

Karl Polanyi[1]

Humanity will only achieve freedom when it knows what its ideals cost.

Karl Polanyi[2]

Karl Polanyi's best-known works were all published in or after the 1940s, but the ideas that found fruition in TGT and later works had begun to germinate in the inter-war period. During these decades he produced numerous articles both as an economic journalist for the *Österreichische Volkswirt* – a periodical that, its sympathy for social democracy apart, resembled the London *Economist* – and in an unpaid capacity as an educator and essayist. Although the volume and range of his output are too great to be summarized in this chapter, I have winnowed out three contributions of particular importance: his intervention in the 'socialist accounting' debate, his philosophical writings on ethics in capitalist society, and his promotion of Christian socialism.

Responsibility and 'overview': the socialist accounting debate

The roots of the socialist accounting debate lay in contemporaneous developments in economic theory and practice. The first refers to Vilfredo Pareto's equilibrium economics, which established the possibility of maximizing utility in a socialist system. As expounded by his student Enrico Barone, general equilibrium, being the solution of a set of simultaneous equations whereby prices bring supply and demand into equilibrium, is at least hypothetically open to realization by socialist or statist administrators. By setting prices at the cost of production and minimizing those costs, these administrators can achieve a degree of approximation to Pareto optimality – meaning that no individual can become better off except at another's cost – similar to that of free markets. The case was taken further by a school of Paretian socialists who demonstrated that a state-run economy could match the efficiency of a market economy if administrators instituted a market-style price system.[3]

In economic *practice* the new departure was the command exerted by European states over economic life during the First World War. Governments actively intervened in the control of labour, organized the supply of raw materials and foodstuffs, ordered factories to produce certain goods, took direct command of strategic sectors such as coal, railways and arms, and nationalized private firms. Socialists, such as the Viennese philosopher and economist Otto Neurath, observed that the war economies achieved impressive results, and efficient economic calculation was demonstrably achieved in the absence of market-determined prices. Liberated from the constraints of profit-seeking, production could be maximized, full employment maintained and the business cycle kept in check. If this worked in wartime, could similar methods not also be applied under collective control in a postwar order? In 1919 Neurath published a case for a non-monetized, centrally planned economy, and the 'accounting debate' began.

The first response to Neurath was penned in 1920 by the liberal economist Ludwig von Mises. Central economic planning, he contends, is unfeasible, for 'where there is no free market, there is no pricing mechanism; without a pricing mechanism, there is no economic calculation'.[4] In a market economy it is prices that provide economic actors with the information necessary to calculate the most profitable employment of the resources at their command, even as relationships between supply and demand continuously fluctuate. In this way the infinitely complex and ever-changing pattern of final demand is organized by the invisible hand of the market, which informs and co-ordinates market actors' calculations. In the course of market competition entrepreneurs advance rival projects in a trial-and-error game, with the efficient winners rewarded and the losers punished. Competition thus serves to bring prices closer to marginal costs. In this a crucial task falls to financial capital. If resources are to be allocated efficiently in an ever-changing economy, capital must constantly shift from one sector to another, from one firm to another. In a market economy the task falls to financial capitalists who buy and sell securities and borrow and lend money. In an industrialized socialist economy, by contrast, the state as owner of the major means of production usurps that role. Because the economy, or at least its commanding heights, are state-owned, the movement of goods and services between the various subsections are internal transfers rather than exchanges. True prices cannot form and a planning authority cannot substitute itself for the price mechanism: the economy is simply too vast for a single administrative centre to cope. Without a price system the co-ordination of plans by ministries is therefore impossible.

Polanyi's contributions to the accounting debate were published in 1922 and 1925, and he developed related themes in articles, seminars and unpublished essays over the rest of the decade. With regard to the capitalist price mechanism, he advances three main arguments. One is that it cannot furnish meaningful data concerning the social effects ('externalities') of economic transactions. Another is that, as an economy in which human actions are co-ordinated by the movement of things, market capitalism is a system that in its opacity undermines individual responsibility. The third is that because capitalist price formation excludes the social consequences of private activity and because incomes are dependent upon atomized private activity, an asocial ethic and an unacceptable degree of distributive injustice result. In a market economy the price system is determined by the original distribution of goods amongst the members of society and there are no precepts whatsoever regarding the recognition or non-recognition of wants. 'From the moral point of view the market system is more arbitrary in the appreciation of wants than a planned economy', for price formation depends upon the distribution of income yielding resources, and that is 'a fact wholly accidental to the principles governing the recognition or non-recognition of wants'.[5]

In noting the absence of any necessary congruence between Pareto optimality and moral justification, Polanyi is rehearsing an argument that has been put recently, and evocatively, by Amartya Sen:

> An economy can be optimal in this sense even when some people are rolling in luxury and others are near starvation as long as the starvers cannot be made better off without cutting into the pleasures of the rich. If preventing the burning of Rome would have made Emperor Nero feel worse off, then letting him burn Rome would have been Pareto-optimal. In short, an economy can be Pareto-optimal and still be perfectly disgusting.[6]

Yet, despite his trenchant criticisms of its distributional injustice and opacity, Polanyi's case is no root-and-branch assault on the market economy. It possesses, he suggests, two important advantages: 'the individual liberty assured to its members' and 'the rationality and precision of its movements as opposed to the inadequate oversight and arbitrary methods of a planned economy'.[7]

What Polanyi seems to be saying is that both market and command economies fail to provide oversight, albeit in different ways. In an economy lacking a price mechanism planners are unable to gain an exact measure of either the *marginal productivity of labour and capital*', '*the rate at which the accumulation of capital-goods shall proceed*' (measured as a function of the relative pressure of present and future wants of individuals), or the relative urgency of consumers' desires. In judging the importance of this last,

> the central authority must rely on intuition, based on sympathy and insight qualified by the conscious will to acknowledge some and to leave unconsidered other wants. Both elements entering into the final judgment – the intuitive appreciation of the wants of other people as well as the amount of recognition accorded to them – lack precision. The first is necessarily incomplete, the second is essentially arbitrary.[8]

Polanyi allows that in a centralized socialist system the arbitrary element may vanish – to the extent that the planning authority is 'constituted on democratic lines' – but the lack of precision would remain.

By way of illustration, consider the case of administrators in a command economy assessing competing locations for a new chemicals plant. Their decision is guided by two paramount considerations: to maximize productivity, and to minimize human suffering by locating it upwind of an unpopulated area. The first, in Polanyi's terminology, involves technical (or 'natural') costs, the second, 'social costs'. Command economies possess no mechanism for bringing these different dimensions together in price terms such that a rational calculation, and thence decision, can be made. Nor are they capable of moving beyond the first stage of an 'overview economy', for where the planning process is centralized in a single apparatus the overview achieved is merely 'external', with the members of society envisioned as objective, calculable units, to be comprehended through statistics.[9] If statistical data may provide adequate information on one of the three elements of economic life, the means of production, they are of little help on the other two: human needs and *Arbeitsleid* (the disutility – literally 'hardship' – of labour).[10]

The thrust of Polanyi's case is that 'internal overview' is indispensable to a socialist economy. It involves 'putting ourselves in [others'] situation and empathizing with their needs and *Arbeitsleid*'.[11] But how can this be achieved in practice? How can economic relations be made visible such that we can see them 'from within', enabling us to appreciate the consequences of, and thereby gain full responsibility for, our own actions? His answer is constructed along two tracks.

The first is to identify a general mechanism for enhancing internal overview through the development of those organizations that best achieve it in existing society: 'trade unions, industrial associations, co-operatives, and socialist municipalities'.[12] To illustrate the point he cites the example of a working-class political party. Its members are sensitive to the political climate in general, to the balance of class forces, to the confidence of the labour movement, and they transmit this knowledge, tacit and explicit, throughout the party organism, enabling it to react flexibly, realistically and decisively, even at times of political crisis and fast-moving events. Or consider trade unions: they are organs not merely of external overview but also of internal overview over *Arbeitsleid*. Here too, both leaders and members have a general idea of the various currents within the movement, enabling them to set goals, evaluate means and act accordingly. Or again, one may think of the consumer cooperative, or the industrial association, which gathers the workforce of an entire industry together. All such organizations should be judged according to the overview available to ordinary members as well as to leaders. Crucially, all are built upon the self-activity of their members, and it is this that enables them to achieve internal overview – as contrasted with the external overview of the administrative state. By bringing individuals together in practical fulfilment of their needs, self-organization produces more vital forms of organization than those based on bourgeois principles of *Recht* and bourgeois or command-economic practices of administration. From self-organization, internal overview naturally flows.[13]

The second track is the sketching of the economic structure of a future socialist society. Here, Polanyi draws upon insights from marginalism, which he believed could be deployed on behalf of socialist economics and against its conservative adherents, and upon the writings of G. D. H. Cole's 'functionalist' wing of Guild Socialism and similar contributions by Otto Bauer.

In the 'functional' society proposed by Cole and Bauer, social obligation would derive from function. The determination of rights and duties by social function would tend to promote a 'responsible society', with the General Will devolved to a network of self-governing functional associations in which the state is merely one *inter pares*. The idea is that human beings establish

> various associations to carry on the functions in which they are interested: the church, the trade union, the cooperative society, the municipal council, and the State. Each can serve its own purpose best by being relatively independent, and by working *in conjunction with, but not under the authority of,* any of the others.[14]

Alongside trade unions, cooperatives, municipal councils and the state, a new form of functional organization would be the guild – in essence, a group of cooperatives or trade union that takes command of an industry or sector. At the root of the guild idea was the attempt to adapt the Owenite concept of small-scale producer community to modern industrial society. Inspiration came from the medieval guilds, the role of which was conceived of as protecting the honest artisan against unscrupulous rivals and guaranteeing social control of production through regulation. While influenced by syndicalism, the Guild Socialists criticized it for neglecting non-producers, and called for producer guilds to be balanced by consumer associations, grouped into a sort of second chamber of Parliament and acting as counterweight to the guild-dominated first chamber. This is in essence the framework that Polanyi proposed in his writings of the early 1920s as the political form of the projected socialist commonwealth.

As regards the *economic* structure of socialism, the Guild Socialist position was less developed. Cole had sketched out some ideas, using a highly simplified model that considered just one commodity, milk. He envisaged an interplay of associations corresponding to four functions: production (the Agricultural Guild), consumption (the Co-operative Society), wholesale (the Distributive Guild) and representation of the citizenry (the Commune). The Distributive Guild distributes the milk it receives from the Agricultural Guild, while the Co-operative Society represents the consumers' standpoint. How is the price of milk determined? The Distributive Guild, after negotiating a price to pay the Agricultural Guild, then estimates its own costs of distribution and proposes a price, which it submits to the Co-operative Society. If the two agree, wholesale and retail prices can be fixed. If not, the issue is referred to the Commune for arbitration.[15] As in a market system, goods and services are priced, consumers use money to exercise choice with regard to their purchase, prices respond to changes in the quantity of goods on offer and in the urgency with which they are sought, and a number of independent centres influence the outcome. Unlike in a market system – including more recent blueprints for a market socialism in which workers' cooperatives compete with one another in conventional markets – the price of a good or service is formed by a process of negotiation and the various co-ordinating bodies respond simultaneously economically, to market demand, and politically, to organized consumer opinion.

Polanyi made use of Cole's blueprint but added a little complexity. Like Cole, he assumes the population as a whole to be represented by a 'Commune', which represents citizens' interests, including those of collective consumption (e.g. local infrastructure, education, health). In practice it could take a variety of forms: 'functional *Rechtsstaat*, territorial democratic authority, Congress of Soviets, socialist state, etc.'.[16] Then there is a Consumers' Association, representing individual consumers, and a Producers' Association, composed of trade unions, guilds or works' councils, or a composite of them all. Overall ownership of the means of production lies with the Commune but firms operate as semi-independent units with day-to-day executive control. Each organization is arranged pyramidically – either along territorial lines or, for the Producers' Association, from individual workplaces upwards. Each economic organization would keep two sets of accounts, charging technical costs – such as use of raw materials and the expenditure of labour – to the account of the Producers' Association and social costs to the Commune. The former would be interested in keeping technical costs down (for instance in maximizing the productivity of the chemicals plant discussed above) while the Commune's remit would be to keep social costs down (insisting on locating the plant away from population centres); between the two a negotiated solution should normally be achievable.

In practice, how would agreement be reached? At the macro level, the various organs negotiate a basic economic plan. Whereas the Consumers' Association seeks better and cheaper goods and services, the Commune calls for increased investment in public facilities – for example, health, education and transport – while the Producers' Association presses for shorter working time. Ultimately they fix a total quantity of labour hours and a series of products, with prices.[17] Wage parameters are negotiated by the Commune, Producers' Association and trade unions, with the Commune playing the key role in determining average pay, as well as a maximum and minimum, while the trade unions have the major say in calibrating the wage hierarchy.[18] Certain prices, notably of strategic raw materials and basic goods such as housing and food, are fixed by agreement between Commune and Producers' Associations and, where appropriate, the Consumers' Association.

For other goods a pseudo-market mechanism kicks in. As explicated by his friend and student Felix Schaffer, Polanyi illustrates this aspect of the model by envisaging two state farms, one producing eggs, the other butter. A number of consumers are then introduced, each of which is endowed with a definite amount of purchasing power in the form of 'token money' – a currency that functions as standard of account and means of payment but not means of exchange.

> Then every consumer can work out for himself how many eggs and/or how much butter he wants to buy. Thus a total demand for eggs and butter emerges. If the demand e.g. for eggs exceeds the supply, the price is gradually increased until supply and demand equalize.[19]

Unlike in Neurath's model, there is in Polanyi's, 'in a certain sense, purchase and sale at agreed prices and therefore, if you will, a "market"'.[20] But evidently it is of a very particular kind, with major branches of production and trade in state ownership and the parameters of wages and controlled raw materials under state control. Money is retained but is 'in part directly regulated and in part re-functioned'.[21] Personal profit is ruled out, for the excess of sale price over cost price is divided, by agreement, between reinvestment and general consumption. In short, the capitalist functions of market, commodities, money, price and profit either die away or undergo a radical change of function.[22] Final decision over prices is in the hands of the Commune and other Associations, leaving to markets the initial determination of the prices of non-essential commodities, intermediate products and non-controlled raw materials.

The beauty of his scheme, Polanyi avers, is not simply that social costs are brought into the heart of economic decision-making but also that prices, because they ensue from producer–consumer negotiations, express conflict not between commodity owners but within individuals. Unless perhaps in a society that divided naturally into hedonistic workaholics and lazy ascetics, conflict could never become entrenched and fundamental, for the Commune and the Producers' Association represent different functions of the same constituents. Each citizen belongs to the major associations, and is able to participate in decision-making processes; each can see that the negotiations between Commune and Producers' Association reflect the tension within individuals between their dual functions of producer and consumer, between the utility of consumption and the hardships of labour. Because an individual's inclinations are aggregated in the process – as a fraction of the total social needs for consumption and exertions in production – she cannot but be aware of the connection between her consumption and production activities within the social whole and, by extension, of the connection between her needs and those of her fellows. Polanyi puts it thus:

> In place of conflicts between the similar interests of different groups of people, as is the case in class society, in socialism one finds that the conflict which animates society and economy is that between the variously constituted aspects of the same body of individuals.[23]

In a system of this sort, 'ideals confront costs within each individual. . . . No state and no market intrudes between the two sides of our consciousness, and no responsibility can be shifted onto others; only we ourselves have responsibility for our fate.'[24] A related virtue of the scheme, finally, is that with producer–consumer negotiations at its heart, it establishes 'internal overview', such that the fetish character of commodities evaporates, the opacity of economic relationships is discarded, and markets lose their appearance as a natural force.[25]

Critique and rejoinder

In bringing questions of the economic and political form of socialism, and of economic calculation and ethics, into such close relationship, Polanyi's blueprint was original and distinctive, and quite unlike other attempts to paint a future socialist economy with Paretian brushes. It is his emphasis on overview that stands out. Only when they have 'an immediate and transparent view, down to the smallest figure, of the cost of sacrifice and the benefit of progress' can human beings have confidence that they are directing their energies towards valuable purposes.[26] For him, 'socialist calculation' is not simply the technical application of Paretian equilibrium equations to a collectively owned economy, but a mechanism for recreating in the complex societies of modernity the sort of overview that had existed in the household (*oikos*) economies of the past.

Although Polanyi's articles are not thought of as the centrepieces of the socialist accounting debate, they did spark some discussion. The *Archiv für Sozialwissenschaft und Sozialpolitik*, which carried his original article, also published responses, by Mises himself and by Felix Weil, the moneyed Marxist who was later to establish the Institute for Social Research in Frankfurt.

Mises finds much to praise in Polanyi's critique of central planning but taxes his model with a serious lack of clarity as to who really owns the means of production. Is it the workforce organized in the Producers' Associations, or the Commune?[27] That the model assigns ownership to the Commune but reserves to the Producers' Association the right of disposal constitutes an insuperable contradiction, for ownership means nothing if not the right to dispose. Mises refuses Polanyi's assumption that the two organizations would be able to avoid irreconcilable conflict. If Producers' Association and Commune could not agree on a price, he asks, which would cast the deciding vote? The stronger body would win: if the Commune, Polanyi's model is simply a socialist order; if the Producers' Association, it is syndicalism; if neither, it is paralysis. Was Polanyi advocating syndicalism or state socialism? He had to choose one or the other.

As for Weil, he begins by insisting, contra Polanyi, that the definitive difference between socialism and capitalism lies in the reliance of the former upon central planning as contrasted with market exchange for the latter.[28] The brunt of his critique, however, centres upon the concepts of technical and social costs. For one thing, it is not an original discovery but a rehash of an old contrast between productive and distributive value that one encounters, *inter alia*, in Dühring. More significantly it is not a useful distinction. Polanyi fails to demonstrate convincingly how the two cost categories can be separated, and nowhere shows how to calculate them; and this is no surprise, says Weil, for many of them can be little more than rough estimates. Ultimately, the allocation of costs to the technical and social accounts is determined administratively in Polanyi's model, by firms and the major associations. And how independent are the firms? Can they retain profits? If, as it seems to Weil – echoing Mises – overall control in reality does reside with those sociopolitical associations, it would in its essentials be the same as a centrally planned economy. Finally, he suggests that prices in Polanyi's model, in the absence of a common denominator and automatic correction, lack any real mechanism of comparability and that attempting calculations based upon them is 'mere amusement'. It is a bit rich on Polanyi's part to criticize centrally planned forms of socialism for their alleged inability to calculate prices efficiently, and yet to assume, with the most meagre of evidence or argument, that two or three associations in a pluralist guild economy would be able to achieve this with success.

Polanyi replied to Mises and Weil, again in the pages of the *Archiv*.[29] He rebukes Weil for failing to understand Guild Socialism and for groundlessly assimilating his concepts to those of Dühring. But the bulk of his reply is directed to Mises, against whom he makes three main points. First, property should not be equated with the right of disposition; it also involves the right of appropriation. These rights need not be invested in the same hands, and in a pluralist socialist society they would not be. Second, Mises is wrong to assume that one institution of power must be able to trump all others. In constitutional governments, for example, political power is distributed among two or three ruling organs, each of which possesses final authority in a specified range of areas but none over them all. In Polanyi's model, moreover, the equilibrium of power mandated by the functional principle involves the various parties entering a binding agreement to cooperate. Third, blinkered by his methodological individualism, Mises fails to comprehend the point that because the various institutions in Polanyi's model represent the different interests embodied in each and every citizen, institutional conflict would not be fundamental and irreconcilable.

In his response to Mises, Polanyi makes some telling points, but there is no evidence to suggest that he emerged from the debate with complete conviction of the superiority of his 'theorem'. Of the reasons for this some were contextual: both Viennese Social Democracy and British Guild Socialism were declining in strength by the time he wrote his response. Yet he was also aware that his model was not the finished article. According to Kari Polanyi-Levitt,

> he believed it was not properly worked out. The evidence for this is contained in a memoir by [his friend Felix] Schaffer, who explains that Polanyi eventually gave up 'the theorem' but later came to express essentially the same idea in a different form, historically, in *The Great Transformation* and subsequent works.[30]

Schaffer's observation is, as we shall see, astute, and it finds some support in Polanyi's own words. His essays on socialist accounting, he writes, contained

> the nucleus of a concept of the economy as a *natural process* in a society – not a separate body or bureaucracy. This was the beginning of my institutional vision, which twenty years later took me into economic history.[31]

This, his work on economic history, is the subject of the next three chapters. However, between his explorations in economic theory of the early 1920s and those in economic history from the mid-1930s onwards there was an intervening period in which, journalistic writings apart, his attention was drawn above all to questions of moral and political philosophy. This shift in focus was not unconnected to the socialist accounting debate, as Michele Cangiani, Kari Polanyi-Levitt and Claus Thomasberger have pointed out.

> Polanyi accepted the [socialist accounting] problematic that Mises had proposed. That his response was different to, indeed the antithesis of, Mises' results from their utterly different conceptions of freedom. Mises, drawing on Mill and Feuerbach, took the principle of utility as the foundation of his conception of objective exchange value as the necessary and indispensable instrument of human cooperation in a complex society, whereas for Polanyi this is precisely the expression of unfreedom, for it *prevents* the achievement of overview.[32]

How the question of overview might be approached from the perspective of the philosophy of freedom was the theme of some of Polanyi's most brilliant writings, written over a ten-year span that followed his 1925 response to Mises and Weil.

The subjugation of moral ends to economic means

In his political philosophy Polanyi's interest was above all in the question, as he formulated it in a letter to a friend,

> *How can we be free, in spite of the fact of society?* And not *in our imagina-*
> *tion only*, not by abstracting ourselves from society, denying the fact
> of our being interwoven with the lives of others, being committed to
> them, but in *reality*, by aiming at making society as transparent as a
> family's life is, so that I may achieve a state of things in which I have
> done my duty towards *all men*, and so be *free* again, in decency, with
> a good conscience.[33]

The most brilliant essay in which this theme is pursued is 'On Liberty'. I shall introduce the heft of its argument before turning to Polanyi's other writings in the same area.

The starting point of the essay is a critique of modern philosophies of freedom. In the process of exploring the limitations of the bourgeois ethic of negative liberty Polanyi revises a belief he had held when young, that moral accountability is only vested in individuals. Indeed, his charge against those who adopt negative liberty as the basis of ethical life is that if freedom is conceptualized as 'owing accountability to my conscience and only to my conscience, . . . state and society are, logically, ruled out as moral subjects'.[34]

'On Liberty' next proceeds to sketch the evolution and limitations of modern ethics. As a pivotal development it locates the arrival, in Europe, of the notion of the individual as the fount of freedom and responsibility, an idea that gained ground as the organic institutions of medieval society dissolved. It achieved its distilled form in Calvinism, with its insistence on the responsibility of the individual at the expense of traditional corporate bearers of moral responsibility: family, community, guild and church. The individual becomes the vessel of freedom, but can only achieve this utopian, extra-social position to the extent that she takes no internal part in objective social powers – civil society or the state. Thus, this vaunting of individual responsibility entailed a rejection of collective forms of responsibility and a denial of the 'social' aspect of the ethical field, even an antagonism to state and society. (One may note here the resemblances to passages in Richard Tawney's *Religion and the Rise of Capitalism*, which highlighted the emphasis in Puritan teaching on 'individual responsibility, not social obligation', as well as the individualistic morality and general 'disparagement of the significance of the social fabric' spawned by its individualistic religious doctrine.)[35]

Calvinism posed the problem of the relationship between individual freedom and the reality of society in an extreme form, leaving philosophers to try to resolve it. Given his admiration for John Stuart Mill, and his importance in this field of inquiry, it is puzzling that Polanyi's 'On Liberty' fails even to mention the eponymous classic of English liberalism. Instead he discusses Rousseau's social contract and Kant's categorical imperative. In Rousseau, the individual's freedoms are dissolved by agreement into the social whole; both the individual's motivation and his connection to his fellow men play a part in his schema, but only a formal one. In Kant's categorical imperative, which represents the 'heroic' form of the contradiction between individualist morality and the recognition of society, both motivation and social connections disappear from the frame; the individual's relationship to her own social function and to the state are conceived abstractly, as a question of duty, thereby becoming a matter exclusively of her 'internal freedom' and evacuated of any real sense of responsibility for society.

Ultimately, Rousseau and Kant failed to surmount the problem, but theirs were brave attempts. In Polanyi's epoch of 'bourgeois decadence' their recognition of the tension between ideals and reality had become occluded. Instead, the tendency was to suppress the contradiction, either through a sceptical turn against the ideals of freedom (as in fascism) or through a variety of specious – individualistic or 'uncommitted' – conceptions of freedom, summarized by Polanyi as 'the freedom of the wild ass in the desert'.[36] These include anarchism's 'frivolous and dishonest' conception of liberty, as well as those who aspire to freedom by withdrawing from society (to, for instance, 'the lonely island of religious delusion'), a course of action that can only harm the ethical self by denying the undeniable: its community with others.

From his reading of this central dilemma of bourgeois moral philosophy Polanyi concludes that:

the idea that our personal participation in the 'lives of others', in social realities, is our responsibility and thereby within the realm of freedom is unrealizable in a bourgeois world. But it is equally impossible to deny this idea, to deny our responsibility, and thereby arbitrarily delimit our freedom. The bourgeois idea of liberty and responsibility points beyond the borders of the bourgeois world itself.[37]

Why is the realm of freedom unrealizable in bourgeois society? If not by liberal means, how can the torch of liberty be carried forward? In addressing these questions Polanyi turned to Marx and Engels, specifically, with two of their three critiques of capitalism: that it is anarchic and restrictive of human freedom. (The third, that it subsists upon relationships of exploitation, was never his focus.) He also appreciated what he saw as their discovery of communism and of society, concepts which he reads as congruent with his own dichotomy of 'transparent and opaque' forms of economic organization and with Tönnies' 'community and society'.

In *Community and Society*, Tönnies argues that the hallmark of modern 'society' is a novel kind of actional disposition characterized by the liberation of individual behaviour from customary norms, a shift that has facilitated the autonomous conception of ends and the calculation of alternative means but at the cost of the marginalization of 'community', with its small-scale, face-to-face relationships – a form of social existence in which individuals, oriented to the purposes of their group, make its ends their own. Tönnies' book advanced a resounding challenge to liberal certainties of the naturalness of possessive individualism, confronting it with the altogether different perspective of man's innate inclination to communal life.[38] The ideal it advanced, as paraphrased by Polanyi,

> was the restoration of community – not, however, by returning to the preindustrial stage of society, but by advancing to a higher form of community that would follow upon our present civilization. He thought of it as a kind of cooperative phase of civilization that would retain the advantages of technological progress and individual freedom while restoring the wholeness of life.[39]

In developing the concepts of 'primitive communism' and 'community' respectively, both Engels and Tönnies had noticed the subversive potential of research by conservative thinkers – Johann Jakob Bachofen, Otto von Gierke and Lewis Henry Morgan – into

a 'primitive' era of human development in which maternal authority or communal legal institutions had held sway, as contrasted
with the impersonal law of late antiquity.[40] If a kinship-based era
had existed historically, this served to highlight the uniqueness of
modern capitalism and to bolster the belief that it is but a phase of
human history, from which a new communal era may ensue. What
appealed to Polanyi in Engels' concept of 'primitive communism'
was his supposition that 'personal, direct, and immediate' relations
characterized 'primitive' societies, as well as the thesis (also found
in Bachofen and Morgan) of the 'unity of human existence in pre-
historic times'.[41] Yet Polanyi reads Engels through a Tönniesian
lens. While for Engels the absence of classes and political organizations of class rule (such as states) demarcates 'primitive communism' from *all* forms of class society, including those in which
exploitative relations take a 'face-to-face, inter-personal' form,
for Polanyi the fault line is between 'impersonal-opaque' and
'personal-transparent' modes of social interaction, and this, historically, translates into the distinction between market society and all
previous formations in which *Gemeinschaft*-type relations prevailed
– including European feudalism.[42]

Alongside communism, Polanyi credits Marx and Engels with
the discovery of 'the reality of society', by which he seems to mean
the external, objective character of inter-personal relations.[43] This
breakthrough formed the foundation stone of modern sociology, he
argues, as manifested first and foremost in the work of Tönnies.[44]
What Marx had discovered, and Tönnies later reworked in his own
unique way, was the contradiction between the emergence of large-
scale social interdependence, regulated by seemingly objective
laws, and the atomization of the social fabric – legally, morally,
politically – into autonomous individuals. It is perhaps in the *Grundrisse* that the point is made most concisely.

> The more deeply we go back into history, the more does the indi-
> vidual, and hence also the producing individual, appear as depen-
> dent, as belonging to a great whole. . . . Only in the eighteenth
> century, in 'civil society', do the various forms of social connected-
> ness confront the individual as a mere means towards his private
> purposes, as external necessity. But the epoch which produces this
> standpoint, that of the isolated individual, is also precisely that of the
> hitherto most developed social relations. The human being is in the
> most literal sense a ζῶον πολιτικόν [creature of the polis], not merely
> a gregarious animal, but an animal which can individuate itself only
> in the midst of society.[45]

In Tönnies' reworking of this dialectic, according to Hüseyin Özel's outstanding doctoral treatise on Polanyi's social theory, even as the possibilities of realizing and developing the potentialities of the individual are augmented, capitalism concurrently deprives human beings of

> direct, personal relationships with other individuals, unmediated by exchange or money, [a] 'fictitious commodity' which reduces them into abstract, functional units. . . . In other words . . . the reality of society is both recognized for the first time, and denied because of the perverse existence of human beings under capitalism which contradicts their very essence. For the problem of this society is that it was only an 'economic' society.[46]

It is because the 'reality of society' simultaneously emerges and is denied under capitalism that the dilemmas of bourgeois moral philosophy become so intractable. Unlocking the problem requires attention to sociological facts. In a society in which productive property is divided amongst independent private owners, where the fates of factors of production and products alike are determined by their encounters on markets, the labour and lives of individuals are dominated by objective, impersonal forces, and the social organism is atomized such that social relations between people take the fantastic form of external relations between things. In Polanyi's rendition of this familiar Marxian argument,

> Useful goods are objectified into commodities; tools into Capital; human needs into demand; creative human activity into labour power; the personal relationship of individuals co-operating with one another into the impersonal exchange-value of the goods produced by them. . . . The laws governing the exchange relationship of commodities dominate man.[47]

But why should economic laws dominate human life in general? Because, Polanyi suggests in his essay 'Community and Society',

> as all human and social ends depend for their achievement on material means, ultimately the blind forces which govern the means determine also the ends. Thus, by the force of things, the means tend to rule over the ends.[48]

From this two consequences flow. First, the realm in which moral freedom can be exerted is diminished, and human self-confidence with it. Second, because human labour, which should be an end in itself, is subsumed 'as a commodity to be bought and sold, like cucumbers' within this system under which economic means usurp moral ends, the dignity of the labourer and the 'fabric of society' are both impaired.[49]

Yet the problem goes deeper still. It is not simply that the sphere of moral choice is restricted and distorted but that, given their condition of systemically generated mutual estrangement, individuals are unable to make properly informed moral decisions. The market so mystifies socioeconomic relations, the world of capitalism – in which all important relationships are created behind the backs of human beings – is so bewitched, that cognizance of the impact of our economic actions becomes nigh impossible, prejudicing moral reflection.[50] Together, the state and market,

> stand today like walls between people such that the effects of individual lives upon one another cannot be followed beyond the limits drawn by law and by price. Our responsibility does not go beyond our citizenship and our market personality.[51]

How conspicuously different this is to liberal moral philosophy, for which capitalist society is one in which ends can be freely chosen by individuals. For Polanyi, the ends in capitalism are given, not chosen. Even for capitalists, or managers of capitalist enterprises, there is scant leeway to consider the moral content of their actions; essentially, they are pre-given.[52]

The ethical consequences of the reified nature of social relations under capitalism are not confined to the restriction in the sphere available to the exercise of moral choice and to the difficulty of securing a moral bearing in the mystified world of the market. There are further implications. First, production, and by implication the producing classes, are denigrated. Given that the only desires recognized by the market are those manifested in effective demand, it is the consumer,

> the person living upon society, who appears as the one rendering a service to his fellows, whilst the producer who toils and creates thereby actually plays the role of a superfluous being, not much better than a parasite. The market does the trick.[53]

Closely related to this, secondly, is the narrow culture of egotism that market society begets. When all economic connections between individuals run through the market, each is isolated as an economic entity, and constrained to orient primarily to self-interest.

The insidious effects of egotism in a mystified society are illustrated by Polanyi through an elaboration of Chateubriand's famous 'killing a mandarin' parable. Readers are invited to imagine that they are given a machine which, in response to the mere push of a button, grants them the immediate fulfilment of their every wish, albeit at the price that each time the button is pressed one person within the vast population of faraway China will die. Balzac had already cited the fable – falsely attributing it to Rousseau – to show that in bourgeois society it is difficult to observe even the most elementary moral obligations.[54] Polanyi pushes the point further. The parable, he remarks,

> provides an exact allegory of the relationship towards his fellow citizens of even the best of people in today's world. Whoever is able to bid the appropriate market price can at once conjure up everything that humanity can supply. The consequences of the trick are felt in the nether world beyond the market. He does not see them, he cannot see them. For individuals today, humanity in its entirety consists of the anonymous Chinamen whose lives can be erased without so much as blinking an eye, whose lives will be erased in order to satisfy one's desires.[55]

With society atomized into market actors and with its economic institutions separated from the political, humanity cannot set itself agreed goals, or unfold its powers in concert. Given that humans are strongly social beings, whose humanity is fully realized through willed, cooperative human relationships that govern the totality of their lives, these separations set the seal on our alienation from ourselves. Worse, with the unleashing of human productive powers combined with the restriction of the capacity for international collective action, humanity is positively endangered. Adapting an image from H. G. Wells, Polanyi warns that human society appears to have taken the disturbing form of 'desperate children trapped in a wagon careering helplessly towards the precipice'.[56]

Having established the ethical contradictions of bourgeois society – that it bears aloft the banners of liberty, equality and fraternity while in reality preventing the fulfilment of all three – Polanyi proceeds to sketch the main lines of a resolution. He bases his argument largely on an interpretation of Marx that highlights themes of human freedom, alienation and the aspiration to render social relations transparent, such that the individual experiences her immanence in the species – the Marx, in short, that was to come to the fore in the 1930s when more of his early writings became widely available. For Marx, in Polanyi's reading,

> *freedom* and *humanity* have the same meaning. His wish is for bourgeois society to be replaced by 'human society'. The more immediate, conscious and close to life is the human involvement in social relationships, the freer is the human being and the more human his society. [For him, socialism is a society] in which the relationships of human beings are distinctively human, i.e., direct, unmediated, 'for their own sake', personal.[57]

The highest stage of freedom, Polanyi continues the argument, is achievable only when social relationships are as transparent as those of a family or communist community; indeed, 'no freedom exists in the absence of overview, for without awareness there cannot be choice'.[58] Ideally, all social life would be sufficiently transparent for us in every instance to be able to exercise the decision 'to act or not – in the knowledge that we have chosen between two clearly delineated and definite options, exercising a responsibility that cannot be shifted onto someone else'.[59] The goal upon which progressives should set their sights is the reabsorption of social relationships from their current condition, dominated by reified states and markets, into the lives from whence they really spring, enabling the realization of internal overview across all social relationships, economic and non-economic alike. Socialism, in this conception, is the institutional framework that enables individuals to direct their purposes towards those of the community and make its ends their own. It 'must always be thought of as a form of life in solidarity, as family life extended to humanity as a whole'.[60]

Positing family life as the metaphor for the desired society harks back to Tönnies or Rousseau, but in identifying the *agency* through which the socialist interpretation of freedom can become effective in world history Polanyi's Marxian filiations are again highlighted. It is in the working class, he insists, that the idea of 'societal liberty' is rooted, for it is workers who experience most acutely both the dependence of society upon its human substance and that of each individual upon society. From this recognition stem the socialist insights that all human behaviour has social consequences and that all social institutions rest upon the actions of individuals, and it is these that underpin the core socialist ethic: that acting in freedom means acting according to the consciousness that we must bear responsibility for our involvement in the mutual relations of people towards each other. Freedom here signifies not freedom from duty and responsibility – which Polanyi sees as the view typical of bourgeois political theory – but rather a communitarian-socialist conception of freedom *through* duty and responsibility.[61]

The 'transparent' society of 'On Liberty' and the other essays discussed above is treated by Polanyi as a regulative ideal; he envisages it not as absolutely realizable but as asymptotically approachable. Distancing himself a little from the more utopian formulations of Marx's early works, Polanyi insists that in such a society not all forms of objectification would be transcended, for any large-scale economy requires mechanisms by which to aggregate individual desires, and this inevitably involves an element of reification. Nor would it be an easy society in which to live, from a moral perspective. Whether heroically or humbly, its members would be obliged to take conscious responsibility for the effects of their actions upon society at large, and could no longer follow the psychologically undemanding path of cathecting responsibility for their failings onto external institutions or forces.

Towards a synthesis of communism and Christianity

In the inter-war period Karl Polanyi's political leanings were unmistakably socialist: in the 1920s he was close to Austromarxism, and in the following decade was a staunch supporter of Stalin's Russia, although without regarding it as a model to be copied in the West. He did not, however, believe that the socialist movement could achieve its goals without a cultural, even spiritual, revolution. His contribution towards that goal centred upon the attempt to create common ground between socialism/communism and Christianity. Although in Vienna he had engaged with the Christian socialist movement, it was following his move to London that this activity took an organized and intensive form.

Polanyi's writings from his British exile overflow with observations on the synergies between the two movements. The tone is captured by these excerpts:

> A Christian should be able to understand the reactions of working class folk better than the communist, and thus make a greater contribution to the working class movement. But to do this, Christians must accept the Marxist economic conception of history, etc. or he can't analyse situations.[62]

In the inter-war period 'a new change in the forms of human consciousness and conscience are creeping in upon us. The Man who
is more than anyone else responsible for the expression of this
change is Karl Marx.' Marx's method was 'scientific' but, more
importantly, was 'prophetic teaching – the most important since
Jesus – a revelation of truth become active in history. . . . He is
reputed to be an economist. This is entirely misleading. Marx's
work was a religious statement.'[63]

In London, Polanyi helped to found the Christian Left Auxiliary
Movement ('Christian Left' for short), a group dedicated to forging
a socialist current within Christianity and to infusing the communist and socialist movements with the Christian spirit. Many of
its members were neither Marxists nor practising Christians, but
all were deeply indebted to both ideologies and would effortlessly
switch from deploying Marxian theory against liberal Christians
in one breath to invoking the words of Jesus against the materialism of communists in the next. The movement's aims included
exposing the 'apostasy' of the churches, preparing 'the minds of
men for the inevitability of the transformation of society', and
showing 'the significance of a life committed to the services of the
working class movement and to the truth of socialism'.[64] Its manifesto, acceptance of which was a condition of membership, makes
four key statements: Jesus proclaimed that man cannot fulfil his
true nature except in communion with his fellows; it is the denial
of this truth that led to the present global crisis; the way forward
is shown by the socialist policies of the Soviet Union; and 'it is the
religious task of the working-class to bring about the Socialist
transformation'.[65]

The best-known supporter of the Christian Left was the Labour
Party intellectual Richard Tawney, but his involvement was sporadic. Its most prominent active voice was that of Polanyi's
close friend, the philosopher John Macmurray. He recently gained
notoriety when Tony Blair revealed that 'if you really want to
understand what I'm all about, you have to take a look at a guy
called John Macmurray. It's all there.'[66] If so, one must wonder
either at the former prime minister's command of philosophy or
at his capacity to speak the truth, for, if Macmurray was not a card-
carrying communist, his socialism was of the deepest red: he held
that political authority must 'assume control of the economic and
financial activities of society', and that the antagonism between
capitalism and democracy is of a fundamental character such that
they cannot co-exist even in the medium term; he was profoundly

influenced by Marxism; and he found much to admire in Stalin's Russia.[67] Macmurray advocated a 'Personalist' philosophy – the term was coined to distinguish it from individualism – that insists upon the communal essence of human beings: people are by nature, and should be understood as, 'persons in community'. Macmurray, as is apparent, spoke a language in which Polanyi was already fluent.[68]

The most important fruit of Polanyi's involvement in the Christian Left was his involvement in its major statement, a volume entitled *Christianity and the Social Revolution*. He was one of its editors and contributed an essay, 'The Essence of Fascism'. The thrust of his philosophy in general and his hopes for the book in particular are outlined in a letter he wrote Macmurray in 1933.

> I SHOULD WANT THE BOOK TO BE A REAL EFFORT TOWARDS A SYNTHESIS OF COMMUNISM AND CHRISTIANITY. As to my own part I am convinced that I have got a long way towards a synthesis of C. and C., both on the philosophical side and (though less clearly) on the practical side. . . . If you are trying to establish a new social order you are trying to integrate a new system of social habits, and you can't do that without a religious symbol for the keystone.[69]

In 'The Essence of Fascism' and a series of other texts in the 1930s, Polanyi pursues an original argument concerning the relationship between Christianity, liberalism and socialism. He begins by identifying a world-historic breakthrough: the Christian doctrine of the soul, which, Polanyi believes, enabled the development of genuine individual moral responsibility and the principle of equality. In one respect, however, Christianity's ethic remained undeveloped – inevitably so, given the simplicity of the society in which it originated. It was 'pacifist' and 'communist' but these were expressions of

> the denial of the inescapable nature of institutional society. Power, economic value, coercion, were repudiated as evil. The discovery of the nature of personal life was thus linked with the refusal to accept the need for permanent forms of social existence.[70]

Thus, in Polanyi's vocabulary, Christianity did not and could not recognize 'the reality of society', and this, in the modern age, was to become a real historical problem. Whereas in the (still 'simple') societies of the eighteenth and early nineteenth centuries liberalism succeeded in representing the Christian inheritance, thereafter, in complex industrial civilization, it proved unable to reconcile moral individualism with moral community.[71] Power, economic value and coercion are unavoidable elements of complex society: 'there is no means for the individual to escape the responsibilities of choosing between alternatives. He cannot contract out of society.'[72] Liberalism, with its ideal of negative liberty, is incapable of mastering the dilemma. Socialism, based as it is upon the ethics of individualism and egalitarianism whilst simultaneously recognizing the reality of society, was well positioned to pick up the baton where liberalism had let it fall.

With this argument, Polanyi arrives at a position that he was to unfold in the pages of TGT, viz., that liberalism's fundamental failure was that it promoted and justified the institutional separation of the economic from the political sphere. Ultimately, the causes of civilizational collapse of the early twentieth century lay not in economic developments *per se* but in the contradiction between the two spheres, given that one was the fief of a small elite while the other was subject to the influence of the working masses through electoral democracy. Two paradigmatic resolutions of the predicament thereupon made their appearance, both of which involve the abolition of the fateful separation of spheres. One, fascism, signified the triumph of capitalism and the abolition of democracy. The other was socialism: 'the extension of the democratic principle from politics to economics', a move that would imply 'the abolition of the private property of the means of production, and hence the disappearance of a separate autonomous economic sphere' such that 'the democratic political sphere becomes the whole of society'.[73]

With these arguments in mind we are in a position to summarize Polanyi's genealogy of socialism. It is a movement that aspires to the integration of individual autonomy and moral community; this goal requires a commitment to the values of individuality, community, democracy, equality and freedom. Ultimately, these shared liberal-socialist values have their roots in Christianity – essentially in the doctrines of Brotherhood (the oneness of humanity) and of Grace. The latter states that all human beings possess souls (hence: equality) that can be saved or lost (hence: freedom and responsibility). That men have souls, as Polanyi puts it,

> is only another way of stating that they have infinite value as individuals. To say that they are equals is only restating that they have

souls. The doctrine of Brotherhood implies that personality is not real outside community. The reality of community is the relationship of persons.[74]

Socialism, in short, inherits the values of Christianity and carries out a social transformation such that these can flourish in a post-liberal world. (In some formulations communism is introduced as an ancillary category, albeit with ambivalence as regards its democratic credentials. For example, 'Communists propose to hand over undertakings to the political State. Socialists really agree fundamentally but regard it as essential that this should come to pass by the *democratizing* of economic life.'[75] Elsewhere, communism is defined as 'the totalitarian version of the democratic principle'. Although prepared to resort to dictatorial methods, its adherents regard these not as an aim but as a means. They aim at 'a free society, a classless society'.)[76]

Ranged against the great tradition of Christianity-liberalism-socialism-communism is fascism. It eradicates freedom, reducing citizens to subjects and abolishing the political sphere by excluding citizens from public life and transferring 'the functions of the political State to the leaders of industries'.[77] It is the extreme expression of the tendency to reduce labour to a commodity, and as such 'robs the human individual of his or her conscious will and purpose, his or her soul'.[78] In pulverizing community and waging war on individuality, democracy, socialism and communism, fascism could not be more antithetical to the tenets of Christianity.

In his lectures from the late 1930s Polanyi returns again and again to the image of an intensifying collision between socialism and capitalism (or 'fascist capitalism'), and goes so far as to predict that 'capitalist nations must decline into the dusty past' and give way to 'an International of Socialist states – a necessity of human development which has been rendered apparent by the emergence of the first socialist state'.[79] In spite of the determinist ring to this prediction, however, Polanyi more commonly formulated it in terms of a choice that faced humanity: in the long run a modern industrial society 'is either democratic or Fascist. It is either based on the ideal of common human equality and responsibility or on their negation.'[80] Given liberalism's responsibility for the predicament, democracy's torchbearer today cannot but be socialism – 'the tendency inherent in an industrial civilization to transcend the self-regulating market by consciously subordinating it to a democratic society'.[81] In order to communicate his message to a wider audience Polanyi began to pull together the various strands of his work in Vienna and London – economic journalism, socialist propaganda and political philosophy – and to integrate them with his researches in anthropology and economic history. The outcome was *The Great Transformation*.

2

The Great Transformation

In order to comprehend German fascism, we must revert to Ricardian England.

Karl Polanyi[1]

What we call labour has not the slightest resemblance to a commodity. It is simply an aspect of man's life, which is neither detachable from him, nor capable of being hoarded, or transported, or manufactured, or consumed.

Karl Polanyi[2]

Polanyi's masterpiece, *The Great Transformation: The Political and Economic Origins of Our Time*, was written in the early 1940s on the basis of theses developed over the course of the previous decade. Initially, it was planned as the first volume of two for the second of which a variety of titles were considered – 'The Common Man's Master Plan', 'Freedom From Economics' or 'Tame Empires' – while the first was to be christened 'The Liberal Utopia: Origins of the Cataclysm'. Due to the ambivalence of 'liberal' this was jettisoned in favour of the title under which the book finally appeared. In America, Polanyi explained in a letter to his daughter,

the title will have to be different, for here *liberal* means progressive, or more precisely what *radical* meant in England until not long ago. (. . . the English term liberal is untranslatable into American unless you say *laissez-faire*, or more often *conservative!*). Hoover, for instance, is called conservative because he is a liberal (in the English sense), while Roosevelt is called a liberal, meaning he is for the New Deal.

Therefore, *Liberal Utopia* would be taken to mean an attack on the supporters of the New Deal, which would be almost the opposite of my purpose.[3]

The title is thought by some to allude to 'the great transformation of European civilization' from a pre-industrial to an industrial phase,[4] and that – or, more accurately, the market's breakthrough in Britain – is indeed a core concern of TGT. But for Polanyi the phrase referred to the sociopolitical drama that had commenced in 1914 and continued throughout his life. At its apogee the liberal system, predicated upon the separate institutionalization of economics and politics, had presided over economic growth and international stability, but with the outbreak of world war, 'nineteenth century civilization collapsed', to quote the book's resounding opening line, ushering in an 'Age of Transformation' towards a new order of 'integrated societies'.[5]

In its search for an explanation of the transition from a period of relative peace and prosperity to political turbulence and economic collapse, and in its conviction that the age of liberalism was rapidly approaching its quietus, with *laissez-faire* economic regimes yielding to state intervention and planning, TGT was representative of a wave of literature written during the Great Depression – including masterpieces by Polanyi's fellow Austro-Hungarian exiles Karl Mannheim, Joseph Schumpeter and Peter Drucker. What sets TGT apart is its identification of 'market utopianism' as the root cause of the crisis. Although it is in many respects a dense and complex book, that thesis is developed single-mindedly and with great conviction, and this has contributed to TGT's abiding influence.

In its structure *The Great Transformation* divides into three parts. I shall postpone discussion of the last, a slender section, until the conclusion of this book. In this chapter I introduce the main themes of TGT, before examining the criticisms that have been levelled against it.

The Liberal Century: contradictions of a golden age

Part One of TGT presents an overview of the nineteenth-century liberal order and its demise. How should the collapse be interpreted? As the product of a concatenation of disparate political and economic processes and contingent events? The causal factors that approaches of this sort typically identify include depressions and business cycles, credit and currency collapses, the colonial scramble, secessionist movements, and the diplomatic bungling that hastened the outbreak of the First World War. In addition, one can point to the collapse of the gold standard and the revolutions in Russia, as well as the gathering conflicts between the bourgeois West and Bolshevism and between Britain's intransigent imperialism and the militarisms of the revisionist powers. Without denying the importance of such factors, Polanyi insists that an adequate explanation must dig deeper: it requires a focus upon the institutions that structure the world economic and political system. In the nineteenth century these were the balance of power system, the liberal state, the gold standard and, 'fount and matrix' of the entire arrangement, the self-regulating market.[6]

There must have been something about the balance of power system of the 'Liberal Century' (1815–1914), ventures Polanyi, that promoted peace. Admittedly, Europe's powers had 'infested the continents of the non-white peoples with cruel wars of conquest and subjugation', yet war within the core had been largely absent.[7] Why, for an entire century, had the balance of power system enabled relative stability? Some would point to empirical facts: that the new order, and boundaries, imposed by the victors at Waterloo could be accepted by the major powers (including France), and that these were consolidated through a system of diplomacy by conference, treaty and the Concert of Europe. The emphasis in TGT by contrast is upon socioeconomic change. Polanyi propounds a modified form of commercial peace theory that identifies the rising European bourgeoisie, *haute finance* in the van, as a potent 'peace interest'. Recognizing that their purposes could be achieved better through the spread of constitutional government and free markets, financiers directed their energies towards non-violent activities. Whereas in previous eras trade had tended to stimulate military rivalry, with the development of world commerce and finance it had become intertwined with and dependent upon 'an international monetary system which could not function in a general war'.[8] As the world's commercial and financial entrepôt, Britain had a vested interest in international stability; on the whole, therefore, its hegemonic power was placed in support of the 'peace interest'.

The balance of power system of the nineteenth century, in this analysis, possessed a pronounced bias towards stability thanks to the growing role of a social class (the bourgeoisie) and a hegemon (Britain) that together promoted the 'peace interest'. Commercial peace theory in its original form predicted a continuation of that happy chemistry but the First World War cut that illusion short. The theory had to be renounced or adapted. In 'The Sociology of Imperialism' (1919) Schumpeter had attempted the latter by attributing imperialist drives – and the causes of the recent war – to pre-capitalist and étatiste social forces. Polanyi's adaptation was altogether different. Although sharing Schumpeter's belief that the rising bourgeoisie had contributed to the peaceful nineteenth century, he introduced a novel thesis: that its crusading drive to universalize capitalist institutions at the global level spawned contradictions that ultimately brought the system crashing down.

The puzzle that Polanyi introduces is why those same institutions that had underwritten the 'Hundred Years Peace' of 1815 to 1914 were thereafter to preside over social breakdown and war. The answer, he suggests, can be found by analysing the nature and history of the self-regulating market system, for it was the common matrix that shaped all the institutions under discussion, including the balance of power system, the gold standard and the liberal state. The crumbling of the institutional framework of liberal capitalism resulted in part from British decline, and the replacement of a fluid, multi-polar, balance of power system by an inflexible bi-polar order based upon Anglo-German rivalry. But the critical change was the yielding of a free trade regime to protectionism, as societies defended themselves against the consequences of adherence to the gold standard. Peace and stability had rested upon the liberal world economy, and its demise precipitated a general cataclysm that included the First World War and its legacy of economic and social turbulence. This conclusion sets the stage for Part Two of TGT, its most substantial section, in which Polanyi turns to examine the origins and dynamics of the market economy, in particular the 'sudden changeover to an utterly new type of economy' that had occurred in early nineteenth-century Britain.[9]

Birth of the market economy

Part Two of TGT is subdivided into two parts: 'Satanic Mill', which deals with the origins and nature of the market economy, and 'The Self-Protection of Society', which focuses upon market deepening and the response by 'society'. 'Satanic Mill' begins by drawing attention to a familiar conundrum concerning the Industrial Revolution: that an 'almost miraculous improvement in the tools of production' was accompanied by 'catastrophic dislocation of the lives of the common people'. What was that satanic mill, asks Polanyi, that destroyed 'the old social tissue' and 'ground men into masses'? The answer is the abrupt institutional change involved in the birth of the market economy, whipped forward at an unsustainable pace by an 'extreme and radical' materialistic creed: liberal political economy.

The term 'market economy', I should point out, is deployed in much of TGT in a distinctive, not to say idiosyncratic, manner to refer to a system that is 'directed by market prices and nothing but market prices' and in which all integral components, including land, labour and money, are commodified. 'If these conditions are fulfilled', writes Polanyi, in his socialist variation on a theme by Jean-Baptiste Say, 'all incomes will derive from sales on the market, and incomes will be just sufficient to buy all the goods produced.'[10] Pure markets of this sort will not clear unless all their elements are commodified, and will therefore adjust smoothly to changes in supply and demand. Distortions will emerge if people command alternative sources of welfare, such as a guaranteed income. For a true market economy to exist, Polanyi adds, it must be based upon commodity money and not token money; nothing can be brooked that inhibits the formation of markets; no measure or policy can be countenanced that would influence their operation; and there can be neither any interference with the prices of any good or factor of production, nor regulation of supply or demand unless such regulation enhances the dominance of the market.[11]

Where the market economy stands out from any previous economic system is that its functioning depends upon the commodification of land, labour and money: 'fictitious commodities' in Polanyi's lexicon. At one level, the term is designed to underscore the moral indecency of treating people and land as fodder for markets. That labour is a commodity like any other was a staple idea of classical liberalism – Ricardo, for example, asked rhetorically of the role of the legislator, 'Why should he have the power to fix the price of labour, more than the price of bread, meat, or beer?' Opposition to the doctrines of Ricardo, Malthus and the Benthamites centred upon this issue, with one typical polemic blasting the political economists for treating 'man as a machine, and the labourer as a commodity'. To call labour 'a commodity that is to be brought to the market like wheat or any other article', the same piece continued, is 'sheer nonsense' for 'the one is a shadow, the other a substance'.[12]

Polanyi draws upon this 'humanistic and common sense argument' but encases it within a Tönniesian framework that alludes to the 'artificial' status of legal contracts and the unnatural, 'utopian' character of the self-regulating market system.[13] With this, the thrust of the 'fictitious commodity' concept shifts from the moral plane to the historical. Because human beings and nature are not produced for sale, they are not commodities, but this delusion provided the foundation of liberal society, with fateful consequences. By appropriating land and labour unto itself the self-regulating market subjects 'society' to its logic and laws, and simultaneously, at the institutional level, it separates itself from the political sphere. The state, deprived of its former regulatory functions and evacuated from substantive economic activity, takes on a narrow, 'nightwatchman' role as enforcer of the rules of the market. Here too, this marks a novel departure from the entire range of previous social formations – including mercantilist Britain of the seventeenth and eighteenth centuries, from the ruins of which free market capitalism arose. 'It is generally characteristic of human society', Polanyi would tell his students, 'that its legal, moral and economic organization is *one*, i.e., that it is artificial to insist upon these differences.' The modern market society forms the exception to the norm, for in it 'a distinct economic sphere has developed which is *separate from the political*'.[14]

In explaining the origins of the self-regulating market, TGT presents two terminologically and conceptually distinct narratives. One, discussed below, is unique to Polanyi while the other bears a strong resemblance to standard accounts of the rise of capitalism, drawing especially upon the work of Belgian historian Henri Pirenne to sketch the gradual but inexorable development of markets in feudal and mercantilist England. In this second narrative urbanization is accorded a central role: towns are assumed to be the centres of commerce; their growth 'induced landlords to produce primarily for sale on the market'.[15] The trend towards the commercialization of land, a proxy for which is the prevalence of negotiated rent, commenced as early as the fourteenth century and gave rise to a Tudor 'agricultural capitalism' that was characterized by the sudden appearance of speculation on a tremendous scale and of profit as a basic motivator of aristocrats' economic behaviour, an aggressive mobilization of land for the market with little if any regard shown for the welfare of the peasantry, and the emergence of a class of wage labourers.[16] By the early eighteenth century the expansion of trade, driven above all by the 'agglomeration of the population in

the industrial towns', was already giving rise to 'industrial capitalism' in England and in France too. This was still capitalism in its
mercantilist phase, but mercantilism, Polanyi reminds us, accelerated the separation of labour from the land and the development
of markets for money and credit; it 'insisted emphatically on commercialization as a national policy'[17] and marked, indeed,

> a tremendous step towards *freer trade*. Innumerable internal tolls
> were abolished and the wholesaler as well as the industrial exporter
> in the towns – *both capitalist by nature* – could now develop produc-
> tion more freely.[18]

The other voice presents a quite different narrative. It, quintessentially Polanyian in tenor, discusses the transition from mercantilist capitalism to its free market liberal successor as a sudden and
traumatic rupture. This voice adamantly rejects the supposition that
mercantilist capitalism was a market economy *in statu nascendi*.
Elites in the mercantilist age, it insists, were united in their opposition to the commercialization of land and labour, and governments,
despite their support for trade, fostered autarky at the levels of both
peasant household and nation state. Markets were strictly regulated, and limited, and the formation of free markets in labour and
land was prevented, most famously by the 1662 Act of Settlement.
Labour was regulated by 'laws against beggary and vagrancy, statutes of laborers and artificers, poor laws, guild and municipal ordinances',[19] while land was owned by the monarch, church and
aristocracy, the privileges of which depended upon land tenure.
Neither labour organization nor systems of land tenure were
entrusted to the market; rather, they were 'immutably fixed by the
traditional organization of society'.[20]

Mercantilist Britain, this 'second voice' concedes, may have
witnessed trends towards economic 'improvement', and some of
these, above all the enclosures movement, demanded of the masses
that they adjust to the new reality. But these processes were supervised by governments that sagely maintained a balance between
'improvement and habitation' and erected institutional safeguards
– statutes, poor laws and ordinances – such that fear of hunger
could not become an individual's motive for economic action.[21]
Generally speaking, rulers acted to ensure that the pace of social
development was such that 'the dispossessed could adjust themselves to changed conditions without fatally damaging their substance, human and economic, physical and moral'. Enclosures were

'constructive' rather than 'degenerative', thanks to 'the consistently maintained policy of the Tudor and early Stuart statesmen'. England was able to withstand 'without grave damage the calamity of the enclosures' because its statesmen 'used the power of the Crown to slow down the process of economic improvement until it became socially bearable'.[22]

The two narratives are not equipollent: the 'second voice' is much stronger. Indeed, throughout TGT, Polanyi spares no effort in detailing the comprehensiveness of the contrast between the market economy and other systems. In none of the latter 'were markets more than accessories of economic life'. In all, the production and distribution of goods were 'secured through a great variety of individual motives disciplined by general principles of behaviour. Among these motives gain was not prominent.' As witnessed by 'its vast extension of state intervention', mercantilism 'thought of markets in a way exactly contrary to market economy'. Tendencies to commercialization notwithstanding, the mercantile period experienced *nothing* that presaged the future control of markets over society. 'On the contrary. Regulation and regimentation were stricter than ever; the very idea of a self-regulating market was absent.' As a result, the transition to the market economy occurred abruptly, exploding the 'unity' of mercantilist society. It was a switch so sudden that it made 'nonsense of the legend of English gradualism'. Out of separate and regulated markets, economic liberalism in 1830s Britain rapidly forged a new and unified market economy. The critical point was reached with the establishment of an integrated labour market, a new type of institution that functioned by threatening the unemployed with starvation: 'As soon as this drastic step was taken, the mechanism of the self-regulating market sprang into gear.'[23]

Malthus, Ricardo and Speenhamland

Explaining why this explosive institutional change took place is not the central task of TGT, but Polanyi does sketch out what he sees as its two primary causes. One is technological-economic in nature. Although Polanyi hails from a tradition of social-scientific thought that privileges the role of markets, he credits 'the machine' (or, to be precise, the cost structures dictated by new technologies) with critical responsibility for the breakthrough. Borrowing a thesis from Paul Mantoux, he proposes that once a 'commercial society' had

come into being, the application of elaborate machines to the production process gave rise of necessity to the self-regulating market: 'For large scale production on modern lines, a free circulation of labour was absolutely necessary.'[24] Expensive equipment was not profitable unless continuously churning out goods; the smooth running of this circuit, in turn, required an assured supply of the factors of production, and this necessitated their commodification.[25] (Ironically, he repeats this claim in a 1947 article that inveighs against economic determinism.)[26]

The other cause, which I shall discuss at greater length, is ideational in character. The market economy, Polanyi explains, was rooted in 'the expectation that human beings behave in such a way as to achieve maximum money gains'.[27] This belief spontaneously gained ground as society became increasingly commercial but was imparted with rigour and popularity by intellectuals – the political economists Adam Smith, David Ricardo and Thomas Malthus and their followers – and gained traction when their theories were adopted by the governing class.

Writing as he did before the transition to the market economy, Adam Smith is seen by Polanyi as a transitional figure. His theory does not rely upon an assumption of self-interested individualism, as had Hobbes' and Mandeville's. Neither is there the slightest intimation that society is or should be ruled by the economic interests of capitalists, nor any sense of 'the economy' as a separate entity subject to laws of its own that furnish citizens with a standard of good and evil. Rather, in the spirit of the Scottish Historical School, he conceives of man as a social and moral being, a member of the civic order of family, state and society. But if in this sense he reflected the ideational fabric of the mercantilist age, Smith also sharpened the knife that was shortly to slice it to shreds. In discovering the market's role as the pivot of economic life and as the spur to competition, and in originating the myth of man's innate propensity to barter, truck and exchange, he gave a decisive impetus to a conceptualization of society as atomistic and driven by self-interested 'Economic Man'.[28]

Adam Smith was not the true prophet of the new order; that role fell to the Englishmen Malthus and Ricardo. Crucial was their 'discovery' of the Iron Law of Wages: the 'law' (in reality a hypothesis, later disproven) that wages tend over the long run towards their 'natural price', by which is meant the wage level necessary 'to enable the labourers to subsist and to perpetuate their race, without either increase or diminution'.[29] By positing a tendency of population growth to outstrip the available food supply, based upon the drives to hunger and sex, Malthus was attempting to re-found political economy upon a naturalistic basis. His central idea was that a demographic-economic self-regulating mechanism exists that generates a strong secular tendency towards a subsistence-wage equilibrium with a constant population. If population growth is, as he believed it to be, a function of the level of wages, higher wages will produce an increased supply of labour relative to demand that, when the new supply comes 'on stream', depresses wages and over time returns the supply of labour to that which is required by capital at the subsistence wage. Ricardo borrowed this influential but invalid theorem from Malthus, although he added two significant caveats: that the natural price of labour is not 'absolutely fixed and constant [but] varies at different times in the same country, and very materially differs in different countries', and that 'in an improving society' countervailing tendencies exist such that the 'market' wage rate may remain above the natural rate 'for an indefinite period', and may in the process 'give a continued stimulus to an increase of people'.[30]

The policy implication of the 'iron law' was that Britain's traditional poor laws should be swept aside. Malthus argued that they interfered with the self-regulating mechanisms that impel the poor towards self-disciplined behaviour and reproductive prudence. These mechanisms exist in the economy only in its 'natural' state – the condition of scarcity. Remove that scarcity and gone is the fear of hunger that spurs proletarians to labour for their employers and to adopt the norms of thrift and frugality. Here too, Polanyi points out, Ricardo was less absolute than Malthus: he conceded that the poor laws had not prevented wages from rising in the early nineteenth century, and proposed their removal 'by the most gradual steps'. Yet Ricardo was no less adamant that they were pernicious or that complete abolition was the aim. 'The principle of gravitation is not more certain', he opined, than the tendency of the poor laws 'to change wealth and power into misery and weakness . . . until all classes should be infected with the plague of universal poverty'.[31]

The thrust of Malthus and Ricardo's new political economy was forceful and unambiguous: the laws of the market, in Polanyi's paraphrase of the case, must and should set the limit of human possibilities. Human laws that interfere with the market, notably the traditional poor laws, could only be counterproductive. With their abolition in 1834, the labour market was established and this 'released' the market economy.[32] The transition was sudden, a chain reaction, in which 'the harmless institution of the market flashed into a sociological explosion'. All dimensions of human life, including 'marriage and the rearing of children, the organisation of science and education, of religion and arts, forms of habitation, choice of profession, the shape of settlements, down even to the aesthetics of every-day life', now had to be moulded according to the needs of the new system. 'Here it could truly be said that society was determined by economics.'[33]

But hold on, says Polanyi. When, precisely, were Malthus and Ricardo producing their studies of the natural laws of capitalism? In the first quarter of the nineteenth century. This *preceded* the establishment of a labour market in Britain. Before 1834 the terms and conditions of labour were regulated, and the unemployed were not threatened with the sanction of hunger: this was 'capitalism without a labor market', and one could speak neither of labour market nor of market economy in any meaningful sense.[34] This prompts the question: what type of economy were they analysing? How is the British economy between 1795 and 1834 best described?

It is best conceived, Polanyi proposes, as a transitional society, torn as it was between 'two mutually exclusive systems, namely, a nascent market economy and a paternalistic regulationism in the sphere of the most important factor of production, labor'.[35] Working people were compelled to earn their livelihood by selling their labour-power, yet in the absence of a labour market the commodity they were offering could not find its market value. The shorthand term by which Polanyi refers to this period is 'Speenhamland', after the Berkshire town where, in 1795, magistrates agreed upon a system of parish relief to alleviate the hardship that a spike in grain prices, caused by bad harvests and wartime limitations on imports, had inflicted upon the poor.

Speenhamland is a contested term. For some it denotes a broad range of relief policies in which able-bodied individuals and their families received assistance, while others use it to refer specifically to the use of a 'bread scale' that provided different levels of support, in relation to family size. Its causes and consequences are contested too. Until relatively recently the tone was set by the account of the 'Poor Law commissioners', bitter opponents of Speenhamland who believed that by obstructing the functioning of markets and preventing the formation of a free market in rural labour it conflicted with the laws of nature, no less. Although intended to relieve the suffering of the poor its effects were ineluctably perverse: they encouraged malingering and idleness, undermining the nation's prosperity and even the life chances of those it aimed to assist. In violation of past precedent, it authorized relief not just to the infirm, the aged or the dependent but also to the 'able-bodied'. By topping up workers' wages it removed the link between income and labour, undermining the work ethic; by providing assistance to parents it discouraged sexual restraint among the poor. The system inadvertently transformed an income floor into an income ceiling, resulting in economic and moral ruination and an unjustifiable burden upon taxpayers. The commissioners recommended it be abolished, which, shortly after they published their Report in 1834, it was.

For the best part of two centuries the market-liberal account of Speenhamland was hegemonic. It served market liberals such as Mises and Hayek as a cautionary tale with which to warn against governmental initiatives to establish a guaranteed basic income, and was even largely accepted by socialists, from Robert Owen through Marx and Engels to Polanyi himself.[36] But in recent times it has been subjected to comprehensive critique. In a pathbreaking analysis Fred Block and Margaret Somers have refuted the thesis that the consequences of Speenhamland were counterproductive. From the perspective of elites in the 1790s, they argue, the system was eminently sensible, given the context of food riots at home, not to mention the revolutionary events across the English Channel. The assistance provided did succeed in buffering the rural poor against unemployment and the loss of other income sources that resulted from collapsing craft industries, land enclosures and falling demand for agricultural labour. It did not engender a widespread disincentive to work, rural productivity did not decline, and, except during famines and the immediate aftermath of the Napoleonic Wars, real wages actually tended upwards. Block and Somers argue, further, that a forgotten cause of rural distress in the Speenhamland period was the profoundly deflationary impact of the 1819 decision to restore sterling to its pre-war parity. With falling prices and a credit crunch, farmers were forced to reduce labour costs, giving rise to chronic rural unemployment, increased use of poor relief and the 'Captain Swing' riots of 1830. More than the rising cost of welfare provision, it was the threat of rural disorder and rebellion that undermined elite support for the old poor laws and inspired Parliament to set up a Commission to reform them. What the Commissioners then attempted was to shift the burden of responsibility for the rural distress away from the macroeconomic policies, which

they had supported and which had created the agricultural down-
turn, and onto the rural poor and the Speenhamland system itself.
Using arguments from Malthus they succeeded in rescuing

> political economy from its responsibility for the plight of the rural
> poor. By effectively blaming the victims for the macroeconomic
> policy mistakes that had intensified rural poverty, they turned a
> potential disaster into a policy triumph. In doing this, they made an
> enormous contribution to the legitimation of political economy. The
> severity of the agricultural downturn might well have undermined
> the whole belief in laissez-faire and self-regulating markets.[37]

The Speenhamland legend, Block and Somers conclude, served 'to
cover up the first major policy failure of the new science of political
economy' and to consolidate the electorate's faith in market
self-regulation.

Most of the historical studies upon which Block and Somers base
their analysis have appeared in recent decades, but when Polanyi
undertook his research on Speenhamland the picture drawn by the
Poor Law Commissioners still prevailed, and it is partially repro-
duced in TGT. In its analysis of the empirical facts this is the least
sure-footed section of the book. Although in notes appended to
TGT Polanyi observes, *pace* the Commissioners, that rural England
during the first two decades of Speenhamland evinced 'exceptional
prosperity' and general wage rises, in the main body of the text he
accepts that 'the inevitable result' of the allowances was to restrict
wages to their lowest possible level (even at times below the
minimum necessary for subsistence), that the adage 'once on the
rates, always on the rates' contained a good deal of truth under
Speenhamland conditions, and that agricultural productivity suffered.[38] Might it not have been this latter, he speculates, 'which
convinced the new urban middle classes of the urgent need of a
complete change in the system'?[39]

The extensive treatment of Speenhamland can seem puzzling to
readers of TGT. Why devote such energy to this fleeting chapter of
English social history? The answer is that in Polanyi's reading the
episode, firstly, provides support for his contention that a market
economy cannot operate efficiently if a safety net is provided to
protect workers from the threat of starvation and, secondly, accounts
for the introduction of the market economy in the 1830s. Speenhamland was 'a kind of "protectionist" measure intended to stave off
the coming of industrial capitalism, with its grievous effects on the
social fabric of rural communities'.[40] So long as Speenhamland was

in force the market economy could not function properly, yet the resulting social and economic breakdown redounded to the benefit of the new system: 'out of the horrors of Speenhamland men rushed blindly for the shelter of a utopian market economy'. Few institutions presiding over a social transition, he concludes, 'have shaped the fate of the civilization that succeeded it' more decisively than Speenhamland.[41]

Having taken a necessary detour via Speenhamland, we are now in a position to return to Malthus and Ricardo. If the fears behind the stampede towards the market derived from the lived experience of Speenhamland, the signposts directing it were put up by the political economists. The conclusions they themselves drew from the Speenhamland experiment were fateful. From it they derived the iron law of wages, and thereby positioned orthodox economics upon 'naturalistic foundations'. By invoking biology in support of the necessity to keep wages low, Malthus had refashioned political economy in the mould of a natural science. The nascent market society, with him and Ricardo as its midwives, 'was founded on the grim realities of Nature . . . The laws of a competitive society were put under the sanction of the jungle' rather than of human decision. Having placed political economy on its positivist footing the architects of the labour market, spearheaded by the Poor Law Commissioners, felt 'steeled to their task by an assurance which only science can provide'.[42] Throughout the 1834 Report their liberal market crusade is disguised as science – claiming, for example, that the old poor laws had represented the repeal by government of '*the ordinary laws of nature*'.[43] Yet this entire edifice, Polanyi contends in heretical spirit, was based upon the 'flimsy foundation' of Speenhamland. A hybrid of paternalism and the market system, in no way should it be treated by political economists as a stable entity from which a serviceable model could be derived. The 'laws' postulated by Malthus and Ricardo were not those of a market economy at all. Neither of them 'understood the working of the capitalist system'.[44] Nor could they have done. It did not yet exist.

Marketization and its backwash

If 'Satanic Mill' charts the birth of market society from the contradictions of Speenhamland, the subsequent subsection, 'The Self-Protection of Society', unfolds the core thesis of TGT: the triumph of economic liberalism and the 'militant creed' of *laissez-faire*, and the response of 'society'. The liberal system 'burst forth as a crusading passion' in the 1830s, became 'the organizing principle' of the British economy and then proceeded to reconstruct the world in its image. It had three central tenets:

> that labor should find its price on the market; that the creation of money should be subject to an automatic mechanism; that goods should be free to flow from country to country without hindrance or preference; in short, for a labor market, the gold standard, and free trade.

These formed a totality. The gold standard acted as guardian of the 'gargantuan automaton' of world commerce, but because its functioning bore the constant threat of 'deadly deflation' manufacturers required the compensatory guarantee of institutions pledged to keeping prices low: free trade and a competitive labour market. In this way the three tenets 'formed a coherent whole . . . The sacrifices involved in achieving any one of them were useless unless the other two were equally secured. It was everything or nothing.'[45]

Although in theory a self-regulating mechanism, there was nothing natural about free market capitalism; a system of that sort 'could never have come into being merely by allowing things to take their course'. Instead, the road to it 'was opened and kept open by an enormous increase in continuous, centrally organized and controlled interventionism' – including the French Revolution, and the Poor Law Reform and associated Benthamite initiatives of the 1830s–40s.[46] In this thesis, TGT is an early and prominent example of a genre of historical writing – other eminent exponents of which include Edward Thompson and Peter Linebaugh – that construes the transition to free market capitalism as coincident with and facilitated by a far-reaching transformation in state capacity and strategy: the rise of consolidated and centralized states that sought to re-engineer the norms and behaviour of working people and the poor, fashioning them into subjects responsive to the needs of capital. In this vein, the Poor Law Reform has been referred to variously as a 'heroic attempt at social planning in the broadest sense' and as a case of that 'shift in thinking about state policy away from largely negative state prohibitions and towards attempts at deliberate social engineering', which, paradoxically or not, characterized the period of 'laissez-faire'.[47]

If one of the best-known theses of TGT is on the role of state power in imposing the market system, its central narrative deals with how society, usually mediated by the state, protects itself against the consequences thereof. The difficulties of theorizing these antithetical purposes of state power are explored below. But first let us attend to Polanyi's double movement theorem.

Its premise is that transforming land, labour and money into fictitious commodities endangers nature, human beings and business respectively, leading to grievances, resistance and the imperative of protection. No society, argues Polanyi,

> could stand the effects of such a system of crude fictions even for the shortest stretch of time unless its human and natural substance as well as its business organization was protected against the ravages of this satanic mill.[48]

Through the extension of the freedom of contract to land – which in Britain was concentrated in just three decades following the Poor Law Reform – nature is transformed into an object of commercial exploitation. Turning labour into a commodity transfers control over people's livelihoods to 'artificial' and volatile market forces and strips away all protection against starvation. Basing monetary systems on commodity money – gold or silver – ensures that if output expands rapidly, the ensuing constriction of the money supply enforces deflation, and the ruination of even robust business enterprises.[49] Thus, the self-regulating market threatened to devastate not only human beings and natural resources but even 'the organization of capitalist production itself'.[50] Its expansion achieved its least restrained form in the colonies, where the disruption of traditional institutions deracinated communities and heaped catastrophe upon native populations – as exemplified in the litany of eminently preventable famines imposed by British liberals upon the Indian subcontinent. Yet if Britain's own experience during the Industrial Revolution differed from that of its colonies, it was in ferocity only and not in nature.[51]

Backed by phalanxes of political economists, entrepreneurs and politicians, the idea of the self-regulating market could appear an irresistible force, but it possessed a critical flaw: it was, quite simply, unsustainable. It 'disregarded the fact that leaving the fate of soil and people to the market would be tantamount to annihilating them', and the resistance that inevitably ensued. No sooner had industrial capitalism secured its footing in Britain, in 1834, than 'a deep-seated movement sprang into being' to protect human society from its perils.[52] This 'countermovement' pressed for state intervention, in the form of factory laws, social legislation, tariffs, central banking and the management of the monetary system, through which the market's destructive effects upon people, nature and money could be checked. Its signal achievement was to empower the state in its roles as regulator of the economy and as guarantor of basic social welfare and a modicum of equality.

The countermovement was not the usual defensive behaviour of a society faced with change; rather, 'it was a reaction against a dislocation which attacked the fabric of society' and which, if left to itself, would have destroyed 'the very organization of production that the market had called into being'. Its prophet – and nemesis of Malthus and Ricardo – was Robert Owen. He was the first to see that, if left to evolve according to its own laws, the market economy would engender grave and permanent evils. And he it was who 'discerned behind the veil of market economy the emergent reality: society'.[53] After Owen, others were to develop related arguments. There was Marx, who, as paraphrased by Tönnies, identified labour legislation in the mid-nineteenth century as 'the first conscious reaction of society against the tendencies of the capitalistic mode of production'.[54] For Tönnies himself, unlike Marx, the accent was upon 'society' qua resisting subject, and this was Polanyi's prism too, with the proviso that society's actions are not those of a transcendental subject but are mediated through historically contingent class-based forces: one-nation conservatives, feudal landlords, peasants, trade unionists and socialists, all combining into a single movement.

As an enlightened bourgeois, landowner and inspiration of the British labour movement, Robert Owen represented three of the four classes that were agitating for social protection. The fourth was the peasantry, and, when considering the world as a whole, Polanyi also mentions a fifth group: the 'exotic peoples [whose] revolt against imperialism' signified the attempt 'to achieve the political status necessary to shelter themselves from the social dislocations caused by European trade policies'. Although these forces shared the general aim of blunting the operation of markets in fictitious commodities, that is not to say that they invariably acted in concert; the protective impulse can be hitched to a defence of the market system – exemplified for Polanyi by conservative movements of farmers and peasants at times of socioeconomic crisis – or to attacks upon it, as with socialist labour movements.[55] This is a paradoxical, not to say confusing, aspect of Polanyi's countermovement, but not one that he develops in TGT. Therein, the primary use to which it is put is not to explore the politics of particular social movements but to explain two sets of general socioeconomic phenomena: the 'double movement', whereby the expansion of market principles governing genuine commodities proceeds in tandem with their restriction in respect to fictitious ones, and those 'disruptive strains' that the double movement engendered and which afflicted market economies in the first half of the twentieth century.

Disruptive strains and the end of elasticity

In itself, the double movement is an uncomplicated notion involving market-generated oppression and the ensuing resistance. But in TGT it is deployed as part of a broader historical thesis concerning the evolving clash between marketization and protectionism. Polanyi traces the tensions between economic liberalism and the countermovement first in Speenhamland and then again in inter-war Europe. The countermovement, he maintains, acted in the nineteenth century as a scaffold that provided necessary support for market expansion by checking its destructive tendencies. In the twentieth century, however, it became a scaffold in the alternative sense: the platform upon which the market system met its end.

But why can state intervention and market expansion not co-exist harmoniously? Why must 'regulated capitalism' be inherently unstable? Polanyi's answer arrives in three interconnected parts. The first is that interference with the price mechanism, whether due to monopolies, tariffs, incomes policy, trade union behaviour, taxation, social insurance or municipal activities, causes 'impaired self-regulation' of the market system, reducing its flexibility and growth potential and begetting economic slump and mass unemployment. Inevitable as government and trade union interventions may be – as reactions to the damaging consequences of the attempted imposition of an artificial, utopian system – they are economically deleterious. Who could deny, asks Polanyi rhetorically, that government intervention in business 'may undermine confidence', that private business 'is injured by the competition of public works', or that deficit finance 'may endanger private investments'?[56]

The second posits a growing inconsistency between the international stage on which market expansion unfolds and the national level at which protectionist policies are implemented. 'While in imagination the nineteenth century was engaged in constructing the liberal utopia' on the global scale, in reality it was delegating management of its affairs to national institutions, notably govern-ments and central banks.[57] The 'need for elasticity' was particularly great at the level of the international economy, but as domestic economy and society became increasingly national in organization their own elasticity, and capacity for adaptation, diminished. This is a complex point to which I shall shortly return.

The third thesis concerns the contradictions engendered by the separation of politics and economics in an age of democratization. Throughout most of Europe the capture of political power by the working classes enabled by the extension of the franchise had gen-erated a conflict between state power and the still-mighty business elite – between 'politics' and 'economics'. For Polanyi – in contrast to consensus sociologists such as Émile Durkheim or Talcott Parsons, for whom social differentiation contributes to functional social harmony – the institutional cleavage between economics and poli-tics maps onto the battle between the major social classes. A society in which the political and economic systems are locked in struggle 'is inevitably doomed to collapse, or to revolution'. While in the 'organized capitalism' of the pre-war period these tensions had been bridged by a system of 'complicated deals and compromises' that cemented 'an uneasy balance between the two main social classes', with the extension of the suffrage after 1918, in a period of acute economic and social dislocation, that precarious equilibrium broke down. Now, with the market economy ceasing to function properly, 'it was inevitable that the workers should make use of their political influence to protect themselves against the insuffi-cient working of the industrial system'. The gain in 'human values' that this brought, however, came at the price of 'increasing difficul-ties in the industrial sphere'. From this, Polanyi derives a general conclusion: 'that in case of a breakdown of the industrial system laissez-faire and popular government would become mutually incompatible. The one or the other would have to go.'[58] Democracy and capitalism had become irreconcilable enemies. Economic crisis and the crisis of democracy exacerbated one another, creating a social and institutional impasse that necessitated the reuniting of economics and politics, a process of re-totalization that could take either a reactionary and bogus form – exemplified by fascism – entailing the suppression of democracy and the total domination of government by business, or a progressive, effective form in socialist planning.

In a series of chapters towards the end of TGT, the accumulation of 'disruptive strains' resulting from these constitutive contradictions is charted by means of a survey of world history from the 'Great Depression' of 1873–96 through to the Great Depression of 1929–39. The importance of the first of these was that it shook public confidence in the self-regulating market. From that moment on, the extension of liberal endeavours, such as the gold standard, was invariably accompanied by protectionist policies such as social legislation and customs tariffs. Indeed, 'tariffs, factory laws, and an active colonial policy [became] prerequisites of a stable external currency'. But market expansion and social protectionism inevitably clashed. Regulation that remained haphazard and isolated, as opposed to being *'disciplined by a higher principle'*, simply slowed the economy down, producing strains that would eventually bring down the international system itself.[59]

If one arena functioned as the locus of accumulating tensions it was the international monetary regime, centred as it was upon the gold standard – the market economy's 'chief institution' at the global level.[60] Generally reckoned to have come into being in 1867, the gold standard may be thought of in summary form as a free trade regime with fixed currencies. Given that token money would not be accepted on foreign soil, commodity money – gold – performed the vital function of stabilizing currency exchange. It was a powerful institution, and participating nation states had little choice but to comply with its requirements, above all the single-minded pursuit of currency convertibility. Its magic was that it assured firms or individuals in one country that the currencies earned by exports and investments abroad would be 'as good as gold'; its effect was to remove obstacles to global market expansion.

The mechanism operated as follows.[61] Each participating country set the value of its currency in relation to a fixed weight of gold; its central bank was obliged to exchange gold for currency at that price. Each endeavoured to give its residents considerable freedom to engage in international economic transactions. The central bank based the domestic money supply upon the amount of gold held in its reserves (its circulating currency was backed by gold). In theory the mechanism was self-regulating, with international trade imbalances automatically correcting themselves: if a country enjoyed a trade surplus it would experience an inflow of gold that would necessitate an expansion of the domestic supply of money and credit, causing interest rates to fall and prices and wages to rise, raising demand for imports and harming prospects for exporters. Conversely, a country in deficit would suffer an outflow of gold, producing a decrease in its money and credit supply, a decline in domestic wages and prices, and decreased demand for imports.

Seemingly simple and smoothly functioning, the gold standard met with support across the political spectrum. That it removed the determination of money's purchasing power from the influence of the policies of governments and political parties explains its particular appeal to right-wing liberals such as Ludwig von Mises, but many socialists thought the same. In the words of the Fabian celebrity George Bernard Shaw,

> You have to choose between trusting to the natural stability of gold and the natural stability of the honesty and intelligence of members of the Government. And, with due respect for these gentlemen, I advise you, as long as the Capitalist system lasts, to vote for gold.[62]

Belief in the gold standard, as Polanyi put it, was the faith of the age; uniting 'Ricardo and Marx, John Stuart Mill and Henry George, Mises and Trotzky, Hoover and Lenin, Churchill and Mussolini'.[63]

With hindsight the limitations of the gold standard stand out clearly. Its effective functioning depended upon a high mobility of labour-power and capital, upon international cooperation amongst central banks (highlighted in Barry Eichengreen's treatise) and the hegemony of a liberal state, Britain, which could impose the necessary rules and conditions upon the rest of the world (an emphasis shared by Charles Kindleberger's and Prabhat Patnaik's otherwise divergent accounts)[64] as well as upon the insulation from popular pressure enjoyed by central bankers and government officials. All of these conditions were eroded either during or in the aftermath of the First World War, with international cooperation undermined, British power waning, the franchise extended and working-class parties demanding that governments act to increase employment levels. Rather than underwriting stability, the gold standard itself posed the paramount threat to financial stability and material prosperity in the inter-war period.[65] Far from representing a solution to economic imbalances, the gold standard could actually exacerbate them: by precluding currency devaluations in the early 1930s it contributed to the swiftness with which the slump spread internationally.

At that time, the pre-eminent critic of the gold standard was John Maynard Keynes. Polanyi's critique borrows from him but adds a distinctive element.[66] With Keynes, he draws attention to the gold standard's axial contradiction: that the measures necessary to maintain the system in equilibrium are implemented by central banks that are inevitably tempted to bend the rules on domestic money supply and credit conditions in order to counteract disturbances. This contradiction, argued Keynes, had intensified in the postwar period, due to a widespread and formidable 'urge' towards 'local autonomy and independent action' and in particular to the 'overwhelmingly strong' resistance of trade unions and the newly enfranchised working classes to the abrupt wage falls threatened by the system's stringent rules.[67] The quintessentially Polanyian supplements to Keynes are that he phrases the contradiction as one between central banks as protective national institutions and the gold standard as a liberal international institution based upon a fictitious commodity; that a fundamental clash between capitalism and democracy is involved; and that in their reaction against the control over society by fictitious forces, entire societies forged tightly co-ordinated national economies, a shift that inevitably undermined the gold standard. In the rest of this section I shall draw out these arguments in more detail, beginning with the contradictions of the gold standard.

Under the aegis of the gold standard, foreign trade was mediated by gold but, as gold could not be increased in line with output, for domestic transactions token money was essential. Central banks, although indispensable to the functioning of the gold standard, used their control of domestic money and the credit system to mitigate the local effects of price fluctuations that (under gold standard rules) were required to keep exchange rates stable. The central bank was thus part of the 'countermovement'; in Polanyi's words, 'essentially a device developed for the purpose of offering protection without which the market would have destroyed its own children, the business enterprises of all kinds'.[68]

That central banking drew monetary affairs into the sphere of politics was unproblematic so long as price movements were incremental. But when they swung wildly, nations adhering to the gold standard felt obliged to secure themselves against volatility, and key to this was the national token currency, 'since it allowed the central bank to act as a buffer between the internal and the external economy'. To the degree that state intervention was able to counter the pernicious effects of the gold standard – for example, via import quotas and capital controls – it interfered with its operation, rendering national economies more rigid and exacerbating economic contradictions. In their domestic role, the central banks began to take on the appearance of 'impregnable bastions of a new nationalism', and as such, they undermined the functioning of the gold standard.[69] It is a dialectic that Fred Block has expressed succinctly in his introduction to the 2001 edition of TGT:

> The gold standard was intended to create an integrated global marketplace that reduced the role of national units and national governments, but its consequences were exactly the opposite. Polanyi shows that when it was widely adopted in the 1870s, it had the ironic effect of intensifying the importance of the nation as a unified entity.[70]

The root cause of the tension, to recap, is that the gold standard, free trade and capital export required a freely fluctuating domestic price formation that was increasingly prevented by capital controls, tariffs and wage rigidities. The resulting strains – domestically, when deflation gave rise to long-term mass unemployment, and geopolitically, as governments sought to deflect social discontent through beating the imperialist drum – eroded the cooperative inclinations of participating states and ultimately 'broke the system'.[71] Already in the late nineteenth century these tendencies were apparent. 'Imperialism and preparation for autarchy', Polanyi ventures, 'were the bent of Powers which found themselves more and more dependent upon an increasingly unreliable system of world economy.'[72] If the First World War had one root cause it was the contradictions that flowed from the 'increasingly inelastic national systems' that states had established in a vain attempt to ease the strains generated as the gold standard conflicted with rigid national economies.[73]

Following the gold standard's disintegration during the First World War, many countries returned to gold in the 1920s, albeit in most cases to a watered down version, the gold exchange standard, under which central banks were obliged to exchange a sum of the domestic currency for an invariable sum either of gold or of a currency fixed to gold (the US dollar and, after 1925, sterling). Across Europe the restoration of the gold standard turned up the heat of class struggle, as profits were squeezed between sinking commodity prices and wage 'inelasticity'. Against Keynes' advice sterling was returned to gold – at an excessively high value – by Winston Churchill's government; the consequences were harsh deflation, a decline in the competitiveness of British exports, and the 1926 General Strike. Under the impact of the Wall Street Crash, and with low gold reserves relative to claims against sterling (in part due to sterling's pivotal position in the gold exchange standard), Britain was forced off gold in 1931, followed two years later by the USA.

These events, Polanyi argues, cannot be understood in purely economic terms but were indissolubly connected to the intensifying conflict between capitalism and democracy. Against the tenacious resistance of liberal intellectuals ('from Macaulay to Mises, from Spencer to Sumner'),[74] workers in the industrialized world won the vote, and they used their newfound influence to win protective regulation. This decreased the elasticity of the price system and the flexibility of markets, with the consequence that the assumptions that had underpinned the gold standard – that national economies adjust and that governments would be willing to enforce this – no longer held. Had the working classes succeeded in pushing socialist demands further, the countermovement would have triumphed over capitalism, bringing the double movement to a terminus. As it was, a stalemate ensued, with political power in the hands of workers, by dint of their numbers at the ballot box, while the economy remained firmly in the hands of a small elite. 'Society' demanded comprehensive protection but received only half measures in the form of social policy, coupled with attempts to marshal the protective impulse behind support for imperialist adventures and immigration control. Economic elites, meanwhile, sought to eliminate working-class influence on the state either through pressing leftist governments to accede to their will, or by helping fascism to power. The trend, or perhaps the imperative, was towards the replacement of 'the haphazard interventionism of the pre War period' by 'full blown national unity of the industrial and economic system'.[75]

In such ways did the various contradictions interlace, with each multiplying the intensity of the crisis as a whole. The attempts of the various social classes to maintain their incomes in the difficult postwar years combined with enormous public debts incurred during the war to stoke inflationary tendencies, exacerbating the general economic dislocation. High tariffs, which in Polanyi's view were never a welcome phenomenon, became downright dangerous as the world economy began to fragment.[76] Reparations and war debts added to the mix, rendering the world economy susceptible to a steep fall when the push came in 1929.

For Polanyi the gold standard functioned as the platform for market expansion in the nineteenth century, and for that reason the importance of the 'snapping of the golden thread' in the early 1930s cannot be overstated. It 'ushered in the end of the market utopia', no less, and was the starting gun 'for a world revolution'.[77] This is the nub of the argument in the chapter of TGT entitled 'Conservative Twenties, Revolutionary Thirties'. To some readers an editorial blunder appears to have been made with this chapter title. Surely Revolutionary *Twenties*! Did that decade not commence with the cresting of a wave of upheavals that had overturned political systems from Russia to the Rhineland, with mass strikes then defeating the Kapp Putsch in Germany, revolutionary movements in Italy, Spain and Cuba, and radical student movements across China and Latin America? Did not the 1930s chart the crushing of those hopes in the torture chambers of Moscow and Berlin, on the streets of Vienna, Barcelona, Beijing and beyond? But no slip had been made. Polanyi's terms refer not to the size or impact of mass struggles or the strength of labour movements but to whether the rules and institutions of the nineteenth century – liberal states and the gold standard – were being restored, as in the 1920s, or were being supplanted by dirigisme and autarky. The 'revolutionary' 1930s may have witnessed ugly repression within particular nation states but at the level of world order the decade witnessed a seismic shift, as the gold standard was killed off by nation states insisting upon their independence. Even the Russian Revolution of 1917–24 did not mark a new departure but was 'the *last* of the political upheavals in Europe that followed the pattern of the English Commonwealth and of the French Revolution'. By contrast, Stalin's revolution, the construction of a socialist society which commenced with the collectivization of agriculture in 1929–30, was begun reluctantly – enforced as it was by the breakdown of the world economy and in particular the inability of external markets to absorb Russia's agricultural produce – and yet in its drive towards autarky it could claim credit as 'the *first* of the great social changes that transformed our world in the thirties'.

If Stalin was in this reading a pioneer of the 'great transformation', Hitler 'hitchhiked' upon it.[78] Polanyi makes some brief remarks upon the immediate developments that enabled the fascist breakthrough – not least the support that the liberal and conservative mainstream gave to authoritarian adventures in the 1920s. The deeper cause, however, lay in the general argument outlined above: that disruptive strains spread from the zone of the market and disrupted the political sphere and society as a whole. Driven on by the countermovement, the formerly separate spheres of state and industry began to intertwine, but because the new integration was partial and incomplete a genuinely renewed social order could not result. At the global level, strains within individual nations destabilized the liberal economy, the disintegration of which in turn destabilized the world's political balance and enabled fascist Germany, alongside its revisionist allies Italy and Japan, to exploit the general dislocation of the times.[79]

At a superficial level, therefore, fascism contributed to the breakdown of liberal civilization, but at the deeper level the latter was explanans to the former. Liberal civilization was not destroyed by fascist movements, or socialism or, as in vulgar Marxist accounts, the innate tendencies of capitalism. Rather, 'It disintegrated as the result of an entirely different set of causes: the measures which society adopted in order not to be annihilated by the action of the self-regulating market.'[80] This is why, if one wishes to explain the rise of fascism or the Great Depression, there is no alternative but to go back to the origins of liberal capitalism. Whereas previous systems maintained 'the *unity* of society' and evolved at a socially acceptable tempo, the liberal utopia of the self-regulating market had generated an unsustainable acceleration of change and the 'disembedding' of the economy from the social fabric, which, together, were bound to wreak civilizational collapse.[81] A cure could only come about if society were to become unified once again, with the scission between politics and economics sutured. Short of that, workers were bound to deploy their electoral power to protective ends and capitalists to use their wealth and influence to weaken political democracy. The result was an impasse characterized by class struggle, economic turmoil and fascism.

The originality of *The Great Transformation*

In analysing the transition from *laissez-faire* economic regulation to state interventionism, Polanyi's was not a lonely voice. But its thesis was unique: in attempting to apply the principle of the self-regulating market to the international economy, classical liberalism was doomed to fail, and bore responsibility for the implosion of 'liberal civilization' in the 'thirty years war' of 1914–45. Given the historical juncture in which *The Great Transformation* appeared, one can justifiably describe it as courageous. Its teachings, Kenneth McRobbie points out,

> must have grated upon not a few readers' ears. Just when Allied armies were breaching the Atlantic Wall of Hitler's Europe, here was a voice proclaiming that the real enemy was the system which the Allies themselves claimed to represent – more, that Berlin and Rome

along with London and New York belonged together in one world system which had 'lost' even before the war had begun.[82]

TGT, in short, is a brave book, but is it also original? Some commentators have argued that its major themes were anticipated by Robert Owen, or by Marx and Engels. Marx, for example, excoriated exponents of the 'economistic fallacy' – as for example in his withering put-down of Ricardo, who 'commits the anachronism of making [primitive hunters and fishermen] apply to their calculation the annuity tables in current use on the London Exchange in the year 1817'.[83] Then there is Tönnies, author of the concepts of 'fictitious commodity' and the 'artificiality' of market society. Yet Polanyi weaves these threads together with numerous others, including anthropological research and marginalist economic theory, and the outcome is unmistakably his own. There is, for example, the couplet 'habitation' and 'improvement', deployed in his argument that the Industrial Revolution accelerated economic growth at the price of cultural decline in the form of the dislocation of the poor from their traditional lifeworlds. There is the linked notion that the aim of increasing wealth through constructing a 'pure' market society would prove to be a Faustian bargain, as it licenses a set of motivations and values that contribute to the ruination of the society in which they prevailed.[84] And of course there is the double movement thesis: that the commodification of land, labour and money results in social disintegration, compelling 'society' to protect itself by delegating the state to regulate fictitious commodities.

Consider, too, Polanyi's oft-quoted idea that the *laissez-faire* system was artificially engineered by the state, as contrasted with the naturally evolving countermovement. This depiction contrasts with neoliberal mythology, most egregiously with the version espoused by Polanyi's near-contemporary, Friedrich von Hayek. Hayek postulates a fundamental dichotomy between spontaneous, evolutionary order (*cosmos*) and constructed organization (*taxis*), the former referring to an unintended yet coherent web of relations within which agents pursued their various ends regulated only by common procedural rules, the latter to purposive enterprises seeking to realize substantive collective goals. Whereas for him, macroeconomic steering and the welfare state represent the trespass of *taxis* onto the ground of *cosmos*, for Polanyi the myriad impulses behind such collectivist interventions have arisen spontaneously in resistance to the market machine.[85]

Hayek's *The Road to Serfdom*, published in the same year as TGT, warns against those such as 'Hegel or Marx, List or Schmoller, Sombart or Mannheim' who advocate restrictions on markets, whether in the form of 'socialism in its more radical form or merely "organisation" or "planning" of a less radical kind'.[86] Like Polanyi, the line Hayek draws is between the liberal market economy (or 'extended order') and any form of regulated society (or 'tribal order'), but for the Austrian the polarity is reversed: a regulated society is anathema, liberal capitalism the ideal. If nineteenth-century liberalism had even a single flaw it was that its triumphant progress encouraged a perfectionist overreach, a culture of utopianism that nurtured its enemies, socialism and fascism, which then joined it in battle. In this way, it may well have been

> that the very success of liberalism became the cause of its decline. Because of the success already achieved man became increasingly unwilling to tolerate the evils still with him, which now appeared both unbearable and unnecessary.[87]

For Hayek, the utopian aspect is not intrinsic to liberalism but is an irrational and unjustifiable leap beyond it. For Polanyi, by contrast, that element is irrational but also innate: economic liberalism is necessarily utopian, for it brings into being an artificial institutional assemblage against which society, understandably and rationally, reacts. The 'disruptive strains' that emerged around the time of his birth and which then led to the dismantling of liberal institutions in those inter-war decades in which the ideas of TGT were germinating were the dragon's teeth sown, inevitably and as a product of its nature, by classical liberalism itself.

Some criticisms of the conceptual framework

Having presented the major theses of *The Great Transformation*, it is time to turn to the criticisms. Many have been levelled against this or that argument, interpretation or fact, and space does not permit me to survey them all. I have selected instead what I believe to be the most important. For the sake of simplicity they can be separated into two areas: historical events and processes, and the coherence and soundness of TGT's conceptual apparatus; it is with the latter that I begin.

In terms of the design and use of concepts in TGT, the bulk of critical attention has focused upon what Polanyi means by the self-regulating market. It is defined as 'an economic system controlled, regulated, and directed by markets alone', but in practice is deployed in three ways: as an ideal type (or model) – a system that operates according to its own rules and no others; as a 'utopian experiment' carried out by economic liberals but doomed to failure because the goal is unrealizable; and as an actually existing system.[88] Polanyi rarely feels the need to clarify which of these uses he has in mind, although he is aware that different definitions are in play. Thus he writes that the market economy 'was always more of an ideology than an actual fact. . . . the separation of economics and politics was never carried completely into effect'.[89] Similarly, in a passage that begins by explaining the necessary dependence of actually existing market economies upon 'artificial' (fiat) money but then appears to claim the opposite – that any society that depends upon such a medium is 'a construction entirely different from market economy'[90] – Polanyi resolves the apparent contradiction by explaining that the latter contention refers to an ideal type.

Is there a tension between the three usages? To a degree there has to be. As ideal type the reference is to a mechanism regulated solely by itself, an impossibility, while as actually existing system it is understood to require continuous state intervention.[91] One way of resolving the difficulty has been proposed by the economic geographer Sally Randles. There is in her estimation a 'great contradiction' at the heart of Polanyi's writings on the 'self-regulated market'. Somewhere during the decade that followed the publication of TGT his definition of market economy appears to have altered. In TGT he presents the self-regulating market as a palpably real institutional form that exerted far-reaching effects upon modern world history. By the late 1950s, by contrast, he 'clearly believes that *all* markets are *instituted* in some way or another such that the "unregulated" market never finds ontological reality, it is no more than an ideology, a utopian dream'.[92]

In fact, as I suggested earlier, both meanings are already there in TGT, and this has prompted other commentators to 'correct' Polanyi by jettisoning one or the other. TGT, they suggest, can be modified such that it makes the simple case that, the purely self-regulating economy being a utopia, actually existing market economies require state intervention. A good example of this argument is advanced by Deirdre McCloskey in 'Polanyi was Right, and Wrong'. The central claim made by her modified Polanyi is that one cannot 'assume the functioning of market laws unless a self-regulating market is shown to exist', and this, she argues, is essentially the same point as was made, albeit with greater rigour, by Lancaster and Lipsey in 1956 and by Rosenstein-Rodan in 1943, namely, 'that an economy without every market functioning does not present to its people the correct relative prices'. It is, further, the nub of the so-called Coase Theorem: that if markets are perfect no interventions are necessary – and, conversely, that in actually existing capitalism certain types of government intervention, such as defining private property, are indispensable. Polanyi, concludes McCloskey, has precisely the same *reductio* in mind.[93] This conclusion is shared by others, including Joseph Stiglitz. In his view the emphasis in TGT is upon the proposition that markets in and of themselves do not lead to efficient let alone equitable outcomes – Polanyi's idea of the utopian quality of the self-regulating market is in line with the findings of recent mainstream economics that, because information is always imperfect and markets are always incomplete, there is always scope for political intervention to improve the efficiency of resource allocation. For Stiglitz, TGT is the story of how the deficiencies of free markets mean that 'government intervention becomes necessary'.[94]

Are Stiglitz and McCloskey right to reason in this way? Certainly, there is no shortage of economists who have argued that a comprehensive depoliticization of market capitalism is unattainable. To McCloskey's list one could add Ha-Joon Chang, Paul Samuelson and Kenneth Arrow, alongside a host of others. The model *laissez-faire* world of total self-interest, argues Arrow, 'would not survive for ten minutes; its actual working depends upon an intricate network of reciprocal obligations, even among competing firms and individuals'.[95] A brief polemic in Adam Smith's *Inquiry into the Wealth of Nations* also warrants mention:

> To expect that the freedom of trade should ever be entirely restored in Great Britain is as absurd as to expect that an Oceana or Utopia should ever be established in it. Not only the prejudices of the publick, but . . . the private interests of many individuals, irresistibly oppose it.[96]

Yet to read Polanyi as making the banal point, in pre-emption of Arrow and Coase, that a market economy cannot be co-ordinated solely by the supply–demand–price mechanism would be to do him a disservice. It only follows if the concepts of TGT are interpreted statically, when they self-evidently need to be read historically. Temporal change is inscribed within the DNA of Polanyi's book. Once free markets in land, labour and money had become established a propensity developed towards the subordination of all economic behaviour to market rules; economic liberalism aimed to push this tendency to its 'utopian' limit; because the free market undermined its human and natural substance, 'society' erected protective barriers against its harmful effects; these helped to sustain the market economy for a time but undermined it over the long run. Read thus, there is no necessary contradiction between the three definitions, and none of them should be privileged as the single operative meaning. In other respects, however – I shall look at state power, fictitious commodities and the double movement – the conceptual apparatus of TGT is problematic.

State power is viewed from two quite distinct angles in TGT. In one tranche we learn about the indispensable role of the nineteenth-century British state in creating and maintaining the market economy and constructing forms of social policy tailored to managing the population in the interests of capital accumulation. In another, we learn of its attempts to protect society against the market's unpleasant effects. The argument is organized around a vision of an interdependence of and enduring contest between 'improvement' and 'habitation', equated roughly to markets and states respectively, but what criteria determine whether a particular state policy should be placed on the 'market' or on the 'protective' side of the ledger? The answer is not clear.

It is apparent that Polanyi does grasp the contradictory nature of the welfare state – that it embodies tendencies to enhance social welfare, to develop the powers of individuals, and to exert social control over the blind play of market forces, yet also represses and controls people, adapting them to the requirements of capital accumulation. He recognizes, too, that even market liberals support many 'protective' measures of public policy. Commenting on the establishment of a fire service in London and compulsory vaccinations for children, he notes that these were supported by 'convinced supporters of *laissez-faire*'.[97] But his theorization of state power is less successful. The central problem, ironically, is that his concept of the market is disembodied: it abstracts from questions of property and control. If these are factored in, many 'protective' measures appear as necessary supports of the market system rather than as contingent, or even counterposed to it. Property owners require workforces that are alive, healthy, educated, stable and reproducing, and they will cheerfully support the expansion of non-commodified institutions to this end. Management of these processes typically devolves upon states. The two principles involved – social policy and profit making – may clash in particulars but share a common basis. In the revealing words of a nineteenth-century Poor Law Commissioner,

> It is an admitted maxim of social policy that the first charge upon the land must be the maintenance of those reared upon it. Society exists for the preservation of property; but subject to the condition that the wants of the few shall only be realized by first making provision for the necessities of the many.[98]

Essentially the same notion, tailored to the conditions of the early twentieth century, was lucidly put by the liberal free trader Winston Churchill in his defence of the introduction of national insurance in Britain in 1909:

> The idea is to increase the stability of our institutions by giving the mass of industrial workers a direct interest in maintaining them. With a 'stake' in the country in the form of insurance against evil days these workers will pay no attention to the vague promises of revolutionary socialism . . . it will make him a better citizen, a more efficient worker, and a happier man.[99]

In championing progressive social policy reform as a means of increasing productivity, Churchill was following in the footsteps of the Poor Law Commissioners, advocating 'habitation' for the poor in the interests of 'improving' the power, wealth and imperial reach of the rich. Polanyi rightly observes that elite interests accepted the need for protective reforms, but is mistaken to suppose that their logic is progressively to undermine and ultimately to abolish the labour market. The growth of states in Polanyi's day was rooted above all in the non-market requirements of capitalism itself.

Another problematic concept in TGT is the 'fictitious commodity'. To begin with, it is open to widely divergent interpretation. For social democrats, for example, it expresses the idea that because labour is not a commodity it ought not to be handled as if it were. 'A genuine commodity falls in price when supply exceeds demand. To treat labour in this way would be iniquitous – its price should be regulated by the state!' A revolutionary socialist pushes the concept further: 'Labour is not a real commodity and we should not pretend that it is. Wage labour – the defining social relation of capitalist society – should be abolished!' A business executive would read it in an entirely different way again. 'We want the local retail environment not to be treated like a commodity' (as a spokesperson from a small supermarket chain recently framed the issue, in justification of his call for regulatory action to restrict the weed-like growth of Tesco, the market leader in British retailing).[100]

A particular source of confusion surrounding the Tönniesian-Polanyian fictitious commodity concept results from the fact that it is commonly assimilated to that of Marx and Engels. That the two theories are sometimes confused is understandable, as they have much in common. They share a polemical edge that voices protest against the determination of human lives by impersonal market forces. Both identify labour(-power) and land as peculiar commodities that are not produced capitalistically and the value of which is determined to a unique degree by political and cultural factors. Where Engels protested that private property 'has turned man into a commodity whose production and destruction depend solely on demand',[101] Polanyi would wholeheartedly agree. However, as Hüseyin Özel has pointed out, the two traditions are constructed upon different premises. Whereas Marx theorizes the commodity as a social relation,

> both Polanyi and Tönnies use the term 'commodity' in its 'empirical' sense; that is, a commodity is a thing which is bought and sold at the market. Both seem to forget the fact that a commodity, being a social relation, is not simply a thing.

By reducing commodities to things, Polanyi's concept contributes to the sort of reified understanding of social reality of which he is otherwise so critical.[102] In Marx's account, the analysis of the commodity's dual nature enables labour to be comprehended simultaneously as use value and exchange value. Generalized commodity production depends upon but also produces the commodification of labour and land: the relationship between 'normal' commodities and the others is reciprocal. For example, volume III of *Capital* analyses how the commodification of land is driven forward by the expansion of markets for agricultural products and vice versa. In Polanyi's view, commodified land, labour or money are contrasted with 'normal' commodities as artificial is with natural. The implication, *pace* Marx, is that generalized commodity production could exist in the absence of commoditized labour-power. The two theories are similar but not identical.

The fictitious commodity – the idea that selling labour, land or money is unnatural – forms the basis of Polanyi's best-known concept, the double movement, and this is the final area that I would like to discuss before moving to historiographical questions. Let me begin by mentioning three important criticisms. The first has been most concisely put by the institutionalist economists William Waller and Ann Jennings. They argue that the double movement concept tends to be reduced to a tautology:

> Whatever does not further the market, reforms it. The normal give and take that is part of any set of viable economic arrangements, or any not obviously economically self-interested struggle, becomes the double movement; any behavior that values fairness and equality in society or that challenges the disadvantaged status of some groups in market society becomes the protective response. Little further explanation is required.[103]

A second objection is that the thesis singles out one form of capitalism, the liberal market economy, as the active form while all others – regulated, corporatist, state capitalist, developmental – are treated as mere responses. Because regulated capitalism is assumed by Polanyi to characterize a transition period and to be inherently unstable, his conceptual apparatus is ill-equipped to deal with it as a lasting phenomenon – or indeed with the devastation to nature and human livelihoods over which its various avatars have presided. He had, it has often been noted, a weak grasp of the internal dynamics of state-capitalist and non-market societies. This is a question to which I return in chapter 4.

The third criticism is that in his reaction against liberal apologetics that contrast the market economy as natural and functional with the wilful and political artificiality of state intervention, Polanyi tends simply to reverse the polarity, emphasizing the 'extreme artificiality'[104] of the market system, when a more fruitful approach would be to deconstruct the dichotomy itself. In a paraphrase of Polanyi, the historian Mohammad Nafissi has put the point pithily:

> Market society had to collapse not so much because its opponents appeared to have gained the upper hand in the 1930s, but because it violated human nature which in turn explains why its opponents had gained the upper hand.

Polanyi's ostensible anti-determinism, Nafissi concludes, not without hyperbole, was underpinned by a naturalist determinism 'as cast-iron as any to be noticed in traditions it is claimed he transcended'.[105]

The dichotomy of 'artificial liberalism' and 'natural protectionism', I would add, provides a clue to a further Polanyian puzzle: why he tends towards voluntarism in his account of the rise of the market and towards functionalism in his explanation of the countermovement.[106] By functionalism I mean the doctrine that holds that societies have needs, and that identifying the ways in which they meet these needs constitutes an explanation of why given social processes are as they are.[107] Ronaldo Munck, among many others, has detected 'a whiff of functionalism' in the way the countermovement is conceptualized as arising spontaneously in reaction to the depredations of the free market. That whiff, the same article suggests, is linked to Polanyi's tendency to leave power relations unspecified – to 'over-sociologize', one might say. There is, Munck suggests, 'a distinct lack of mediations' to explain how the countermovement might operate. 'Who precisely would "spontaneously" move against the unregulated, disembedded market system and why?'[108] Others, by contrast, maintain that Polanyi has a chronic propensity towards voluntaristic explanation. 'With a typically intellectual overvaluation of the influence of ideas in political and economic decisions', writes Alberto Martinelli, Polanyi 'held economists directly responsible for the rise and fall of liberal capitalism.'[109]

Both Munck and Martinelli identify real tendencies in TGT; it exhibits leanings simultaneously towards functionalist and voluntarist explanation. This apparent contradiction, I would suggest, is best understood in the context of Polanyi's characterization of economic relations in Britain before 1795 as 'natural' and after 1834 as 'artificial'. For, if the change from natural mercantilism to the artificial market system occurred so abruptly, it is incumbent upon the theorist to find as instigator and promoter of the transition a *rapidly emerging* force – and it is this that Polanyi locates in Malthus and Ricardo (and Bentham), in their influence upon movements for poor law reform, free trade and *laissez-faire*, and upon state policy. By the same token, if 'society', tending as it does to rebound to a natural condition of unity, is naturally prone to resist the artificial market economy, functionalist explanation is difficult to avoid.

Some criticisms of the historical argument

The problems in TGT at the conceptual level overlap with, yet are
analytically distinct from, debates over historiographical exegesis
and interpretation. Areas of dispute include the interpretation of
nineteenth-century protectionism and twentieth-century 'disruptive strains', but the most contested claim, and the one that I shall
discuss at greatest length, is that in Britain before 1795 the nature
of markets, and of thinking about markets, was diametrically
opposed to that which prevailed in and after the 1830s.

There are four aspects of Polanyi's case to which I would draw
attention. First, that in the earlier epoch elites opposed the commercialization of land and labour; that markets in these were so
strictly regulated as to be effectively 'embedded' in society. Second,
that the motive of gain was not prominent in the production and
distribution of goods, and markets were thought about in a way
diametrically contrary to the economic liberal view. Third, that the
transition to the market economy occurred abruptly in the 1830s, as
a result of technological change and the ideas of political economists. Finally, that Adam Smith originated the myth of man's innate
propensity to barter, truck and exchange, giving impetus to the
notion of self-interested 'Economic Man', which, in turn, enabled
Ricardo and Malthus to reposition political economy upon a naturalistic basis.

Polanyi's critics, of both the admiring and hostile kinds, have
long been probing at weak spots in his reading of British history.
In an early book-length assessment of TGT, Allen Morris Sievers
took issue with its presentation of the market economy as 'a *novum*,
completely without ancestors' and argued that already in mercantilist England the enclosures, with their dispossession of the
agricultural labourer, represented 'something of a renunciation of
the ancient "embeddedness" principle'.[110] In the first book-length
survey of Polanyi's economic thought, Ron Stanfield proposed that
the decisive break with the traditional economic mentality occurred
some two centuries prior to the date given in TGT. Already the
sixteenth century had witnessed 'a dramatic growth in the scope
and strength of market forces', which engendered in the following
century 'a profound crisis in the meaning and guiding principles
of everyday British life. From this crisis emerged the market mentality.'[111] Polanyi was familiar with this chronology. As outlined
above, the less prominent (and less 'Polanyian') of his two narratives adheres to it. He will have encountered a similar chronology

in Marx, and certainly knew it from the writings (which he described as 'brilliant') of Richard Tawney. In *Religion and the Rise of Capitalism* Tawney drew a picture of mercantilist England fundamentally at odds with the dominant narrative in TGT. In his depiction, the intensive development of markets in late medieval Europe acted as a solvent to feudal structures, enabling a radical departure as early as the sixteenth century: the 'swift rise of a commercial civilization' that could be observed in rapidly expanding foreign trade, an outburst of joint-stock enterprise and the development of modern money markets.[112]

The mercantilist transformation of social relations, Tawney shows, was accompanied by revolutionary changes in thinking about economic and social policy. The question of pauperism came to be viewed increasingly through the lens of the new individualism. Although writers on political economy for the most part supported the 'old' poor laws as a means of preventing the degeneration of the able-bodied poor, in the Elizabethan era some had already begun to disparage them, using similar arguments to those 'the reformers of 1834' would towards Speenhamland, and by the seventeenth century the theory that distress could be put down 'to what the Poor Law Commissioners of 1834 called "individual improvidence and vice", was firmly established'. The attitude of elites to the new industrial proletariat in the decades following the Restoration had 'no modern parallel except in the behaviour of the less reputable of white colonists towards coloured labour'. The dawning era was one in which individuals should fend for themselves and not rely upon the state. It was one, moreover, which viewed in the pursuit of economic self-interest the operation of a providential plan – a point that Tawney neatly illustrates with a couplet from Alexander Pope: 'Thus God and Nature formed the general frame / And bade self-love and social be the same.' By the time these lines were penned the drive towards an economy run according to market principles was well under way.

Tawney's chronology of the rise of the market mentality has found support in subsequent historiography, notably Joyce Appleby's *Economic Thought and Ideology in Seventeenth-Century England*. With reference to a cornucopia of documentary evidence, Appleby's prize-winning book demonstrates that seventeenth-century England was no stranger to the motive of gain, and that *Homo oeconomicus* and a market mentality had been vigorously present in England since the early seventeenth century, if not before. She introduces the reader to the likes of Thomas Culpeper, who declared in 1622 that 'private gain is the compass men generally saile by', and John Wheeler, who, nearly two centuries before Smith, mused that 'there was nothing in the world so ordinarie, and naturall unto men, as to contract, truck, merchandize, and traffike one with an other', adding that it was nigh impossible 'for three persons to converse together two houres, but they wil fal into talk of one bargaine or another, chopping, changing, or some other kinde of contract'. The same period saw acquisitiveness, hitherto suffered as a barely repressible vice, become respectable and the language of 'improvement' come to the fore. The new mentality was swept along by economic change, notably the abolition of feudal tenures, which, confirmed in 1660, 'emancipated the principal landowners of the country from most forms of external control in the use of their property'. As land and labour entered the commercial system, with individuals selling labour-power as well as (or rather than) products, 'the principle of competitive pricing spread to every element in the economy, replacing custom or authoritarian direction with the market's aggregation of individual choices'.[113]

Reflecting these developments, a conceptualization of what Polanyi might have called 'One Big Disembedded Market' was present in the seventeenth-century literature and it formed the basis of new ways of theorizing economic behaviour. Numerous writers 'explored the role of demand, the importance of consumption and the economic stimulus of individual initiative. They saw England not as a giant workhouse but rather as a giant market.' There was a general awareness of the existence of a labour market, and an understanding of how wages and rents interacted with costs of production and prices. Endorsers of a liberal economic order began for the first time to differentiate economic factors clearly from their social and political integument. By reasoning as if society did not control the production and distribution of its material resources, Appleby observes, they were denying 'the very composition of society'. A powerful notion arose to the effect that economic relations form a natural order 'impervious to social engineering and political interference', and a new conception of trade developed, one that emphasized the interrelatedness of the myriad discrete acts of sale and purchase.

> Implanted and propagated as a part of this concept of commerce was a new vision of man's essential nature. What began as an explanation became a rationale for market practices. The uniform propensity to seek gain was turned into a constant in human behaviour that permitted calculation and prediction.

When the supposedly natural law that every individual should preserve himself by gain-maximizing action was posited as the underpinning for automatic price formation in the market, a range of concrete behaviours was flattened into a formal definition that simultaneously laid the groundwork 'for a science of economics based on predictable laws of human behaviour' and legitimated that behaviour. Fully two centuries before Malthus and Ricardo, writers

> were choosing to ignore the capricious in commercial transactions and fixing on the regularities, derived from the tendency in a market situation to seek gain. They created an abstract model, wherein the pattern of exchanging was consistent and thus law-governed; that the behaviour of people in market transactions was predictable, therefore market behaviour inhered in human nature; that the flow of goods and payments continued without human interference and was therefore automatic.

Furthermore, and still in the seventeenth century, additional ammunition for the conception of economics as based upon natural laws beyond the reach of political authority was provided by John Locke, with his definition of the value of gold as part of the natural order of things.[114]

Polanyi is on firm ground when he claims that mercantilist England did not know *free* markets in land and labour, or in his location of the mid-nineteenth century as the highpoint of economic liberalism – this was after all an age in which statesmen and scholars were prepared to believe that the laws of the free market were 'the cornerstones of God's plan for mankind'.[115] However, some of his formulations are, at best, open to misunderstanding – for example, that in mercantilist England the idea of a self-regulating market was absent and that 'labour and land had no markets', that policy-makers prevented land and labour from becoming commodified, and that a commercial middle class did not 'gain a standing' until 1832.[116] That he underestimates the degree to which free wage labour had become the norm in rural England conceivably stems from an overreliance upon the writings of the British historian John Clapham, which radically underestimate the pace of formation of an agricultural proletariat in the period between the Restoration and the Napoleonic Wars. Clapham, and mainstream liberal historiography in general, deployed a narrowly drawn definition of the proletariat according to which every owner of a plot of land, however small, was categorized as a non-labourer.[117] With only a slightly broader definition a very different picture

emerges: according to one estimate the proportion of English peasants employed as wage labourers soared from 12 per cent in the
third quarter of the sixteenth century to 56 per cent in 1688, and
continued its ascent in the century that followed.[118]

A deeper problem with the historical account in TGT is that its
two narratives explaining the rise of market society contradict one
another. One, we may recall, describes how mercantilist states dissolve local particularisms in the process of clearing the way towards
a national market. The other insists that there was 'nothing' in mercantilism to presage the self-regulating market: the 'freeing' of trade
liberated it from local boundedness but at the same time extended
the scope of regulation, reaffirming the submergence of the economic system in 'general social relations' and relegating markets to
mere accessory status. The drawbacks of the latter narrative, the
dominant one in TGT, were examined above. To recap: the mercantilist period witnessed pronounced tendencies towards the accumulation of wealth and property, and of a free labour force, such that
by the middle of the eighteenth century the nation's productive
property was owned by a small minority, with the mass of the
population obliged to work for hire. In short, a market society
began to emerge centuries earlier than is suggested in TGT. And
this has implications for a further argument: on Speenhamland and
the rise of the market economy – for the other side to Polanyi's
underestimation of the extent to which labour markets had emerged
in mercantilist England is an exaggeration of the rupture experienced in 1795–1834.

Polanyi's account of the 1795–1834 period of British history was
already subject to searing criticism before the manuscript was complete. One bone of contention was his thesis that the requirements
of expanded factory production necessitated a transition to the
market economy. His friend Richard Tawney, commenting tersely
on draft chapters, criticized this argument as technological-
determinist: it failed to provide a coherent explanation as to why
technological change occurred, and overstated the role of 'hard-
ware' innovation.[119] In reality, changing *social relations* preceded
the Industrial Revolution; the leaps in productivity, and resulting
changes to cost structures, were enabled as much by an altered
organization of production – of control, oversight and the division
of labour – as by new technologies, and the response of workers
to the new organizational structures in industry was also a
critical factor that shaped the pace and direction of technological
change.[120]

A more sustained commentary came from the pen of G. D. H. Cole. While commending certain of the theses in TGT as original, notably with regard to 'the comparative novelty of individual fear of hunger as an organizing factor in industry [and] the Speenhamland origins of classical economics',[121] Polanyi's Fabian friend raised grave objections to the Speenhamland section as a whole:

> I still think that you immensely over-stress the importance of Speenhamland, with the result that you spoil . . . part of a really excellent book by giving the impression of having a bee in your bonnet.[122]

Polanyi, argues Cole, goes astray in treating Speenhamland as a widespread, even universal phenomenon, in underestimating the extent of the wage labour force in agriculture, in ignoring county differences in wage policy, and in failing to cite the war with France as a central explanatory factor. Speenhamland, he insists, 'was essentially a war measure, designed to avoid the necessity for adjusting wages to war prices on the assumption that the war would not last long. It then perpetuated itself because the war did last long.'[123] *Pace* TGT, it did not exist in the industrial towns, 'save as an occasional measure in periods of abnormal distress'.[124] But Cole reserves his most stinging rebuke for the notion that no labour market existed under Speenhamland.

> Frankly, this strikes me as monstrous exaggeration. I think there was a highly competitive labour market in the coal fields and in the textiles long before, [and] over most of the field in which the Industrial Revolution was then operating.[125]

Rural labour markets, he concludes, were well developed even before the loosening of the restrictions upon the movement of labour that occurred at the end of the eighteenth century.

On many of these issues a consensus exists in Cole's favour. This is particularly so with regard to the geographical and temporal scope of Speenhamland: there is no doubt that in the postwar years it was retained in only a few parishes. Polanyi himself took some of Cole's objections on board, and added notes to the second edition of TGT that took into account factors related to the war with France and to Speenhamland's absence in the northern industrial zones.[126] In the same process of revision, however, he injected a further element of confusion. Whereas in the body of TGT Speenhamland is presented unambiguously as 'protect[ing] *labor* from the dangers of the market system',[127] in the notes appended to the second edition a quite different meaning of 'protection' is introduced. Here the system is described as 'a protective move of the *rural community* in the face of the threat represented by a rising urban wage level', where by 'community' Polanyi means the employing class.[128] In this reading Speenhamland aimed above all at maintaining a rural reserve army by preventing labourers from absconding to the urban factories. Two entirely distinct forms of protection – of workers' living standards and of rural employers' labour reserve – are rolled into one.

This yoking of utterly dissimilar policies and motives under the single heading of 'protection' is not limited to Speenhamland but is endemic in TGT. For example, when discussing nineteenth-century protectionism the starting points are eminently reasonable: a critique of reductive approaches that explain tariff and trade policy in terms of successful lobbying by economic interest groups, and a thesis that protectionism developed in part as the result of the incorporation of the lower classes into the body politic.[129] What is less defensible is his leap to the conclusion that the various species of protectionism can be conflated: that business protectionism or import duties are cut from the same cloth as trade union struggles. Consider, by way of illustration, the case of Wilhelmine Germany. Polanyi describes the late nineteenth-century spike in tariffs on agricultural products there as the manifestation 'of a societal tendency toward self-protection set in motion by the ravages of uncontrolled market forces'.[130] Yet the higher tariffs were demanded by the *Junker* class, as a result of their concern to counter the threat that cheap imports posed to their revenues, and were resisted by the organizations of the working class – a class that, according to Polanyi's script, was destined to act as the 'protectors of society' against the market economy. Protectionism, in other words, was imposed from above against working-class interests – a fact that the Social Democrats and unions repeatedly bemoaned.[131]

The same historical conjuncture saw a 'new protectionism' gain ground in Germany and across the industrialized world, with tariff policies re-engineered to help technologically advanced corporations punch their way into external markets. The new tariff regime enabled them to raise prices on the domestic market, in effect imposing on domestic consumers the paying of a tribute with which to subsidize export offensives. That the new protectionism induced economic globalization was widely commented upon at the time, for example by Rudolf Hilferding in *Finance Capital*. A business in one country, he wrote,

> that is menaced by the protective tariffs of foreign countries now makes use of these tariffs for its own purposes by transferring part of its production abroad. . . . Thus the export of capital [is] promoted by the protective tariff of other countries, and contributes to the penetration of capital into all parts of the world and the internationalisation of capital.[132]

In this way protectionism acted to stimulate economic globalization, a fact that cannot easily be incorporated into the Polanyian model, which sees protectionism as tightening the cords of national organization while market expansion span its global web.

Protectionism, and state intervention, Polanyi believed, impaired market self-regulation, producing 'disruptive strains' that were ultimately to overwhelm the world political and economic system. In this argument there are sizeable grains of good sense: it rightly identifies a tendency towards more rigid price and wage structures, locating its causes in corporate monopolization, in working-class militancy and trade union strength and in the expansion of the suffrage, which raised the pressure upon governments to prioritize the stability of incomes, prices and employment. Where Polanyi erred was in predicting that intervention which offers protection to the working class must, over the long run, obstruct the mechanism of the self-regulating market. Such intervention, as Marx and Keynes demonstrated convincingly, not only need not have deleterious economic consequences but can even produce the opposite result. For the overall health of the capitalist system the critical issue is the general rate of profit; it may at times vary inversely with wages or labour regulation but the relationship is not automatic: profitability is not a function of wage flexibility.

A similar argument applies to Polanyi's thesis on the clash of democracy and capitalism. He was of course right to observe a determination amongst conservatives and right-wing liberals to reject democratic reform, fearful as they were that it would usher in populist governments opposed to the rule of the propertied classes, and to perceive that the radical workers' parties that entered governments in postwar Europe were able to use their political leverage to win material concessions for labour. However, he greatly overstates these trends, confusing the entry of labour parties into bourgeois governments with the actual gain of state power, and he fails to notice that large swathes of ruling-class opinion had, in the early twentieth century, swung round to an acceptance of parliamentary democracy: they had come to recognize that, if suitably controlled and tamed, it was eminently compatible with the continuation of the market economy and with the preservation of a great deal of the inherited structure of power and values.

On the basis of his theses on the perverse consequences of state economic intervention and the irreconcilable clash between democracy and capitalism, Polanyi predicted that regulated capitalism was an unstable formation that was doomed to collapse. He published this forecast, as *The Great Transformation*, in 1944, shortly before regulated capitalism entered its golden age. From the late 1940s until ten years after his death, the world economy enjoyed its greatest ever boom under relatively vigorous regulation, and it was not until that phase gave way to a resurgence of classical liberalism, in the 1980s, that interest in TGT took off. Polanyi himself turned away from analysis of twentieth-century capitalism and immersed himself in the study of 'primitive', ancient and archaic economies. He was guided by a political purpose, to demonstrate the novelty of the market economy, and an intellectual aim, to lay the foundations for a new comparative economic history. In the next two chapters I outline and assess the merits of that ambitious project.

3

The descent of economic man

The conception of the Primitive Economic Man, it appears, still haunts economic text-books and even extends his blighting influence to the minds of certain anthropologists. Rigged out in cast-off garments of Mr. Jeremy Bentham and Mr. Gradgrind, this horrible phantom is apparently actuated by no other motive than that of filthy lucre, which he pursues relentlessly, along the line of least resistance.

James Frazer[1]

The Turu economy is no longer viable in an expanding world economy. The Turu will be demolished one way or another and replaced by a national Tanzanian system. I feel that the necessarily painful readjustment will be less painful for them and maybe even enjoyable if we recognize that the Turu are economic men who can be made to desire what is inevitable if it is made profitable.

Harold Schneider[2]

The bulk of *The Great Transformation* consists of an account of the European and North American liberal system as it hit the buffers in the early twentieth century, and an investigation of the cause of the collision. The inquisitorial light is shone upon the market system, and in particular the pioneering liberal hegemon, Britain, but implicit is a series of tenets that have wider methodological implications. A good example is the 'economistic fallacy' (also known as the catallactic fallacy), a concept that Polanyi introduces to account for the failure of contemporary scholarship to grasp the novelty of market society. The fallacy consists in the assumption that a complex division of labour implies market exchange, with the riders that humans are by nature market-oriented beings and that economic behaviour should be universally modelled as if it were market-oriented individual action. Imbued with such assumptions, liberal economic theorists such as Adam Smith and Herbert Spencer took pre-capitalist societies to be rudimentary forms of market society, when the latter was in fact a singularity. ('Never in all known history was society organized in this peculiar fashion.'[3]) But the worst offenders were the neoclassical economists; they analyse all forms of economic behaviour through a formal choice-theoretic framework built upon the postulate of rational calculating individuals – where 'rational' is understood as acting to deploy resources so as to maximize desired outcomes in a given situation. The trans-historical scope of this proposition and the conceptual tools derived from it together imply that economic *theory* applies universally, ergo no general economic *history* is necessary.

The belief in 'economic man', the prevalence of the economistic fallacy and the methodological blind alleys that issued from it troubled Polanyi. He had touched upon them in TGT but they demanded further attention. Empirically, the thesis on the novelty of market society prompted the question of how precisely the economies of non-market societies were organized. This is the concern of the next chapter. Theoretically, there was work to be done in critiquing the neoclassical approach to non-market societies and constructing an alternative. In this chapter I introduce these theoretical and methodological issues by way of a presentation of Polanyi's critique of the neoclassical (or 'formalist') tradition, as well as his 'substantivist' alternative. But the nature of his project can be grasped better if first the preceding debates in economic theory from and against which it was constructed are brought into view, and it is with this that the chapter begins.

Homo ~~oeconomicus~~ *communisticus*

If there were a single foundation stone of Polanyi's critique of *Homo oeconomicus* (economic man) it was laid in the late nineteenth century by Karl Bücher, the German economic historian. Bücher overturned the presumption that exchange was a natural feature of every economy and argued, against the Smithian consensus, that 'primitive man, far from possessing an inborn propensity for exchange, rather has an *aversion* for it'.[4] By the time Polanyi had begun to

search for evidence with which to demonstrate the historical specificity of the market system and of *Homo oeconomicus*, this insight
was widely shared in the field of 'primitive economics' (later to
become known as economic anthropology).

For Polanyi it was fortuitous that the 1920s witnessed the heyday
of this subdiscipline, with the publication of the magna opera of
Richard Thurnwald, Bronislaw Malinowski, Raymond Firth, Marcel
Mauss and Wilhelm Koppers, as well as Robert Lowie's *Primitive
Society* and A. R. Radcliffe-Brown's *The Andaman Islanders*. The ethnographic findings contained in these works and the theoretical
generalizations drawn from them rippled far beyond the discipline.
They were seen as debunking the utilitarian myth of *Homo oeconomicus*, a creature motivated by self-interest, desirous only to
maximize 'utility' and guided rigidly by the rational calculation of
opportunity costs. In his synthetic account of economics in 'primitive communities', Thurnwald identified a characteristic feature as
the absence of any desire to make profits from either production
or exchange and the concomitant 'harmonization of all aspects of
life into a complete whole'.[5] The economic activity of the 'primitive
peoples' (*Naturvölker*) he surveyed possessed a spirit that contrasted with market society: it was geared to the 'act' rather than
to 'acquisition'.[6] Many did not know commodity exchange and
those that did held it at arm's length, through 'silent trade', in
which agreement on prices and quantities is reached without either
party communicating directly with its counterpart – a phenomenon
that Polanyi pursued further in the writings of the anthropologist
Bódog Somló, as well as in Herodotus. Another anthropologist
whose work attracted him was Malinowski's friend and student
Raymond Firth. As summarized by Richard Tawney in his preface
to Firth's *Primitive Economics of the New Zealand Maori*, the book
dealt a swingeing blow to that monster *Homo oeconomicus*, for
whom every effort is a 'cost' the incurring of which is motivated
only by the individual's desire to satisfy their wants.[7] It depicted
Maori economic activity not as occurring within a separate sphere,
suitably set apart for study by economists, but enmeshed within 'a
framework set by the family, the tribe, the class system, the institution of property, the powers and duties of chiefs'. To isolate it from
these social institutions, Tawney concluded, would be 'to give a
quite abstract and misleading picture even of the economic aspects
of Maori society'.[8]

Polanyi was inspired by his anthropological studies to pursue
several interrelated lines of inquiry: into the role of cultural beliefs

in structuring economic behaviour, the institutions that guided economic behaviour in non-market societies, and the question of
how to categorize these. He gleaned particular satisfaction from
Malinowski's *Argonauts of the Western Pacific*, which was regarded
as having debunked the myth of economic man by revealing 'the
communistic tendencies' of the Trobriand Islanders. Whether or not
the Trobriand Islanders knew egotism, their reproduction and stability depended crucially upon a sense of community, to which
self-interested economic behaviour posed a threat. In his notes,
Polanyi inserts an exclamation mark next to the Polish anthropologist's observation that 'giving for the sake of giving is one of the
most important features of Trobriand sociology, and from its very
general and fundamental nature, I submit that it is a universal
feature of all primitive societies'.[9] Malinowski's Trobrianders
appeared to be more concerned to fulfil moral obligations than to
maximize gain; they may have valued material goods but chiefly in
order to safeguard their social standing or social assets.

Generalizing from the ethnography of the aforementioned
authors, as well as Radcliffe-Brown and Margaret Mead, Polanyi
concluded that

> the legend of the individualistic psychology of primitive man is
> exploded. Neither crude egotism, nor a propensity to barter or
> exchange, nor a tendency to cater chiefly for himself is in evi-
> dence. . . . As a rule, the individual in primitive society is not threat-
> ened by starvation unless the community as a whole is in a like
> predicament. It is the absence of the threat of individual starvation
> which makes primitive society, in a sense, more humane than nine-
> teenth century society, and at the same time less economic.[10]

In this summation he is pushing the point further than his sources
had done. Malinowski's scotching of the legend of *Homo oeconomicus*
was tempered by his own tendency to accept the utilitarian depiction of society as consisting of utility-maximizing individuals, and
he relativized his findings on the prevalence of altruistic behaviour
with observations that the Trobriander's motivation in giving
included ambition and vanity – that, indeed, 'whenever the native
can evade his obligations without the loss of prestige, or without
the prospective loss of gain, he does so, exactly as a civilized business man would do'.[11] But Polanyi, more than Malinowski, was
deploying the new ethnographic data towards general theoretical
ends. That 'primitive' people lacked a primary orientation to material gain, he reasoned, was evidently a function of the structure of

their society, and this recognition opened a window onto new ways of envisaging the relationship between community and economy: the latter did not dominate the former but was 'embedded' in the totality of social relationships.

In positing a stark dichotomy between the modern market system and all previous societies, Polanyi situates himself as the inheritor of a line of sociological thinking that was 'first mooted by Hegel and developed by Marx' before its 'empirical discovery in terms of history by Henry Sumner Maine'.[12] In their different ways, these authors presented a schema of an ideal-typical evolutionary progression from agrarian subsistence economies to modernity. The former are technologically basic, with conditional property rights and a limited division of labour; if they evolve at all, it is at a slow pace. Because organized through kinship relations, social cohesion is intense, with restricted scope for individuality and intense cultural uniformity. They are particularistic ('wrapped up in themselves'), with little awareness of counterparts elsewhere and still less of interdependencies that may link them to others; in their ethical outlook they are relative and situational – a given act is not good or bad as such but depends upon who the 'Alter' is.[13] Modern societies, by contrast, are industrialized, technologically advanced, with absolute property rights and a complex and rapidly changing division of labour that cuts across social groups. Each individual is engaged in criss-crossing networks of interpersonal and impersonal relations in which a variety of sets of norms apply. Social cohesion is more diffuse, with unity and order achieved through economic interdependence, central administrative power, and identification with abstract symbols; the dominant ethical systems tend to espouse and privilege absolute and universal values. Different institutional sectors and individuals enjoy a high degree of autonomy, and great scope is afforded to behaviour of a utilitarian kind.[14]

This general style of historical-sociological dichotomy was adumbrated by Marx and Maine and elaborated, each in his own way, by Tönnies, Weber, Durkheim and of course Polanyi. For Marx, the prospect was of the '*Aufhebung*' (transcendence or sublation) of modernity through a rediscovery of community, a thought that he expresses most vividly in a letter of 1843 that looks forward to the day when 'that self-reliance, that freedom, which disappeared from earth with the Greeks' will be awakened again in the hearts of men. 'Then only can men move from society [*Gesellschaft*] to a new community [*Gemeinschaft*], uniting them for their highest ends – a democratic state.'[15] In the *Grundrisse*, similarly, he opposes 'the old view, in which the human being appears as the aim of production', to 'the modern world, where production appears as the aim of mankind and wealth as the aim of production'.[16]

A less utopian purpose underlay Henry Maine's rendering of the issue. A conservative thinker, in studying antiquity he was searching for resources with which to defend 'tradition' and confront social contract theory. His *Ancient Law* charts the evolution of 'progressive societies' from kinship-based organization, where ties between individuals are based on 'reciprocity in rights and duties' (or 'status'), via the gradual dissolution of family dependency 'and the growth of individual obligation' to new social formations governed by 'contractus'.[17] He has no patience with those who seek to explain the present without understanding the radical otherness of societies past: they who would judge previous civilizations by contemporary morality are committing no less an error than are those who suppose 'that every wheel and bolt in the modern social machine had its counterpart in more rudimentary societies'.[18] With this sentiment Polanyi wholeheartedly concurs, but where Maine located the beginnings of a contract-based society in Roman law, for him the transition occurs much later and more abruptly, and where Maine sees in status society 'the dark ages of tribalism', Polanyi identifies much more closely with Tönnies, who reversed the poles of Maine's distinction, envisaging status society (*Gemeinschaft*) as a natural and cohesive realm ('a condition where the lives of men were embedded in a tissue of common experience', in Polanyi's paraphrase), as contrasted with modern *Gesellschaft*. The latter, for the German sociologist, refers to an artificial realm of inauthentic experience in which the advantages of individual freedom and political equality are balanced or even outweighed by the costs of the individual's alienation from traditional customs and social networks.[19]

Tönnies' renowned couplet draws upon both Marx and Maine but unlike them he situates it within a framework of ideal types constructed around postulated differences in willed behaviour.[20] In essence, these are models that represent modal forms of human action. In the case of Tönnies' antipodes they enable us to set our normative compasses, alerting us to the dangers of travelling too far towards a pure capitalist culture whilst drawing attention to past precedents as harbingers of its communal transcendence (*Aufhebung*) in a social-democratic *Gemeinschaft*.[21] As developed by Tönnies and later by Max Weber, ideal types are not 'typical' in the sense of representing the average qualities of a given phenomenon, but constructions created through deliberate exaggeration of one or more of its features. They are not attempts to represent reality photographically but have a heuristic function as diagrammatic, pared-down representations against which reality can be compared and with reference to which hypotheses can be prepared. By dint of their conceptual purity – they do not reflect the real world – they assume the character of what Weber termed a 'utopia' through which 'by way of *mental* comparison particular elements of reality' may be apprehended.[22] Weber, together with Tönnies and their confreres in the German Historical School, advocated a method oriented to the *verstehen* of the distinctive constellations of values that motivate human behaviour in different societies: they construct typologies organized around the characteristic ends of the individual actions of which a given social form is composed and the means by which those ends are achieved. (For example, to apprehend 'capitalist culture', its ideal type is constructed by abstracting from selected aspects of an empirical culture dominated by capitalist interests.) The ambiguities to which this method can lead, and which certainly also intrude into Polanyi's work, are in respect of whether the referent – say, 'pure capitalism' – denotes an ideal type or an actual stage of empirical history.

With Tönniesian and Weberian methods integrated into his toolkit, Polanyi set out to re-interpret non-capitalist economic history and, by way of comparison, to comprehend the distinctiveness of the modern market system better. But in the process he came up against an increasingly hegemonic orthodoxy in the shape of mainstream economics, one that laid down a challenge both to his empirical premise – the novelty of the market system – and, methodologically, to his institutionalism and historicism. In order to situate properly the challenge he faced, an excursus on neoclassical economics, the 'German Historical' tradition and the 'debate over method' between the two is required.

The debate over methods

If, during Polanyi's childhood and youth, anthropology and sociology were pushing the boundaries of knowledge in charting the variability of human social behaviour, a very different path was being cut by the new discipline of economics. The branch of neo-classical (or 'marginalist') economics with which Polanyi was familiar was the Austrian school, founded by Carl von Menger, whose other senior figures included Friedrich von Wieser, Eugen von Böhm-Bawerk, Joseph von Schumpeter, Ludwig von Mises and Friedrich von Hayek. Its emergence occurred not only by way of evolution from classical political economy and disciplinary demarcation against sociology but also in methodological repulsion from the German Historical School (GHS).

The GHS was the prevailing school of political economy in Central Europe for the several decades that followed the publication of Friedrich List's *National System of Political Economy* and Wilhelm Roscher's *Grundriss* in the early 1840s. List and Roscher, followed by a younger generation around Gustav Schmoller and Karl Bücher, rejected the naturalist-positivist quest to discover trans-historical laws of social behaviour, emphasizing instead the uniqueness of time and place, the variability of economic systems, the determining role of ethics and the necessity of inductive method. Against the English economists' postulation of the market economy as a natural phenomenon they stressed its historical specificity and constructedness (in Tönnies' terms, 'artificiality'), drawing attention to the historical novelty of the profit motive and to the pivotal role of states in engineering conditions conducive to market formation. Anticipating Polanyi, they brought the eye of the historian and social theorist to anthropology, refusing the distinction between economic anthropology and economic history and engaging in a systematic theorization of the shifting role of economic institutions in different societies. In every phase of history, in Schmoller's conception, the determining part in economic development is played by a political organ, whether tribe, village or state.[23] Bücher, meanwhile, constructed an evolutionary schema, with the taxonomical criterion being the role played by exchange: in low-surplus economies actors are averse to exchange; these were succeeded by the *oikos*-dominated economies of antiquity in which goods moved from producer to consumer without intervening exchange, medieval towns with a limited amount of exchange, and finally the exchange-dominated modern *Volkswirtschaft*. What appealed to Polanyi in Bücher's approach was that it 'makes exchange only a phenomenon of a particular stage of economic development, while the essence of the economy has to do with actual production, or, as one might say today, with the substantive element'.[24]

In line with their historicist and institutionalist method, the GHS theorists proposed that economics focus on three tasks: sketching a comparative history of economic institutions, identifying a typology of the social conditions relating to these in different economic orders, and presenting the historical sequence of these economic orders as stages of economic development. For Schmoller, institutions should be comprehended as expressions of historically specific mentalities ('psychische Erscheinungen') grounded in shared language, memories and a collective ethos. Some have dubbed his model of human behaviour *Homo sociologicus* in recognition of the role of custom and morality in steering individual needs and passions, but *Homo mass-psychologicus* would be more accurate, given that he prioritizes human feelings and drives, considered in the aggregate, as the foundation of human behaviour. All economic and political life, he writes, 'rests upon psychical mass-movements, mass-sentiments, and mass-conceptions'.[25] Economic phenomena such as capitalist activity should therefore be understood psychologically, as mentalities that express themselves as sets of ideas and moral systems, customs and laws, specific to a people of a certain race or nation. Economic life is transacted within political and social organs that achieve their unity not simply through borders and an integrated territory but in the first instance as a 'spiritual unity by the socialization of the actors, with law, morals, and religion . . . as their prime expressions'.[26] The common element that unites the particular economies of a nation or a state, he elaborates, 'is not simply the state itself, but rather something deeper: the community of language, of history, of memories, of customs and ideas. It is a world of common feelings and ideas, a more or less harmonious tension of all psychological drives', comprising pleasure and pain, sex, self-preservation, social acceptance and a rivalry instinct – but not an acquisitiveness drive.[27] Given that economic life is embedded within cultural systems, historicists such as Karl Knies and Schmoller argued, a moral perspective is indispensable: economics is a normative science. (Schmoller, indeed, thought 'ethical economics' – a term coined by the Swiss economist Jean Charles Léonard de Sismondi – a more appropriate designation for his school than its conventional soubriquet.)

In the closing decades of the nineteenth century the GHS's ideological sparring partners were Marxism and neoclassical economics, although the boundaries separating the three camps, as discussed in the introduction, were flexible. In contrast to Marxism, the historicists disregarded the relationship of social classes to the means of production, concentrating instead upon economic institutions, understood as psychologically based phenomena. On the relationship between social being and consciousness the historicists' position was the inverse of that of Marx. For them, 'the causes of all economic behaviour are to be found solely in the realm of psychology', which is taken to embrace also those epiphenomena of psychological drives: ideas and moral systems, institutions, customs and law.[28]

The other great debate in which the GHS engaged was with the Austrian school of marginalist economics. At issue was not the innovation for which marginalism is best known, its subjective-psychological theory of value. Rather, the dispute centred on the methodology of social-scientific research and in particular on the trans-historical validity of marginalist analysis. Where the historicists proposed that economic behaviour is shaped by social norms and conventions that alter over time, and that economic analysis begins with institutions and must therefore be grounded in empirical inquiries in psychology, anthropology, statistics or history, the Austrians discerned underneath the variety of cultural skins a consistent skeleton of given and unchanging laws. On this basis they developed a formal, deductive, rule-governed economic theory in contrast to the inductive approach of the historicists, for whom the behaviour of particular collectivities can only be understood by studying the answers to political and ethical questions – how does each define the common good, and how is behaviour consistent with the common good enforced? In contradistinction to the GHS, for which institutions are 'the backbone of the economy',[29] the focus of the Austrians was upon elementary exchange processes as transacted by individuals. The methodological purpose in stripping away society, history and psychology was to reveal how rational individuals and firms behave in their natural economic condition and how prices are determined in an ideal world of perfect knowledge, perfect foresight, perfect competition and pure 'rationality'.[30]

Alongside and linked to deductivism, the other hallmark of neoclassical theory was its methodological individualism: the axiom that the foundational impulses of all economic activity emanate from rational, self-interested, economizing individuals. This can be broken down into two claims. One, ontological, is that self-interest is an elementary human drive. The other, epistemological, is that the basic unit of analysis in the social sciences is the individual, which, in economics, means the economizing, cost–benefit-calculating individual from whose psyches and endogenously derived preferences all relevant decisions, behaviour and forms of organization flow. This second claim stems from what is sometimes described as the 'method of isolation'. It is a methodological recipe involving two simple steps: first, discard the accidental, leaving only the essential reality; next, break it down into its most basic, typical and enduring components.[31] Applied to the social sciences this procedure reveals that human behaviour at its most elemental and essential is individual – and it is symptomatic that Menger and the Austrians had repeated metaphorical recourse to robinsonades. Social patterns, culture and institutions are construed as, at most,

> the aggregation of innumerable sovereign individuals exercising free choice on the basis of personal preferences. Most importantly, there is no feedback onto the individual, separately or collectively, from institutions, culture or theory that might variably influence or shape who or what individuals are and do.[32]

Taking the abstract, atomized individual as the unit of study, the task for the social scientist is to discover the individual foundations of social institutions, with the result that institutions are understood as unintended outcomes arising from spontaneous individual action, notably through market processes (the invisible hand).

It is important to note that the ontological and epistemological claims are separable, and while the neoclassical approach tends to envisage the market economy as a natural institution this need not necessarily entail naturalistic explanation. Liberal or conservative aristocrats all, the Austrians believed that egotism and competitiveness are fixed attributes of human nature. But this hypothesis is smuggled into the system as a methodological axiom, with the supposition that when reduced to their 'essential reality' for economic analysis, humans are not social but self-interested 'rational' individuals – where rationality is behaviour that validates their model, enabling economists to explain away any mismatch between theory and reality with reference to 'irrational' behaviour.

When accounting for what they see as the naturalness of market behaviour, the Austrians do not for the most part allude to an innate human propensity to barter and exchange but arrive at the same conclusion by combining the atomistic-individualist axiom with a structuralist logic. Individuals, they reason, are irreducibly diverse, they necessarily place different subjective values on goods and services, are rational and therefore seek to maximize their preference-fulfilment; hence in any society of human individuals an incentive for exchange will inevitably arise. Market exchange will tend to prevail, but this is due to the indirect consequences of individual human rationality in conditions of scarcity (whereby individuals tend to maximize utility by making rational choices that bring them nearer to the margin of indifference) and not, or at least not primarily, to any intrinsic feature imputed to human nature.[33] It is significant that Schumpeter, in one of the most distinguished works of the Austrian school of marginalist economics, *Das Wesen und der Hauptinhalt der theoretischen Nationalökonomie*, explicitly rejects the *Homo oeconomicus* model while arguing that because the subject matter of economics is individual choice, the proper approach, at least for the narrow purposes of economic theory, must be methodological individualism.[34] (Indeed, it is he who coined the term.) Intelligent marginalists, Schumpeter insists, are aware that their *Homo oeconomicus* assumption is an intentionally unrealistic construct, a heuristic model designed to reveal the logic of economic behaviour and not a statement on human nature.[35]

Menger and his co-thinkers were aware that their abstractions did not directly correspond to the real-world economies. Rather, they represented an ideal world against which reality could be measured and against which proposed reforms could be evaluated – this ideal world was the free-market 'utopia' against which Polanyi inveighed in TGT. Economists, in their view, are builders of parsimonious models; they need not necessarily hold human beings to be rationally calculating egotists, but this aspect of human behaviour can be modelled in their terms. Despite the appearance of avoiding naturalistic explanation, by abstracting the economic actor from the social relations of capitalist society 'and so in treating those social relations as the natural substratum and not as the social foundation of economic action in a capitalist society', Simon Clarke has perceptively argued,[36] marginalism naturalizes capitalist social relations, accounting for the institutions of capitalist society – absolute property, market exchange, money, and the separation of the labourer from the means of production – in terms of the imputed behaviour of the rational individual. Thus, for Menger, 'the phenomena of private property, of barter, of money, of credit are phenomena of human economy which have been manifesting themselves repeatedly in the course of human development',[37] while Böhm-Bawerk, in similar vein, defines capital as anything added to the 'original' factors of land and labour, such that any tool-using society becomes, by definition, 'capitalistic' and is considered subject to the same universal and timeless principles.[38] Unlike the classical political economists, for whom historically specific institutional, social and political factors were relevant in analysing the development of any particular economy, for marginalism these should be bracketed out of consideration; all effective social organizations are merely disguised versions of the 'ur-market'.[39] If definitions at this level of abstraction take centre stage in historical-economic analysis it becomes futile to attempt, as Marx or the historicists had done, to distinguish among diverse social formations in which different rules for the conduct of economic life apply.

Where, vis-à-vis the *Methodenstreit*, was Polanyi positioned? As I discussed in the introduction and above, Polanyi was close to the GHS and even closer to its sociological brother, Tönnies, and cousin, Max Weber. He cites Schmoller and especially Bücher as his precursors in approaching economic history from the 'institutional and historical' perspective, and in its broad outlines adhered to the perspective on capitalism developed by Schmoller, Tönnies and Weber, one that highlights the 'spirit' embodied in capitalist rationality.[40] He commends Bücher for having overturned the presumption that exchange was a natural feature of every economy and for originating the thesis that the growth of markets cannot be understood without reference to the central role of state power. On one issue, however, the nature of economic value, the GHS split between a minority (including Tönnies) who advocated a Ricardian labour theory and a majority who adopted the marginalist conception. The latter group included Schmoller, Bücher, Weber and Oppenheimer, who sympathized with the subjective individualism of Menger and company but, working within the German tradition of *sozialpolitik*, were more sensitive to the social injustice and anomie generated by rampant capitalism. For Weber, marginalism offered an adequate account of economic behaviour in capitalist society only, one that had to be situated in a broader framework; he also took issue with marginalism over its 'naturalism' and its subordination of moral and political purposes to the single ideal of economic rationality. For Oppenheimer, similarly, the problem with the marginalists was neither their application of a *Homo oeconomicus* postulate nor the assumption that 'pure economics' is a valid pursuit, but their faith that economics can explain human behaviour in its complexity, when its proper role should be as a subdiscipline of sociology.[41]

On this divide Polanyi followed the majority. He took particularly seriously the marginalist arguments laid out by Oppenheimer, by Schumpeter in *Wesen und Hauptinhalt*, and by Menger in the second edition of *Grundsätze der Volkswirtschaftslehre*. During his early liberal-socialist phase Polanyi went so far as to propose that economics 'does not deal with raw materials, labour or production as such, but with the act of choice', and that 'pure economic theory' applies trans-historically: the 'economic laws' that govern the behaviour of individuals, whether in Crusoesque isolation, as participants in a market economy or indeed in a planned economy, 'are the same in every case'.[42] The neoclassical tenet that resonated most directly with his *Weltanschauung* was its argument that prices result 'from human activity' and its repudiation of the belief 'that value was intrinsic in a thing'. Price, he insisted, is a subjective product; it is 'not an attribute of the item but of the person and of the social relationship'.[43] Only where free human will is found can one also find responsibility, and only those economic categories are valid that can be interpreted as the free expression of human will.[44]

In the 1920s, while retaining marginalism's value theory, Polanyi grew increasingly critical of its interpretation of the ethics implicit in the market system. In a perceptive discussion of this issue, Hüseyin Özel observes that for Polanyi the human being is a 'strong evaluator'. That is, he is

> endowed with the capacity to evaluate his desires strongly in the sense that they are not only concerned with the outcomes of the motivations but also with the 'quality' of the motivations. In other words, he goes 'deeper', i.e. characterizes his motivations at greater depth. However, since an 'individual in the market' must behave only on the basis of the hope of gain or fear of hunger (or pain and pleasure for that matter), he is forced to be reduced to an individual who lacks 'depth', as we ordinarily use this metaphor for people. . . . Thus, the market economy violates our very essence, for it forces us to behave like those 'shallow Utilitarians', by identifying hunger and profit as the only two motives that guide our lives.[45]

On the basis of his historicist conception of institutions as the embodiment of ethics, Polanyi identifies the market economy as the generator of a pernicious utilitarianism. In a market society the need to agree collectively upon ethical ends is obviated – and this was welcomed by the Austrians in the belief that collective agreement about ethico-political ends in modern societies is utopian. In construing the market as a mechanism by which individuals seek to achieve their economic goals – a value-free, technical instrument – the Austrians eliminate social and political considerations from the picture. Dealing only with decisions that directly determine individual gain, with ethical decisions devolved to the individual and as such of no interest to economics, they sanction an amoral orientation toward economic life.

In addition to this ethico-political blast at the marginalist paradigm, Polanyi advanced a methodological critique. He lambasted it for taking as its premise the imaginary isolated individual, arguing that the discursive constitution of the individual as private individual is a phenomenon specific to a mode of economic relations in which the co-ordination of labour occurs via the market exchange of its products. He challenged its premises that individuals act rationally to pursue selfish ends that are determined on the basis of intrinsic desires, that welfare is maximized and efficient institutions emerge if individuals are permitted the latitude to pursue their selfish interests, and that social institutions evolve spontaneously when particular sets of individuals demand them. The error consists not in the stripping away of social relations but in the notion that the workings of actually existing economies can be adequately theorized in their absence. In particular, because institutions are assumed in the theory it cannot explain why one set of institutions is present and not another. In addition, he objected to the economic essentialism inherent in the marginalist model, in particular the idea that there exists an analytically autonomous economic sphere that possesses a logic and rationality of its own. Economics, he sighed, was 'perhaps the only societal discipline that never freed itself at all from the influence of atomistic rationalism', a method that inevitably led to the 'hypostatization' of the market system.[46]

Given the force of his critique of the neoclassical framework, it is puzzling that Polanyi accepted marginalist value theory. In so doing, it seems to me, he was buying into a methodology that could not be assimilated into his broader philosophy. He cannot but have been aware that the apparent contribution of subjective value theory to a de-reified view of economics and to the exercise of human responsibility was a chimera, given its embeddedness within a general approach that so relentlessly hypostatizes the market system. Be that as it may, he stuck to his project of rejecting marginalism's methodological integument while retaining its value theory. Although characteristically innovative, his attempt to chop the value-theoretical branch from the neoclassical trunk and to graft it onto a historicist stem yielded, as we shall see, not a little confusion.

From marginalism to formalism

If in its first phase of development marginalist economics decanted itself from the wider pool of the social sciences by eliminating social and political relations from its purview, in its second phase –

conventionally dated as beginning in 1932 – it pushed outward, asserting its applicability to all realms of human behaviour and to some that lie beyond. As the domain claimed by economics expanded to include analysis of all forms of human behaviour, Schumpeter's insistence that the logic of behaviour studied by economics is not to be confused with a model of man grew increasingly difficult to uphold. In this section I summarize this disciplinary revolution of the inter-war epoch before turning to Polanyi's critique of the application of neoclassical concepts to non-market societies.

When the rudiments of the neoclassical framework were established in the late nineteenth century, its pioneers operated with a traditional definition of their subject. 'Economics is the study of mankind in the ordinary business of life', was Alfred Marshall's matter-of-fact definition; 'it examines that part of individual and social action which is most closely connected with the attainment and with the use of the material requisites of wellbeing'.[47] It was a definition that, like that of classical political economy before it, invited the critique that it relies upon seeing the economic sphere as autonomous, and 'vulgar' material aims as paramount. But in his 1932 *Essay on the Nature and Significance of Economic Science,* Lionel Robbins famously rejected the restriction of economics to one domain of human activity that the traditional definition had implied. His redefinition was rooted in marginalism's method, with its focus on the hypothetical behaviour of rational, economizing individuals rather than the empirical behaviour of individuals-in-society, but he pushes this to the limit. In his hands economics became the 'science of choice'. Its domain was now the logic of maximization subject to constraints on available means; in scope, economics was now universal – except in one respect: the institutional moulding of, or psychological origins of, individual preferences were excluded from investigation.

The revolution associated with Robbins' essay served to re-found the discipline of economics upon 'the logic of choice' (otherwise known as 'logic of preference' or 'rational choice'). No domain of social activity now existed from which it was barred. All that was now required for something to be deemed a subject for economic analysis was the presence of four conditions: a variety of ends, variety in their importance, limited means for achieving them, and the possibility of alternative applications for these means. As Polanyi summarized it, the task of attaining the greatest satisfaction through the rational use of insufficient means is not restricted to the traditional domain of the economic but is present whether a general is disposing his troops for battle, a chess player is scheming to sacrifice a pawn, a lawyer is marshalling evidence to defend a client, an artist is husbanding his effects, a believer is earmarking prayers and good works to attain the best grade of salvation in his reach, or a thrifty housewife is planning the week's purchases.[48]

Polanyi, as we shall see, greeted the near-infinite expansion of the declared domain of economics with scepticism, but neoclassical economists welcomed Robbins' redefinition. It opened a rather tempting door to disciplinary aggrandizement, and unleashed what its critics were to call 'the imperialism of economics': the intrusion of utility-maximizing economic man into the other social (and, with adaptations, ethological) sciences, together with the assumption that the appropriate framework for analysing behaviour exists universally as a matrix formed by scarcity, competition and rational self-interest.

In subsequent decades the limits of economics expanded throughout human society and psychology and – breaking beyond even Robbins' disciplinary definition – into the biosphere beyond. For Gary Becker, 'economic analysis is a powerful tool not only in understanding human behaviour but also in understanding the behaviour of other species', while Gordon Tullock claims that all organisms, from bacteria to bears, being utility-maximizers, can be treated as if they have the same general type of preference function that the micro-economics textbooks attribute to human beings. Another salient example is Janet Tai Landa, who, in an essay entitled 'The Socioeconomic Organization of Honeybee Colonies', argues that 'an efficient bee organization is one that economizes on the sum of setup costs, information costs, and defence costs'. Wendell Berry goes one step further, asseverating that 'rats and roaches live by competition under the law of supply and demand', and, even as I write, the newswires are buzzing with reports of a scientific discovery: that male Java apes 'pay for sex' by grooming females, such that where fewer females are present the 'price of sex' rises, demonstrating conclusively the market orientation of our nearest neighbours on the evolutionary tree.[49] It is only a matter of time before research projects will be set up to investigate the market-driven behaviour of sharks. (Clue: in barren expanses of ocean the 'price' of fish rises.) This is imaginative stuff, no doubt, but is devoid of sense – for prices, markets, trade, supply and demand are determinate concepts only where goods take the form of commodities, and this occurs only in human society.

Such has been the success of the imperialism of economics that bookshop shelves groan under the weight of tomes with titles such as *Uncovering the New Economics of Everything* and the more modestly named *Why Economics Explains Almost Everything*, works that apply marginalist techniques to all aspects of social life, behavioural and institutional, not to mention psychology and human evolution. In *The Economic Naturalist: In Search of Explanations for Everyday Enigmas*, to give one example, marginalist solutions are provided to the abiding puzzles of daily life, such as 'Why does social courtesy sometimes lead to inefficient outcomes on one-lane bridges?', and 'If attractive people are more intelligent than others, and if blondes are considered more attractive, why are there so many jokes about dumb blondes?'.[50] In *The Logic of Life*, to give another, Adam Smith's hoary myth is yoked to an argument to explain why *Homo sapiens* supposedly drove *Homo neanderthalis* to extinction: 'computer-based simulations' show that it was the propensity to truck, barter and exchange that enabled our ancestors to wipe out *neanderthalis* in a mere few thousand years.[51]

In Polanyi's day, 'economic man' had not descended to quite these depths but the process was well under way, not least via the sowing of marginalist seeds in economic anthropology, seeds which took root in the 1930s and produced a fruit that Polanyi called 'formalism'. The term, as he put it in a letter to a student, 'should *not* be confused with the mathematically (or otherwise) formalized character of much of theoretical economics'.[52] Nor should it be mistaken for formal model building in the social sciences – or indeed with Weber's use of 'formal rationality' to refer to a society's ability to quantify and calculate its economic activities. Rather, it is an approach in economic anthropology that incorporates three marginalist propositions. First, the unit of analysis is the rational choosing autonomous individual, evaluating alternative courses of action and adopting the one that maximizes 'utility' – i.e. the fulfilment of their goals. ('All forms of social behaviour', as the US anthropologist Melville Herskovits put it, 'must be referred to the behaviour of individual members of a given society'.[53]) Second, given that people always want more than they can have, the condition in which resource allocation decisions are made is ineluctably characterized by scarcity, which means that the pursuit of one utility necessitates relinquishing another. The prerequisite for systematic economic analysis is not, therefore, the belief that human individuals naturally incline to increase their own pile of possessions but simply the recognition that they respond to the condition of scarcity by seeking to improve efficiency – they economize. On the whole, and across cultures, argued Herskovits,

> the individual tends to maximize his satisfactions in terms of the choices he makes. Where the gap between utility and disutility is appreciable, and the producer or consumer of a good or service is free to make his choice, then, other things being equal, he will make his choice in terms of utility rather than disutility.[54]

Individuals, everywhere, are constantly weighing up the opportunity costs involved in the pursuit of one utility as compared to others: 'a Bushman setting out on a hunt for meat or for buried tubers has to choose a direction and distance to travel that have direct and opportunity costs in terms of energy and time',[55] while even 'the savage can be careful to the last basket of grain and can bargain to the last goat-skin'. 'It has been shown', according to another formalist anthropologist, extending Robbinsian analysis to Robinson's fictional island, 'that Robinson Crusoe has something more than a strictly methodological significance; that an individual in his position would indeed feel the pressure of needs upon resources', would choose between different applications of resources, 'would encounter varying returns and would have to choose between present and future and between work and leisure'.[56]

Third, given that all individuals exhibit rational, utility-maximizing behaviour and that utilities are preferences of any kind, marginalist analysis applies to all human societies. It retains its validity even with respect to unpriced goods such as warmed air – for lighting a fire involves a choice: whether or not to gather, lay and light the kindling. Not only is the use of natural resources, labour-power and technical knowledge an economic universal, Herskovits emphasized, but so is that of 'capital equipment'. Also universal is the division of labour, and hence some kind of exchange of services and of the goods they produce, as well as 'the profit orientation'.[57] Indeed, in any given society the individual 'can be regarded as an entrepreneur, manipulating those around him, trading his products of labor, attention, respect etc. for the most he can get in return'.[58]

The policy implications of the formalist approach were unmistakable. It is premised upon the assumption of an environment of pervasive natural scarcity in which constraints imposed upon the individual by competition are assumed to reflect not particular social relations but the relative scarcity of goods in relation to human wants. On that basis it envisages perfectly functioning markets as the optimal framework in which to enable rational individual actors to maximize their 'utility' and to reconcile the inevitable conflicts of interest that take place among them. The conclusion is that maximally free markets should be constructed in order to optimize individual freedom. Non-market societies will and must become free – with the application of force if need be. It is a conclusion that is succinctly summarized in the quotation from the eminent formalist Harold Schneider with which this chapter begins.

Given that neoclassical economics rapidly advanced into the mainstream, was considered the orthodoxy by the end of the nineteenth century and was adopted by anthropologists from the 1930s onward, the puzzle that presented itself to Polanyi is apparent. On the one hand, ethnographic findings had confirmed that 'primitive societies' operate according to fundamentally different principles from those of modern capitalism; that their economies are 'submerged' in wider social relationships, with neither production nor distribution linked to specific economic interests attached to the possession of goods.[59] On the other, the ascendant paradigm in economics claimed that, in conditions of scarcity, human beings must and will economize, rationally calculating opportunity costs as supply-and-demand curves change in ways that can be studied with the same tools of economic analysis that apply to fully fledged market economies.

In grappling with this puzzle Polanyi began to reflect upon the meaning of the term 'the economy'. Nineteenth-century thinkers, he observed, had noted a discrepancy between two different meanings to which they attached contrasting definitions, one indicating substantive content, while the other pointed to their exchange (or 'catallactic') connotation. As an example he cites Marx's 'means of production' and 'titles to property' (although the more relevant distinction in Marx is arguably that between the material appropriation of natural resources and the social organization through which this occurs).[60] A more direct influence, I would venture, was the aforementioned work of Somló, structured as it is around a distinction between forms of exchange, understood juridically, and the material circulation of goods.[61] As is well known, however, the principal resources to which Polanyi himself refers are Max Weber and, perhaps surprisingly, Carl Menger.

Two meanings of economic

From Weber, Polanyi borrowed a frame upon which to structure his research, and two words. 'For economic anthropology no "sub-discipline" is more relevant than the sociological approach', he proposed, 'rather on the lines of Weber and institutional analysis.'[62] In approaching the problem of the changing place of the economy in human society, Weber

> needed terms which would distinguish between the element of rationality in the economy and its natural elements, such as human wants and needs, which are, by definition, irrational. The distinction between formal and substantive root meanings offered such a conceptual tool.[63]

In his lexicon rationality is substantive in so far as it is shaped by political, moral or religious values (or 'affectually determined'). It is formal in so far as it is quantifiable, calculable and based upon means–end reasoning; it reaches its fullest extent in a pecuniary culture – modern capitalism – which thus represents the culmination of the 'rationalization' process.[64] But Weber, argues Polanyi, was unable to use his couplet to distinguish correctly between the substantive and formal meanings of 'economic'. That Weber failed to do so was due to his 'trite selfishness theory of economic motives' and his tendency to identify the economy with the market. In the belief 'that the separating out of the scarcity elements from the natural and social process of subsistence was either impossible or, if possible, useless', Weber consciously preferred 'to keep to the current (compound) meaning of the term economic'.[65]

Weber's terms, however, could be usefully matched with concepts that Polanyi found in the second edition of Menger's *Grundsätze*, in which the Austrian economist identifies two basic 'directions' of human economy: the 'technical' and the 'economizing'.[66] The former refers to the demand for goods, the creation of the means of production necessary to meet that demand, and their organization in time and space, while the latter denotes the choices predicated upon a scarcity of goods and the processes that flow therefrom: the creation of a hierarchy of preferences, and the attempt to achieve the desired quantities of preferred goods with a minimal input of resources. These distinct dimensions of the economic are normally elided, but they arise upon different bases and have different implications: only scarce goods are economic in the second sense, a sense that therefore need not make an appearance where the means necessary to produce a given range of goods are available in abundance.[67] Menger thus avoided Weber's error of applying the scarcity notion to non-capitalist periods of history; his concept of the economy, Polanyi proclaimed, was sound, innovative, and could be consistently applied throughout the social sciences.[68]

In Polanyi's schema, which marries Menger's concept to Weber's vocabulary, the 'substantive' meaning of economics encompasses human society's interaction with its natural and social environment in so far as this results in supplying it with the means of material want satisfaction (including all material commodities, as well as the services required to supply physiological needs such as food or shelter).[69] It deals with how human beings make their living, whether or not this entails rational decision-making or economizing behaviour and whether or not production is for use or exchange. Unlike formal economics it 'is capable of yielding the concepts that are required by the social sciences for an investigation of all the empirical economies of the past and present' – with the proviso that those concepts are generally rather than universally applicable: they admit of exceptions, unlike universal propositions, which admit of none.[70]

In its formal meaning, economics denotes the logical character of the means–end relationship, as apparent in terms such as 'economizing'. Although borrowed from Weber, for Polanyi 'formal' does not refer to calculability but to the logic of economizing: the rational choices between alternative ends induced by an insufficiency of means. If the rules governing rational choice in conditions of scarcity are trans-cultural and trans-historical, the extent to which they apply concretely in a given economy depends upon whether or not it takes the form of sequences of price-oriented acts induced by choice in a context of insufficient means – a market system, in other words.

Armed with the substantive–formal distinction Polanyi was able to develop a rigorous critique of neoclassical economics, or at least of its application to pre-modern societies. He was scathing about formalist anthropologists such as Herskovits for their assumption that trade, money, markets, capital and investment occur in 'primitive' and modern capitalist societies alike.[71] In addition to published critiques he versified his derision privately in the form of a Gilbert-and-Sullivan-style lyric, the 'Model of a Classical Economist'. Its first stanza captures the essence of his position.

I am the very model of a classical economist;
I've information on the subject making me an optimist
I know the pricing system, so I ignore the historical
From Paleolithic to Neolithic in order categorical.
I'm very well acquainted though with matters mathematical;
For fuller understanding I'll just supply the quadratical.
Any problem is answered by my marginal analysis
When you grant my assumption of a 'ceteris paribus'![72]

In terms of the details of his critique, arguably Polanyi's crucial move is an assault on a core neoclassical axiom: that economic transactions are necessarily characterized by scarcity. If scarcity means that a given economic actor is not in possession of all possible means to achieve her goal, this applies everywhere but is analytically fruitless. Correctly employed, Polanyi suggests, it refers 'to *situations* in which *insufficiency* induces choice between the alternative uses of the goods', and should be used to denote a relationship between means and ends rather than 'as an adjective appropriate to qualify things or goods' in which the element of choice is absent.[73] Conceived thus, not all economic decisions are made under conditions of scarcity: in reality there may or may not be sufficient means available for an end to be achieved, and there may or may not be more than one use for the means. The concept of scarcity, Polanyi's friend and student Harry Pearson added, can be used productively only where 'the natural fact of limited means leads to a sequence of choices regarding the use of these means, and this situation is possible only if there is alternativity to the uses of means and there are preferentially graded ends'.[74]

A second prong of Polanyi's attack on the scarcity postulate comes in the form of ideology critique. Far from being an ancient wisdom, the postulation of a condition of generalized scarcity in which humans, in the absence of a state, perpetually compete for resources (and ultimately 'tear one another to pieces like a pack of famished wolves') is peculiar to modernity. It originates with Thomas Hobbes, whose atomistic conception of society, realized in the market system, brackets out man's irreducibly social condition and assumes 'the insufficiency of all things material', thus initiating a line of thought that misconstrues the satisfaction of material wants and scarcity as a single issue. As Hobbes' adversary, Polanyi champions Aristotle, who, 'by rejecting the scarcity postulate explicitly, made himself the philosophical fount of the position we represent'. In so far as the scarcity postulate springs 'from the demand side', the Greek philosopher attributes it 'to a misconceived notion of the good life as a desire for a greater abundance of physical goods and enjoyments'.[75] Related to this, he conceives of the economy as an instituted process through which sustenance is ensured: like any other animal, human beings are naturally self-sufficient. As Aristotle's heirs Polanyi cites Rousseau and many a contemporary sociologist too. In contrast to Hobbes their premise reads: 'if there is not enough, men will act in accordance with the instituted values'.[76]

Scarcity, in this analysis, is an empirical and socially constructed matter; its presence depends upon natural and social factors and cannot be assumed *a priori*.[77] Two conditions in particular render scarcity more likely. One is the presence of money qua generalized means of exchange: because so fungible it can legitimately be seen as invariably scarce.[78] (The same cannot be said of, say, parsnips or cathedrals, with their limited fungibility.) The other is the extent to which cultural definitions and social control permit the exercise of 'free choice'. Whatever the range of uses to which an item can be put, individuals may not be free to choose among the formally envisageable alternatives. Rules may govern their choice in the matter, and in societies that do not deem natural and human resources to be 'generalized means or facilities adaptable to a variety of ends' the notion of scarcity has little purchase.[79]

In short, scarcity cannot be assessed independently of its meanings in a given cultural context. In modern market economies scarcity becomes generalized: since everything is interconnected, everything is scarce. By contrast, consider the Mbuti Pygmies, who, the anthropologist Colin Turnbull discovered, envision their forest habitat as benevolent and lavish, or the Trobriand Islanders, who normally grow

> twice as much yam fruit as they need and allow it to rot. They phrase their economic life in terms of plenty, while according to our standards they are surrounded by scarcity. We, according to their standards, are surrounded by plenty but phrase our economic life in terms of scarcity.[80]

Indeed, Polanyi continues, ethnographic research demonstrates that there is no starvation in societies living on the subsistence margin except where nature ordains.[81] (This perspective was to achieve a more celebrated expression in the work of Marshall Sahlins, a neo-evolutionist anthropologist who attended Polanyi's seminars at Columbia. A good case can be made, Sahlins argues in *Stone Age Economics*, 'that hunters and gatherers work less than we do; and, rather than a continuous travail, the food quest is intermittent, leisure abundant, and there is a greater amount of sleep in the daytime per capita per year than in any other condition of society'.[82])

The ideological aspect of the neoclassical/formalist construction of scarcity, Polanyi argued, was one facet of a broader problem: the universalization of the assumptions peculiar to a unique historical conjuncture, Western Europe and North America following the Industrial Revolution, in which there reigned 'an organization of man's livelihood to which the rules of choice happened to be singularly applicable'. Given such an economy, consisting of a sequence of scarcity-induced choices taken by instrumental utility-maximizers, the methods of neoclassical economics indeed have traction, but these conditions do not obtain trans-historically. Elsewhere, indeed, 'economic analysis loses most of its relevance as a method of inquiry'.[83] The qualitative differences between 'tribal' or peasant societies and industrial market societies are such that the economic principles designed to analyse the latter have only limited application in the former. That this is not common sense is due to the profound ideological impact of the market system: the justifications on its behalf have come to shape the way we perceive society, in particular through the utilitarian assumption that all other values are subordinated to that of efficiency as defined by market behaviour, but also in the beliefs that material motives dictate social behaviour, that social institutions are moulded by the economic system, and that these tenets apply throughout human history. The last fallacy in particular was a product of Enlightenment 'atomistic rationalism', with its image of society as the product of contracting individuals. When economists applied this method universally they were able to 'discover' the potential existence of a market system in any and every society, whether empirically present or not.

> Thus economic analysis sometimes seemed to be endowed with a formal scope that transcended the empirical limitations set to it by the actuality of a market system. All human economy, then, could be regarded as a virtual supply–demand–price mechanism, and the actual processes, whatever they were, could be 'explained' in terms of this hypostatization.

Economics, Polanyi laments, continues to adhere to the 'atomistic-individualistic model of society' even though that model is obsolete, 'and the contract theories of the origins of state and economy smack to us of the kindergarten'.[84] Individuals communicate and co-ordinate and – perhaps most visibly in tribal societies – incorporate the interests of others into their considerations; their behaviour cannot be modelled as that of isolated selfish decision-makers except perhaps in present day market society.[85]

If, in so far as it is applied to non-market economies, neoclassical economics is ideology, can a scientific, general theory of the economy be constructed so as to provide a secure foundation for comparative economic analysis? This was Polanyi's goal: to reformulate the field of general economic history, using comparative research into social institutions to chart the 'changing place of the economy' in human society systematically. Serving as an indispensable conceptual floor is the substantive definition of economy. Premised on the recognition that economy is inseparable from 'culture', it reminds us 'the functioning of the economic process as such is therefore a problem for the sociologist and the cultural anthropologist to resolve'.[86] It should, he concludes, 'be consistently adhered to throughout the social sciences, with the single exception of market phenomena, where the formal or scarcity definition alone can lead to an effective theory'.[87]

Mechanisms of integration

Having laid out Polanyi's critique of formalism and the basic contours of his substantivist alternative, I can now turn, more briefly, to explicate two further concepts that are central to his approach: 'the economy as instituted process' and 'mechanisms of integration'.

From his substantive definition, Polanyi derives an approach to economies as instituted processes. His chain of reasoning goes something like this. The economy is a social process that organizes a continuous supply of material means. This process 'consists of *movements* of material things: locational and appropriational, i.e. in relation to other things and to persons'.[88] Location and appropriation are near synonyms of, respectively, production and distribution (or ownership). Location includes the creation and transportation of goods and services, while 'appropriation', following Weber, denotes rights of disposal over resources: 'it refers to opportunities, chances, influences, positions, situations, titles, privileges, etc.' and includes two-way transactions (circulation) as well as simple control (disposition).[89] These movements are *integrated*, to the extent to which they are interdependent. They form an economic process in so far as they are integrated, and the forms of integration, in turn, 'depend upon the manner in which the interlocking movements are institutionalized'.[90] Each consists of 'an aggregate of elements embodied in economic institutions', and institutions are not 'economic' unless they comprise a concentration of economic elements – 'It is in this sense that we may describe a factory or a granary as an economic institution, while Christmas or Congress are not economic institutions, in spite of their economic importance, in the substantive sense.'[91]

In summary, by instituted process Polanyi means that economies consist of a sequence of functional movements that are embedded in 'social relations' (or 'institutions' – he uses the terms interchangeably), their function being to supply a group of individuals with a flow of material goods. The 'social relations in which the process is embedded invest it with a measure of unity and stability',[92] and this enables the student of comparative economics to turn to the next task: the construction of a taxonomy of mechanisms of integration and the classification of economies according to which of these is dominant.

An analytical and not a descriptive concept, 'mechanism of integration' describes ideal patterns of locational and appropriational movements each of which corresponds to a particular pattern of economic co-ordination and institutional structure. Drawing upon materials from anthropology and ancient and modern history, Polanyi identifies three basic mechanisms: exchange, reciprocity and redistribution. The movements of redistribution are centric, its typical institutional locus is the state; those of reciprocity are symmetrical, its locus the community; those of exchange are polydirectional, its locus the market. The *loci classici* of market exchange are the capitalist societies of nineteenth-century Europe and North America, where economic intercourse centres upon goods and services changing hands in vice-versa movements amongst isolated actors within an economic realm that is 'disembedded' from non-economic institutions. Polanyi's understanding of the market economy is discussed in previous chapters and there is no need to retread that ground. But what of non-market societies? How are goods distributed, asks Polanyi, where there is no 'motive of gain', no 'principle of labouring for remuneration', and no 'separate and distinct institution based on economic motives'?[93] The answer lies in reciprocity and redistribution.

Polanyi derived the term reciprocity from Malinowski, although it was also used by Maine, Thurnwald and, in a different sense, Marcel Mauss.[94] In Polanyi's conception the paradigmatic reciprocal relationship is gift exchange, which is in central respects antithetical to market exchange: in the latter, the relationship is entered into for the sake of the commodity, in the former, the product is exchanged for the sake of the relationship.[95] It is to be found primarily in relations of kinship, friendship, cooperation and chieftainship, and refers to situations where 'members of one group act towards members of another group as members of that group or a third or fourth group act towards them',[96] the movements typically involving the transfer of equivalently valued resources between correlative points of symmetrically arranged groups. As an example Polanyi mentions 'the striking "duality" which we find in tribal subdivisions' (such as moieties) that 'lends itself to the pairing out of individual relations and thereby assists the give-and-take of goods and services in the absence of permanent records'. As an example, consider the Arapesh of New Guinea, as recounted by Margaret Mead. If there is meat cooking on an Arapesh man's fire,

> it is either meat which was killed by another, a brother, a brother-in-law, a sister's son, etc. – and has been given to him, in which case he and his family may eat it, or it is meat which he himself killed and which he is smoking to give away to someone else, for to eat one's own kill, even though it be only a small bird, is a crime to which only the morally deficient would stoop.[97]

Or take the Trobriand Islands, where each coastal village is paired with an inland village, enabling the reciprocal exchange of breadfruit for fish to operate smoothly, while in the kula trade each individual pairs up with another on a different isle, facilitating a sophisticated pattern of circulation of armbands, necklaces and other valuables.[98]

After market exchange and reciprocity the third term is 'redistribution' (or, as Polanyi occasionally calls it, 'storage-cum-redistribution'). An adaptation of Thurnwald's 'distribution'[99] and synonym of *Verwaltungswirtschaft* ('administered economy'),[100] it refers to economic co-ordination through appropriational movements towards and away from a centre (a chief or state), organized through 'custom, law or *ad hoc* central decision'. Despite the prefix it would be an error to suggest, with David McNally, that it connotes the systematic transfer of resources from rich to poor – indeed, in most societies that Polanyi deems redistributive the flow is in the opposite direction.[101] As its prototype he cites a hunt that requires a division of labour: in technical terms, goods (here, game) are acquired, collected in a central place, then distributed for consumption; in social terms, the divided labour is reunited and community is established. But 'redistribution proper' begins with storage, and the presence of a central individual or group that takes charge of the collection and reallocation of goods. It occurs 'on all civilizational levels, from the primitive hunting tribe to the vast storage systems of ancient Egypt, Sumeria, Babylonia or Peru'.[102] What is common to all of these is a significant measure of 'centricity': the concentration of power in central hands. As Sahlins was to put the point, 'redistribution is chieftainship said in economics'.[103]

If Polanyi's three mechanisms are ideal types, or models, actual societies evince a mix of two or all of them. However, in any given movement of a good, one of the forms can be seen as the system that determines it, and at the aggregate level one form of integration will normally prevail.[104] For example, the 'Christmas trade of Western cultures' is organized along lines of reciprocity, albeit with the assistance of market exchange and in a market-dominated society. That mechanism is dominant 'to which the integration of the factors of production, land and labour is primarily due'.[105] Thus, exchange is integrative where land and food are mobilized as commodities within a system of price-making markets such that the effects of prices are spread to other markets. In such societies non-economic institutions are embedded in the economic framework, and the primary sanctions that govern relations between participants in the economic process are those of price movements. In those where market prices are fixed, by contrast, 'the economy is integrated by the factors which fix that rate, not by the market mechanism'. In redistributive societies, political institutions prevail and sanctions take the form of formal rules, while in their reciprocity-dominated counterparts sanctions are organized primarily through custom, and the economy is completely submerged in society.[106]

Inconsistencies and ambiguities

Polanyi's new conception of the economic and his reciprocity-redistribution-exchange schema proved to be highly influential. His theses were taken up and developed by anthropologists and ancient historians who collaborated with him on the edited volume *Trade and Market in the Early Empires* (including Terence Hopkins, A. L. Oppenheim and Walter Neale), by others in his circle such as Moses Finley, Paul Bohannan and George Dalton, by a range of other anthropologists including Marshall Sahlins and Morton Fried, and – side-swipes at Polanyi's 'radical institutionalism' apart – by the sociologist Neil Smelser.[107] Inevitably, in the process of the dispersion of the model, and his own elaborations of it, a number of ambivalences and tensions came to light. I introduce a selection of these, before presenting an overview of the formalists' response.

There is, firstly, the methodological status of the model. It changed over time. In his earliest uses of reciprocity and redistribution Polanyi used the terms descriptively, for classificatory purposes – as Malinowski and Thurnwald had before him. Later, however, he refashioned them as cornerstones of a general model of 'economies across cultures'. This conceptual evolution has created confusion and inconsistencies with regard to usage by Polanyi himself and interpretations by others. Secondly, at times he applies redistribution to groups smaller than a society, such as a hunting band or the self-sufficient 'household' economy – he had in mind the ancient Greek *oikos*, the Roman *familia* and the medieval manor, but also self-sufficient peasant families[108] – while elsewhere these are referred to as a fourth mechanism, 'householding'. In Rhoda Halperin's view, householding should not be referred to as a subset of redistribution because it need not involve the two-way collection of goods into and away from a centre.[109] Other objections have been raised to the effect that households, being self-sufficient, do not fit into Polanyi's schema at all, given that it is organized around modes of *exchange*, and that, being applicable to restricted social groups, householding cannot define an economy *in its totality*.[110]

A third and more serious difficulty is that Polanyi vacillates over whether attitudinal factors belong to the schema, with each form of integration linked to a modal type of intention. When developing his general economic history he referred to no thinker more than to Max Weber, whose sociology centred upon the composing of typologies of organizations according to the ends that motivate their construction and inform their direction, the means available to those ends, and the value orientation of action that typifies them.[111] Weber's ideal types are distinguished according to psychological dispositions (which, when generalized, are cultural values), as well as the social-relational contexts of the actions to which these dispositions are appropriate motivational forces. Robert Owen, Polanyi's lifelong idol, also placed motivation at the centre of his analysis of economic organization. Whether or not Weber or Owen were direct influences, Polanyi's concepts steered a similar course. Like them, he saw the orientation to individual gain as the distinctive feature of modern market society – by gain he does not mean a profit made in exchange at set prices but one made where prices fluctuate and are subject to bargaining – in contrast to its feudal predecessors, in which economic integration was established on the basis of the peasants' ties of fealty to their lords.[112] More emphatically, in unpublished notes from 1944, he suggests that

> the economic system is organized in different societies at different times, in very different ways. The motives range from duty, compulsion, love of activity, joy of competition, social conformity, vanity, to the thirst of gain and pursuit of profit. . . . Explaining an institution means being able to point to the motives which make individuals participate in it.[113]

However, he was forceful in his disavowal of the postulation of the individual's desire to 'truck and barter' as explanation of the emergence of markets, and the occasions in which he succumbs to the psychologistic fallacy of explaining institutions by actors' motivations are relatively rare. On the whole, his focus was upon the role of institutional arrangements in structuring individual behaviour. At the core of TGT, for example, is the idea that in order to establish a labour market the fear of hunger must be made actual: the individual motives are engineered via the creation of institutions. Haggling, he remarks elsewhere, 'is not the result of some human frailty, but a behavior pattern logically required by the mechanism of the market'.[114] Ultimately, Polanyi sought to finesse the dilemma by relegating the issue of motivation to the domain of scholarly taste. In studying economic institutions, he wrote in 1960,

> one can choose between values and motives on the one hand and physical operations on the other – either of which can be regarded as linking the social relations with the process. Perhaps because I happen to be more familiar with the institutional and operational aspect of man's livelihood, I prefer to deal with the economy primarily as a matter of organization.[115]

Polanyi's primary purpose, then, is not to describe a superficial pattern of the movement of goods and services or the motivational attitudes linked thereto, but to model specific types of economic organization and social structure. Yet the nature of his model tends to hinder fulfilment of that aspiration. Because constructed around formal patterns of locational and appropriational movements, the mechanisms of integration group together forms of behaviour that exhibit a particular pattern even where the social relations that express themselves in this way are utterly diverse. By way of illustration, consider redistribution. Polanyi finds it amongst hunter-gatherer band societies but also as the dominant mode in tributary systems such as ancient Egypt and in the later Roman Empire. As if that range were not already encompassing enough he identifies the Soviet Union as 'an extreme instance' of redistribution and, in the 1950s, observes that the redistributive mode is gaining ground in other 'modern industrial states'.[116] His students detected it as the dominant mode in egalitarian societies (Kalahari bushmen, Congo pygmies) and hierarchic societies (Pharaonic Egypt, Homeric *oikos*, medieval manor) as well as in the public sectors of Western Europe and North America.[117] That the net is cast so wide obscures crucial differences, as Joachim Voss has pointed out.

> Polanyi's definition of redistribution ignores the fact that the same centralising phenomenon – the concentration and dispersion of goods – can have very different results and intentions. For example, in the case of Hawaiian chiefdoms, ritual redistribution clearly includes an element of taxation. This makes possible the existence of a class of political/religious specialists who are not themselves involved in the material process of production. On the other hand, amongst the !Kung San the redistribution of game acquired by one or a few hunters, to the rest of the community, is clearly a form of sharing supported by strong institutional levelling mechanisms. These are instrumental in preventing the emergence of hierarchical social distinctions such as those found among the Hawaiians.[118]

It is no coincidence that Voss's critique echoes that of Weber by Lukacs in his *Destruction of Reason* – that, because framed at such a high level of abstraction, Weber's ideal types become empty formal categories around which sprawling segments of history are assembled, and because they do not require reference to specific types of social relation they can bring entirely disparate institutions under one rubric. Weber, writes Lukacs, 'formally equated ancient Egyptian bureaucracy with socialism, soviets (*Räte*) and estates (*Stände*)', and 'in speaking of the irrational vocation of leader (charisma), he drew an analogy between a Siberian shaman and the social democrat leader Kurt Eisner, etc.'.[119] His method, in short, is formalistic, in the sense that it describes formal properties that summarize superficially common features that in reality are profoundly different. It is guided by what a recent critic has called a 'categorizing imperative' dedicated to the construction of, and cataloguing of phenomena within, ideal types selected and arranged through a formalistic technique of analogy.[120]

There is a further zone of ambiguity in Polanyi's model that demands attention. Its origin, I would speculate, lies in different understandings of reciprocity. Does reciprocal behaviour exist in all forms of society, as Mauss believed? Or is it the hallmark of 'primitive' societies, as Maine and Malinowski maintained?[121] These two perspectives are not necessarily incompatible, but which one is emphasized tends to relate to the question of what is involved in the 'dominance' of a mechanism of integration: does it refer to preponderance, such that one mechanism is more significant but *inter pares*, or to dominance in the sense that it determines the operation of the whole? There is ambiguity in Polanyi's writings on this issue, and it relates, in turn, to his vacillation over the degree to which the mechanisms of integration slot into a framework of evolutionary progression. At times he is adamant that they 'do not represent 'stages' of development. No sequence in time is implied.'[122] Yet he could not easily shake himself free of the sway of that traditional conception of historical progress which posits an evolution from a primordial society of kin or tribal relationships through political society, characterized by the rise of the city-state, to advanced industrial society. Polanyi maps reciprocity, redistribution and exchange to 'primitive', archaic and modern economies respectively, and this enabled neo-evolutionist anthropologists such as Sahlins, Halperin and Morton Fried to interpret the model in evolutionary terms. In Halperin's judgement, Polanyi 'worked within an evolutionary framework', placed transformations in economic processes at the centre of his analysis, and 'emphasised that these transformations involved changes in the institutional arrangements organising economic processes'.[123]

Finally, Polanyi occasionally betrays unease with regard to the meaning of another core concept, the institution. He tends to assume that institutions exist in order to serve communities, but this caused him difficulties when writing TGT, in which the subject is not the integrative function of the institutions of market society but their disintegration. Could social disintegration be theorized within a functionalist understanding of institutions, he asked his brother Michael in 1943? Social institutions, his letter explains, are traditionally seen as existing to serve the community – its 'organs or functions'. In TGT, however, this perspective brought little traction; deploying it would have rendered 'my treatment meaningless. For unless an institution can, potentially, destroy a society, it's no use arguing the self-protection of society, etc., as I do.' Hence, he opted to redefine institutions 'in terms of mechanisms. An institution which "serves" a society could never destroy it – that is why I must eliminate the functional (or organic) definition of institutions altogether.'[124] Following the publication of TGT, however, Polanyi reverts to his earlier (traditional, or communitarian) view. In 1944 he defines institutions as 'Recognisable patterns of law, custom or habit which can be associated with some purpose or function', whereby 'the purpose or function is what [the institution] achieves from the point of view of the community, in other words the *service which it renders* to the community'.[125] Similarly, in 1960 he theorizes economic institutions as mechanisms of social unification and integration, whereby each of the three patterns – reciprocity etc. – 'is capable of integrating the economy, ensuring its stability and unity'.[126] For non-market societies, institutions are seen as their organs, implicitly defining the research agenda as explaining social integration, stability and unity. For liberal market society, institutions are mechanisms, and the emphasis of research is explaining disintegration, instability and disunity. Unless institutions may be defined, like light, in two manifestly different ways, Polanyi had snagged himself in a definitional tangle.

In both conceptualizations, domination and compulsion are noticeable by their absence. Substantivism is not a consensus sociology but, with the partial exception of its analysis of market society, it is no conflict theory either. This, according to critics such as the anthropologist John Gledhill and archaeologist Mogens Larsen, predisposes it to a static, institutional and functional analysis. Because its historical surveys are essentially descriptive, the problem of explaining the genesis and evolution of the 'embedding institutions' is not broached directly. Explanation of institutional change, when it appears, relies upon comparative statics and *ad hoc* arguments, while as deeper explanation unanalysed concepts such as 'moral order' or 'custom' are smuggled into the scheme, opening it up to the charge of functionalism.[127] For the sociologist Alan Jenkins, similarly, Polanyi's integrative mechanisms are purely descriptive indices: why one, singly or in combination, is dominant at one time or the other is left untheorized. The various modes of integration are seen as the accidental consequence of particular histories, obviating the need to look for mechanisms governing the transition from one form to another. In effect, 'the historical incidence of the operation of the mechanisms is conceived as the empirical realisation of "essences" in diverse form', in the manner of idealist philosophies of history.[128] This argument has been taken to its limit – and in my view made to squeeze too much out of a valid insight – by the historian of antiquity Mohammad Nafissi. In elucidating the static quality of Polanyi's schema he proposes that

> the putative exhaustive patterns of pre-capitalist socio-economic integration were conceived as harmonious entities (or eternities) immune to historical change. These concepts and the societies which they designated were so constituted because they were at the same time conceived as (theoretical and societal) manifestations of the 'unchanging essence of man as a social being'.[129]

In this sense, Nafissi suggests, the model is pre-sociological; it expresses Polanyi's religious conception of humanity. The exception, the market system, proves the rule: in Polanyi's view it does have historicity and is dynamic, but this is precisely its flaw – its dynamism is self-destructive, and it is so because it violates humanity's collectivist essence.

Evidently, and as is to be expected of major theoretical innovations, substantivist economics did not step onto the public stage fully rehearsed and with the i's and t's of its script dotted and crossed. It was worked on over time, drew upon a range of sources, and was taken up and reworked by Polanyi's students and others. Inevitably there was much to be ironed out, and there is room for discussion regarding its appropriate purposes. Party to these debates, the main lines of which have been summarized in this section, have been Polanyians as well as a range of thinkers who, while critical of his model, regard it as fertile and suggestive. The same could not be said, however, of formalist scholars. Their critique of substantivism was head on: a take-no-prisoners approach. And it is to their response and the wider debate that it catalysed that we now must turn.

The formalist rejoinder

With hindsight one can locate the prehistory of the formalist–substantivist clash of the 1960s and 1970s in earlier eras, for example in the *'oikos* debate' over the existence of capitalism in the ancient world, which I outline in the next chapter, or in differences amongst anthropologists in the inter-war period. For better or worse, the

debate raged for about twenty years following the publication of
Trade and Markets in the Early Empires. As in many such quarrels
some of the memorable points scored were against the adversary's
weakest positions, which highlighted the importance that those
involved attributed to the debate but was less well adapted to
addressing the issues of interest to non-partisan observers.

The chief allegation that formalist anthropologists and economists, such as Harold Schneider, Scott Cook and Robbins Burling,
threw back at the Polanyi school was its blindness to the universal
presence of gain-motivated behaviour, exchange and markets, a
topic that I shall postpone to chapter 4. In this chapter I shall look
at the four other major charges that they level against substantivism: it is unscientific, ideological, restricted in scope to a dwindling
subject area, and relativist.

In a reprise of Menger's position in the *Methodenstreit*, the formalists argue that the creation of models on the basis of induction
(generalizing from observation) is not a scientific procedure. The
proper method for economic analysis is deduction, where each
phenomenon is understood as an example of a general law. For
economic anthropology the aim should be to understand behaviour
in accordance with the canons of logical reasoning, which requires
the application of models based upon a set of assumptions deduced
from the universal conditions that govern human behaviour –
'simple postulates relating to choice of means and ends (e.g. "scarcity," "economizing," "maximization")'.[130]

On the second point, concerning ideology, the formalists con-
tended that human behaviour prior to the nineteenth-century institutionalization of the self-regulating market economy was not
innately altruistic, cooperative and essentially devoid of conflict
and competition, as Polanyi and his followers appeared to maintain. In fact, the pursuit of profit, or 'gain', is ubiquitous. In denying
this, the substantivists were resurrecting Romantic mythology.
Their 'intransigent' refusal to accept the cross-cultural applicability
of formal economic analysis, consequent upon their denial of the
universality of gain-seeking behaviour, was not the result of rational reasoning but the 'by-product of a romantic ideology rooted in
an antipathy toward the "market economy" and an idealization of
the "primitive"'.[131]

The formalists' third riposte was less a critique than a prediction
of dwindling scope for substantivist analysis. Given that the
substantivists accepted the validity of formalist analysis in market
situations, as the world market expands the scope for application

of their model inexorably decreases. With this point, unlike the others, there were substantivists who concurred. George Dalton, to name one, conceded that substantivism applied only to 'aboriginal' (pre-colonial) economies in stateless societies and tribal kingdoms, as well as 'early, traditional, and pre-modern sub-sets of peasantries in states'. It was a concession, Barry Isaac advises, that 'left substantivism largely stranded when sociocultural anthropology turned increasingly towards the study of contemporary populations during the 1980s and 1990s'. These populations, after all, 'had economies that both the formalists and Dalton, the leading substantivist spokesman, agreed required "formal economics" for their analysis'.[132]

Finally, the formalists claimed they had been misunderstood on matters of human psychology. Typically with reference to Malinowski, substantivists insisted that rational, maximizing behaviour directed to 'economic ends' is not an anthropological universal, where by 'economic' they assume the production and distribution of goods. But this, since Robbins' reformulation of neoclassical economics, was to miss the point. What Robbins had clarified is that the contention that human beings maximize is a formal proposition that does not refer to particular 'economic ends' such as acquiring money or exchanging material goods.[133] What is 'economic' is the form of behaviour: allocation towards desired goals in a situation of scarcity. The goals to be preferred (i.e. maximized) could include the intensity of religious epiphany or of the feeling of security just as much as the value of a real-estate portfolio or the size of a collection of vintage automobiles. As Burling formulated it, each of us is ceaselessly striving 'to maximize our satisfactions' but such goals are 'colored by the values' of our society, and these may include 'prestige, love, leisure, or even [!] money'. Indeed, he goes on,

> the relationship of a mother to her baby is just as much an economic one, or rather has just as much of an economic aspect, as the relationship of an employer to his hired labourer. A farmer hoeing his yams is being no more economic than when he is chatting with his cronies in the men's house. The economic aspect of behaviour – choice, allocation of scarce means, including time and energy and not just money – is present in all this behaviour.

It should be possible, he concludes, to subject to economic analysis the 'supply of prestige', the 'demand for power' and the 'cost of authority', not to mention 'the marginal utility of loving care'.[134]

Giving their case an ethico-political edge, the formalists depicted themselves as upholders of liberal values, contrasting their position with the substantivists whose Romantic relativism is blind to human universals. Underneath our cultural skins we are all essentially the same, the formalists said; crucially, we all experience the same imperatives to economize, maximize and exchange. 'Even the savage who is normally near starvation', as D. M. Goodfellow put the case, 'has freedom of choice to "waste" those resources which he has, and a correspondingly greater need to apply them with due care.'[135] Nor can this be refuted by pointing to peoples who happen not to be imbued with an ethic of thrift or hard labour. As a case in point Goodfellow invites readers to consider the peoples of Latin America, 'whose main occupation appears, at least to the superficial observer, to be to lie in the sun'.[136] Far from contradicting neoclassical analysis, these Latinos are rationally choosing to maximize not income but something else (the details of which he does not spell out: leisure, pleasure or the brownness of their skin, the reader is left to assume). Human preferences may vary, but we all maximize in constrained conditions, and it is this that grants the assumptions of neoclassical economics their universal validity. Economic anthropology, Goodfellow concludes, will consist either of neoclassical economics or of nothing at all.

> The proposition that there should be more than one body of economic theory is absurd. If modern economic analysis . . . cannot cope equally with the Aborigine and with the Londoner not only economic theory but the whole of the social sciences may be considerably discredited. For the phenomena of social science are nothing if not universal.[137]

To those who cavil that, if not the brownness of skin then at least pleasure or leisure are nigh impossible to measure, the formalist reply is that the ethnographer can deduce individual preferences from observed economic behaviour, notably the exchange of goods and services. To the substantivists who attempt to sequester reciprocal and redistributive forms of circulation from the formalists' purview, they respond that all such mechanisms are, ultimately, less complex versions of market exchange, and as such are eminently available to the techniques of marginalist analysis. 'Conceptually, at least', Leonard Joy explains,

> there is no problem. For example, ritual exchange, reciprocal exchange, redistributive exchange, and market exchange can each be included separately in the pattern of activities open to individuals or

groups. To be sure, one could not calculate an individual's optimizing behaviour unless one knew both his utility function and the rates of return to different activities in respect of each of the dimensions of the utility function. But one could say something about implicit revealed preference from the observation of behaviour.[138]

Such bravado notwithstanding, the formalists were alert to the problems posed by the application of neoclassical techniques to 'primitive societies'. Explaining how members of non-monetized societies calculate marginal productivity is no easy task; it requires experimentation with various factor combinations and estimation of the opportunity costs of withdrawing factors from one use in favour of another. The trouble is, Burling admitted, in such societies 'there seems to be little prospect for quantification'. The economic anthropologist must therefore employ concepts such as cost, value, demand and supply 'in a much broader context' than is the custom for economists and 'over a range of meaning far wider than that which is priced' – or else 'he had better stop talking about economics'.[139] Even in societies where neither regular commodity exchange nor barter is present, individuals still display a hierarchy of preferences, and these determine what types of products are exchanged – for example at potlatches or other ceremonial occasions. This insight enabled formalist anthropologists to deploy game theory, econometrics, price fixing and other models from orthodox economics to the behaviour of individuals in 'primitive' and other pre-modern societies,[140] and, since the advent of the new institutional economics, the potential scope for the application of such models has extended to include explanation of the evolution of institutional structures 'as ways to reduce transaction costs' (as Douglass North put it in his critique of Polanyi).[141] Even the kula trade of the Trobriand Islanders has been widely reinterpreted as profit-oriented behaviour: a method of organizing markets and reducing transaction costs across tribal boundaries.[142] It would seem, then, that the formalists had 'won' the debate. Whether that is so, I touch upon below. In the meantime, however, it is necessary to introduce a third major school that entered the fray.

Marxist interpositions

From the mid-1960s, the formalist–substantivist dispute was triangulated by the intervention of Marxists; indeed, for a decade or two, questions raised from this quarter occupied centre stage in economic anthropology. For scholars writing in the 1960s and 1970s a

worldwide social-movement upturn, including large-scale industrial struggles, was lived reality and, with its attention to contradiction and conflict, Marxist theory suited the times. Althusserian
anthropologists in particular developed conceptual tools for investigating the articulation of modes of production, and these had an
appeal for ethnographers researching the impact of the world
market upon hunter-gatherer and agrarian societies. On a number
of basic methodological and empirical issues Marxist and substantivist positions converged, on others they diverged. I briefly consider the former before turning to the latter.

In their critiques of neoclassical economics and formalist anthropology, the two schools of thought have a good deal in common.
Together, they repudiate formalism's identification of 'the economy'
with its market form, its belief in a trans-historical economic
rationality and its concomitant lack of conceptual tools that would
permit the recognition of different economic systems. Both traditions agree that there is no universally applicable economic theory,
and that the conditions conducive to market behaviour (notably
commodification) and to capitalism in particular (crucially, the
generalized commodification of labour-power) are far from universal. Maurice Godelier, a distinguished Marxist anthropologist of the
postwar era, welcomed the substantivists' research into forms of
market, trade and money in non-capitalist societies and applauded
Polanyi and his school for asking questions about the 'shifting place
of the economy', not least because this stimulated the study of issues
considered vital for a Marxist research programme – specifically, the
reasons for, and the conditions which historically have generated,
changes in the forms and effects of production relations.[143]

These areas of agreement would seem to outweigh any differences, yet the latter were of sufficient import for Marxist anthropologists and economists to be seen, quite understandably, as
throwing down a gauntlet to substantivism. Their charges can usefully be grouped under three headings: the referent of the term
'economy'; the critique of neoclassical economics and the analysis
of market capitalism; and the conceptualization of economic institutions and relations of production.

The first point concerns Polanyi's definition of 'the economy' as
an arena of material wants satisfaction. The formalists, according to
Godelier, have a valid point in their critique of this formulation, to
wit, that because services are immaterial 'the economy' cannot be
defined as a material field. Their alternative, that all rational activity
in a context of scarcity is economic, is still less satisfactory, he

argues, for it dissolves the economic 'in a formal theory of purposive action in which it is no longer possible to distinguish between economic activity and activity directed towards obtaining pleasure, power or salvation'. Godelier addresses this problem by suggesting a reformulation of the substantivist definition, such that the economic aspect of, say, a singer's performance may best be defined by the extent to which she makes a livelihood from her activity: the economic aspect consists in the exchange of her performance for money. Provided that one does not reduce the significance and function of a service to its economic aspect this enables the economic to be defined,

> without risk of tautology, as the production, distribution and consumption of goods and services. It forms both a domain of activities of a particular sort (production, distribution, consumption of material goods: tools, musical instruments, books, temples, etc.) and a particular aspect of all the human activities that do not strictly belong to this domain, but the functioning of which involves the exchange and use of material means. The economic thus appears as a particular field of social relations which is both external to the other elements of social life and also internal to them.[144]

This suggestion could, one suspects, readily be taken on board by substantivists without damage to their framework.

In their challenge to formalism, secondly, many Marxists adopt a significantly different tack from that of substantivists. On one point they defend formalism from criticism: it does not – or at least need not – rest upon the premise that individual behaviour is hedonistic, asocial or ahistorical.[145] The concept of maximization need not therefore be interpreted as a statement concerning human nature. Its weakness, rather, lies in its emptiness: in so far as utility theory relies upon the concept of preference maximization it is vacuous and non-falsifiable.[146] As the US anthropologist Donald Donham argues, borrowing from Amartya Sen, 'if you are consistent, then no matter whether you are a single-minded egoist or a raving altruist or a class conscious militant, you will appear to be maximizing your own utility in this enchanted world of definitions'.[147] Substantivists are therefore wrong to propose that individuals in market societies maximize while others do not; the opposite of maximization is not constrained production but unintelligible disorder.[148]

A related line of reasoning has been pursued by the British economist Simon Clarke. For him, it is not in itself a repudiation of marginalism to say that it abstracts the analysis of exchange from the historically specific relations of production that it entails, for this is exactly what neoclassical economists claim to be their scientific accomplishment. But neither should it be accepted as valid within its own sphere subject to correctives from sociology and anthropology, as substantivists maintain. More effective than criticizing the disconnect between formal deductive analysis and real history is to challenge its premises. Here the task should be to show that its abstractions are illegitimate by establishing the incoherence of marginalist economics in its own terms, viz., 'that the *formal rationality* of the fetishised forms of appearance of capitalist social relations cannot be abstracted from the *substantive irrationality* which derives from the irrationality of the social relations of capitalist production which they articulate'.[149] The consequence of this argument is that Polanyi errs in seeing the formalist method as applicable to the market system; his critique of attempts to apply neoclassical theory to other systems would have been more robust if he had been alive to its manifold inadequacies in explaining the nature and dynamics of the modern market economy. (This point finds support amongst non-Marxists too. The anthropologist Keith Hart, for example, notes that Polanyi's concession to formalism 'represented a retreat from the splendid iconoclasm of [TGT] into an academic division of labor respecting the economics profession's monopoly in "market" economies'.[150])

A third concern for Marxists, and the last to be looked at here, concerns the institutionalist method. Polanyi's basic term of reference is the mechanism of economic integration, set within a Weberian identification of typologies, in contrast to the Marxist perspective that envisages a society's institutional arrangements as arising upon the basis of a particular mode of production, integrated within a social-relation-centred explanation of change. At no point, Godelier claims, does Polanyi really ask why it is that a given institution, or mechanism of integration, prevails in one society rather than another.[151] Rather, he limits himself to describing the manner in which trade, money or markets are institutionalized in societies dominated by this or the other mechanism. This enables him to chart the shifting 'place of the economy' but 'without ever really being able to pose the theoretical problem of its effect upon the functioning and evolution of societies, and therefore of its role in history'.[152] Why, within a certain society, should one or other social structure be found? Why should the production process be embedded in kinship relations in one historical epoch and not another? For Marxists, it is insufficient to see that kinship has many functions among primitive hunters in order to conclude that it plays a dominant role in social organization. For that, an institution must function as the social relation which organizes the material process of the given society.[153]

The nub of Godelier's critique is that Polanyi's method in determining the role of the economy in society is empiricist: that he never seeks to discover whether the hierarchy of causes that determine the reproduction of a social system is the same as the hierarchy of the institutions which visibly dominate its functioning. Polanyi, Godelier argues, 'observed different hierarchies of institutions and he then concluded, as an empiricist, that in all these hierarchies, whether dominated by kinship relations, religion or politics, the economy each time played a subordinate role in the functioning and evolution of their societies'. Not all forms of social behaviour are equally decisive in the reproduction or transformation of a social system. This 'unequal importance', Godelier continues,

> this hierarchy of effects of the forms of social practice supposes, and at the same time reveals, the existence of a different causality of these levels and these forms of social practice, the existence of a hierarchy of causes. One should thus try to discover which causes rank highest in this hierarchy, which social relations determine the reproduction of social systems, not all by themselves, but in the highest instance, and thus ultimately.

Social relations, in short, only play a determinant role at the institutional level if they assume the function of production relations.[154]

A degree of confusion entered this particular debate thanks to a blunt formulation put forward by another French anthropologist, Claude Meillassoux, when he reproached Polanyi for restricting his model to the *circulation* of social product and neglecting the sphere of production.[155] It is a contention that has been frequently repeated, most recently by Michael Burawoy with his quip that Polanyi 'did not know anything about production'.[156] For Godelier, however, this critique is unwarranted. Strictly speaking, Polanyi does not neglect the social relations of production. Rather, he conflates them with the forms of circulation of the product.[157] His 'locational movements' approximate to 'technical relations of production' in the Marxist lexicon, while his 'appropriational movements' – including, in the case of market capitalism, the buying and selling of labour-power – resemble what Marxists term the 'social relations of production'. But this latter correspondence is inexact. For Marxists, the relations of production in class-divided societies involve the questions of how a surplus is produced, who controls its distribution, and to what ends. Polanyi's focus is upon the shuttling of goods and services between various individuals or other centres of appropriation rather than upon the framework of social relations that enables the transfer of goods and services over sustained periods from one social group to another. In short, Godelier regrets the absence in Polanyi's schema of 'any theory of exploitation of man by man', as a consequence of which his criticism of the capitalist system is weakened.[158] (Polanyi himself expressed the point concisely by contrasting Marx's account of the role of economy in society, 'an exploitation theorem – class war', with his own, 'a market theorem – no class war'.)[159]

The debate scatters and dissolves

The formalist–substantivist debate fizzled out in the 1970s with neither side able to claim victory – although if the quantity of published texts penned by scholars on one side who feel not the slightest need to refer to the other's arguments is an index of success, formalism 'won' by a country mile. And while the term itself has fallen into disuse, formalism's progeny continue to thrive. They include a number of approaches that draw upon 'information theory, game theory, cost–benefit analysis, rational choice, agricultural development and a host of other spin-offs from mainstream economics'.[160]

During the debate, the substantivists did land some memorable blows upon their adversary's weaker positions. (My personal favourite is a quip by George Dalton: 'if it is thought that Western price theory is relevant to primitive economy, the question arises, why not other branches of Western theory – say Keynesian income and employment theory – as well?'[161]) Those formalists who clung to the neoclassical precept that what individuals maximize is the satisfaction of having more of one commodity than the other were unable to explain satisfactorily how this applies in societies that lack a price system and thus possess no common yardstick which can be applied to all 'utilities'. Those who attempted to address the wider difficulty of calculating non-economic preferences by adapting their models to include a wider range of variables saw their theory become decreasingly parsimonious, ever less falsifiable, and ever further adrift from the neoclassical paradigm. Equally, however, few would deny that some of formalism's favoured techniques – from decision trees to multiple regression analysis to game theory – can be usefully applied to certain situations in non-market societies.[162] As champions of these methods, formalism's spin-offs naturally attract support from those anthropologists who aspire to elevate their discipline's status to 'hard science'. More importantly, formalism and its parent, neoclassical economics, have long been beneficiaries of prevailing power structures. As Philip Mirowski has shown – in *Machine Dreams*, that mazy masterpiece of gonzo intellectual history – neoclassical economics was sponsored and supported by the Western (including Israeli) military-industrial-political complex during the Cold War, and since then has retained its position at the ideological core of neoliberalism, advancing the propositions that economics is about consumer choice and not relations of class or power, that its techniques are ethically neutral, that its proper remit is 'problem-solving' rather than 'critical' theory, and that, as the overriding policy implication, states should retract their tentacles from the market place.

Formalism is sometimes said to have 'triumphed' in the debate but this is surely hyperbole.[163] One, admittedly impressionistic, index is that, in one of the few surveys of opinions on 'which side won', when Richard Wilk put the question to members of a feminist economics email discussion group they unanimously awarded the laurels to substantivism.[164] Whether or not that is representative, there is no doubt that in economic anthropology the influence of substantivism has been profound and abiding. In the US, before the publication of *Trade and Market*, the prevailing approach had been empiricism. Polanyi's interventions stimulated a reaction: a turn towards theoretical generalization, comparative research and the analysis of 'big' structures. This assessment by a hostile critic is exaggerated – for much the same reason that US analysts during the Cold War persistently overstated Soviet missile numbers – but is none the less indicative of Polanyi's tremendous influence.

> *Trade and Market* together with the Columbia seminars had an enormous impact on United States economic history and economic anthropology. . . . One might say that beneath the surface of an American social scientist of that generation, you will find a Polanyist, just as beneath the surface of a British social scientist of that period you will find a Marxist.[165]

Among social anthropologists in particular, Polanyi and his co-thinkers galvanized interest in trade, money and markets, helping to loosen their discipline from its fixation upon purportedly isolated societies.[166] His idea that the economy is best treated as a subsystem 'bounded' by, or 'embedded' in, a social system, together with his systematization of the concepts of reciprocity and redistribution, entered the anthropological and archaeological repertoires. And, for its long-term influence of unmistakeable importance, the sharp dichotomy he drew between contemporary capitalism and all other societies connected to a deeply ingrained need amongst anthropologists: to establish the 'otherness' of other cultures and thereby legitimate their field as a separate and independent discipline within the academic division of labour – in contrast to formalist anthropologists, who are obliged to see their subdiscipline as a hand-servant to economics, its role being to supply the master discipline with exotic variations upon the theme of man's original nature.[167]

In addition to directly influencing a generation of anthropologists the substantivist school has been effective in indirect ways, of which I shall mention two. First, it was one strand within that broad critical backlash against neoclassical economics in its mid-twentieth-century phase, to which the latter responded by retreating from some of its weaker positions and engaging in a process of revision. Behaviourism was diluted or jettisoned, with notions of 'social norms' introduced to refer to the reactions of economic actors to stimuli that cannot be captured by the calculus of individual cost and benefit.[168] In response both to the challenge emanating from substantivism and other species of 'old' institutionalism and to critiques of the assumptions of perfect information, costless and instantaneous transactions, perfectly competitive markets and unbounded rationality, neoclassical economists crafted a 'new' institutionalism, the anthropological adaptation of which has been dubbed the 'new institutional economic anthropology'.[169] Co-ordination of economic activity, those who sit on this branch of the neoclassical tree recognize, involves more than simply transactions on markets; rather, institutions play a vital role.

Although substantivism, an avatar of the 'old' institutionalism, may take some credit for spurring this revision, it cannot claim parentage of the new. Whereas the latter 'sees institutions as simply "constraining" individual *behaviour*' the former sees them, in addition, 'as being "constitutive" of individual *motivations*'.[170] Whereas the new institutionalism believes that institutions matter because they reduce transaction costs, thereby enabling individuals to maximize their utilities, the old sees them as playing an active role, in interdependence with individuals and their behaviour – human beings are social and cultural beings as well as individuals.[171] To summarize, the new institutional economic anthropology represents a continuation of the economistic fallacy by other means. Although ditching the discredited assumption of egotistical *Homo oeconomicus*, it retains from the neoclassical tradition its other core postulates, notably methodological individualism and instrumentalist rationality (an assumption that the object of analysis is the means–ends calculations of sovereign individuals).[172]

Substantivism's second indirect influence was upon the emergence of a new current within social anthropology: culturalism. Indeed, some see it, with reference to the background of its best-known exponent, Stephen Gudeman, as a continuation of substantivism. As a callow researcher in rural Panama, Gudeman recalls, he started out in formalist fashion.

> Wearing the hat of a neoclassical economist, I intended to apply concepts from the theory of markets to the activities of subsistence farmers. My goal was to elicit their agricultural choices and plot them on decision trees, attaching their subjective valuations and probabilities to the outcomes. I anticipated that this exercise, intended to explain their behavior in terms of rational choice and self-interest, would open the way to a full exploration of their economy.[173]

Yet the 'puzzlement and gentle incredulity' of his interviewees, as his questions failed to elicit the right sort of answers, forced him to rethink. Initially he fell under the spell of Polanyi and Veblen, for whom actors' *meanings* took centre stage. But he then took this principle a decisive step further. The task of economic anthropology, he came to believe, is to investigate the cultural *understandings* that shape and suffuse economic behaviour: 'I began to see economy as constructed through folk models and metaphors.'[174] In order to do this the anthropologist must not only understand the local language, practices and culture, but, in analysing these, apply indigenous norms and perspectives. In this, culturalism applies to substantivism its own critique of formalism and Marxism, to wit that it is illegitimate to apply social-scientific concepts developed in the West – such as utility, relations and powers of production, surplus, exploitation or class struggle – to non-Western societies that, being so radically other, require an entirely different set of analytical concepts. To culturalists, substantivism, as much as formalism or Marxism, appears as a theory the purely local validity of which is disguised by its imperial pretensions.[175]

This chapter has introduced the methodology and core concepts that Polanyi developed during his postwar decades in North America. The main force of his intellectual efforts during that period, however, was devoted to applying his new method to empirical research. How, he wanted to discover, are economic processes, particularly markets, trade and money, institutionalized in archaic societies? An umbrella term, 'archaic' includes the meanings of subcategories such as 'medieval' and 'ancient', economies that are characterized, loosely, by institutions that had not made their appearance in 'primitive communities' but which 'are no longer found in societies where the use of money as a means of exchange is already common'.[176] In chapter 2, his analysis of one of these, mercantilist Britain, was touched upon. In the next chapter we turn to look in detail at Polanyi's writings on a range of other examples, notably the empires and city-states of Mesopotamia, ancient Greece and pre-colonial Dahomey.

4

Trade, markets and money in archaic societies

There are a number of different modes of subsistence; and the result is a number of different ways of life, both in the animal world and in the human.

Aristotle[1]

The Greeks and the other civilized peoples of antiquity were unfamiliar with the idea of a supply–demand market, especially for food. Such an institution would have horrified them. They would have regarded it as being in the nature of famine, anarchy, or corruption, since it meant to them the breakdown of the community.

Karl Polanyi[2]

Introduction: the *oikos* debate

The theses for which Polanyi is best known, the 'double movement' and substantivist economic anthropology, are geared primarily to market modernity and low-surplus economies respectively. In the last two decades of his life, however, his intellectual attention was primarily geared to a third category, 'archaic' economies. On its critical edge, his research was targeted at a set of historical arguments that flow from the economistic fallacy, the best known of which were advanced by the 'modernizers' in the *oikos* debate. On its constructive side he drew upon and modified a set of arguments associated with Maine and Tönnies as well as economic historians that entered the lists in the *oikos* debate on the 'primitivist' side. Tönnies' merit, in Polanyi's judgement, had been his ability to 'reconstruct the outlines of ancient and medieval civilization with the help of the "community–society" dichotomy', but he failed 'to apply the distinction to the actual history of economic institutions such as trade, money, and markets'.[3] The 'primitivists' had done precisely that, but Polanyi was not satisfied with their results.

The opening salvo in what became the *oikos* controversy was a theorem advanced by the German economist Karl Johann Rodbertus in the 1860s. The economies of antiquity, he claimed, were organized around self-sufficient estates or households (*oikoi*); they lacked a taxation system of the modern kind and did not distinguish between types of revenue such as are formed in modern land, labour and capital markets.[4] The controversy itself, which in various guises is still with us today, erupted in the 1890s, with as chief protagonists the primitivist Karl Bücher and the modernist Eduard Meyer. At its centre was the question of whether or not the economies of antiquity – Greece in particular – were highly developed prototypes of the modern market economy. Were the fifth and fourth centuries BCE better described as an age of international trade with vigorous industrial enterprises organized along capitalistic lines, or as an overwhelmingly agrarian and non-monetized period in which economic intercourse was restricted to autarkic *oikoi*? For Bücher, generalizing Rodbertus' *oikos* to the ancient economy as a whole, the answer was clear: it was geared to consumption, and the limited role of markets testified to poorly developed trade and monetary systems. Even when productivity increased, deeply entrenched anti-commercial values blocked the development of capitalistic behaviour. Such were the discrepancies between modern capitalism and the ancient world that classical historians should be wary of transposing economic categories (such as wages, prices and profit) from one to the other.

Meyer's approach was the diametric opposite. For him, even the economic institutions of third-millennium Babylonia resembled modern capitalism, as evidenced by the numerous documents referring to private business transactions in slaves, land and buildings, the division of property at death, and a developed system of accountancy, while the later period of antiquity, with its highly developed transportation and trading networks, was 'in essence entirely modern'. Trade and money 'were of fundamental importance in the economic life of the ancients',[5] and their presence testified to the organization of economic life through markets. Indeed, it was entirely normal for individuals to engage in production and exchange for the purpose of profit. Classical Athens, he went so far as to say, 'stands as much under the sign of capitalism as England has stood since the eighteenth and Germany since the nineteenth century'.[6]

The next major contributor to the debate, Max Weber, attempted a synthesis. On the one hand, he accepted the modernist contentions that the *oikoi* were centres of commercial exchange and that acquisitive activity, the trade of goods on markets and non-market-oriented capitalist profit-making (such as tax farming) were all widespread, allowing the thesis to be ventured 'that capitalism shaped whole periods of antiquity, and indeed precisely those periods we call "golden ages"'.[7] On other issues, however, he hewed more closely to the primitivist path, and was adamant that 'nothing could be more misleading than to describe the economic institutions of Antiquity in modern terms'. Emphasizing that until modern times markets were generally kept apart from mainstream society, he concurred with Rodbertus that ancient society was a slave society, with the *oikos* as its defining centre, that the expansion of international trade was connected to the consolidation of slavery, and that trade was no more than 'a thin net spread over a large natural economy'.[8] Capitalist enterprise there was, but Weber was careful to stress the dissimilarity from its modern variants. Ancient capitalism was essentially agrarian and dominated by political rather than economic motives; its protagonists were not 'sustained by any positive justification of the profit motive'.[9]

Weber's approach was defended and extended by the classical historians Johannes Hasebroek and Moses Finley. In a seminal work from the 1920s, the former argued that ancient Greek and Roman citizens behaved as *Homo politicus*: they disparaged market activities, holding that these should be subservient to political considerations – as contrasted with the likes of Venice, Holland or the Hansa towns, where 'trade was imbued with the aristocratic spirit'. Counselling against viewing ancient society through lenses ground in our own, he ventured a number of novel theses, notably that the primary motivation behind the extraordinary Hellenic colonizing thrust of the seventh and eighth centuries BCE was not commercial, as modern minds are wont to assume, but conquest and the securing of supplies, and that Athens' imports should not be categorized as peaceful trade but 'plain robbery and exploitation'.[10] Several years later, Finley elaborated upon these themes, paying particular attention to the problem of translating ancient terms into modern parlance: modern, market-centric concepts of banking, investment and credit, he insisted, cannot be applied to antiquity; indeed, the attempt to do so has been positively harmful.[11] Terms such as 'firms', 'joint stock companies', 'capital', 'capitalists' cannot fail to invoke elements which either did not exist or took a fundamentally different form in ancient Greece.

During and following his time at Columbia, Finley was to build upon this youthful critique of the modernist case. He highlighted the paucity of evidence in ancient records of money-lending for business purposes (bottomry loans apart), of contemporary commentary on price fluctuations (other than for reasons of natural catastrophe or political troubles), of contemporary justifications of land-holding in maximization-of-income language, and of any systematic drive to create capital (as distinct from the amassing of wealth).[12] According to one survey of his oeuvre, the flaws in the modernist case that he exposed include, *inter alia*, 'the persistent reliance on unrepresentative evidence; . . . the absence from ancient society of "vast conglomerations of interdependent markets"; the absence from ancient affairs of state of anything resembling "economic policy"; and the absence from Greek literature of economics'.[13]

In developing his own distinctive position, Polanyi took Bücher and Weber as his principal guides but learned much from Rodbertus and Hasebroek, and from Finley too. He applauds Rodbertus for rejecting the assumption that economic intercourse and market activity are coterminous, and Bücher for his appeal to economic historians to learn from social anthropology and for his insistence that the system of price-making markets sets modern economies apart from all others. He concedes that some of their positions were mistaken. In conceptualizing the *oikos* as a strictly self-sufficient household Rodbertus and Bücher were at the very least culpable of 'crass exaggeration'. Their image of autarkic antiquity could not be sustained in the face of the incontrovertible evidence of Minoan international trade as early as the middle of the second millennium BCE and of Phoenician international trade, not to mention the vast geographical scope of classical Greek trade – 'from the Atlantic to the Azovian Lake, from the Danube to the Nile'.[14] Assessed against the empirical record, however, the modernists' case fared even worse. Gazing at antiquity through modern eyes had steered them into a thicket of confusions. For example, where we think of banking as a sophisticated form of dealing in money and credit, in antiquity it involved no credit instruments, and where we think of world trade as the culmination of foreign trade, in antiquity it was its starting point. As a result, the modernists grossly exaggerated the scale of manufacturing and trade in antiquity, the scope of private business enterprise, and the sophistication of banking and finance. A more profound problem, however, was their failure to recognize that modernity's distinctive feature is neither trade nor money nor markets but the supremacy of the market mechanism. But in this failure there lies a twist: it was not theirs alone. Albeit with qualifications, it was a myopia shared by the primitivists. Rodbertus and Bücher – and Marx[15] and Weber with them – conceived of trade, money and markets as interdependent exchange institutions, such that evidence of trade or money use could be taken as an index of price-making markets. This error left them vulnerable to modernist swipes: if each new discovery of evidence of trade or money use was a sign of price-making markets, the primitivist position would be inexorably undermined.

The *oikos* debate, Polanyi declared to an audience at Yale, had reached an impasse. 'While ancient society – its colonies, its wars, its classes – appeared anything but "modern," trade and the use of money undeniably existed on a scale comparable to the beginnings of modern times.' The controversy had suffered from the fact that none of the protagonists, with the partial exception of Weber (and, Polanyi might have added, Hasebroek), was able to conceive of an economy with market places and extensive trade and money use as co-ordinated in any manner other than through market mechanisms. This was an error that Polanyi, working alongside Finley and others in his 'Columbia Interdisciplinary Project', set out to rectify. In so doing they amended, indeed re-invented, the primitivist case. One modernist contention was accepted: that antiquity knew extensive trade networks and developed forms of money and markets. But this apparent concession was accompanied by the thesis that trade, market places and money need not be co-ordinated through a price-making market mechanism and that their presence, therefore, need not betoken a market system. 'The debate started by Rodbertus and Bücher', Polanyi concluded, 'has broadly led to a vindication of their essential position, though only with the help of institutional insights which were still hidden from them.'[16]

In revealing those insights not only was Polanyi proposing a resolution of the *oikos* debate but in so doing he was beginning to chart a general economic history to rival Weber's pioneering efforts. The aim was, with the forms of integration detailed in chapter 3 as the conceptual basis, to present a coherent analysis of the institutional arrangements governing the production, exchange and valuation of goods other than by the market system, in a diverse array of societies. The principal findings appeared in three volumes, two of which were published posthumously (Polanyi's *Dahomey and the Slave Trade; An Analysis of an Archaic Economy* and *The Livelihood of Man*) while the third, *Trade and Markets in the Early Empires*, was published in 1957 and comprised essays by Polanyi and his collaborators. In this chapter I present the main findings of these works, commencing with an examination of Polanyi's general approach to trade, markets and money before moving on to a range of historical case studies, from Babylon and archaic Greece through pre-colonial Meso-America and Dahomey to twentieth-century rural India and the Maghreb.

'Primitive' and archaic trade, markets and money

Why, you may be wondering, does Polanyi choose to build his research programme around these three institutions? Essentially it is for two reasons. First, as the basic institutions of economic exchange they provide a crucial test for his general approach. The form they take varies with the dominant mechanism of integration; and to account persuasively for that variance in empirical economies is the necessary first step towards the mapping out of a substantivist general economic theory.[17] Second, they are the most misunderstood of economic institutions. Because in modern times the three had merged into a single interlocking market system, historians tend to read that pattern into earlier epochs, and to assume markets to have been the generative and co-ordinating instance, with trade conceived of as a movement of goods through markets, facilitated by money as a means of exchange.[18] But rather than as a seamless whole, Polanyi suggests, they are better seen as distinct components that are 'institutionalized separately and independently of one another'.[19] Defined as separate forms, what are trade, money and markets? As a simple first step, trade may be defined as the carrying of goods over a distance: a two-sided relationship between economic actors in which neither party applies direct force. Markets require a place, a stock of goods, a group of persons with goods to dispose of (supply) and a group willing to receive them (demand), a price, and a regulating authority.[20] As to money, it may be defined as 'fungible things in definite uses, namely payment, standard, and exchange', where fungible refers to durable and quantifiable objects.[21] Defined in these terms, it is apparent that none of the three needs to be institutionalized within a single supply–demand system. Let us unpack this argument, via closer analysis of trade, markets and money, in that order.

Trade, for Polanyi, is defined broadly as 'a method of acquiring goods which are not available on the spot'.[22] Unlike piracy or plunder, what distinguishes it is its two-sidedness, and this is linked to its peaceful character. (There is some room for disagreement here, for as trade Polanyi includes flows of tribute, which, arguably, represent a systematic form of plunder.[23]) In market economies its prevalent form is 'market trade'; geared towards making a profit, it requires monetized accountancy. Familiar to us, it requires no further elaboration. In low-surplus economies, by contrast, the typical form is gift trade. Organized ceremonially and often involving treasure, gift trade links partners – such as guest friends or kula partners – in reciprocal relationships. The exchange involved is construed as an indissoluble part of a wider web of reciprocal relations; it involves a relationship 'of a permanence and warmth not known in a market', as Polanyi's student Paul Bohannan put it, and hence 'it is bad form overtly to count and compute and haggle over gifts'.[24] In archaic trade, thirdly, the market and gift forms are marginal; it is predominantly 'administered' by states, or by semi-political bodies such as chartered companies. Prices and other terms (including provisions for the safety of trade routes) are negotiated, in a process that involves 'diplomatic higgling-haggling', but once the treaty is signed all bargaining ceases.[25] Because the import interest was dominant, i.e. trade was geared primarily to the acquisition abroad of luxury goods that are not obtainable at home, administered archaic trade was less influenced by cost differentials than is competitive trade in the modern world economy. Much of it consisted of sporadic expeditions rather than a continuous activity – indeed, one Polanyian anthropologist points out, 'except for specialist trading peoples like the Phoenicians and the Hausa, trade was rarely basic to livelihood' in pre-modern times.[26] Often, the monarch or chief alone would be formally entitled to trade even though the actual operations were organized by employed traders, or factors.[27] Money was not necessarily involved at all – as witnessed, for example, in the imports into ancient empires of tribute in kind. Where it was, prices 'were fixed largely by custom, statute, or proclamation, and perhaps should not generally be called prices at all'[28] – as an alternative, Polanyi suggests 'equivalents', a term that denotes agreed rates at which goods and services are exchanged (either in the discharge of an obligation or in exchange transactions) but without implying either an exchange of equal values or the causality of autonomous forces of supply and demand.

In the absence of market mechanisms, how could administered foreign trade, particularly between cultures with different economic systems, take place? Coining a new concept, Polanyi suggests that the characteristic institution and site for such exchanges was the 'port of trade'. Its genesis lay in 'silent trade', which evolved via sophisticated forms of 'passive' external trade into complex, institutionalized 'ports of trade'.[29] The port of trade, he summarizes, was

> the paradigm of a type of arrangement for foreign trade comparable in economic efficiency to the international market places of latter days, while embodying administrative principles and operational methods foreign to the supply–demand–price mechanism with which we are familiar.[30]

Its efficiency is explained by the fact that the goods involved were typically either luxuries intended for a small elite, or goods, such as corn, slaves or precious metals, which lend themselves to administrative control.[31]

The 'port of trade' is one of the many Polanyian terms that have taken on a life of their own, and its meanings have diverged somewhat in the process. Whereas for Polanyi it 'is a specific organ of foreign trade in nonmarket economies',[32] others, such as German historian H. G. Niemeyer, define it rather more stringently as an institution of professional trade 'situated in geographic and structural terms on the border between a non-market-oriented society and a market economy'.[33] All agree, however, that it refers to sites at which travelling merchants and other traders would gather, for which political authorities – whether monastery, city or empire – guaranteed the security of business, organized a judicial system, and provided facilities of anchorage, debarkation and storage.[34] They commonly fulfilled a buffer function, insulating trade in a non-commercial society from commercial activities and ensuring that foreign influences did not pose a danger to the hinterland. Other characteristic features include a polyglot, polyethnic and polysocial population; a focus on long-distance luxury commerce, and administered prices.[35] They were typically coastal, as in the cases of Goree, Rhodes, Carthage or Byblus, but some, including Kandahar, Acalan, Palmyra and Timbuktu, were located inland on the 'desert border, at a river head, or where plain and mountains meet'.[36] As a rule, the authorities that presided over them were – as for instance in Ugarit, Sidon or Tyre – small or weak, ensuring that the site was a 'no-man's land', not dominated by any overweening political power. Some, however, were the possessions of a hinterland empire, the more sophisticated of which adopted a 'hands-off' policy. The port of trade *par excellence*, wrote one contributor to TMEE, was Alexandria. 'Neutrality was its *raison d'être*. Although situated on Egyptian soil, and erected under a Greek government, neither the Egyptians, nor even the Greeks themselves were to wield power in it.'[37]

Unlike trade, Polanyi's typology of *markets* is not triadic. Rather, an axial distinction is divined: between *the* market economy – a self-adjusting system of markets that comes into being with the generalized commodification of labour and land – and all others. In the latter, markets may exist, they may even be integrated (rather than isolated), but they are not the dominant co-ordinating mechanism. Applying these methodological strictures to the historical record, Polanyi finds that although market places may have existed as early as the Neolithic, the price-making market system did not make its appearance until the first millennium of antiquity, in Greece, and then only to be eclipsed swiftly by other forms of integration. In medieval times something approaching a 'market system' emerged in urban Europe, to be followed in the sixteenth and seventeenth centuries by 'a national system of markets', but in none of these did markets play a role even faintly comparable in scope or scale with their nineteenth-century successor.[38]

What form, then, did archaic markets take? These were, for the most part, agrarian societies, in which those who depended for their livelihoods upon incomes generated through buying and selling on markets were greatly outnumbered by peasants whose self-sufficiency insulated them from any meaningful market dependence. Because their survival was not market reliant they were under no economic compulsion to conform to market standards. They could bring their surplus to offload on local markets but this is a very different matter from producing for the market: except where prices were regulated by custom or decree, peasants were likely to accept virtually any price for their wares, there being no advantage in keeping the surplus at home. As a result, the supply–demand–price mechanism could not be said to function; deliveries of goods would on occasion respond to demand, but this would typically entail shortages attracting existing goods to a specific spot rather than anticipated demand determining their production. In such 'peripheral markets' – a term coined by Polanyi's students Paul Bohannan and George Dalton – prices exerted little or no feedback on production decisions.[39] Especially in rural areas poor communications isolated markets from one another; these were often sites of social interaction as much as economic exchange.

As with markets, Polanyi's approach to *money* centres on a dichotomy between its traits in modern market societies and in 'primitive' and archaic times. In this, one might say that he was following in the footsteps of those such as Marx, Tönnies and Weber who emphasized the uniqueness of the modern 'money economy': the way in which it feeds off and into that 'calculative exactness of practical life' – to borrow Georg Simmel's felicitous phrase – such that human life itself is transmuted into an 'arithmetic problem'. Yet in all other essentials, Polanyi's theory of the nature, and especially the origins, of money deviates from his usual reference points, including Marx and Weber but also Menger and Malinowski. Following Smith, they all construe money's defining function, even in low-surplus economies, to be its mediation of exchange, and believe that only quantifiable objects serving this purpose can be properly regarded as money, and that money originated as a means of exchange. For Marx, money is the embodiment of exchange value, the universal equivalent 'into which all commodities as exchange values are transformed'; it develops from regular commercial exchange between societies. (In the *Grundrisse* he goes so far as to state that it 'arises naturally' from the social and economic relations between 'foreign' commodity owners.[40]) Weber follows Marx in this, and while Menger stands out from the others by theorizing money's origins in barter relationships within rather than between communities, he too prioritizes its exchange function.[41]

Polanyi dissents from the 'money as exchange' approach. In his view its exchange function develops, as a rule, within the framework of organized trade and markets; as 'status-free money' it is of little importance under fully 'primitive' conditions. Indeed, money need not function as a means of exchange at all. Historically, that role emerged only subsequent to the other three (unit of account, means of payment and store of wealth), each of which originated and was institutionalized independently of the others – and each role, he adds, may be simultaneously served by different money objects or material units.[42] Broadly speaking, then, Polanyi belongs to that school which, following James Steuart, considers money to have originated as a unit of account. However, he is also close to those such as Hamilton Grierson who deem money to have emerged in the payment of compensation for social and individual wrongs and that, from such origins, its use spread to other practices (such as bride-wealth) and ultimately to facilitating commodity exchange.[43] The Cambridge prehistorian Alison Quiggin was heavily indebted to Grierson, and her *Survey of Primitive Money* is a key source in Polanyi's own discussion. Money in 'primitive' societies, she maintains, is not primarily a means of exchange and rarely possesses an all-purpose character. Rather, one type of money buys, for instance, food, another a canoe, while a third may function as a medium in secret societies or in marriage payments. In contrast to Marx and especially to Menger, she ventures that barter was not the main factor in the evolution of money, and adds that 'the objects commonly exchanged in barter do not develop naturally into money'. Rather, its primordial form was as a means of payment, for example in the almost universal customs of bride-price and wergild; these 'established standards of value and regularized certain media of exchange, which are two of the three main functions of money'.[44]

Building upon the work of Grierson and Quiggin, Polanyi proposes a heuristic by which money's character in modern market societies can be distinguished from its incarnations elsewhere. In *market* societies it resembles language and writing in that it is 'organized in an elaborate code of rules concerning the correct way of employing the symbols' – money objects in the one case, sounds and letters in the other. Circulating throughout the economy it fulfils exchange, payment and other functions, and in order to do so must be uniform in quality: it is 'all-purpose' and 'status-free'. The various money uses in *archaic and 'primitive'* societies, by contrast, may be supplied by different money objects.

> Consequently, there is no grammar with which all money-uses must comply. No one kind of object deserves the distinctive name of money; rather the term applies to a small group of objects, each of which may serve as money in a different way. While in modern society the money employed as a means of exchange is vested with the capacity of performing all the other functions as well, in early society the position is rather the reverse.[45]

For example, slaves, horses or cattle may be used as a standard for assessing prestige-conveying wealth, while cowrie shells are the money object used for lesser goods. This 'special-purpose money' measures and compares only a restricted assortment of material goods and services on a common scale; it is not interchangeable and

circulates in only part of the economy – accordingly, archaic economies tend to be multi-centric, with two or more 'spheres of
exchange'.[46] Primitive and archaic money, thus, may be described
as 'heterogeneous', in that its use in one role need not extend to
another. For example, money in the form of prestige goods (including valuables and ceremonial objects) may be deployed as a means
of paying tribute but not as a means of exchange. It tends to be
safeguarded against usury and profiteering and bound up with
status.[47] By setting limits to consumption for the poor and sanctifying the higher living standard of the leisure classes, money, as
we shall see, contributes to the consolidation of archaic class
structures.[48]

Such, then, is Polanyi's general account of trade, markets and
money in non-market societies. Up to this point I have presented it
at an abstract level, with the scantiest of empirical references and
without analysis of its strengths and weaknesses. In the rest of this
chapter I look at its application to empirical economies – from
ancient Mesopotamia to postwar India – by Polanyi and his followers, exploring the originality of the project and assessing the criticisms that have been levelled against it.

Ancient Mesopotamia: three theses

The nature of economic life in the states and empires of ancient
Mesopotamia was long debated as one arena within the wider *oikos*
controversy. From the modernist perspective, which Polanyi
regarded as a consensus, second-millennium Babylon was in his
paraphrase 'a capitalistically-minded business community, in which
king and god alike engaged in profiteering, making the best of their
chances in lending money at usury and imbuing a whole civilization with the spirit of money-making over millennia'.[49] In partial
contradiction of this, Max Weber's approach had centred on the
theorem that the irrigation systems upon which Near Eastern agriculture relied required continuous supervision, a condition that
selected in favour of large, complex and unified bureaucratic structures capable of organizing forced labour on a grand scale – despotic states that tended to dominate civil society in general and
economic life in particular. 'The economic activities of the Mesopotamian monarchy', he proposed, 'constituted an *oikos* which far
surpassed in size the private sector.' The palaces and temples 'effec-

tively regulated the conditions and rates of private lending', and it was they, not market competition, that set the prices at which goods were sold. Weber did recognize, however, that the age of Hammurapi in particular witnessed a remarkable development of private trade, and, in a significant feint towards modernism, he conceded that Babylonian society was from the outset 'shaped by economic institutions propitious to capitalism'.[50]

Following Weber, a number of Assyriologists in the inter-war period advanced interpretations of the southern Mesopotamian states and empires that highlighted economic centralization in the hands of super-*oikoi*: the temples and palaces. Anton Deimel – with whose work Polanyi was familiar – concluded on the basis of the records from a Lagash temple that *all* land and enterprise in early Bronze Age Sumer (or at least in Lagash) was temple-controlled.[51] His conclusions, along with those of his compatriot Anna Schneider, contributed to a revised understanding of the Near Eastern economies. They were, the evidence suggested, 'dominated by large palace- or temple-complexes, which owned the greater part of the arable land and virtually monopolized anything that can be called "industrial production" as well as foreign trade (which includes inter-city trade)'.[52] It was a revision of the previous consensus that enjoyed its heyday in the mid-twentieth century, when Polanyi and the Assyriologist Leo Oppenheim were researching their contributions to TMEE. It was also extended, in a rather different direction, by Polanyi's colleague at Columbia, Karl Wittfogel. Borrowing Weber's theorem on 'hydraulic-bureaucratic official-states' he proposed that a rigid dichotomy should be drawn between Occidental freedom and Oriental despotism, a fissure that could be viewed as having carved its way throughout subsequent history. With this proposition, Wittfogel initiated the Cold War polemic that elevated the 'West' as heir to Hellenic private economy and democracy in opposition to the stagnant, despotic and dirigiste empires of the 'East'.[53]

Roughly speaking, this was the state of the debate when Polanyi commenced his studies of Mesopotamia. What is distinctive about his position is that it reconciles the evidence of a monetized trading culture with the primitivist model, thereby refuting the consensus supposition that the birth of civilization must have been coeval with the birth of market exchange. In the process he also repudiates the thesis that the redistributive systems of Mesopotamia were overseen by bureaucratic tyrannies. Although in agreement with

Wittfogel that 'the market' was born in Greece and not Babylonia, he points to the constitutional limitations on the exercise of power enjoyed in the latter, and adds that

> the absence, or at least the very subordinate role, of markets did not imply ponderous administrative methods tightly held in the hands of a central bureaucracy. On the contrary, gainless transactions and regulated dispositions, as legitimized by law, opened up a sphere of personal freedom formerly unknown in the economic life of man.[54]

In opposition to modernist readings, Polanyi proposes three main theses, on trade, money and markets. The first, on trade, is specific to the Assyrian city of Assur, on the upper Tigris, and its trading colonies during the Old Babylonian period (around 1900–1800 BCE), evidence concerning which had recently come to light in the form of an archive of business records and correspondence unearthed at Kültepe in central Anatolia. The new data excited Polanyi, for they revealed extensive trading activity on a non-market basis, with equivalencies established not through market competition but by custom or treaty. Embedded within a redistributive system, this was 'in all essentials' unlike market trade. Whereas the latter, considered in its elementary form, involves two actors and results in a negotiated contract, the early Assyrian trader operated 'dispositionally', by which Polanyi means that the defining element in his behaviour was 'a sequence of one-sided declarations of will, to which definite effects were attached under *rules of law* which governed the administrative organization of the treaty trade he was engaged in'. Much Assyrian trade was state-controlled and where it was not it was strictly regulated; but this did not mean – contrary to liberal expectations – that it was bureaucratically administered or unfree. In Old Assyria, Polanyi explained to a correspondent, economic behaviour was regulated by law, which meant that there was

> no bureaucracy, no administration, no command, no shifting of responsibility: instead the organization of trade is free, spontaneous, undirected *but* within an institutional frame which leaves it to the individual to act at will as long as he keeps to the law.

Keeping to the law meant, for example, storing contracted goods at the guild hall, sticking to agreed prices, or refusing to sell on credit. The Old Assyrian trader, in this interpretation, was a variant of the Akkadian *tamkārum*: a salaried quasi-public individual acting on behalf of a state organization and tasked with engaging in commercial exchange or, on occasion, with financing it. *Tamkāru*, although free agents, retained a public status within, and operated within the framework of, the palace hierarchy, and engaged in risk-free trade – wholly unlike market-oriented merchants who profit (or lose) in the competitive process of buying and selling.[55]

Polanyi's second set of arguments concern money and banking, which, despite the absence of markets, originated and flourished in Mesopotamia's irrigational empires. Money was, however, of the 'special-purpose' kind, with grain serving for the payment of wages, rent or taxes, and silver as a standard of value. Banking enterprise centred upon the 'staple finance' practices of large estate managements, and included the provision of harvest credit. Dealing with staples on a large scale involved inventories and accounting, for the purpose of budgeting, balancing, controlling, transfers and clearing in kind. Again, these operations required the use of money in the 'special-purpose' sense, with one staple selected as the standard of value. The essential point for Polanyi is that Mesopotamian banking developed not as an expedient in exchange economies but as the means by which to make redistribution more effective – and as such, a chasm separates it from its modern counterparts.[56]

The third thesis, on markets, is presented in two versions. One maintains that 'Babylonian trade and business activities were not *originally* market activities'.[57] The other goes much further, with the claim that from the Old Babylonian period right up until the fifth century BCE, Babylon 'possessed neither market places nor a functioning market system of any description'. It is important to note, however, that although Old and New Babylonia were essentially 'marketless', Polanyi admits of the possibility that 'capitalist activities' flourished – for he defines them, following Weber, as those 'which, in a relatively peaceful way, employ economic means to get monetary gain, or rather gain made in relationship to prices', as contrasted with capitalist *economies*, which are recognized by the presence of institutions dependent upon markets and by exchange as the dominant mechanisms of integration.[58] Accordingly, both Old Babylonia a century or two before Hammurapi and New Babylonia in the middle of the first millennium BCE can be said to have hosted the first ever 'successful periods of private business activity' organized along capitalist lines. In the latter period in particular, Polanyi's collaborator Leo Oppenheim ventured, significant privatization dynamics were in play, centred on the palace bureaucracy.[59] In each such epoch, a capitalist upsurge would last for one or two centuries before public business activity regained its customary upper hand; it was a pattern which cropped up repeatedly in subsequent history – in classical Greece and Rome, and then, following a long interval, in Western Europe in the tenth and eleventh, fourteenth and fifteenth, and nineteenth centuries. That said, if the nineteenth-century West was an unambiguous instance, 'capitalistic' could only be used to refer to Old and New Babylonia in a heavily qualified sense, 'since the equivalencies from which profits sprang did not originate in *markets*'.[60]

Mesopotamia: evaluation and critique

How well have Polanyi's analyses of ancient Mesopotamian economies stood up in the light of subsequent scholarship? The short answer is, less successfully than his other forays into comparative economic history. He has been accused of understating the degree to which they evolved – and this is particularly so with respect to the Tigris–Euphrates region from the middle of the fourth to the middle of the first millennium BCE. In my view, however, if one carefully parses his statements – not least those on 'capitalist upsurges' – one discovers a detailed awareness of institutional evolution. But what of the three theses? In assessing these, particularly with respect to the earliest phases of Mesopotamian civilization, caution has to be exercised, for the paucity of evidence encourages resort to the imagination, as we shall see below. Despite that proviso, however, there is no doubt that two of them were overstated, if not downright false.

Before I turn to evaluate the three theses, some preliminaries concerning post-Polanyian Assyriology are of relevance. To begin with, subsequent to the publication of Polanyi's research the 'palace–temple' model came under sustained challenge, principally from Igor Diakonoff and Ignace Gelb. They argued that the temples were less dominant than Weber, Deimel and Schneider had assumed, and that considerable control over means of production was exercised by village communities and individual households. Others proposed that as early as the third millennium the long-distance exchange of certain items had taken the form of market trade. In 1975, the Czech-American Assyriologist Carl Lamberg-Karlovsky published an influential paper on the soapstone trade, arguing – in explicit rebuttal of Polanyi – that it was unquestionably market trade, connecting areas of supply and demand via 'market networks'. A recent paper by Audrey Bossuyt goes further, asseverating that third-millennium Mesopotamia 'formed a strongly integrated market'. Still others have suggested that market mechanisms existed during the Sumerian Renaissance, also known as Ur III (which is by common consent the period of Mesopotamian history that is most refractory to modernist interpretation), as evidenced by a substantial degree of commodification of goods, fluctuations that closely tracked supply shortages, as well as private landownership and the sales of family houses and even orchards to individuals.[61]

With regard to Ur III, the modernist perspective has been hotly disputed, with a number of Assyriologists insisting that the documented evidence of immense tracts of arable land held by temple, palace and provincial administrations precludes a major presence of other large estates of whatever property form, and that, where smaller private plots did exist, ownership rights were vested in families and not individuals.[62] Temple-owned lands were not bought and sold, and the sale and purchase of other lands were rarely, if at all, a 'modern' market phenomenon involving buyers and sellers calculating income streams, capitalizing them at the going rate of interest and deriving a fair price. Rather, land sales were a last resort at times of duress: before selling their land families would sell their animals, and pledge their own labour (or even their children, as bond-servants for sex or other labour).[63] As regards the artisanal sphere, the foundations of the temple-economy model remain robust: as Lamberg-Karlovsky himself points out, the state had a virtual monopoly on trade and on handicraft production.[64] No data exist,

> for the *free* outside sale of finished products manufactured by the artisans of the temples and/or palaces before the mid-2nd millennium; both production and distribution were in the hands of the 'Great Organizations', the temples and palaces.

The business of the merchant in making money/profit, he adds, is not to be found in Sumerian documents.[65]

What of the claims regarding 'market networks' and a 'strongly integrated market' in the third millennium? One should, I think, treat these with caution, bearing in mind the influence, not least in our neoliberal age, of the economistic fallacy. Lamberg-Karlovsky defines 'market networks' as 'institutionalized transactions of commodities and services channelled from an area of high supply to one of high demand'[66] – a broad-brush characterization that would, for example, have included most transactions within the Soviet Union. On the crucial question that his essay purports to answer – that such networks were not administered trade but privately organized and geared to individual profit – Lamberg-Karlovsky provides no empirical evidence but only guesswork and speculation. A more egregious case is Bossuyt's 'strongly integrated market': it is a bold assertion, but is deduced from the assertion – as nebulous as it is meaningless – that 'cities, often very far from each other, maintained close contacts' with one another.[67] Or consider the claim, advanced by Maria Aubet, that 'the accumulation of huge stores of grain and metal in Babylonia in the second to first millennia BC clearly indicates the existence of a market'.[68] It is true that for this period a good deal of evidence attests to market behaviour, however that is defined, yet the existence of huge grain stores is emphatically not clear evidence of markets.

A still more arresting illustration of the economistic fallacy in operation has come from the pen of Morris Silver – an economic historian who seemingly regarded himself as Polanyi's nemesis. Ancient Mesopotamia, he asserts, 'experienced lengthy and significant periods of *unfettered market activity*',[69] but much of his case attests rather to a propensity to unfetter polemical speculation from solid empirical evidence. For example, Silver invites readers to reflect upon the way in which the landscape of southern Mesopotamia was planted 'with large groves of female date palms', and deduces that the effort involved in artificially pollinating them 'makes little sense except as a response to market opportunities'. Or consider the metals trade conducted by the merchants of Assur. Written evidence suggests that the town shipped some 1.6 tons of tin each year, which, if used to produce bronze, would require in addition over 14 tons of copper. 'Can we imagine', he asks rhetorically, 'that tin and copper in such quantities would have been mined in the absence of a market orientation?'[70]

Assyriologists and anthropologists sympathetic to Polanyi have delivered meticulous rebuttals of Silver's captious case. They highlight in particular his tendency to infer institutionalized market behaviour from the sketchiest of data. The date palms, one response points out, could easily have been pollinated for non-market reasons; in any case, artificial pollination is hardly a time-consuming chore. Assurian tin and copper could unquestionably have been mined in the absence of a market mentality, and that Silver cannot recognize this attests to nothing more than the power of 'economic solipsism'. The same ailment underlies his adoption of translations that unthinkingly reflect the market mindset: 'price' is used where 'proceeds' would suffice, and 'wage' where 'ration' may be the appropriate term. As Anne Mayhew and her colleagues have pointed out, terms like 'price' or 'sale' derive their substantive content from operations and roles within particular sorts of economic system. 'To choose to translate a word as *commercial* – as opposed, say, to "delivery against silver" – or to translate another word as *merchant'*, with its connotation of private ownership of merchandise, 'as opposed, say, to "agent" or "bailee" – necessarily implies that the translator has a particular socioeconomic system in mind'.[71] An even more uncompromising response, by the German Assyriologist Johannes Renger, accuses Silver of committing the most elementary errors. For example, his claims for the existence of markets in the ancient Near East lack 'a clear account or explanation of the criteria which could serve as proof for the existence of markets'. The assumption, Renger adds,

> that a simple reference to something sold or bought, to a hiring contract or a loan given is sufficient evidence for markets in credit, labor, land or commodities, respectively, is a completely unacceptable method of historical research.[72]

Having laid out some relevant co-ordinates of late twentieth-century Assyriological debate, we are now in a position to evaluate Polanyi's three theses. One of these, the 'strong' formulation on 'marketless Babylon', can be swiftly despatched. It was contested from the start – even by his own research assistant, Moses Finley, who accused him of confecting the idea that new evidence had shown markets to have been absent. These supposedly new historical insights, he wrote to Polanyi, 'are exclusively your own, unknown to nearly all Assyriologists and shared by none' – apart from Oppenheim, and his view on the matter was tentative and off the record.[73] Today, the Assyriological consensus is that evidence does exist of market places at which consumer goods were indeed traded.

Nevertheless, at least for lengthy phases of Mesopotamian civilization the weaker formulation, that markets were marginal to economic life, still holds up well. For this there is a simple underlying reason: the factors necessary to a market-dominated economy were lacking – in particular the presence of a class of 'free' workers, able and obliged to sell their labour-power to the owners

of productive property. These were primarily subsistence economies in which producers had little incentive to exceed their consumption needs, and this left relatively little surplus available for
exchange purposes. Towns there were, but their denizens typically
owned plots of land outside, resulting in a snail's-pace development of town–village economic exchange.[74] There was bulk trade,
and there were standardized prices, but these did not respond to
supply and demand 'in ways that reflected costs and consumer
utility. Rather, formal exchange at standard prices (rather than
negotiated informally on a person-by-person basis) occurred mainly
within the large public households.'[75] Rather than fluctuating to
reflect shifts in risk or supply and demand, prices were essentially
administered and customary, reflecting the internal accounting
practices and standardized rules of the big institutions. In consequence, Michael Hudson has observed, good harvests

> did not have the modern consequence of depressing prices and hence
> causing agricultural poverty. Bumper crops did not collapse rural
> incomes and drive cultivators into debt... Rather, their proceeds
> were used to pay off debts, or perhaps to exchange for temple and
> palace handicrafts. This left only negligible room for market forces
> to operate, mainly at the margin, above all for the barley sold by
> individuals to the large institutions in times of crop failure.[76]

Polanyi's second thesis, that Old Assyrian trade was conducted
by *tamkāru* along non-market lines, has proved more susceptible to
criticism than at least the weak formulation of the first. Since his
death many more of the Kültepe tablets at Kanesh have become
available, and these appear to show that a major portion of Assyrian
commerce was conducted by merchants on their own account and
for purposes of personal gain.[77] According to Aubet, the tablets
reveal 'orders to "sell at any price"', the weighing up of costs,
margins of gain and profits, and numerous 'allusions to the poor
demand for tin, to a fall in prices, . . . to the fluctuation of prices and
to changes in supply and demand', all of which lend credence to
the notion of a substantial market element in Old Assyrian trade.[78]
Pace Polanyi's reference to risk-free trade, a second study points
out, the documents repeatedly refer to losses as well as gains,[79]
while a third goes so far as to describe Assur as 'a clear instance of
a . . . merchant-capitalist city-state'.[80]

All that, however, does not amount to a consensus on Old Assyrian trade, as alternative readings are available. Mario Liverani, in
particular, has defended the claim that it was administered, and

contends that it is best understood as embedded within a redistributive economy. According to him, the Kültepe data reveal that trading operations were subdivided into three segments: the initial relationship between a temple or palace and its merchants; their activities after leaving their home base; and, finally, the settling of accounts between merchants and central agencies at the end of the process. What Polanyi overlooked was that in the middle stage merchants could indeed freely trade and play on price differentials to augment their individual gains. In the first and third parts, however, an administered relationship, using fixed values, did indeed obtain, with merchants receiving silver and processed materials from the central agency and returning after six or twelve months with the equivalent in exotic products or raw materials.[81]

As regards the third thesis, I shall consider it in two parts: money, and then banking. On money, a number of Polanyi's claims find support amongst economic historians and Assyriologists today. Throughout Mesopotamian history, writes Raymond Goldsmith in his overview of pre-modern financial systems, monetization was minimal, with rents and taxes being paid on the whole in goods or labour services (although towards the middle of the first millennium this begins to change, with long-distance market trade gaining in importance and with it a greater intensity of money use). Metals were employed 'to a limited extent in pensatory payments and in the incurrence and discharge of debts, but were never coined'.[82] Hudson's more fine-grained analyses also concur with Polanyi on the central issues. In accord with Polanyi, Hudson theorizes money's origins in multiple processes, and accords a seminal role to Sumerian staple finance. Specifically, he cites three separate tributaries of the money form in archaic societies: wergild-type debts to compensate victims of manslaughter or injury; food and related contributions to common-meal guilds; and third-millennium Sumer, where money evolved as a unit of account by which commensurability, and thence prices, were established in order to assist the various departments of the temples and palaces in administering their transactions. It was thus, he observes, in public institutions that a common monetary vehicle, silver – as well as investment at interest – first appeared.[83]

The Sumerian monetary system centred upon a common schedule of values assigned to various commodities used within temples and palace for internal book-keeping between departments; it was based upon special-purpose monies for the denomination of debts, settling of balances and payment of interest charges. Barley for cultivators and silver for merchants were the two chief money tokens, but other commodities were assigned standardized proportions too.[84] Silver's role, and here Hudson diverges from Polanyi, spilled out beyond those 'special-purposes'. With an assortment of goods assigned prices, these were rendered commensurable, which facilitated exchange transactions that were mediated by silver, which, being bought and sold like any other commodity, came to resemble a general-purpose money[85] – even if its circulation was far 'stickier' than that of all-purpose money today, given the rudimentary monetary and credit system of the time.

Turning, finally, to the credit system and banking, here too Polanyi's propositions have found support amongst Assyriologists, albeit, as we shall see, in amended form. According to Hudson, Renger and others, temple and palace were major providers of harvest and consumptive loans. In southern Babylonia, as in the ancient world generally, loans took the form of silver or merchandise advanced to traders, as harvest loans or consumer loans to strapped cultivators, or for the hiring of dependent labour; in all of these the loan was a means to a determinate end. There is scant evidence of productive loans to industrial entrepreneurs for achieving gain through the accrual of interest – an end in itself.[86] Nor is there evidence of 'a loan-market where supply and demand would have influenced the conditions for loans (e.g., interest rates, etc.)'. The rate of interest on silver loans was set by royal decree and remained fixed for over a thousand years, from Hammurapi through to New Babylonia. Although in practice there was doubtless some fluctuation in interest on silver loans, and more on barley loans, across the centuries the rate was essentially static and this, Renger points out, 'constitutes a strong argument against the existence of a credit market. If there had been a credit market in the true sense of the word, one would expect changing rates according to supply and demand.'[87] The banking and monetary system, in short, was rudimentary. Debts were non-transferable, banks did not engage in credit creation, and money was not potential credit but simply the means of denominating debts in terms of weighed pieces of metal to which a value was assigned.

Where Polanyi's thesis requires emendation is in its underestimation of the role of private money-lending, especially in northern and central Babylonia but in the south too, even including Ur III.[88] Arguing along similar lines to Liverani, discussed above, Hudson has suggested that interest charges arose at the interface *between* the public institutions (the temples and palaces) and 'merchants', who operated simultaneously in both a public and private context. The major creditors were the large institutions, followed by their officials acting in their own interest. What appeared to Polanyi at first sight to be a taxonomy of different types of economy thus turns out to be a distinction between different kinds of market pricing within Mesopotamia's 'mixed economy'.[89]

One suspects that Polanyi would not have demurred from the characterization of Mesopotamia as a 'mixed economy'; after all, referring to archaic societies in general he recognized that palace business was prone to being extended 'to the favored few'.[90] However, whereas Polanyi devotes only the odd passing remark to structures of property and class, Hudson and others have developed a detailed picture thereof. That palace and temple property was in essence a type of private property, different from and antithetical to communal property, was an argument pioneered by Diakonoff. More recently, the historical sociologist Michael Mann hypothesized that private, state and familial property

> *emerged together*, encouraged by the same processes. When our records begin – the excavated tablets of the early city of Lagash – we find a complicated mixture of three property forms in land administered by the temple. There were fields owned by the city's gods and administered by the temple officials, fields rented out by the temple to individual families on an annual basis, and fields granted to individual families in perpetuity without rent.

In contrast to the customary liberal conception of private and public sectors as antithetical, Mann stresses that processes of property accumulation in the hands of 'public' officials and private individuals in Mesopotamia 'were connected to, and in the end mutually supportive of, one another'.[91] Moreover, given that 'the earliest system in civilized societies by which exchange value could be conferred on an item was the weighing, measuring, and recording system controlled by the central-place irrigation state', the preconditions for market exchange may well have originated in the temples of Mesopotamia.

But it is Hudson who has given the closest scrutiny to the complexity of property forms across Mesopotamian history, as well as to the dynamics of politico-economic change to which they relate. Following Diakonoff, he envisages palace and temple as 'specialized public utilities, set corporately apart from the kinship-based communal sector'. Whereas the latter produced for subsistence, the bulk of economic surplus found its way into the 'public' sector. Far from trade having evolved historically from a small private scale to a larger, and ultimately public, scale, as the hoary liberal postulate has it, the reverse appears to have been the case. It was Bronze Age Sumer's public enterprises that squeezed out civilization's first continuous and regular economic surpluses,[92] and sustained investment and capital accumulation were first legitimized therein, not in a private market system. Sumerian temples acted as the catalyst for key entrepreneurial innovations, including the first regular land rents and bulk trade for profit, as well as the basic array of institutions upon which profit-making business depends: standardized pricing, interest-bearing credit, contractual formalities, account keeping and its requisite measures and weights.[93] By distributing goods at standard prices the temples also created conditions propitious to the emergence of independent merchants and market exchange.[94] Whereas Polanyi believed that markets first emerged at the lower margins of society, amongst military camp followers, foreign merchants and money-lenders, in Sumer and Babylon markets arose within elite-dominated sectors.[95]

Building upon these insights, Hudson advances a theory of what could be called (forgive the pun) ur-privatization. Rulers and their bureaucracies, he points out, behaved simultaneously in public and private ways. Their 'public' position could readily be transmuted into private advantage, with temple and palace officials exploiting their powers for personal material gain; indeed, the temple and palace archives reveal 'a bureaucracy engaged in personal gain-seeking to a degree not dreamed of a century ago'.[96] Endemic corruption underpinned a privatization process that was initiated and propelled by ruling families, warlords and other powerful individuals at the apex of the social pyramid. 'Private' enterprise thus emerged from the 'public' sector: it developed at the top of society, as self-seeking proliferated among the *tamkāru* 'merchants' who in their official positions belonged to the public bureaucracy.[97] As palace rule weakened, 'royal and public land-holdings came to be privatized by palace subordinates, local head-men, creditors, and warlords',[98] and by about 2300 BCE, land sales involving individuals were becoming more common. The heirs of the twenty-third-century BCE King Sargon of Akkad, for example, purchased land from the families of subject communities.

Although the orientation to personal gain that Hudson highlights diverges substantially from Polanyi's account, on the more fundamental question they agree: a wider societal ethic of individual gain-seeking did not come into being. In market societies norms of this sort may be viewed as the mainspring of progress but in archaic societies, including Mesopotamia, they were:

> perceived to sow the seeds for economic polarization, and hence social discord and decay. . . . Wealth was seen to make its possessors drunk with arrogance . . . , addicting them to seeking riches without limit in predatory ways.

It was to avoid this form of egoism, Hudson adds, 'that social pressures led citizens to consume surpluses conspicuously in public feasts, gift-giving, funerals, and similar rites of passage'. In so far as market forces did make themselves felt they were, in the interests of social cohesion, repeatedly overridden by states on matters as diverse as credit, private wealth-seeking, and the prevention of creditors foreclosing on the land of insolvent debtors. In Hudson's conclusion, an arresting inversion of Wittfogel's, it was 'the palace that played the role that most economists today assign to the private sector: preserving economic freedom for its citizens, a liberty that subsequently was lost in "the West", that is, in classical Greece and Rome'.[99]

Naturally, new evidence and reinterpretations have altered the field that Polanyi had ploughed. What is left of his furrows? How well does his contribution stand up in the light of the Assyriological research that has appeared since his 'Marketless Trading in Hammurabi's Time'? To begin with the negative, Polanyi tends to understate the degree of market development and the extent of private enterprise in Mesopotamia (albeit with the caveat that in unpublished notes he tentatively describes Old Babylonia as a 'period of private business activity' imbued with a capitalistic mentality).[100] In drawing too firm a line between private and public power and between administered and market trade, his radar struggles to pick up processes of privatization and the emergence of markets within the 'public' sector. That said, as was made clear in the above discussion of his specific theses, there is much to be said for his contribution. Empirically, his theses on the role of markets, and his observations on banking, finance and administered price equivalencies find significant support among Assyriologists today. Perhaps more importantly, his admonition against assimilating the past to the present through the anachronistic application of modern categories is methodologically indispensable. It was an approach that he pursued, on the whole with more successful results, in his studies of other archaic civilizations, beginning with Bronze and Iron Age Greece.

Trade and markets in Bronze and Iron Age Greece

Mesopotamia was not, in Polanyi's judgement, the birthplace of 'market methods'. Rather, that was Greece.[101] Athens' *agora* was the first market place of which we have definite knowledge, and the laurels for inventing market trade can be awarded to its citizenry. Given the common misconception that Polanyi abhorred market trade it should be emphasized that he admired the Athenians for this innovation. At least in part, it was an outgrowth of their democratic revolution, for a defining issue in the 'class war' between democrats and oligarchs was whether the principal agency of redistribution was to be the state or the 'overgrown households of the rich'. That in this confrontation the polis prevailed, at least for a time, served to establish an organic link between democracy and the market. 'The democratic form of redistribution depends on the market for its full effectiveness', as Polanyi put it, for payments by the polis took a monetary form, which provided food markets with their vital stimulus.[102] But if democracy synergized with market trade, did this not risk affirming the 'Plato to Nato' polemical tradition that erects a contrast between Mesopotamia's non-market despotisms and the democratic market system of ancient Athens? The answer, of course, is no. We have already seen that Polanyi detected remarkable spaces of liberty in the 'Eastern' monarchies. In addition, although he saw Athens as an innovator of market methods, this did not make it a market system. The quintessentially Polanyian question to ask is: did markets *integrate* the economy?

Before addressing that question directly, I shall circuit it historically through a brief summary of Polanyi's understanding of Athenian ancestors: the Neolithic and Bronze Age economies of the Aegean. In his nomenclature, these were essentially reciprocative and/or redistributive, with at most an element of small-scale market exchange. From the third millennium BCE onwards the tendency was towards redistribution, its culmination being Mycenaean Greece of 1600–1100 BCE, a 'palace economy of an extreme type' in which the circulation of commodities was an internal, non-monetized process that involved staple accounting. Taxed goods were collected at the centre and stored or disbursed – first and foremost to palace personnel, who were charged with providing intercession with the gods, organizing protection from attack, and supervising disaster relief. Drawing upon the Linear B sources published by Michael Ventris and John Chadwick, Polanyi suggested that Mycenaean Greece 'may well be the only case on record in which a literate community eschewed the employment of money for accountancy'.[103] No word on any existing tablet, Finley added, 'can confidently be taken to mean "to buy", "to sell", "to lend", or "to pay a wage"'.[104]

Following the implosion of Mycenaean civilization, large-scale redistribution subsided as the dominant organizing principle for the movement of goods, and thereafter it was, according to a recent and ground-breaking Polanyian treatise, 'probably very limited, restricted to instances of the divisions of the production from a hunt or following the slaughter of livestock'.[105] Half a millennium elapsed in which, in Polanyi's view, economic exchange was primarily reciprocal in nature and the small household was the basic economic unit – even if gift exchange between nobles was also of significance.[106] Of the earlier part, the 'Dark Ages' (1100–800), little is known, although it is generally held that the Homeric epics originated during and reveal something about that period (even if they may, additionally, transmit folk memories of the Mycenaean era). Economic activity centred on household production and consumption, although the epics indicate that there were also larger estates controlled by the elite and worked, especially at harvest time, with the help of hired landless *thetes*.[107] In the Homeric poems there is no mention of money, and no indication of rural–urban trade, while long-distance maritime trade was clearly reserved almost exclusively for luxury items.

Of the later 'archaic' part of the period (800–500), a little more is known. In Polanyi's interpretation, it was a period in which reciprocity was on the wane, with kin relations yielding to those of neighbour and citizen, and competitive individualism in the ascendant.[108] Compared with the small-scale production and minimal exchange of the Dark Ages, what a transformation had overtaken Greece by 600 BCE, and still more by 400! In the economy that had come into being, slavery played an important role; it represented, indeed, what one historian has termed 'the most drastic urban commercialization of labour conceivable'.[109] Commodification and monetization had made giant strides, and loan transactions were now an integral part of economic life. Coins had come into general usage. Both local markets (*agorai*) and international trade were thriving: in Aristotle's time, writes Polanyi, 'Delos and Rhodes were developing into emporia of freight-insurance, sea-loans, and giro-banking compared with which the Western Europe of a thousand years later was the very picture of primitivity.'[110] The question that confronted him is evident: given that the modernists had correctly identified the vigorous condition of markets, money and banking in classical Athens, were they mistaken to theorize it as a prototype of modern market capitalism? In the introduction to this chapter I sketched the general lines of his answer; now we can look at the finer points.

Polanyi's approach to the problem relies upon applying his conceptual apparatus, including his differentiated understanding of trade, markets and money, to a detailed examination of the known facts regarding economic behaviour – including, not least, the degree to which classical Athenians held values consonant with market behaviour. On this latter, he rehearses a number of familiar arguments from the primitivist canon. The ruling class of Athens and the other Greek city-states was predominantly agrarian, and trading was not regarded as a virtuous activity – as is apparent from the fact that 'traders were foreigners [while] citizens were as a rule *not* traders'. Positive attitudes towards self-sufficiency and a disdain for money-making activity were held by philosophers such as Aristotle ('the philosopher of *Gemeinschaft*') and, if less trenchantly, outside the Academy's walls too. The axial questions, however, concern the workings of economic institutions: 'To what degree are markets price-making? Can they be said to produce one price? And do they represent primarily a meeting of private persons and firms as against that of the representatives of public authorities?'[111]

To the first two of these his answer is unequivocal. With reference to Athens' key import, grain, he maintains that 'at no time was its price increased in order to attract supplies. The grain supply was secured by other means'[112] – i.e. imperial power. Indeed, Athenians held to the view that the price of wheat was essentially fixed (at five drachmas per medimnus), and this was 'a normative principle of great effectiveness' that could not have held such sway in the context of a price-making market. Within Athens itself, market trade in the *agora* was subject to strict supervision by the polis, for example with laws regarding fair dealing and enforcing its separation from the *emporium* of Piraeus, Athens' port of trade. In the *emporium* there was competitive price determination and this did affect prices in the *agora*, but only to a degree, for the latter was shielded from the full force of external fluctuations. Overseas trade was mostly administered trade and gift trade, and although the price of wheat and other grains could and did experience violent fluctuations, these were not market-driven but correlated with political events that impacted trade routes. And while the *agora* price could remain 'tied to the *emporium* price, so long as the latter remained within reasonable limits', that connection would be severed when prices rose to a dangerous level. When supplies fell abruptly the solution did not centre upon movements in price but upon appeals by magistrates and other citizens to the prestige of merchants: these were persuaded to sell their grain at the conventional price. At these junctures,

> we find the correlation between supply and price snapping: instead of the price rising steadily as supply drops, we find the reverse – the price suddenly drops. It is at this critical point that the mechanism of state control came fully into operation. Athens could link its *agora* to the emporium so long as the emporium price fluctuated within certain limits; to abandon itself completely to the vagaries of the external prices would have been suicidal.[113]

Markets, such examples demonstrate, were subject primarily to 'political and moral discipline' rather than 'market laws, which is what the economic historian unfortunately still means by "economic"'.[114] Although market laws were not entirely absent, and changes to equivalencies did in certain cases 'happen precisely as if a market mechanism had been acting', the point that Polanyi drives home is that such a mechanism 'had not yet been instituted'. Rather, market forces remained contained within the social and political fabric. Even the *agora* itself 'was hardly more than a device, facilitating the operation of the redistributive system, which remained dominant'.[115]

With this we have arrived at the final question, concerning the role of individuals and firms vis-à-vis the public authorities. Here Polanyi focuses upon the extraordinary economic role of the polis. Far from being simply a lawmaking body, it was also the indispensable economic actor, one that took an overarching responsibility for the livelihood of its citizens, organizing the import of basic goods and furnishing a large slice of the average citizen's income. A decisive push to this dynamic was given by democratization, for the provision of wages for public service upon which democracy depended required commodity markets at which that income could be exchanged. To finance the operation the state was able to draw upon tax revenues but, in addition, it commanded

> the resources and the energies and services of all its citizens through the liturgy principle – the obligation of citizens to provide public services from their private purses or time. Goods, service, and money thus were collected, or alternatively the rights over their disposal. Money and treasure were stored in the state treasuries; precious metals were cast into statues and other works of art which could be melted down when needed; grain, the staple food, was kept in state storehouses.

Ultimately, that the reach of the polis could extend so far was down to the authority it exercised over individuals, not only in the political and military but also in the economic and social spheres. 'It was this discipline', Polanyi observes, 'which made it possible for the polis to rely on a market for the provisioning of the citizens. For in an emergency, the market could be – and was – transformed at a moment's notice into a redistributive device.' In short, the *agora* was much more than a market, and classical Athens, although no *oikos* economy, was no market economy either. Rather, elements of redistribution – in both familial *oikoi* and the polis – and of market exchange 'were fused in an organic whole which should be taken as a distinctive type of empirical economy'.[116]

That is, I think, the thrust of Polanyi's argument. But there is a coda, concerning the final quarter of the fourth century BCE, with an intriguing twist. At that juncture, Polanyi maintains, a supply–demand–price mechanism with a 'genuinely capitalistic character' can be said to have arisen, at least in certain commodities – slaves, grain, luxuries and manufactures, and shipping. Throughout the eastern Mediterranean, grain supplies did begin to be transported on a major scale 'in response to the movements of relative prices', and prices did tend 'toward uniformity in the entire area'.[117] (There are Polanyian historians, indeed, who refer to the Hellenistic world of the third and second centuries BCE as the only other market-dominated society in history apart from our own.[118]) Yet what is, from a modern perspective, remarkable about this, the high point of the market's development in classical antiquity, was that far from being a spontaneous outgrowth from Attican markets it was the creation 'of the superplanners of Ptolemaic Egypt, who adapted Greek marketing methods to the traditional redistributive techniques of the Pharaohs'.[119] The Greeks, Polanyi never tired of pointing out, were the originators not only of market trade but also, in

Ptolemaic Egypt, of 'the elaborate type of planned economy', such that the centuries that followed Alexander's conquest of Asia marked the meridian simultaneously of 'ancient "capitalism" and of "non-capitalist" economic activity'.[120]

Greece: evaluation and critique

If one begins at either end, chronologically, of Polanyi's analyses of Hellenic antiquity, a good deal of support for his interpretations by subsequent scholars can be found. On Ptolemaic Egypt, with the exception of one or two exaggerations – notably the use of the polemically loaded term 'superplanners' and the thesis of a sharp shift towards price-setting markets – he gets the essentials right: the government undoubtedly did dominate economic life, exercising control over the bulk of productive land and of important manufacturing processes (such as olive oil production) too. Skip back one and a half millennia and a similarly affirmative assessment can be given. His description of Mycenae as a redistributive economy without significant market networks and lacking credit, debt and even the issuing of interest-bearing loans was to all intents and purposes accurate. Although it seems likely that certain periods of Mycenaean history witnessed a greater extent of local market behaviour and a larger private or communal sector than he believed, it is beyond question that the economy was centred upon palace redistribution, with palatial elites exerting rigorous control over the production and distribution of a range of goods, above all but not exclusively of the prestige kind. The Polanyi–Finley model, alongside Colin Renfrew's adaptation of it, remains today an important reference point in Mycenaean studies.[121]

With regard to Dark Age and archaic Greece, the contributions of Polanyi and especially of Finley have been subjected to intensive critical parsing, and on some topics they surely overplayed their hand. Finley's *World of Odysseus*, to take a celebrated example, has been criticized for understating the degree to which the Homeric elites engaged in commerce: it was not trade as such that they frowned upon, his critics point out, so much as the dishonesty and fraud that have accompanied petty retailing since time immemorial. Such exaggerations notwithstanding, the basic substantivist analysis of the period remains robust.[122] Market exchange was not the primary vehicle for the circulation of goods; these moved principally through gift exchange and plunder. Polanyi's interpretation of the Homeric epics on questions of trade and local markets is solid: they do not refer to local markets, and they do attest to the gathering of food at the centre for the purpose of feasting (albeit not as a permanent 'central store' of food). The dominant form of integration can legitimately be described as 'balanced reciprocity', to use Sahlins' term.[123] Foreign trade, in the sense of trade beyond Greece, was almost non-existent for most of the Dark Ages, while trade with strangers was regarded as an 'unsociable' activity.[124] And throughout the period, most of what limited maritime shipments occurred were not trade in the narrow definition. (For example, one historian has pointed out that when a sculptor, in order to execute a commission, travelled to a distant quarry where he paid for a quantity of marble that he then brought home, that was not an act of trade in the strict sense of 'the purchase and movement of goods without the knowledge or identification of a further purchaser'.)[125]

When we turn to classical Athens the picture becomes more variegated. One criticism of Polanyi comes from an unexpected source: Finley himself. If anything, Polanyi's research assistant insisted more adamantly than did his elder colleague on the marginality of markets in the Greek city-states and, famously, disagreed with Polanyi's interpretation of Aristotle to the effect that an embryonic market economy existed in Athens. And yet, Finley maintained, Polanyi errs in denying the existence of significant price variations according to supply and demand in the fifth and fourth centuries; these were a commonplace, and they bespeak the development of a supply–demand–price mechanism in international trade earlier than Polanyi had claimed.[126] To this empirical objection Finley adds a methodological one. Peasant markets, administered trade, ports of trade, conventional 'prices' and barter, he notes, are to be found in both 'primitive' and archaic/ancient worlds.

> But the intrusion of genuine market trade, on a considerable scale and over very great distances, into the Graeco-Roman world had a feedback effect on peasant markets and the rest to such degree as to *render the primitive models all but useless.*[127]

Some have taken this to mean that Finley underwent a conversion to modernism, and came to embrace its critique of the primitivist tradition, but I see it otherwise. The passage does indeed repudiate Polanyi, but not for his *primitivism* as such. Rather, the criticism is specifically of his transposition of Thurnwald's categories of exchange, distilled as they were from observation of *'primitive'* economies, into systems of 'integration' applicable to *archaic* civilizations. For Finley, Polanyi's model neglects to distinguish adequately between archaic and 'primitive' societies, but this does not equate to a rejection of its emphasis upon the unique character of the modern market system.

With respect to both Finley's empirical and his theoretical points, similar objections have been voiced more recently by the classical historian Mohammad Nafissi and the philosopher Scott Meikle. Polanyi failed to give due weight either to the evidence attesting to the spread of high-risk international market trading or to the impact of fluctuations in supply and demand upon variations in the rates of pay for hired labour, and he stands accused of 'lamentable exaggeration' in comparing Aristotle's thoughts on *koinōnia*, *philia* and *autarkia* with the reciprocity institutions of the Trobriand Islanders.[128] Far from being a defence of archaic reciprocal gift exchange, Aristotle's concern with the cohesion of the polis represented an attempt to specify reciprocity as a relationship of equality between proportions of products being exchanged.[129] From a quite different viewpoint, Edward Cohen's 'banking perspective', the ancient Athenian economy, although arguably 'embedded' in the fifth century, had by the fourth at the latest evolved into a fully fledged 'market economy' in which banks (*trapezai*) created credit, and productive loans (in the form of bottomry loans) advanced by banks, temples and landowners were a prominent element within a flourishing circuit of finance. Private property was respected and a *laissez-faire* policy prevailed, at least in the financial sphere. In an eye-catching inversion of the primitivist case, Cohen contends that the *trapezai* were 'unincorporated businesses operated by individual proprietors or partners, almost entirely free of governmental regulation', in contrast to modern banks, which are 'almost always corporate institutions, invariably governed by official regulation'.[130]

Still others have criticized Polanyi for generalizing from a spokesperson for the decaying aristocracy, Aristotle, to the Athenian citizenry as a whole; for failing to recognize the existence of regular rural food markets in the fifth and fourth centuries;[131] for his claim that the Greeks invented market trading; for overstating the separation of domestic and external trade;[132] and for exaggerating the degree to which ancient Greek ports of trade were politically neutral.[133] A greater number of Athenian citizens, it seems, engaged professionally in trade than Polanyi assumed, although their primary motivations were likely to have been considerations of status, the quest for honours and privileges, or gift giving, as contrasted to the profit-motivated professional merchants (typically, metics).[134] Finally, Polanyi stands accused of overestimating the degree to which prices were administered in classical Athens – except for grain and its derivatives, and even here, he exaggerates. Although the retail price of bread was fixed in proportion to the wholesale price of grain (in Aristotle's day, by a board of thirty-five guardians), there is no evidence that the wholesale price was subject to the same regime. 'In fact, Athens set the retail price of grain in relation to a wholesale price on imports that was determined by the impersonal market mechanisms of supply and demand', and even during severe shortages traders bringing grain to the city were permitted to charge the going rate.[135]

It seems to me that many of these criticisms hit the target, and yet, for all that, Polanyi's approach retains important strengths. It is fair to say that his recasting of the *oikos* debate stimulated new interpretive approaches, and the amended primitivism that he developed still finds considerable support amongst classical historians, in part due to its methodological commitments – notably, its critique of anachronistic reason – but also because many of its empirical propositions remain persuasive. Fifth- and fourth-century Athens was fundamentally a subsistence economy; for the most part production and consumption were not mediated by market exchange. The polis lived off the produce of its hinterland, and trade was overwhelmingly local. Polanyi's categorization of Athenian foreign trade as administered may be an exaggeration but it does capture a significant truth: that much of this trade was determined by contractual ties between Athens and other polities or by gifts from their rulers, or was quasi-decreed by the Athenian polis.[136] Indeed, in the case of its grain imports, a substantial proportion of what might appear to be market trade was in fact imperially enforced tribute payments. Trade, in the sense of imports, was vital to Athens and the other Greek cities, but only in that sense – and Athens' exports were greatly outweighed by its imports.

Across Greece in the classical era, markets in consumer goods could hardly be described as 'fully integrated', for, had they been so, situations could not have arisen whereby desperate grain shortages in individual cities coincided with plentiful supplies to others. In such cases, hungry urban dwellers did not depend solely upon higher prices to draw increased supplies from elsewhere in the empire; they resorted to imperial intervention. As to the extent of marketization within Athens and other similar city-states, it is of course the case that many artisans and other producers owned their productive property and sold their output on markets, but on the whole this was petty commodity production. Markets in the chief means of production (land) and in labour-power were weakly developed: land did not become alienable until around the end of the fifth century, and the propertied classes extracted surplus primarily by means of rent and unfree labour, not wage labour. There was no market in capital, for the simple reason that there was no market in labour that was anything other than seasonal and casual; without a significant pool of people needing to hire out their labour-power in order to acquire the means of life, there cannot be a significant market in capital for establishing productive enterprises.[137] A monetary system there was, and money-lending, by landowners and temples as well as by *trapezai*. But the credit system was rudimentary, and the only financial instrument of major importance, the bottomry loan, was a hybrid of loan and insurance contract.[138] Bankers did not systematically collect deposits and other spare funds in order to advance these as loans to promote business activity; unlike that of banks today, the socioeconomic context within which they operated was one in which wealth expansion primarily occurred through direct exploitation or war.[139] Bankers were often manumitted slaves and their social status was low, in contrast to the present day in which, to a far greater degree than in antiquity, status is a function of wealth. (Although, were it determined by *vox populi*, today's bankers would of course be in an altogether less elevated position.)

If the just-listed arguments affirm Polanyi's position in respect of economic organization, something similar applies to the parallel question of economic mentality. Although individual merchants aspired to profit, the Greek city qua collectivity 'was not interested in the very slightest in whether "its own" traders and merchants made profits through commercial exchange', in the judgement of Geoffrey de Ste Croix. Nor, the same historian adds, 'did any Greek city known to me ever show any concern whatever about exports: whenever we can see foreign trade becoming a factor in Greek city policy, it is always the import aspect which is predominant'. Commercial activity flourished, but the pursuit of profit for its own sake was regarded as a threat to social order. With this in mind it is perhaps not surprising that in Athens and the other Greek cities 'no single statesman is known to have been a practising merchant, and no merchant is known to have played a prominent part in politics'[140] – and yet, in so jarring with the modern market mindset, does not this aperçu bespeak a gulf between the two worlds?

Finally, the centrepiece of Polanyi's case with respect to the 'archaic' character of ancient Athenian society concerned the relationship between polis and economy. That these were somewhat more differentiated than he allows is a criticism that I find to be persuasive, but it does not alter the fact that the state played a central role in economic life.[141] In late fifth-century Athens the share of public property in total wealth, at 55–60 per cent, was so large that Raymond Goldsmith, who calculated the figure, doubts 'whether as high a ratio can be found anywhere else except in some of the theocracies of the ancient Near East'.[142] Less measurable but more important is the question of regulation. Political institutions 'contained' markets in such a way that no clear separation of state and market could be discerned – their relationship was one of 'indistinction', to use Perry Anderson's term, and this is doubtless the reason why the ancient Greeks did not conceive of economics as a separate discipline. The *agora* was not simply a site of commerce but one of political exchange, and litigation. In contradistinction to the previous aristocratic order, in which politics happened privately in the great rural households, the *agora* embodied the democratic principle that politics had to be done in public and in the city.[143] It is simply not possible to overstate the degree to which ancient Greek life was politicized, Paul Cartledge has noted, adding that

> it is this politicization which explains ... the necessity (rather than the mere desirability) of alienating market-exchange as far as possible beyond the tight bonds of the civic community, displacing it for preference onto sub-citizen classes excluded from full civic participation by reason of their legal status as women, aliens or unfree.[144]

With these thoughts in mind, it seems to me that Polanyi's description of ancient Athens as essentially a redistributive economy (albeit with burgeoning market elements), has merit, and this is acknowledged by a significant number of contemporary classical historians.[145]

West Africa: Dahomey, Whydah and Tivland

If there was one single feature of democratic Athens that excited Polanyi's admiration it was, he often remarked, its success in reconciling 'economic planning with the requirements of markets'.[146]

In this it was a pioneer but not a singularity. Subsequent history was to see numerous variations on the theme, and the one towards which Polanyi elected to direct his attention was the West African empire of Dahomey – a kingdom whose territory, translated into today's geography, occupies much of Benin and part of Togo. Working in collaboration with his former students Abe Rotstein and Rosemary Arnold, he prepared a volume, posthumously published as *Dahomey and the Slave Trade: An Analysis of an Archaic Economy* (hereafter, DST), while Arnold also contributed two essays on Dahomey and its port of trade Whydah (or Ouidah) to TMEE.

The image of eighteenth-century Dahomey presented by Polanyi and Arnold is refreshingly free from condescension and full – perhaps too full – of admiration. Although non-literate, its people constructed ingenious accounting and counting systems and used 'trade, money and markets with sophistication'[147] – a fact that Polanyi explains, invoking a notion akin to his brother Michael's 'tacit knowledge', in terms of its belonging to 'a forgotten phase of civilization which we might call "operational", owing to the gadgets by means of which complex mechanical and organizational feats may be performed without a conceptualization of the successful process'.[148] Its leaders' accomplishments in statecraft were legendary, demonstrating that this skill is 'not a white man's privilege'. (Indeed, Polanyi elaborates, the expansion of the market system in modern times has been to the detriment of the political arts in general.[149]) They excelled at war, and proved adept at running a 'planned economy of an advanced type'.[150] In fact, Dahomey's martial and command-economic prowess belong together: as with most of the societies admired by Polanyi (including Sumer, classical Athens, Ptolemaic Egypt and the Soviet Union), its dirigisme arose in large measure from the exigencies of coping with the pressures of a threatening security environment, its first century having been 'an almost continuous struggle for survival'.[151]

Yet what Polanyi and Arnold hold in the highest regard of all is the cohesion of Dahomean society and the stability of its state. In accounting for this, they refer to its religious customs such as ancestor worship, which 'internalized the emotional foundations of the rule of law, making superfluous the governmental apparatus of constraint with the masses of the people'.[152] Another factor was the structure of political and economic governance. The crown, at the head of an exceptionally centralized state bureaucracy, organized the affairs of war, foreign trade, taxation and currency. The king 'annually reviewed economic conditions, formulated plans for the future, distributed a minimum of cowrie to the population to buy food, set certain equivalents, received and dispensed gifts, and levied tolls, taxes, and tribute'.[153] Yet this was no bureaucratic despotism; rather, centralized bureaucracy and local autonomy existed in judicious combination, not least in Dahomey's 'ordered' and redistributive economy, which Polanyi describes as displaying 'an almost perfect balance of central administration and local freedom through a subtle tissue of reciprocating and householding institutions supplemented by local markets'. The monarchic state was formally separate from, and its powers were checked by, familial and local networks ('that cradle both of tradition and freedom'), with local autonomy rooted in ancient customs 'which the king himself did not dare to offend'.[154] Centrally directed agricultural production articulated with 'village freedom' such that the allocation of labour and land, the organization of the production process and price-setting were all determined not by the market mechanism but by monarchy, sib and guild.[155] Although rural areas teemed with 'big and small market places', the choice of crops to plant 'was directed from the capital, according to the overall requirements of planning'.[156] Dahomey was patently 'a country of markets', but these were isolated and did not link together into an integrated system. Markets were not price-making: movements of goods were not the product of price differentials between local markets, and prices did not fluctuate according to supply and demand.[157] Instead, the king and his ministers set general price levels, decreeing alterations in response to shortages or abundance of stocks – 'when there was an overproduction of one crop and an underproduction of another, the crop of an entire district might be changed at [the Minister of Agriculture's] command'[158] – and local variations on these general rates were implemented by producers' organizations, including those of the market traders themselves.[159] Overall, despite 'the absence of the equilibrating mechanism of the market', this system of equivalencies evinced an 'amazing stability' – and one, moreover, that spared Dahomey from suffering famine, of which only one was recorded in its history.[160]

Turning to foreign trade, it 'breathed', in Polanyi's evocative phrase, 'through local markets while avoiding a market system'. The bulk of trade in the key exports of slaves and palm oil was 'channelled through an administrative network quite separate from markets, acting through the intermediary of the "port of trade"'– the coastal slave-trading entrepôt of Whydah.[161] A classic instance of a port of trade, Whydah was initially independent but, after incorporation into Dahomey, was granted extraterritorial status. Not all of Dahomey's laws applied there, and its inhabitants were permitted to retain their traditional customs, such as snake worship. The inland state traded 'passively', entrusting the organization of 'active trade', and trade over long distances, to Whydah. It was a symbiotic relationship that enabled Dahomey to divest itself efficiently of slaves captured in war whilst resisting the penetration of those alien influences which commerce inevitably brings – here, in the form of European slave traders. To account for the conduct of trade in Whydah, Polanyi and Arnold insist, there is no need to refer to markets.

> From start to finish, the trading operation is an affair of state, administered from the palace, and conducted by the dignitaries of the land under terms of treaty. The presence or absence of markets makes no difference to the trading operations described. . . . Export–import transactions are conducted in separate places of trade completely removed from the market place.

In Whydah and Dahomey, trade, in contrast to markets, was organized by and for elites. To trade in slaves, other export goods or luxuries was a prerogative attached to high-status positions: trade stocked the palace, the army, and the houses of the great, while markets catered to 'the common wants of the population'.[162] One of the advantages of the arrangement, Polanyi believed, was that high- and low-status individuals were positioned within entirely separate economies, yielding that rigid, status-defined class hierarchy which he held to be the chief cause of the kingdom's remarkable social solidity. Economic differentiation applied not only to trade but to money too: the poor used one kind, the rich another – and prestige goods such as precious metals could only be obtained by exchanging their like. In contrast to modern society, upon the social relations of which general-purpose money acts as a solvent, the fact that money was 'state-made' and existed in different forms, each with its appropriate function, served to buttress the status order.

Writing of the use of 'status money' in pre-colonial West Africa in general, Polanyi explains that separate monies established 'limitations of consumption for the poor, while the higher standard of life of the leisure classes was automatically safeguarded. Without unfairness one can here speak of *"poor man's money"* as an instrument of maintaining upper-class privileges.'[163] In Dahomey specifically, he notes, money was 'connected with status, creating powerful invisible linkages in the social tissue'; it strengthened status identities and obligations and, as such, served to 'solidify the social structure' and to strengthen the state.[164] With its clear demarcations of social position and its ethics of patriotism and deference, Dahomey was for Polanyi – perhaps surprisingly given his socialist views – 'an unbreakable society, held together by bonds of solidarity'.[165]

Polanyi's thesis that special-purpose money serves to cement the status hierarchy in archaic societies was developed in tandem with perhaps his most gifted student, the anthropologist Paul Bohannan. In his research on the Tiv people of the Benue, in the Cross River region of Nigeria, Bohannan drew attention to their differentiation of commodity exchange into three hierarchically organized spheres. At the bottom, a subsistence category included raw materials, everyday comestibles, household utensils and some tools, while the top group consisted solely in rights to non-enslaved human beings, primarily women. These bracketed a third sphere, prestige goods, which included slaves, cattle, a type of large white cloth and metal rods, and 'was tightly sealed off from the subsistence goods and its market'. Within this middle sphere brass rods functioned as a general-purpose currency (i.e. it fulfilled all three major functions commonly attributed to money); outside it they were used as a means of payment but not exchange. Strict rules of conversion applied, so for instance one could not 'buy' a wife no matter how many sesame seeds one was willing to offer. In his earliest research findings, Bohannan desists from using the term 'money' to describe the brass rods, for they 'never provided a standard gauge against which the exchangeability value of all commodities was reckoned, as is the case with the coinage issued by [the colonial authorities]'. In Polanyi's terms, however, they represented a paradigmatic instance of special-purpose money, as contrasted with the general-purpose money introduced by the colonial administration, and this nomenclature was adopted by Bohannan in his later writings.[166]

Dahomey and the Tiv: evaluation and critique

Half a century after its publication there is much in the Polanyi–Arnold analysis of Dahomey that remains non-contentious, including its assessments of the efficiency of Dahomey's military and political apparatuses, the economic divide between bureaucratic state sector and egalitarian civic sector, the special status of merchants, and the orientation of royal trade towards the acquisition of necessary goods rather than the securing of profits by their resale. On the question of the relative absence of famines there is more room for debate. If its policy framework of 'flexible redistribution' did help to prevent famine, Dahomey would not be alone. In his *Late Victorian Holocausts*, Mike Davis has skilfully traced the cause of the devastating increase in deaths from famine across three continents during the final quarter of the nineteenth century to the destruction of redistributive mechanisms, with their flexible policies, stronger ethic of provision for poor, lack of suspicion of 'welfare cheating' and preparedness to bend the rules when famine looms. Millions of lives could have been saved, he argues, had it not been for the liberal resolve that the rules of the market prevail over the interests of the starving, combined with the imperial refusal to grant them a tax holiday. That said, it should also be pointed out that for climatological reasons Dahomey occupies a comparatively famine-free belt of the African savannah, and, furthermore, that a major contributory cause of its one recorded severe famine, in 1780, was directly political: the overexploitation of the peasantry.[167] Polanyi's silence on this may be symptomatic, for he displays a persistent blind spot towards the brutal, exploitative and acquisitive character of Dahomey's ruling class. (One caustic critic remarks that he 'casually mentions that after a military victory 4,000 captives were sacrificed to Dahomey's gods', which invites the reader to consider such questions as 'How would Polanyi have felt if he had witnessed these killings?' and 'What would he have thought of the training procedure for future Dahomeyan executioners, where girls and boys were given knives to hack at the heads of their living victims?'.[168])

As regards economic organization, two principal criticisms have been advanced of Polanyi and Arnold's contributions. The first concerns an ambiguity in their treatment of the separation of trade and market. If by 'market' we are asked to understand local food markets and the main market place at Whydah and to overlook their external connections, the point is well made but limited in scope. What is bracketed out is the influence of the world market upon Dahomean trade: in the eighteenth century the international market in palm oil and slaves was flourishing, and in the following century Dahomey was at the epicentre of the international clandestine slave trade. Hence it is one-sided to conceive of prices of slaves or palm oil as being centrally administered. If the king and his advisors had set the asking price too high, purchasers (European traders) would have made themselves scarce. More generally, as Robin Law has put the point, Polanyi was right that the Dahomean political authorities set prices administratively, but he exaggerated their success in fixing them over long periods.[169]

Polanyi's work on West Africa has also been subjected to scrutiny by the economic historians Philip Curtin and Patrick Manning, and the sociologist K. P. Moseley. Curtin provides additional support for Polanyi's thesis that currency exchange in the region was organized around ideal values to which actual market exchanges did not necessarily conform, but takes him to task both for his assumption that the state monopolized the slave trade and for his denial that the prices of slaves fluctuated significantly.[170] As to Moseley and Manning, they contend – convincingly, in my view – that Polanyi and Arnold exaggerate the isolation of the slave trade from other commercial intercourse, and present a static image of Dahomey when in fact it evolved significantly from one century to the next. Thus, Moseley suggests, Polanyi's depiction of the administrative control of trade is considerably less applicable to Dahomey in its old age than in its youth.[171]

Turning, finally, to money, the tide of anthropological opinion over the last three decades or so has been flowing against the Polanyi–Bohannan position. The general tendency has been to deconstruct the assumed antitheses between 'us' and 'them', 'moderns' and 'traditionals', '*Gemeinschaft*' and '*Gesellschaft*'; to restore, in Arjun Appadurai's phrase, 'the cultural dimension to societies that are too often represented simply as economies writ large, and to restore the calculative dimension to societies that are too often simply portrayed as solidarity writ small'.[172] As part of this general trend, anthropologists of money have been paying greater attention to its liminal and hybrid forms – for example, in studies of colonization processes, in cases in which elements of special-purpose money were retained despite the intrusion of colonial monies[173] or, in modern times, in instances of special-purpose money, such as cheques, which serve only one money function.[174]

As regards Polanyi and Bohannan's theses on special- and general-purpose money, subsequent scholarship can usefully be divided into two currents: the icy polemics of the economic historian Anthony Latham, and a still critical but decidedly warmer group, represented by the economic anthropologists Mary Douglas and Jane Guyer and the economic historian D. C. Dorward.

Latham identifies an empirical flaw in Bohannan's case and leaps from this to a grand statement: that if the logic of this recognition is followed, the 'Polanyist' model *in toto* is revealed to be flawed.

The metal rods of eastern Nigeria, he claims without indicating his reasoning, are no minor case study but form the foundation of 'the whole Polanyist interpretation' of 'primitive' and archaic societies: if the rods are pulled from beneath it, the entire edifice will fall. His case, in brief, is that the metal rods did not circulate within the 'prestige' sphere only but were commonly subdivided for petty purchases and were therefore in reality a general-purpose currency; that such currencies pervaded 'primitive' and archaic societies; that they are a sure sign of a market economy; ergo, that Polanyi and Bohannan were wrong to theorize the existence of non-market mechanisms of integration.[175] *In nuce*, his argument is this.

> The rod currency was the principle [sic] Polanyist example of a status exchange unit operating within a system of reciprocity, and key to their interpretation of primitive and archaic societies. But if it turns out to have been a true general purpose currency operating within a market economy as appears to be the case, then the whole Polanyist interpretation is thrown into question. How many other systems have they misleadingly labelled as reciprocity based? It must be emphasised that if a currency contains both large units, and small units which can be used as small change for petty transactions, then it is almost certainly a true general purpose currency. If it is a true general purpose currency, then it is operating in a market economy and not a reciprocity system. True general purpose currencies and market economies are synonymous. Money based market economies pervaded primitive and archaic societies, not systems based on reciprocity and redistribution.[176]

This is a passage crammed with such transparent and risible non sequiturs that it would be condescending to the reader to devote space to the refutation of individual points. I would observe, however, that in spite of his unshakeable belief that Right is entirely on his side and none whatsoever on Polanyi's, Latham unwittingly confirms a central Polanyian thesis when he turns to discuss another eastern Nigerian group, the Efik. Because Efik chiefs invested the returns from trade they were 'acting in a truly capitalistic manner', in his judgement. And yet, 'surprisingly', he adds,

> there was no development of capitalistic means of production, despite the capitalistic commerce. . . . So the profits of commerce were not invested in capitalistic production. Instead, any surplus above the demands of commercial liquidity was converted into slaves, the most desired and status-conferring possession in Cross River society.[177]

Latham has, in short, railed against Polanyi and his followers only to reveal inadvertently that they are correct on the key issue. In the absence of the subordination of labour-power and the main instruments of production to capital, market trade may develop and flourish but a market economy will not.

Despite Latham, Polanyi's and especially Bohannan's work has been widely admired by anthropologists and economic historians of western Africa. Dorward and Guyer identify empirical defects in Bohannan's research but treat them as just that: flaws, rather than as blows fatal to the Polanyian research programme. Dorward's interest is specifically in the Tiv's use of *Tugudu* cloth, which, he maintains, served as a general-purpose currency, cutting across the ostensible spheres of what Bohannan believed to be a multi-centric economy.[178] Bohannan's focus on the subsistence economy, Dorward suggests, led him to ignore the importance of artisanal production and the Tiv's involvement in trading networks. That said, Dorward accepts that the concepts of special-purpose money and multi-centric economy in general may well be useful tools. Guyer, an anthropologist generally critical of the modernization paradigm, is on the whole favourably disposed towards Bohannan's work, and proposes that his model, to be defensible, requires but two modifications: first, that many items in Tiv exchange were vital components within regional trade networks (into which *Tugudu* cloth and brass rods offered entry); second, that in this process the strict boundaries around the spheres of the Tiv domestic economy could be altered or breached.[179]

Further towards the appreciative end of the spectrum one finds Mary Douglas, an anthropologist who studied at Oxford with Paul Bohannan and who cites his work as an inspiration for her exploration of the connections between special-purpose money and status hierarchies.[180] With reference to the status-preserving effects of the Tiv exchange hierarchy – that metal rods were used primarily for the purchase of prestige goods and status symbols and only exceptionally for other purposes – she notes a similar system in her own area of research, amongst the Lele of the Congo. However, she asks, can the Tiv's metal rods or the raffia cloth with which the Lele pay fees, fines and tribute really be designated 'money'? Unlike Polanyi and the later Bohannan, she is reluctant to apply the term to such tokens, the use of which is restricted to the purchase of specific items, notably prestige goods and status symbols. Their underlying socioeconomic purpose is less exchange than the preservation of status divisions and, as such, they are more accurately seen as coupons operating within a rationing system. Using a lexicon that evokes Menger and Simmel more than Polanyi, Douglas conceives of money as an instrument of freedom, oriented to possibilities, in contradistinction to coupons, those instruments of control, rationing or licensing that are oriented to restrictions – whether with egalitarian purpose or to shore up status hierarchies.[181]

To sum up this section, there seems to be general agreement that Polanyi was in error to suggest that general-purpose money did not circulate in archaic societies, and few today would support his claim that only in the last few centuries has 'money as a means of exchange become general'.[182] Exaggerating the contrast between general- and special-purpose money hampers our understanding of the processes by which, as exchange becomes more regular and widespread, money evolves into its contemporary form. That said, the critics of the Polanyian paradigm should not push the point too far. Yes, we can study the moral, embedded and special-purpose functions of 'modern market money' and the calculative and rational dimensions of other forms.[183] But the former does tend to be remarkably fluid, interchangeable and abstract, and caution is to be advised when designating some of its forms – such as cheques – as a type of special-purpose money, for they are readily, generally and continuously converted into other forms, unlike the metal 'hoes' of the West African coast that were deployed chiefly as bride-wealth, or the cassowaries, hand drums and bone head-scratchers of the Mae-Enga in upland Papua New Guinea.[184] In drawing attention 'to the ways in which money objects have their origins in quite specific cultural practices that are distinctive from the process of market-based exchange', the Polanyian distinction between general-purpose and special-purpose money is analytically valid and has been applied usefully by anthropologists in the field.[185]

From Meso-America to rural India via the Berber Highlands

In its essentials, the substantivist model that Polanyi applied in his studies of Mesopotamia, Greece and Dahomey was adopted and developed by his colleagues in the Interdisciplinary Project at Columbia. Several of these we have already encountered, but it would be remiss not to mention the work of three others: Anne Chapman, whose essay on the pre-colonial civilizations of Central America is one of the jewels of TMEE, Francisco Benet's ethnography of the rural Maghreb, and Walter Neale's contribution on Indian village economy.

Chapman's essay is on the political economy of the Aztec and Maya, with a focus, naturally, on markets, money and trade. In both of these civilizations her researches revealed that market places, though prominent, were tightly regulated. Restricted to certain places and days and with prices set and supervised by state bodies, 'the market' did not extend beyond the market place. As in many other archaic economies, a variety of money objects were utilized. For the Aztecs the principal money token was the cocoa bean (hence the title of one essay on the subject: 'When Money Grew on Trees'). Others included small cotton cloths, gold dust, feathers and, possibly, small copper axes and pieces of tin. For the Maya, a similar set of objects was employed: cocoa beans, cotton cloths, strings of red shells, copper hatchets, bells, jade beads and salt. The bulk of Chapman's essay, however, is devoted to trade, with particular focus upon the Aztec *pochteca*, long-distance traders whose activities were 'to a remarkable degree separate' from market institutions. In contrast to the local markets, their transactions typically took the form of barter. The *pochteca*'s trade 'was the highly structured occupation of persons dedicated to performing their duties under the authority of their professional organizations'. Those organizations

> possessed a tight-knit structure, with their own hierarchy, special gods, distinctive rites, particular feasts and religious celebrations, unique insignia and a strict moral code, as well as an ethical point of view on the hazards and rewards of the profession, and a high regard for honesty and group solidarity. They had courts to judge their own members . . . They also sacrificed and ate slaves in honor of the god Huitzilopochtli.

That the practice of trade involved elaborate organization and ritual behaviour was evidently connected to the insecurity of the occupation. Even the return to home base, with slaves or hired workers laden with foreign goods, could be a risky venture. The *pochteca* therefore made sure to return from their trips on a 'good luck' day: 'They waited until night-time before entering the capital [Tenochtitlan] and came in secretly so that no one should notice them'; they would thereupon deposit the goods with a relative or other person of confidence before repairing to their homes. As regards the ports of trade at which most trading took place, some were administered by the Aztec or Maya Empire itself while others were run autonomously by the trading community, after usurping authority from the local inhabitants. As this implies, far from the 'purely economic' image of the peaceful merchant, the *pochteca* participated in the conquest of the non-Aztec territories with which they dealt.[186]

An altogether different form of economic integration is to be found in the rural Maghreb of the nineteenth and early twentieth centuries, discussed by Francisco Benet in one of the shorter pieces in TMEE. The Berber Highlands of Algeria and Morocco, he discovers, evinced a co-ordinated nexus of market exchange and in-group reciprocity that permitted market individualism and communal reciprocity to mesh in a unique way. Berber villagers store grain in the *agadir* – a solid (and sometimes fortified) structure, typically at the centre of the settlement – but keep their heaps in strictly separate cells, which Benet believes to be 'a remarkable demonstration of economic individualism'. Although they bring their produce to market as individuals, the market place functions as the centre of community. 'The markets are the forums of the tribe', remarked one nineteenth-century traveller in the region;

> Ideas and business affairs are dealt with here once a week between individuals who live at a considerable distance. It is here that collective sentiments form and manifest themselves. Villages and families fuse their emotions into that often entirely different product which grows from mass contacts. . . . The egotism of the tribe or the *douar* [village] takes the place of the egotism of the individuals.

Nowhere else, another analyst of Berber society has offered, can a combination be found 'which is nearer equality and farther from communism'.[187]

The exact converse might be said of the economy of rural India, the subject of the final chapter of TMEE that I shall review here, by Walter Neale, student and friend of Polanyi. Neale begins his essay with the observation that Indian village economies had long been a conundrum for Western scholars, for they could see that a complex division of labour was in place yet distribution was evidently not organized through markets. 'There was no bargaining, and no payment for specific services rendered. There was no accounting, yet each contributor to the life of the village had a claim on its produce, and the whole produce was easily and successfully divided among the villagers.' For British colonial administrators this had proved a practical headache when, applying liberal market preconceptions, they attempted to calculate taxes based upon market rent. Given that this did not exist, they sought instead to calculate the 'imputed rent' – an estimated figure for the rent that would be paid if a market existed. But this was hardly a practical solution. After all, asks Neale,

> how can the value of a product be computed when so much of it is consumed by the producer and never reaches the market? . . . How can one compute costs when virtually all the costs are implicit and there is no such thing as a standard wage for agricultural labor?

Economic rent, he continues, 'is a quantity that requires a market system, and could not therefore have meaning in the context of the Indian village economy', so to inquire as to whether revenue from land was a rent or a tax 'was to misconstrue the economic organization of pre-British India. It falsely assumed that the use of market terminology would prove revealing', when in fact it occluded the issue.[188]

The colonialists' critical error lay in their failure to distinguish between market *places* and the market *system*. The latter, as we have discussed above, is not a location but a mechanism that connects supply and demand to produce prices, involving markets for a range of products that interconnect, such that each change in demand or supply conditions ramifies throughout the whole. Indian villages did indeed possess market places to which, for example, cow-owning families would bring milk surplus to domestic requirements. But the surplus milk would be sold at the customary price, and would not determine the number of cows a family kept – the supply.[189]

At this juncture Neale turns to ask the standard Polanyian question: if not through market mechanisms, how then was the Indian village economy organized? The answer he finds is in a blend of redistributive and reciprocative elements, centred on the distribution of the essential foodstuff, grain. Redistribution operated within the village unit, with each villager participating in the division of the grain heap, as well as at higher and lower levels. 'Below, the share remaining to the cultivator's joint family was managed by the head of the family and parcelled out to the members of the family.' Above, princes, kings and emperors all took their portion. Under the Mughal Empire, for instance,

> there was a hierarchy of redistributive centers with the village grain heap at the bottom and the king's storehouses at the top. In between, the local powers and provincial governors maintained their own

storehouses, retaining a share and passing on the remainder to the level above. In regard to grain, the whole political and social structure was founded on redistribution.[190]

In other economic sectors, however, particularly services, arrangements were of a reciprocative nature, organized through kinship and caste and sanctioned by religion. Each member of each caste 'contributed his services and skills to the support of every member of the other castes. . . . Each caste was economically entirely dependent upon the performance of their duties by the other groups.'[191]

As with his mentor's perspective on Dahomey there is much of value in Neale's research, yet it can be criticized for projecting an image of the Indian village economy that focuses so narrowly upon explaining economic integration that its exploitative character is obscured from view.[192] The other principal criticism that has been levelled against his account will come as no surprise to those who have read thus far: it underestimates the role of money in rural India. According to the anthropologist Chris Fuller, the majority of cultivators in most of the subcontinent had been paying their land taxes in cash, not kind, long before the onset of colonial rule. In his fixation upon the division of grain on the threshing floor, Neale 'fails to give due weight either to the importance of money in the pre-colonial revenue systems, or to the degree to which the most sophisticated of these systems had been detached from the actual harvest'.[193]

Conclusion

Between the publication of *The Great Transformation* and his death in 1964, Karl Polanyi devoted his energies to developing a comparative and non-ethnocentric 'general economic history', a framework capable of making sense of modes of economic organization even where systems of interconnected price-making markets are absent. The case has, as we have seen, elicited some illuminating criticisms. But mixed with the wheat there is no shortage of chaff. In sifting one from the other I would recommend, as a rule of thumb, that four questions be asked. First, to which of Polanyi's writings is the comment directed? If the answer is *The Livelihood of Man*, one should bear in mind that this was published posthumously, on the basis of unfinished manuscript fragments. Of course they convey his ideas, but the texts were not definitively approved for publication by the author. Second, has care been taken to select for interrogation his stronger positions? Wearisomely often, critics seize upon Polanyi's occasional comments that deny the existence of markets (in Mesopotamia, notoriously), when his central point was not their non-existence but their marginality and separate institutionalization. Third, has the critic understood that the mechanisms of integration are ideal types, not detailed models of entire social systems, and that in actual societies Polanyi recognizes that they co-exist? (By way of illustration, the historian of antiquity Peter Bang dismisses Polanyi's notion of 'redistribution' because it cannot capture the more complex economic arrangements of the Roman Empire – but Polanyi never once suggested that it did.[194]) Finally, have the conceptual distinctions that Polanyi makes between market places, price-making markets and the market system been properly grasped? All too often, critics infer from Polanyi's hostility to modernity's 'One Big Market' an antagonism to all forms of market and commerce. One of them chides him for drawing a crude contrast between pre-monetary communities and a 'nightmarish view' of modern commerce.[195] But charges of this sort – and they are legion – are crass misrepresentations that cannot withstand scrutiny. Unlike opponents of market exchange *per se*, if such persons exist, Polanyi maintains that, historically, it 'permits a flexibility in the elements of the economy that causes a sharp rise in their usefulness in production and consumption alike'.[196] And, far from having an aversion to money, he credits it with extending 'the scope of our intellectual and moral experience'.[197]

Nevertheless, Polanyi did have, as we have seen, a persistent tendency to push his case too far. His dichotomy of administered prices, treaty trade and inert ports of trade in archaic economies vis-à-vis the fluctuating prices of trade in market economies is overdrawn, as is the insistence that outside market economies 'no supply–demand–price mechanism can be effective'.[198] In addition, his account of archaic societies downplays their internal contradictions and hence, as numerous critics have pointed out, is poorly equipped to explain socioeconomic change.[199] With his predilection for a comparative approach geared to the construction of taxonomies based upon ideal types, the method is ill-suited to charting the development of economic behaviour and concepts both from less to more commercial phases of antiquity and from the pre-capitalist world to modern capitalism.[200]

Once again, it is worth pointing out that the range of criticisms directed at Polanyi's project is testament to its significance. It was a pioneering and ambitious enterprise, one that produced new conceptual tools, outlined in the preceding chapter, as well as a series of original empirical studies surveyed in this one. In the process Polanyi revolutionized the *oikos* controversy, revamping and revitalizing the primitivist case. His reworking of the primitivist position was original, and many of its basic contentions remain persuasive. In most ancient and archaic societies markets were marginal. They were restricted mainly to goods (and in some cases slaves), rather than land or labour-power, and were not the primary determinants of the distribution of wealth in society. Manufacturers generally produced for known buyers in known quantities rather than competing on an uncertain market, and if their decisions were affected by price fluctuations the feedback mechanism did not operate with anything approaching the alacrity of its modern counterpart. Financial instruments were largely limited to evidences of debt (i.e. claims and liabilities), while deposit banking, the transfer of debt and organized financial markets were noticeable either by their absence or by their rudimentary nature. His writings on the ancient and archaic worlds, as we have seen, have stimulated the work of numerous classical historians and archaeologists, of which Moses Finley, Colin Renfrew, Carlo Zaccagnini, Michael Hudson, Johannes Renger and Mario Liverani are among the most distinguished. Alongside the double movement thesis and substantivist economic anthropology, it is the third of the major contributions for which Polanyi is remembered.

5

'Disembedded' and 'always embedded' economies

Where there is a separate economic system the requirements of that system determine all other institutions in society. No other alternative is possible, since man's dependence upon material goods allows of none other.

Karl Polanyi[1]

The fascist era appeared to herald a total crisis of a market organized industrial society. I sought to move into focus the separating of the economy out of the social whole. This led me to primitive society as an approximation of embeddedness, i.e. an antithesis of market society.

Karl Polanyi[2]

If in the first two decades that followed his death Karl Polanyi's ideas circulated chiefly among anthropologists and classical historians, more recently the running has been made by political economists and economic sociologists. One theme on which his ideas have provided inspiration may be summarized as 'neoliberalism and its discontents' and is the subject of the next chapter. In this one, I examine a concept that has, more than almost any other, become identified with Polanyi: the 'dis/embedded economy'. It is a notion around which much debate has revolved, generating some light and not a little heat. I begin by looking at three reasons that account for some of that 'heat': the divided sociological terrain upon which it stands; Polanyi's shifting relationship to that terrain; and the diverse purposes to which economic sociologists have put the term.

Embeddedness: a genealogy

'Embeddedness', a metaphor denoting a state of dependence upon or subordination to, refers to the relationship between 'economy' and 'society', that defining question of a discipline the founders of which approached it in diverse and inevitably clashing ways. For Marx, whose works are often cited as stimuli to Polanyi's use of the term,[3] economic behaviour cannot be studied as if it is isolated from society. That 'the economy', as a separate analytical category, came into existence, Marx explained, was consequent upon the emergence of a new matrix of class relations centred on the relationship between the owners of money and the means of production, on the one hand, and free workers, the sellers of their own labour-power, on the other. Separated from the necessary instruments and materials of production, workers must contract with other parties in order to produce; they must sell their labour-power to secure the means of survival. It was on the basis of this historically novel separation that the central dynamic of capitalist society – the drive to infinite accumulation, with social purposes subordinated to market imperatives – comes to appear as if emanating from a particular 'sphere', the economic.

Marx's theses on alienation and on the separation of the political and economic spheres are both rooted in the same theory of class in capitalist society. The worker is alienated from the object he produces because it is owned and disposed of by another, the capitalist. The class relationship, although centred in the sphere of production, extends in its effects to other social institutions, in particular to the distinction between private and public domains. That the exploitation relation in the new society was enforced primarily through the effect of propertylessness on the workers' 'voluntary' decision to hire out their labour-power, rather than by direct coercion within structures of personal obligation or ownership, had implications for the form taken by state power. Because the 'political' nature of the relationship between capitalists and their representatives on the one side and their employees within the farm, factory or office on the other came to appear as the strictly 'private' realm of civil society, a space distinct from civil society could emerge in the shape of the modern 'political state'. The production and distribution of goods and services appear to be situated within the 'economic' realm, giving the appearance of 'society' dominated by 'economy', with social purposes and humankind's metabolism with nature subservient to narrow economic ends dictated by market imperatives.

Despite their separate institutionalization, state power and capitalist markets are, for Marx and Engels, *internally related*. For, as one Marxist economist has put it, market exchange involves 'not only exchange but also the mobilisation and deployment of commodities as useful things', and as such 'relies on and continually engenders non-market social relations'. These reciprocal and redistributive relationships arise alongside and in interaction with the narrowly 'economic' relations of money-making, comparison of returns, and the utilitarian reckoning of costs and benefits. Some will involve 'trust, custom, solidarity and moral obligation in ways reminiscent of the gift, but they also embody hierarchy, power, authority and rivalry deriving from capital as a set of exploitative economic operations'.[4] If commodity exchange is to function systematically, a rule-governed system of property ownership must exist, as well as a coercive apparatus to constrain transgressions of property rights. In this way, property, and therefore exclusion and force, are essential to the generalized commodity form: 'economic' processes demand as a vital presupposition the consolidation of a system of 'rights' and 'freedoms', and a set of means by which they may be maintained.[5] In modern capitalism, the constitution and guarantee of property rights and the management of population are tasks undertaken by states.

Marx's theories of alienation and the separation of politics and economics were important reference points for Polanyi, but in an earlier age they had provided similar inspiration to Tönnies. With its adoption by him, the notion that the economy in capitalist society is instituted in a historically singular manner became a staple of the nascent discipline of sociology, with his *Gemeinschaft und Gesellschaft* becoming a touchstone for German sociology in particular. But on several points he parted company with Marx. He was infuriated by the thesis that capitalist states are structural supports for capitalist society such that the first step towards overcoming the latter must be the deconstruction of the former and their replacement by workers' democracy, and singles out the work in which Marx develops this argument most fully, *The Civil War in France*, as 'pathological' and motivated by 'dark anger and bitterness' – his worst, in short, by far.[6] Working within the German tradition of *Sozialpolitik*, Tönnies theorized states as class-neutral instruments that should be bent towards the reform of capitalism along collectivist social-democratic lines through the incorporation of the working classes via welfare measures and the vote.

Like Tönnies, Max Weber was closely linked to the German Historical School. With that tradition he shared the postulates that economic behaviour is grounded in the cultural realm of customs, language and the collective ethos, and that the dominant ethic in capitalism contrasted sharply with that of previous systems, as well as a sense of disquiet over two aspects of capitalist society: the domination of means over ends, of things over human beings,[7] and its unstable character (which in his view derived principally from the clash of substantive and formal rationalities). For him, 'the market alone was not an adequate basis for the realisation of a rational and harmonious social order'; its operation had to be confined within limits set by morality and by states – the latter conceived as benign, impersonal entities that guarantee civil order and progress. The social preconditions for stable capitalist society could not be discovered in the self-interest of market actors alone; economic analysis had to be supplemented with a theory of institutional structure.[8] In its theorization of the relationship between 'economy' and 'society', Weber's work stands out in its comparative approach, entailing a profound awareness of the variability of human institutions and the unique character of the contemporary Occident; in its attention to the moral and psychological foundations of capitalism and the cultural anchoring of modern, 'rationalized' social existence; and in the concept of the differentiation of social subsystems necessary to the functioning of market economies. If his core intellectual interest was in the social structure and dynamics of modern Western society, his political commitment was, as Jan Rehmann has shown in impressive detail, to the redirection of German capitalism along Fordist-American lines. On this basis Weber advocated the development of autonomous power centres alongside Bismarck's patrimonial state and the subordination of the working class through integration into the bourgeois political order. In contradistinction to Tönnies, he advocated the further differentiation of economic and political realms, not least because this would strengthen the hand of conservative layers within the labour movement who wished trade unionism to be restricted to 'purely industrial' issues.[9]

Such, very roughly, were the sociological materials from which Polanyi's embeddedness thesis was constructed. As to the term itself, his first usage that I know of was in a 1934 essay which explains that no system of labour ('Arbeitsverfassung') can be understood without first making sense of 'the social system in which it is embedded ('eingebettet').[10] Later that decade he wrote that in all systems other than modern market society 'economic life is embedded in social relations'.[11] In these early incarnations the usage is Marxian–Tönniesian. (If anything, it is closer to Tönnies in that it locates the font of alienation and disembeddedness in the separation of politics and economics, rather than in the separation of labour from productive property.) The context was formed by the ongoing crisis of the inter-war decades, which, Polanyi believed, was caused essentially by the sundering of the 'unity of society' under the impact of the separation of economics and politics induced by the market system.[12] Later, as he was to explain to his student Abe Rotstein, he shifted away from that theory while retaining the concept of embeddedness[13] – albeit now in a Weberian–Tönniesian mould. A case can be made that already in TGT the concept of 'disembedded economy' had come to rely upon a Weberian notion, that economic behaviour in capitalism is determined by particular types of psychological motivation, hunger and gain, although as we saw in chapter 3 this perspective was not unique to Weber but was shared by others, notably Owen. Either way, the nub of the argument in TGT is that a society in which individual drives motivate economic behaviour will be atomized, a *Gesellschaft*, in contrast to societies in which economic behaviour is steered by irreducibly social-cultural motivations such as status, religion and morality.

Polanyi's classic formulations on embeddedness arrived in a series of texts written between 1947 and 1957: 'Our Obsolete Market Economy', 'Aristotle Discovers the Economy' and LOM. In these he equates societies based on 'status' or '*Gemeinschaft*' with those in which 'the economy is embedded in non-economic institutions'. Policy in such societies is geared to satisfying socially determined needs; their individual members tend to suppress egotistical behaviour in favour of their role within the collective whole. In Trobriand society, for example, 'the production and distribution of material goods [was] embedded in social relations of a noneconomic kind' and neither labour nor distribution was undertaken 'for economic motives, i.e., for the sake of gain or payment or for fear of otherwise going hungry as an individual'.[14] In pre-colonial West Africa the 'slave trade was embedded in the medley of their practically sovereign bodies' – i.e. territorial states.[15] These regimes are contrasted to those based on '*contractus*' or '*Gesellschaft*', in which the sphere of economic exchange is 'institutionally separate and motivationally distinct'.[16] In *Gesellschaft*, the economy is governed by laws of its own and 'motivated in the last resort by two simple incentives, fear of hunger and hope of gain'.[17] Priority within *Gesellschaft* is accorded to

> the chrematistic needs of personal acquisitiveness. Individuals within such a society are subjected to socialization pressures that [encourage them to] respond solely to their own wants, irrespective of the standards of justice that are infringed while satisfying those wants. In short, they are individuals who act as *homo oeconomicus*.[18]

This entailed an inversion of the historical norm: instead of the economy being enmeshed within society, social relationships *'were now embedded in the economic system'*.[19]

Given the cross-cutting intellectual and political currents upon which it draws, it is no surprise that Polanyi's use of the term 'embeddedness' can appear indistinct, or beset by contradiction. There exists, for example, an ambiguity as to whether the counter-movement successfully 'embeds' the market economy. There are passages in TGT that imply that it can so do but that, given the inherent tension between protective measures and a market system, any such victory would be pyrrhic; yet elsewhere in the same book, and more so towards the end of his life, Polanyi's use of the term tends to drift towards the commonplace that 'the economy is embedded in institutions'[20] and that because markets depend upon non-economic conditions they can never be completely self-regulating. At a methodological level there is some uncertainty as to whether the dis/embedded economy is a descriptive empirical term or an 'ideal type' (a structural-analytical concept for the purposes of comparison). Should 'embeddedness' be understood as a methodological axiom, that *all* economic behaviour is enmeshed in non-economic institutions, or as a theoretical proposition referring to differences in the degree of that 'enmeshment'?[21] In this, the Polanyian ambiguity directly follows its Tönniesian predecessor. *Gemeinschaft* and *Gesellschaft* can be taken to refer to different types of society – one based on contract and interest, the other on feeling and custom. Alternatively, the dichotomy can be applied to the customary and contractual relations that exist symbiotically within every society.

If the term is used in the empirical sense, further ambiguities emerge when one examines precisely what societies come under which bracket. Polanyi left no room for doubt that nineteenth-century Britain exemplified the 'disembedded' end of the spectrum with, at the other, the Trobriand Islands, closely followed by ancient

Athens and Dahomey, and Stalin's Russia, yet his student Terence Hopkins, in a contribution to TMEE, disagreed. Hopkins concurs that embeddedness is a matter of degree, with one extreme being represented by 'economies whose constituent actions are patterned through their occurrence in non-economic roles'. But at the other end of the spectrum he finds economies 'organized through such economic institutions as fluctuating prices *and centralized planning'.*[22]

On the question of the Soviet Union it seems to me that the student's grip was firmer than the master's. Stalin's Russia was a far cry from the Trobriands: in most respects a typical late-industrializing society of the early twentieth century, Russia used state power as a lever for implementing land reform, marshalling resources and concentrating capital in its drive to catch up, economically and militarily, with the advanced powers. Military competition from a position of backwardness during an epoch of world-market disintegration stamped it with its characteristic 'war-economic' form: relative autarky, an emphasis on heavy industry and a high savings ratio. Stalin's revolution, in this light, entailed the conversion of the Soviet state, under the whip of geopolitical competition, into an agent of accumulation that presided over a no-holds-barred exploitation of peasants and workers and despoliation of the environment. Far from being embedded in social custom, labour-power in 1930s Russia more closely resembled a commodity than did its counterpart in Western democracies. As György Konrád and Ivan Szelényi once put it, in a departure from their otherwise Polanyiesque approach,

> [T]he great turning point in the history of the Eastern European economy was the introduction of Stalinist economic policy, which found a country where three-quarters of the population were small peasant producers and in a few years' time transferred all available labor to the 'socialist labor market'. Stalin and his entourage realized that neither extorting capital from individual peasant holdings through a system of forced deliveries of crops, nor giving free rein to the open marketing of peasant production, could greatly increase the surplus available ... That objective would be served only by curtailing the peasant's self-sufficiency, treating all labor as a commodity, and extending the range of consumer articles that could only be obtained with money as rapidly as possible. Thus, far from abolishing commodity relations, Stalin universalized them.[23]

A similar point was made at the time by Keynes, with his remark that it was only in authoritarian societies like 1930s Russia, in which 'sudden, substantial, all-round changes could be decreed, that a flexible wage-policy could function with success'.[24]

Stalin's Russia, then, was not a society in which 'politics' dominated 'economics' but one in which decisions at the apex of power were attendant upon the imperatives of global competition and these were passed downwards through the state-controlled transmission mechanisms. It is true that the mobilization of society behind the accumulation drive occurred by way of an unprecedented empowerment of a 'political' organ, the party state, but this was simultaneously experiencing a process of 'economization'. For the Communist Party, as Soviet historian Moshe Lewin has described, the process involved its cells being refunctioned as

> brokers in the service of their branch of the economy, sometimes even of just one enterprise. . . . The economy was declared to be the most important 'front' . . . In this way the country's cultural, artistic, and other activities were 'economized'. Everyone, from writers to judges and procurators, had to contribute to the battle for the productivity of labor, the quality of industrial products, or the building of dams.[25]

Institutions such as the traditional peasant commune and factory committees that offered genuine protection against the diktat of capital accumulation were incorporated into the state or destroyed. From this vantage point it is ironic, Wolfgang Streeck has observed, that the Stalinist 'economy-*cum*-state' bore an uncanny resemblance in its core dynamic to free market capitalism – that self-regulating market which 'Karl Polanyi suggested was driven to subordinate the social order entirely to rational-economic objectives', and to marginalize any and all 'social institutions capable of representing a logic other than that of economic accumulation'.[26]

Further adventures of a concept

'Embeddedness' has come a long way since Polanyi coined the term.[27] It exercises a general appeal for those who are dissatisfied with the narrow focus of orthodox economics, serving as a doorway to explorations of the relationship between economic behaviour and the social integument. In economic sociology it has become a key conceptual tool with which to explain those social and psycho-social features of human behaviour that are ignored or marginalized in orthodox economic analysis – for example, relations of trust, which lubricate market transactions, or those such as fraud and malfeasance which represent distortions of the market ideal. It is deployed as 'a categorical instrument', in Jens Beckert's formulation, 'for describing those ordering processes that lead to a reduction of the uncertainty of the action situation and the social structuring of decisions in market contexts'.[28] In the new institutional economics it has found favour as shorthand for the ways in which the choices of individuals are conditioned by the institutional context in which they find themselves.[29] From these theoretical beginnings it has migrated into the realm of policy debate. Broadly speaking one can discern, with Gillian Hart, three distinct 'pathways out of Polanyi'. The first is the use of the term 'embeddedness' to shore up the argument that the 'developmental state' was the decisive factor in the East Asian 'miracles' – against the neoliberal explanation that they were market-led. The second, a neo-Weberian perspective, is deployed in the projection of a 'kinder, gentler' capitalism that is associated in particular with the World Bank during the transition from Washington to post-Washington consensus. The other 'asks a more Marxist set of questions that have to do with the slippages and contradictions that emerge within the "neo-liberal thrust" of the 1980s and 1990s'.[30]

The term's primary portal into economic sociology and institutional economics was through the work of a neo-Weberian sociologist, Mark Granovetter, in 1985. Granovetter's article brought embeddedness its current prominence but at the cost of considerable confusion. If Polanyi influenced him at all it was subconsciously, for he recruits the concept to a quite different purpose, and did not intend his usage to be seen as a reappropriation.[31] His aim was to chart a route between two 'extreme' positions: the utilitarian, 'undersocialized' conception of man, which neglects the influence of non-economic norms and institutions upon economic behaviour, and the 'oversocialized' conception, represented by Polanyi's argument 'that the behaviour and institutions to be analyzed are so constrained by ongoing social relations that to construe them as independent is a grievous misunderstanding'.[32] In what one may charitably assume to have been a slip of the pen, at different stages in the argument he identifies both the Polanyian 'extreme' and his own middle course as '*the* embeddedness approach'.[33]

Granovetter reserves his sharpest criticisms of Polanyi for the postulation of a rupture between pre-modern embedded societies and disembedded market society.[34] For him, economic behaviour in market societies is rooted in socialized networks: all societies are 'embedded'. Sometimes known as the 'network approach' – because embeddedness is taken to refer to the meshing of economic activity with networks of social relations – his case is that explanation of the behaviour of market actors should focus upon structures of social networks and the positions individuals hold within them rather than upon ethical commitments or institutional arrangements. This approach, he suggests, can serve to broaden the basis of rational choice theory: what may appear to be non-rational behaviour or the automatic following of cultural rules may be seen to be a perfectly sensible individual calculation when 'situational constraints, especially those of embeddedness, are fully appreciated'.[35] This, the neo-Polanyian economists Jérôme Maucourant and Michele Cangiani have pointed out, is not so much a critique of Polanyi as a wholly different concept, deployed at a different level of abstraction: it refers to the fact that economic agents are always already socialized, and to the connectedness of individuals in social networks, and not to the institutional arrangement of the economic system as a whole. Granovetter's approach is not concerned with the larger social systems in which economies are located but instead

> reste individualiste et microsociologique. Il en vient donc à une généralisation de l' 'embeddedness', entendue à sa manière, qui réduit au minimum la différence entre le 'système de marché' et les autres 'organisations institutionnelles' de l'économie.[36]

Embeddedness, in short, only became recognized as a pivotal Polanyian concept as a result of widespread interest in a quite alien concept, Granovetter's. Given that the dominant usage of the term is so unlike Polanyi's, the fact that he is widely cited as its originator is the cause of not a little confusion – and some avowedly Polanyian scholars use his sense and the Granovetterian recoinage interchangeably, seemingly unaware of their dissimilarity.[37]

Since the late 1980s 'embeddedness' has taken on a life of its own. Its proliferation would appear to suggest that it fulfils a useful role, yet the directions it has followed have been semantically so divergent that, as Granovetter recently remarked in explanation of why he himself rarely uses it any longer, 'it has become almost meaningless, stretched to mean almost anything, so that it therefore means nothing'.[38] Its critics argue that it was always problematic, for it encourages the misleading view that there exists a dichotomy between social relations, grounded in trust and reciprocity, and

market relations, based upon free exchange between rational egotists. In this regard, Greta Krippner suggests, the term is paradoxical: 'the basic intuition that markets are socially embedded has led
economic sociologists to take the market itself for granted'.[39] Those
who follow Granovetter in isolating the 'network' aspect of markets
neglect the underlying social content. It is, Krippner goes on, an
approach that obscures the fact that

> congealed into every market exchange is a history of struggle and
> contestation that has produced actors with certain understandings of
> themselves and the world which predispose them to exchange under
> a certain set of social rules and not another. In this sense, the state,
> culture and politics are *contained* in every market act.

By directing attention to the layers of social behaviour outside the
market, the concept of embeddedness desociologizes the market
itself.[40]

For Krippner, such objections do not apply to Polanyi, for whom
markets are not networks of structurally equivalent producers but
'rather fully social institutions, reflecting a complex alchemy of
politics, culture, and ideology',[41] but others believe that they do.
John Lie, of UCLA, goes so far as to describe Polanyi's concept of
market exchange as 'disembedded'.[42] From his heterodox – not to
say heretical – perspective, Polanyi offers a moral critique of the
sociologically empty market concept of neoclassical economics
without probing its weakness by way of investigating 'the concrete
social relations of those who buy and sell'. The weak point of the
model is its equation of market exchange with commodification,
for this renders invisible the underlying social relations through
which commodity exchange is organized. Another California-based
sociologist, Kurtuluş Gemici, has suggested that Polanyi employs
embeddedness in two contradictory ways: as a 'gradational concept'
and as the holistic principle that 'all economies are embedded'. The
former 'reifies the market economy' by acceding to the misleading
notion that social life consists of separate spheres. With this move
'the market becomes a social sphere devoid of all social content'.[43]

On the whole these criticisms miss their target. It is misleading
to suggest that Polanyi's analysis divides social life in market society
into reified spheres; his point concerns, rather, the separate institutionalization of economic and political activity. Moreover, he uses
embeddedness not only as an analytical term but also to allude to
the political goal of ensuring a stable democratic society through
the regulation of markets in land, labour and money. The term's

reference point, as Beckert has argued, is not the economy as such but

> the larger social systems in which all economies are located . . . In *The Great Transformation* Polanyi did not aim to understand the functioning of market exchange in order to explain the social preconditions for market efficiency; he was concerned with what happens to social order and political freedom when economic exchange is organized chiefly through self-regulating markets.[44]

It follows that a sociological theory of the economy that claims Polanyi as its inspiration cannot limit itself to examining the preconditions for designing economic institutions adapted to 'efficiency' but must also attend to the effects of the organization of the economic system on society at large.

Even amongst neo-Polanyians substantial disagreement exists as to the meaning and appropriate usage of the term. Probably the most influential position has been put by the political economist Fred Block in a series of papers and articles that meld the Polanyian and Granovetterian usages. With detailed reference to the development of Polanyi's ideas propaedeutic to TGT, Block argues that because Polanyi was exiting from his most Marxian phase as he began to write TGT, a clash of conceptual frameworks exists in that book that generated conceptual ambiguity. One lens in TGT, a survival from Polanyi's Marxian period, frames its subject as the logic of market forces that disembed economy from society. Coupled with this is another, much more original, lens through which Polanyi begins to glimpse something startlingly new. By observing that for most of their history market societies are constituted by two opposing movements, with the strength of protection effectively re-embedding the economy, he begins to see that there can be no such thing as a disembedded economy: a pure market economy is an illusion that may be pursued but never attained. It therefore makes no sense to speak of the 'logic' of the market economy, for economic processes cannot but result from a mix of cultural, political and economic forces. From these observations Block infers that the non-Marxian Polanyi should be hailed as the originator of the notion of the 'always embedded economy', the recognition that functioning market societies must maintain some threshold level of embeddedness – of interrelation with the other social-structural and cultural-structural elements of society – or else risk social and economic disaster; that 'markets must construct elaborate rule and institutional structures to limit the individual pursuit of gain or risk degenerating into a Hobbesian war of all against all'.[45] Given that a moral and institutional framework is invariably present, this approach directs attention towards the different degrees and characteristics of 'marketness' and of 'embeddedness' in different economic structures.[46] In what ways are transactions and contracts embedded in social relations such as family ties, friendships or long-term supplier–contractor relations? To what extent do non-economic goals such as moral or spiritual commitments shape economic behaviour? Such questions may then guide comparative research into the social and moral underpinnings of market behaviour in different states and regions – a project that Block himself has pursued in his subsequent research.[47]

Polanyi's supposed discovery of the 'always embedded economy', for Block, also connects to overtly political questions. It shows, against Marxism, which in Block's depiction (some would say caricature) insists that 'reforms of capitalism that interfere with the logic of capital accumulation' are futile,

> that there are no inherent obstacles to restructuring market societies along more democratic and egalitarian lines [and] that the multiple forms of dependence of business groups in market societies on state action provides [*sic*] a critical resource or lever for those seeking political change. Even those business interests who profess to believe in the most extreme forms of *laissez-faire* doctrine need the cooperation of the state and this often disguised dependence can be employed to renegotiate the legal underpinnings of market society.[48]

There are therefore, he concludes, no systemic obstacles to changing the rules of international order (as occurred at Bretton Woods) so as to enable the flourishing of progressive reform.

Reasons of space prevent me from discussing the debate on Polanyi's understanding of the postwar world economy, embedded liberalism and welfare states, but I do so in detail elsewhere.[49] What I can do here is briefly sketch the general lines of debate on the question of the 'always embedded economy'.

That there is a sense in which a free market economy is 'embedded' is uncontentious. As one Polanyian economist has put it,

> The economy is always instituted by a socialization process which moulds individual character toward the ethical, aesthetical, and instrumental norms, standards, and practices which are needed to participate in it. This much is true of all social economies in that all must integrate economic activity by means of systems of

communication and sanction. These systems inform individuals as to the behaviour expected of them and of others, and of the rewards and penalties that they can apply to others or expect to be applied to themselves in cases where expected behaviour is or is not forthcoming.[50]

At this level of abstraction it is hard to dispute the institutional and normative embeddedness of market capitalism: of course the market requires an array of institutional supports (property rights, forms of law, means of enforcement of contracts, etc.). But surely Polanyi was not voicing the commonplaces that 'marketeers are people, too',[51] that economic behaviour is always woven into legal, political, customary and ideological fabrics, or that the stability and predictability of markets depend upon their connections to wider webs of social relations? Given, to mention only a few examples, the traditions of sociological thought and both the Scottish and German Historical Schools, with their explorations of the market economy's institutional preconditions, that would represent one of the more tiresome attempts to reinvent a late second-millennium wheel. This was a point 'that Adam Smith devoted his life to making',[52] as one economist has pointed out, knocking for six the notion that the 'always embedded' thesis is original to Polanyi. No, say Block's critics, his reading obscures the freshness and theoretical richness of Polanyi's case. The novelty of the market economy is that its institutional embedding entails a diremption from non-economic institutions in a manner that negates both social control over economic institutions and moral behaviour within them. For Polanyi, as Matthew Watson has put it, skilfully drawing out the connectedness between the moral, motivational and structural aspects of the term, embeddedness

> is the social control of economic relations through institutional means, where a link can be drawn between embeddedness and the social obligation to act in a morally dutiful manner. Insofar as 'the market' imposes purely functional character traits on individuals, the moral dimension of economic activity is increasingly dissolved.[53]

To grasp this, one has to step a little way into Polanyi's mental universe. He disagrees with the liberal theorization of the market economy as embedded in norms of individual liberty, egalitarianism and pluralism. He recognizes its links to these principles but perceives at a deeper motivational level the values of acquisitiveness and self-interest that it sanctions and by which it is underpinned, and they are reprehensible: they atomize society and dissolve its moral fabric, spawning egotism and anomie. To say that the liberal market is 'embedded' in the sense of 'instituted', then, does not negate its 'disembeddedness' at other levels. The term does not denote the economy's separation from *society* but from non-economic institutions, a separation that produces a rift between individual and society and a consequent moral degeneration. (Polanyi's argument here has been perceptively likened by Peter McMylor to Alasdair MacIntyre's understanding of liberal ethics: that liberalism cannot do without a moral discourse and is in the abstract sense 'ethically embedded', but is best grasped as an *incoherent* moral tradition because it arises from within a compartmentalized social order.[54])

What Block's critics emphasize, against the 'always embedded' concept, is the uniqueness of the modern market society. Its peculiarity consists in the degree to which its customs and values are shaped by imperatives that pulse from a distinct market sphere. As Walter Neale once framed the issue, the self-regulating market 'takes a large portion of human activity and sets it aside from all other activity, gives it a set of rules to live by and permits the whole of this activity to be governed by the supply–demand–price mechanism'. Relieved of higher restraint, the market tends to influence everyday life far more assertively and overtly than do the economic institutions of reciprocative or redistributive societies. Consider by way of illustration the demand for labour. It, Neale continues,

> has a direct effect upon the locality in which one lives, the kind of economic activity in which one engages, and the security of one's bodily survival. . . . Religious faith, social status, political belief, family life, loving, hating, gossiping, do not decide what shall be done, except as they are part of the complex of motives and emotions creating demand for products.[55]

This is why it does make sense to speak of a disembedded economy, and even to conceive of it as one in which society is embedded. Such a system, in the words of Maucourant and Cangiani,

> reste *dis-embedded*, précisément à cause de ses *caractéristiques institutionnelles générales*; elle est donc typiquement autonome et constitue la contrainte fondamentale du développement de la société. C'est alors la société qui tend à être, comme dit Polanyi, *embedded* dans son économie.[56]

This is an altogether different interpretation from Block's. It brings Polanyi's concept closer to the outlook of Marxists, who view the rise of the market economy less as the outcome than as the primary cause of that set of legal and cultural changes which includes the generalization of contractually based economic behaviour, the emergence of norms associated with absolute property rights, and separate legal systems geared to enforcing those rights.

Embeddedness and decommodification in the mid-twentieth century

Block is undoubtedly correct to identify Polanyi's post-1930s shift further away from Marxism's orbit, and yet even in the inter-war period Polanyi's conception of the relationship between economics and politics was at least as Tönniesian as it was Marxist. Consider, for example, his article from 1928, 'Liberale Sozialreformer in England'. In it, he discusses the rise of the New Liberals in Britain around John Maynard Keynes and Ramsay Muir. It contains this suggestive passage.

> In a pure exchange economy, in utopian capitalism, in Ferdinand Tönnies' *Gesellschaft*, nothing but contract matters; its content is the cash nexus: payment for labour power. In the *Gemeinschaft*, of the future and of the past, it is status that counts; its essence is not money or monetary value but power, rank, influence, respect, responsibility, freedom – the reality of socio-cultural values. Just as the Liberal Party's economic programme represents an attempt, while staying within the framework of private property, to build the public economy [*Gemeinwirtschaft*] into the societal order [*Gesellschaftsverfassung*], its accompanying social reform has as its aim to transform wage labour from a mere contractual relationship into a juridically guaranteed status position, determined by social values, all without any fundamental supplanting of private property in the means of production.[57]

This excerpt is of interest, I would suggest, in part because it provides evidence of Tönniesian precursors of two concepts, 'utopian capitalism' and 'embeddedness', that were later to be developed in TGT, but also because it expresses the assumption that a greater role for state regulation within a capitalist economy, under the right sort of government, represents a significant stride towards *Gemeinschaft*-type embeddedness. (To the ear the link is clearer in

German: '*Gemeinwirtschaft*' means public sector.) The Liberal Party, Polanyi reports, was significantly modifying its approach to fundamental values and policies, including individualism, social justice, public ownership and the market economy, and there is no reason, he claims, why it should not, in alliance with Labour, push beyond the limits of liberal capitalism such that wage labour in Britain would cease to be a merely contractual relationship.

In this supposition he was not alone. In the inter-war period the corporatist shift in economic policy-making then under way was widely viewed as propitious to, if not direct evidence of, a transition to socialism. To name but two famous examples, this was the leitmotif of Hayek's *Road to Serfdom*, which detected the hydra of socialism in almost every act of government regulation, while Hayek's compatriot, Joseph Schumpeter, believed as late as 1949 that in the USA and Western Europe *laissez-faire* capitalism was giving way to policies that in some respects 'differ but little from genuine socialist planning', in respect of government intervention, redistributive taxation, public control over the labour and money markets, and expansion of the public sector and of social security.[58] As for Polanyi, he maintained that history's rudder was set firmly towards regulation, decommodification and planning. In the assumption that this trend would on the whole be salutary, with democratic socialism a likely development, he can often seem to approve of regulation, planning and decommodification *per se*. Read his texts more closely, however, and a differentiated position emerges.

Crucially, he does not equate decommodification either with re-embedding or with socialism. In his usage, the 'de-' of decommodify carries the weak charge of the prefix in words such as 'demote' and 'deflate', not the stronger force of 'depose' or 'deracinate'. In TGT he avers that the decommodification of money had already been largely realized with 'the creation of deposits', and that 'social legislation, factory laws, unemployment insurance, and, above all, trade unions' have as their purpose the removal of human labour '*from the orbit of the market*'.[59] He believed that labour in Britain prior to 1834 was decommodified, as it was in fascist Italy, and in the USA in the early 1940s.

Decommodification proceeded in tandem with movements towards the reunification of economy and society, yet Polanyi does not see this as synonymous with the trend towards embeddedness, for the reunification of economy and society could take a variety of guises, and, as fascism revealed, these included the possibility of a morbid 'disembedded' outcome in which economy and society were unified but under the domination of the former. Other forms of capitalist corporatism were possible too, as pioneered by the 'conservative planners' around Harold Macmillan – and here again, Polanyi was under no illusion that the object of corporatist reform was not the supersession of capitalism but its restoration.[60]

That said, he was optimistic that the global drift was on the whole towards 're-embedding'. After the defeat of fascism, he opined in the early 1940s, 'capitalism will be unable to thwart progress towards democracy and socialism'. 'We are witnessing a development', TGT proclaims, 'under which the economic system ceases to lay down the law to society and the primacy of society over that system is secured', and this may occur 'in a great variety of ways, democratic and aristocratic, constitutionalist and authoritarian'.[61] The Soviet Union was his favoured exemplar, alongside Clement Attlee's Britain and Roosevelt's New Deal. The market economy was disappearing across much of the world, he assumed, plausibly enough, towards the end of the war, a claim that he repeated at regular intervals, with decreasing plausibility, until the end of his days.[62]

As we have seen, Polanyi was careful to distinguish between capitalist-corporative trends and socialist transformation, at least when the plans of conservatives or fascists were under discussion. On the whole, this also applies to his analysis of the New Deal: although Roosevelt's reforms offered the prospect of a different, 'independent solution of the problem of an industrial society', they were evidently 'not meant to supersede private enterprise, but on the contrary to save it from monopoly and modernize its working'.[63] Yet when it came to governments that deployed socialist rhetoric, notably Attlee's, Polanyi threw caution to the wind. Britain, he enthused in 1946, was undergoing 'a rapid transition to a Socialist society – the only alternative to war and depression'.[64] This was thinking at its most wishful, for Attlee's government showed no sign of developing an alternative to market capitalism and every sign of continuing Britain's liberal-imperialist traditions: it joined NATO and the Bretton Woods institutions, diverted a higher proportion of GDP to arms than did even the US or France, secretly set up a nuclear bomb-making programme, deployed troops to fight left-wing and national liberation movements in Korea, Greece, Malaya and Vietnam and, domestically, to break strikes, and supported Apartheid South Africa.

The failure of Polanyi's predictions with regard to the Attlee government did not in the least douse his faith that the great transformation remained on track. In the early 1950s he continued to believe that a shift to a new socioeconomic paradigm was coming to maturity, the 'postulates' of which were 'full employment at home, regulated trading abroad, [and] a controlled development of the national resources'. ('Nothing less than a shift of the place occupied by the economy in society as a whole was involved', he opined.[65]) But this was surely an exaggeration, as Peter Drucker pointed out to him at the time. It is the case, Drucker conceded, that the belief in the omnipotence and benevolence of the market 'has all but been given up', that the boundary between the self-regulating market and political organization had been greatly blurred, and that in sizeable sectors of Western economies the market had been altogether replaced. And yet the previous twenty or twenty-five years had none the less 'seen a fantastic expansion of market-organization' into territories such as Africa, India and even China, which, 'as late as the end of World War I, [had remained] almost entirely outside the scope of the market'.[66]

In the West too, whether or not Drucker and Polanyi were right that the market system had been rolled back during the postwar decades of 'embedded liberalism', the socioeconomic system remained capitalist. For all the reforms of Roosevelt, Attlee and their confrères, they left intact the entrenched power of capitalist classes, a crucial point that is neglected in Polanyi's writings. The bulk of the means of production remained in the hands of existing business elites whose primary goal remained the accumulation of capital. Increasingly, they were able to use their wealth and power to evade regulations that restricted them in that end, lobbying politicians and influencing public opinion. For them, ably assisted by rightwards-moving social democracy, the crisis of the 1970s and the failure of Keynesian policies to restore profit rates provided an opportunity for revanche. The upshot was a US-led campaign to prise open foreign markets, the rise of finance capital, the drive by revenue-squeezed states to sell assets, and a campaign to restore profits (entailing reductions in corporation and upper-end income taxes and in welfare expenditure, assaults on union organization, and the imposition of market mechanisms within the public sector). In short, we have arrived at the 1980s neoliberal turn. It is the subject of our sixth and penultimate chapter.

6

At the brink of a 'great transformation'? Neoliberalism and the countermovement today

There is nothing in today's global market that buffers it against the social strains arising from highly uneven economic development within and between the world's diverse societies. The swift waxing and waning of industries and livelihoods, the sudden shifts of production and capital, the casino of currency speculations – these conditions trigger political counter-movements that challenge the very ground rules of the global free market.

John Gray[1]

If a 'double movement' – the deregulation of world trade in the nineteenth century, and its reregulation in the twentieth – can serve as a model, then we may once again be standing at the brink of a 'great transformation'.

Jürgen Habermas[2]

By common consent, what gives Polanyi's work its contemporary relevance is his analysis of the pathogenesis and malign consequences of free market globalization. In the market-fundamentalist climate that prevailed across much of the globe in the 1990s and 2000s, the motif in *The Great Transformation* that has resonated most widely is that *laissez-faire* liberalism represents a utopian attempt to apply the principle of the self-regulating market to the international economy, a project that sowed the seeds of its own destruction. Almost without exception, those for whom Polanyi serves as inspiration are united in their antipathy towards the neoliberal belief system. An 'excess of markets', they say, generates socioeconomic instability, and where 'the intensity of a market mentality increases' social solidarity declines. Countries such as Britain and the USA that are characterized by a 'high degree of market mentality' and in which the pursuit of individual self-interest tends to trump social obligation are likely to suffer high rates of social disintegration, crime, and 'deviance'.[3]

Neoliberalism, Polanyians agree, is bad for your health. But what led to its ascendancy? How secure is its reign, and wherein lie its contradictions? How have Polanyi's teachings been applied to these questions? Can we already observe, or should we expect to see, a new countermovement, and if so, what forms is it likely to take? In what ways might it compare to the 'protectionist' movements of 1870–1940, discussed in TGT? And if neoliberalism is doomed, how will it fall and what sort of policy regime could replace it? In this chapter I discuss all of these questions, with particular focus upon the nature and dynamic of 'countermovements' in the neoliberal era.

Explaining the neoliberal ascendancy

The distinctiveness of Polanyi's explanation of the advent of the nineteenth-century free market regime, we may recall from chapter 2, lay in its weaving together of four arguments: altered cost structures contingent upon new technologies dictated market expansion; the protective regulations that represented a haphazard response to market expansion stalled the economic engine; in response to the ensuing crisis, elite opinion swung behind the political economists' case for a free market *laissez-faire* regime; and the new order, far from being an inevitable consequence of economic trends, was actively 'made' by state policy. Of Polanyians today, few would privilege the first, technological, argument in explaining the return of a free market regime, but updated versions of the others abound. Neoliberalism, in the neo-Polanyian optic, is explained essentially as the product of three ingredients: a crisis induced by the clash between political regulation and market imperatives, the intervention of free market economists, and their influence upon policy-makers.

The first proposition is that during the post-1945 age of welfare state Keynesianism, 'social control' over the economy reached its apogee, and demonstrated what is widely (but erroneously) believed to be Polanyi's thesis that 'markets tend to work most efficiently in a regime of robust regulation'.[4] During that golden age, institutional reforms successfully embedded 'Fordist social systems of production' within both nation states and 'regional orbits of trust', of which the Third Italy and the German *Länder* were outstanding examples.[5] The success of this social-democratic mode of regulation, however, set in motion two dynamics which combined to erode the coherence and strength of those national and regional institutions. That the Bretton Woods system served to re-establish a competitive global economic arena underpinned intensified rivalry between nation states and unevenness within and between national economies. Meanwhile, rapid output growth generated full employment, and this translated into 'excessive wage increments',[6] which 'caused the capitalist market economy to seize up',[7] as became manifest in low profit rates and high inflation. The upshot, ultimately, was a loss of confidence in the prevailing Keynesian orthodoxy.

At this juncture the other two propositions enter, concerning the role of ideology – the intellectual and propagandistic role of the New Right – and of the state. Hayek, Friedman and their followers promoted the pursuit of the free market utopia, a project that, against the backdrop of the crisis of Keynesianism, quickly gained supporters in high places. This is uncontroversial but deserves mention because it occupies a privileged position in Polanyian accounts. For ideas to become a material force, however, they had first to grip the business and political elites. Just as Polanyi's discussion of nineteenth-century Britain draws attention to the aggressive political intervention required to impose *laissez-faire*, so, in our own age, the adoption of the neoliberal case by the likes of Pinochet, Carter and Thatcher was indispensable to its success. Government power was at the heart of the construction and globalization of the new order.[8]

In my view this explanation of the neoliberal turn has two weaknesses. One consists in the proposition that the 1970s crisis was induced by excessive wage growth. In fact, real wages in the advanced capitalist world rose more quickly in the 1950s than in subsequent decades, but without inducing a recession. Then, in the 1970s, all major economies entered crisis simultaneously, even though levels of labour organization and militancy varied greatly. Rather than wage pressure being the problem that caused the crisis, it was the crisis which made wage pressure into a problem, or at least one that could no longer be tolerated.[9] The other consists in an overemphasis upon the ideological, with neoliberalism deemed a utopian project of universal marketization. That commitment which seemingly defined neoliberalism, as David Harvey and others have argued, functioned in reality as ideological cover for a drive, pioneered in the US and adopted in much of the rest of the world, to restore corporate profit rates at the expense of workers and welfare recipients and to lever open protected markets in industrializing countries.

The focus of Polanyian theory during the neoliberal age, however, has not been upon its origins but upon the nature of the system that could or should replace it. It is a question that is best discussed under two separate headings. One, discussed below, concerns the contradictions that may undermine the neoliberal order and the social forces that appear best placed to make good its demise. The other, to which we turn now, is the type of alternative economic arrangement that is possible and desirable.

Alternative futures: participatory planning and the mixed economy

For a critique of market society and neoliberalism to be persuasive one must be able to identify realizable alternatives. In Polanyian discourse the bulk of such discussion concerns alternatives to neoliberalism alone, but in the space where Polanyian and Marxist currents converge, alternatives to capitalism have also been adumbrated. Both Marx and Polanyi held capitalism to be inherently undemocratic, because the wielders of economic power are unaccountable to either their employees or the general public, and anarchic, with decisions regarding resource allocation taken on an *ex post* basis and without systemic concern for their impact upon 'externalities' (essentially, society at large and the environment). For both, the alternative would be democratic, including in the economic sphere. Those who create society's wealth would deliberate and decide upon what is to be produced and to what purposes, and at least the major investment decisions would be co-ordinated *ex ante*. Socialists have tended to avoid discussing the detailed institutional arrangements capable of serving that end, on the grounds that that would be to pre-empt the outcome of a long and uncertain process of transformation. But speculative models none the less serve a useful purpose in deliberating upon the feasibility of alternative futures; and a number have been proposed, including Polanyi's own (as we saw in chapter 1).

One recent attempt to imagine the economic mechanisms of a 'self-governing society' has been developed by Pat Devine, together with Fikret Adaman.[10] In its original incarnation, no mention was made of Polanyi; Devine's sources were Marx and Eurocommunist economists as well as Włodzimierz Brus and Rudolf Bahro. That it merits attention here is both because in his later work a distinctly Polanyian thread has emerged and because even the original version evinces remarkable parallels with Polanyi's own.

In its general lineaments Devine's is an example of a standard model to which many socialists and not a few anarchists would subscribe. The self-governing society would abolish the social (although not the functional) division of labour, such that over the course of their lives people would be able, and expected, to special-ize in a variety of activities, skilled and unskilled. Ownership of productive enterprise would be social, with ownership bodies comprising 'stakeholders' – representatives of groups affected by the use of the assets involved. Economic decision-making would be democratic, with bodies of stakeholders negotiating the major decisions regarding what to produce, where to target investment and how to allocate society's resources. The system's benefits would include the expansion of democracy and the transcendence of narrow self-interest, the reduction of inequality, and the promotion of efficiency in regard to the fulfilment of human needs. The specific sense in which Devine's system resembles Polanyi's is that it accords an integral place to market exchange while ruling out the operation of market forces. The former refers to the sale and purchase of the output of existing productive capacity, the latter to the process through which changes in the structure of productive capacity are co-ordinated in capitalism (or market socialism) via atomistic decisions on investment and disinvestment that are coordinated *ex post*. Unlike in capitalism (or market socialism), major investment decisions in Devine's model are not made at the level of the enter-prise, since they affect a wider set of individuals and groups. Yet a constrained form of market does operate, with goods offered for sale on markets and consumers able to choose between them. In this way, the information required for effective decision-making arises, without recourse to market forces.

As Devine's model demonstrates, Polanyian theory can contri-bute fertile thoughts on alternatives to capitalism, yet its major preoccupation today lies in the narrower and nearer-term field of alternatives to its neoliberal phase. On this, a consensus exists among Polanyians that the desired medium-term goal is some sort of 'mixed economy', but there is a diversity of opinions as to what this would in reality entail. The past provides abundant examples of mixed economies from which some gain inspiration, while others identify redistributive and reciprocal mechanisms operating within present societies and advocate their consolidation. For the former, the typical references are to Keynesian policies and 'Fordist' regimes in their heyday – the long postwar boom. A paradigmatic example, the British political theorist Maurice Glasman has suggested, is the Federal Republic of Germany, where land, labour and money were so far from being fully mobilized as commodities that from its foundation in 1949 until at least the mid-1990s it was no market society but a 'substantive society underpinned by non-market institutions'. Agricultural production and housing were (and still are) subsidized and regulated, and 'the status of the human being in the labour market' is juridically secured through rights of consultation and joint decision-making as institutionalized in the Co-Determination Acts of the 1950s and 1976. As to money, the fiscal orthodoxy and Central Bank autonomy championed by ordo-Liberalism represented nothing other than a façade that served to conceal a very real form of democratic economic governance, exemplified in the facts that the board of the *Bundesbank* included elected representatives of the Federal States and that at no point 'was the deutschmark allowed to find its market price outside a guaranteed fixed rate'.[11]

For Glasman's compatriot, the anthropologist Chris Hann, an altogether different optic applies. For him, approximations to a Polanyian mixed economy did not exist during the postwar boom but did emerge in its aftermath. In the late 1980s, for example, he greeted its arrival in Central Europe. In Hungary at the time, the market principle was gaining sway but this was ('contrary to what Polanyi sometimes implies') eminently compatible with a substantial reciprocal sector.[12] Indeed, Hungary

> is developing the sort of mixed economy which [Polanyi] identified with approval in Dahomey and in the ancient Mediterranean, but which he never observed during his lifetime. It has a lot of redistribution, a lot of market exchange, and it even creates quite a lot of room for genuinely 'reciprocal' social exchanges between individuals.[13]

More recently Hann has made an analogous case on behalf of China, which he conceives as an 'embedded socialism' of which Polanyi himself would have approved.[14]

Another seam in which extended Polanyian treatments of the 'mixed economy' can be found is in papers presented at Polanyi-related conferences, many of which have appeared in a series of published volumes. In one, *Karl Polanyi*, Margie Mendell discusses the 'liberatory alternatives' that continually bubble up within and against the dominant market paradigm – the Grameen Bank in Bangladesh is one example; others are the participatory budget in Porto Allegre, and the 'fair trade' movement.[15] In an earlier volume, *The Life and Work of Karl Polanyi*, the Swedish political economist Björn Hettne proposed that although 'redistribution' (state interventionism and welfare states) was in decline and the market principle was experiencing its second wind, that was far from the whole story. Alongside these vectors of change one could begin to descry a third trajectory, of ultimately greater moment: the rise of 'reciprocal' arrangements (which others would call 'civil society' or the 'Third Sector'). 'After the present phase of neoliberal hegemony and social marginalization', Hettne predicted, reciprocity was bound to become more important, 'simply as a mode of survival when the protective redistributive political structures break up'.[16] In a third volume, *Karl Polanyi in Vienna*, Larissa Lomnitz observed that the tide that Hettne claimed to predict had in fact long ago flowed into the cities of Latin America and other parts of the Global South, in the shape of an informal economy. It invariably tends to be 'embedded' – i.e. reliant upon reciprocal solidarity organized through face-to-face social networks – and this, she adds, expresses a long-term trend. As modern states develop, 'the increasing volume of regulations leads people to find informal ways to by-pass them', and the informal economy acts as an increasingly vital complement to the redistributive and market sectors when these prove incapable of satisfying human needs.[17] Somewhat later, in yet another Polanyi conference volume, the Turkish political economist Ayşe Buğra expressed her enthusiasm for the 'successful network structure of Asian economies' in which reciprocal arrangements thrive within 'a highly viable alternative economic order'. Unlike Lomnitz, however, she takes pains to distinguish between two contrasting types of reciprocal relationship: those that are geared to group survival ('helping people to cope') and those that are directed towards individual gain (serving as a means to 'grab'). Even 'coping' strategies, she notes, 'are likely to acquire an economic character defined by the reality of the market'. In much of the Global South the informal sector tends to 'provide sustenance to a large portion of the population but it has not done so without becoming, at the same time, a fertile ground for illicit wealth accumulation'.[18]

Buğra's observation that relationships that appear superficially to be reciprocal are subject at a deeper level to the formidable gravitational pull of market forces has been taken further in other studies, notably *Informalization: Process and Structure*, edited by Faruk Tabak and Michaeline Crichlow. If the informal economy – in which reciprocity is prevalent, if not predominant – expands within a context of a shrinking commodified sector, this volume's contributors argue, this need not betoken the rise of an 'alternative economy'. Decommodification may be symptomatic of social disintegration rather than the emergence of vital and durable economic relations capable of reproducing and sustaining themselves in opposition to capital. In Aníbal Quijano's sobering assessment, the organizations within the informal economy are predominantly engaged in activities of immediate use and consumption, especially in foodstuffs and family services; as such they are often wholly dependent upon external financial or institutional support, and many involve little more than the socialization of family activities – in short, they colonize not the commodified sector but the existing subsistence sector. The great majority of the units and actors within Latin America's informal sector, he concludes,

> are organized around waged work and around groups unequally situated in relation to control of the means of production and thus to production or profits. Their activities are geared to the acquisition of profits and accumulation, and they consequently operate, completely or in part, within the logic of capital. In many cases this amounts to a capitalism of the poor.[19]

In her contribution, similarly, Michaeline Crichlow argues that 'informalization', far from being a recent phenomenon associated with the breakdown of distribution, is endemic to capitalist society. To grasp its nature requires a break with the one-sided conception of capitalism as a modernizing, rational force which homogenizes and shapes the labour process and relations of distribution into a legally codified and efficiently administered mould. Instead, in manifold ways it generates, utilizes and has 'evidently thrived on the seemingly "shadowy gray world" of informal economies or informal sectors'.[20]

The generic approach outlined by Quijano and Crichlow can be extended to the other cases introduced above. Whether Co-Determination and *Bundesbank*, post-communist Hungary or rural Xinjiang, the Grameen Bank or the informal sector in Latin

American favelas, the critical question is to what extent these institutions or institutional complexes provide support for forces that are capable, over the long term, of manifesting a challenge to the power of capital. If they do not provide this support, are they not merely complementing or even entrenching the structures of a market society? What use is the reciprocal re-division of the crumbs if the bakery is ruled by market forces? In the case of the Grameen Bank, for example, does it herald the emergence of a new 'embedded' economy, or is it mere micro-capitalism – or even, as some critics suggest, neoliberalism for the poor?[21] Polanyian champions of the 'mixed economy' concede that these are real concerns but respond that such cases should not be looked at statically or in isolation but with reference to the overall dynamic of the double movement; that an institution or set of social relations which in a period of rampant neoliberalism flows down the gradients formed by market structures may in the context of a rising countermovement track an altogether more progressive course. With this in mind, let us turn to look in detail at Polanyian treatments of the double movement today.

No dearth of countermovements

Of the various Polanyian concepts discussed in this book, arguably the best known and most widely discussed is the double movement, and the central question with which Polanyi-influenced social scientists have engaged in recent decades has been its applicability to contemporary circumstances. As mentioned above, the parallels between nineteenth-century market society and our own neoliberal age are inescapable. Since the demise of Keynesian regulated capitalism we have seen a yawning gap between rich and poor, financial crises galore, and growing pressure on the natural environment. According to Polanyi-inspired analyses, dangerous tendencies towards the 'disembedding' of economic life have been unleashed, including the commodification of everyday life, the ideological naturalization of commodity relations, and the subordination of society to the casino rhythms of finance in particular and of the world market in general.[22]

As diagnosis is a prelude to prognosis, one may ask what the likely consequence of these destabilizing developments is. A countermovement is the short answer, but plotting its co-ordinates is no simple task. At a superficial level, it is true, identifying specific historical moments at which neoliberal reform has provoked a 'protective' response can appear perfectly straightforward. By way of illustration consider a slice of contemporary Venezuelan history, beginning in 1989 with the neoliberal 'Great Turn' introduced by President Carlos Andrés Perez. The ensuing suffering of the poor was a contributing factor first to the 'Caracazo' (Caracas revolt) and subsequently to Hugo Chavez's coup, which was followed further down the line – following his overthrow, and further social crisis and mass impoverishment – by his election on a 'protective' platform. Few Polanyians would deny that this is an uncomplicated case of the double movement in operation. However, when it comes to identifying other instances there is much scope for disagreement. A brief literature review serves to illustrate the point.

An appropriate place to begin would be with a clutch of essays that appeared at the outset of the 1990s. In one, Björn Hettne ventured that that decade, notwithstanding the liberal triumphalism with which it commenced, 'may mark the end of free market ideology just as the 1920s did. After all, the foundations for the global market (Bretton Woods) are falling apart and there is still no substitute.' A protective countermovement was emerging, the global architecture of which would consist of a 'regionalized world-system'. At its heart would be the European Union – so long, at least, as it avoided treading the neoliberal path and constructed instead a 'Fortress Europe', which Hettne defined as 'a social project to create a true European region, based on a domestic market, a shared culture, and historical identity'.[23] Further EU integration based on an overarching strategy of 'benign mercantilism' would bring the elites and wider populations of Europe signal advantages. 'For Western Europe, there would be an enlarged "domestic" market; Europe's position in the world would be strengthened; and the "liberation" of Eastern Europe would be achieved.'

In Canada, the social theorist Robert Cox was thinking along similar lines. The world had returned 'to the beginning of Polanyi's first phase of movement'[24] in the form of neoliberal post-Fordism, but had almost immediately faced a legitimacy crisis due to the intensified suffering and exclusion of the poor, the widespread erosion of respect for politicians and, especially in the post-communist world, a creeping nostalgia for the comparative stability and equality of yesteryear. If ongoing processes of social breakdown were to reach an extreme, malignant movements such as fascism could not be ruled out, but there was also good reason to look forward to the launch of a benign alternative. Harking back to early twentieth-century countermovements against the self-regulating market and to the 'Fordist' economic regimes and Keynesian ideology to which they had given rise, Cox suggested that those achievements at the national scale could be repeated on the scale of the global economy in coming decades.

> By polarizing the satisfied and the deprived within and among national societies, and indeed across territorial boundaries in an increasingly global society, post-Fordism could well arouse a reaction by the disadvantaged and the dispossessed with support from a segment of the competing dominant groups.

This heralded opportunities for 'reregulation and repoliticization', as national and regional polities insulated themselves from the world economy, and through recharged institutions of global governance – a revival, ideally, of the New International Economic Order of the 1970s A countermovement of this sort would occur from above, by way of 'the struggle between rival forms of substantive economy – rival capitalisms', but also from below, through a 'recomposition of civil society' inspired by peace, democracy and environmental movements, churches, trade unions and movements of women and indigenous peoples.[25]

Not long after the publication of Cox's essays a cognate agenda involving countermovements from above and below was presented by the American political scientist James Mittelman. Forecasting that the return of liberal-economic globalization would generate large-scale disruptions – perhaps on a similar scale to those of the 1930s – he envisaged that 'sustained pressure for self-protection' would ensue, with blue- and white-collar workers, clerics, homemakers and middle managers as its primary agents.[26] As in Cox's account, resistance from above would be expressed in the emergence of different 'varieties of capitalism' and also in splits within and between business and political elites. 'Even state functionaries can resist the wholesale implementation of neoliberal development paths', Mittelman pointed out, citing advocates of an 'Asian-style democracy',[27] Malaysia's prime minister Mahathir Mohamad, critics of globalization from the business community (such as George Soros), and – surprisingly perhaps – the globalization boosters Klaus Schwab and Claude Smadja, president and managing director respectively of the Davos forum.[28]

Although the countermovements projected by Cox, Mittelman and Hettne are typical of the genre, the list of candidates for inclusion can be extended further. Fikret Adaman, Pat Devine and Begum Ozkaynak identify 'the anti-capitalist, anti-globalization movement' which heralds, it is hoped, a new era of regulation,[29] while the theologian Gregory Baum perceives a swelling counter-movement in the shape of 'neo-corporatist' forms of cooperation between company managements and their workforces as well as 'micro-economy' projects such as communal kitchens, cooperatively run retail outlets, and gardeners growing vegetables in their allotments.[30] Erik Ringmar identifies, *inter alia*, the family, trade unions, religious sects, Chinese Triads and Japanese corporations.[31] Still others cite intergovernmental organizations as institutional expressions of the countermovement, including the EU's Common Agricultural Policy[32] and the European Monetary System. For Eric Helleiner, the Bank for International Settlements qualifies for countermovement status because, in the 1970s and 1980s, in tandem with the G10 central banks, it created a regulatory regime that supposedly reduced international financial instability. The same author also invokes the campaign for the Tobin tax as a potential component of the dawning countermovement.[33] As an example of forces that 'embed economy in society', Sally Randles cites stock market actors and their advisors who, out of a recognition of 'the risks to the capitalist system' posed by overheated merger booms, mark down businesses that rush into mergers.[34] Another Polanyi-inspired theorist, writing on the transition to the market in 1990s Russia, makes a case for the inclusion of the Mafia as a protective organization (apparently without reflection upon the euphemistic twist this gives to the phrase 'protection racket'). 'The traditional conception of the mafia as guarantor of minimum personal rights and defender of the common man against the uncaring state', he argues,

> does seem to make a great deal of sense. Had Polanyi known more about the organization of the mafia he might have categorized it as a defence mechanism by which society attempted to protect itself from the ravages of excessively rapid change to a market system.[35]

One might think that stockbrokers and Mafiosi represent a limit case, but they do not. In his 'Der Mechanismus der Weltwirtschaftskrise', Polanyi implied that immigration control is 'protective' of 'society', and there are Polanyians today who have updated the argument. One study refers to campaigns to restrict immigration as 'Polanyi-esque movements' of self-protection. 'National-protectionism with racist and xenophobic overtones', it suggests, expresses workers' resistance to their treatment as fictitious commodities.

> Insecure human beings (including workers) have good reason to insist on the salience of nonclass boundaries and borders (e.g. race, citizenship, gender) as a way of making claims for privileged protection from the maelstrom. . . . Indeed, one could argue that the living standards of First World workers [depend upon] their ability to keep out competition from Third World labor by imposing import and immigration restrictions.[36]

Expanding the reaches of the countermovement to the farthest perimeter, Ron Stanfield, author of *The Economic Thought of Karl Polanyi*, includes imperialism, nationalism and the corporation as forms of social provisioning and protection:

> Imperialism and nationalism are banners of protective ideology, their practice is the political, diplomatic, and military administration of economy. Combinations, trusts, and cartels are protectively motivated and operated. Even the modern corporation, the central economic institution of modern capitalism, can be viewed as part of the protective response. The principal animus behind the corporate revolution is the urge to stabilize and control the exigencies of the corporate environment, and these exigencies are largely the uncertainties concomitant to the operation of the market mechanism. . . . the image of the corporation as an institution intent upon ensuring the orderly operation of the vital provisioning function is not only more correct but also far more salutary than the traditional typification of the corporation as a profit-mongering monopolist.[37]

That Polanyian social scientists can assemble this sprawling smorgasbord of policies, movements and institutions under the rubric of the 'protective response', with some cheering the alterglobalization movement for attempting to reassert social control over the market economy while others applaud its adversaries – imperialist states, capitalist corporations and stockbrokers – on exactly the same grounds, must give pause for reflection. Does it make sense to lump together the alterglobalization movement with xenophobic reactionaries – and does this not play into the hands of those who seek to discredit the former by conflating it with the latter?[38] How precisely does one determine whether an act of economic protection – for example, the state provision of export guarantees to armaments firms – is contributing to marketization or to the protective countermovement? As to the contention that the living standards of indigenous workers are protected by immigration controls, there is abundant evidence that suggests otherwise.[39] One wonders why labour should be conceived of as a *fictitious commodity* such that, in so far as workers attempt to reject this status through targeting other workers, they are engaging in *self-defence*. Would it not be more sensible to reverse the terms, with labour-power theorized as a *commodity* and workers who target foreign colleagues theorized as engaging in *fictitious* self-defence?

For Polanyian social scientists there is debate to be had on these problems. Although these writers distinguish between progressive countermovements and their degenerate half-brothers, such as neoconservatism or fascism, they have not paid sufficient attention to the problem that many so-called countermovements, including neoconservative and fascist administrations, have themselves been energetic agents of marketization and commodification – including, in the case of the neocons, the implementation of raft after raft of neoliberal reform. Another area that proves recalcitrant to discussion in 'countermovement' terms is those progressive movements that rebel against 'protective' regimes, such as the West German student movement in the late 1960s, or the Czech general strike of 1968. Are they part of the countermovement, or is there no place for them within the double movement framework?

To my mind, the countermovement does make sense but as a heuristic that refers to the way in which, when the self-regulating market undermines the security of their livelihoods, human beings look to political ideas and organizations that claim to defend society against market excesses. If given any more determinate content than that, for example when used to imply that those ideas and organizations actually do rally 'society' against the market, the concept tends to collapse under its own weight: it comes to function, if you will, as a 'bad abstraction'. This is a point that I shall develop below. But before I do so, it would be negligent were I not to discuss what are arguably the two most important works of the last two decades to have applied the double movement concept creatively: Giovanni Arrighi's *The Long Twentieth Century* and Beverly Silver's *Forces of Labor: Workers' Movements and Globalization since 1870*.

Pendular forces

Arrighi and Silver belong to that galaxy of thinkers, discussed in the introduction to this book, whose work weaves together concepts from Marx and Polanyi. To begin with the more recent of the two,

Silver's *Forces of Labor* is an investigation into the structural changes that have affected workers' bargaining power across the world since 1870. She divides workers' movements into two categories: 'Marx-type labour unrest', which refers to 'the struggles of newly emerging working classes that are successively made and strengthened as an unintended outcome of the development of historical capitalism', and Polanyi-type labour unrest, 'the backlash resistances to the spread of a global self-regulating market, particularly by working classes that are being unmade by global economic transformations'. The latter includes workers' opposition to 'the disruption of established ways of life and livelihood', to economic and cultural insecurity, and above all to being treated as a commodity – this includes hostility towards the visible incarnation of labour-market competition (i.e. other workers), as well as the struggles of those who had benefited from established social compacts that are in the process of being dismantled. In Polanyian mode, Silver charts 'a pendulum-like motion' of labour struggles. In the first two-thirds of the nineteenth century, labour commodification and economic globalization provoked a protectionist countermovement that reached well into the next century and was institutionalized in national and international social compacts between trade unions, capital and states that partially protected labour from the vagaries of an unregulated global market. 'But these compacts protecting livelihood came to be perceived as a growing fetter on profitability – a fetter that was broken with the late-twentieth-century wave of globalization.' To the extent that we observe contemporary processes of globalization through the Polanyian lens we would now 'expect a new swing of the pendulum' – and there has indeed been a panoply of Polanyian struggles, of which riots protesting against IMF-drafted austerity programmes are a salient example. However, despite her invocation of the pendulum, Silver is careful not to predict a recapitulation of past patterns. There are 'good reasons to think that processes of contemporary globalization and labor unrest are not simply retracing the path followed in the late nineteenth and early twentieth centuries'. For one thing, a revival of growth-based 'Fordist' regimes would be ecologically unsustainable; for another, workers' bargaining power is strongly affected by the unpredictable events of world politics in general and of wars in particular.

Where Silver parts company with Polanyian theory is in her treatment of changes to the organization of production, the ways in which these continually transform the terrain on which labour movements grow, and the dependence of workers' bargaining power upon their recognition of their own strength. Her most serious critique is that:

> the concept of 'power' is largely missing. For in Polanyi's analysis, an unregulated world market would eventually be overturned 'from above' even if those below lacked effective bargaining power. This is because the project of a self-regulating global market is simply 'utopian' and unsustainable on its own terms – it is one that is bound to wreak such havoc as to be replaced from above regardless of the effectiveness of protest from below.[40]

In TGT this is most explicit in the chapter entitled 'Conservative Twenties, Revolutionary Thirties', which accounts for the supplanting of market mechanisms in the 1930s by étatiste structures of accumulation in terms of elite initiatives. In the schema in TGT, change from below is desirable but unnecessary. By overturning established social compacts the self-regulating market provokes popular resistance, but this is not essential to 'society's' protective response. The term 'countermovement', in short, is misleading, conjuring as it does a social movement with the inevitable connotation of collective action 'from below'.

The other outstanding Marxian–Polanyian contribution is by Silver's sometime co-author, the world-systems theorist Giovanni Arrighi. In my view the most impressive and unquestionably the grandest attempt to knit Polanyian concepts into a systematic analysis of modern history is his *The Long Twentieth Century* – a work whose subtitle, *Money, Power, and the Origins of Our Times*, deliberately echoes that of TGT. Arrighi shares with Polanyi an ability to theorize grand historical trends without losing focus on the detailed intersections between economic history, international relations and social movements. A sweeping survey of much of the last millennium of European and US history, it would be impossible to summarize his tome adequately in the small space available, but I shall do so just enough to bring out its Polanyian thread.

Arrighi's starting point is Fernand Braudel's concept of systemic cycles of accumulation, the economic cycles that characterize the development of capitalist hegemons. Each cycle commences with the revolutionizing of productive technique, centred within a particular geographical territory; economic success encourages the consolidation of the new structures of accumulation, including hegemonic leadership; there then follows an era of overaccumulation and financial expansion. In the latter phase – in which we find ourselves today – the hegemon reaps the fruits of bygone investment in its world leadership; it is described, following Braudel, as 'autumnal'. *The Long Twentieth Century* identifies four 'systemic cycles of accumulation', each characterized by a unity between hegemonic agency and the prevailing structure of global accumulation: Genoese-Iberian, Dutch, British and American. This narrative of economic cycles threaded into hegemonic succession, Arrighi suggests, is intertwined with 'the long-established pattern, first observed by Henri Pirenne, of alternating phases of "economic freedom" and of "economic regulation"'. Together, these two macro-historical processes – one cyclical and sequential, the other pendular – have produced a succession of hegemonic thrusts, each of which corresponds to a particular form of economic organization. The complete (serial-cyclical-pendular) chronology commences with the formally organized and regulated capitalism of Venice, the success of which called forth as a countertendency the informally organized, unregulated and 'cosmopolitan-imperial' capitalism of Genoa. Entering its period of proto-hegemony, Genoa found its role usurped by the formally organized 'corporate-national' capitalism of the Netherlands – the first true hegemon. As its growth attained its limits, a cosmopolitan-imperial and 'informal capitalism triumphed once again under British free trade imperialism, only to be superseded in its turn by the formal capitalism of US big government and big business'.[41] To the extent that the US government practised free trade during its hegemonic ascendancy, its strategy centred upon

> bilateral and multilateral intergovernmental negotiation of trade liberalization, aimed primarily at opening up other states to US commodities and enterprise. Nineteenth-century beliefs in the 'self-regulating market' – in Polanyi's sense – became the official ideology of the US government only in the 1980s under the Reagan and Bush administrations ... Even then, however, the unilateral measures of trade liberalization actually undertaken by the US government were very limited.

In common with some realist international relations theorists, Arrighi associates hegemonic breakdown with periods of world-systemic chaos.[42] Since the 1970s we have been living in just such a phase, as US hegemony declines. But what will replace it? The development he charts – in sharp contrast to the realists – is of

> successive hegemonies of increasing comprehensiveness, which have correspondingly reduced the exclusiveness of the sovereignty rights

actually enjoyed by [the members of the modern inter-state system]. Were this process to continue, nothing short of a true world government, as envisaged by Roosevelt, would satisfy the condition that the next world hegemony be more comprehensive territorially and functionally than the preceding one.

Signs of just such a development can be observed in 'the withering away of the modern system of territorial states as the primary locus of world power' and in the 'tendency to counter escalating systemic chaos with a process of world government formation', as exemplified in the 1980s and 1990s by the revitalization of the Bretton Woods institutions, the UN and the G7.[43] This process will tend to accelerate as US power continues to drain away while East Asia's grows. As regards the prevailing form of economic organization, Arrighi concedes that 'it is entirely possible that the revival of previously superseded beliefs in free markets and individualism typical of the 1980s is the harbinger of yet another long swing in Pirenne's pendulum towards "economic freedom"'.[44] For

> the very success of administered markets in promoting economic expansion in the 1950s and 1960s has disorganized the conditions of 'economic regulation' and has simultaneously created the conditions for the enlarged reproduction of the 'informal' capitalism typical of the sixteenth [Genoese-Iberian] and nineteenth [British] centuries. . . . The 'regulatory' thrust of the US regime developed in response to the dysfunctions of the 'deregulatory' thrust of the British regime. . . . As in all previous swings, an organizational thrust in one direction has called forth an organizational thrust in the opposite direction. . . . And so today's 'deregulatory' thrust may well be indicative of a new swing of the capitalist world-economy towards 'economic freedom'.

It is also possible, however, 'that this new swing towards "economic freedom" will be nipped in the bud by the countervailing tendencies that its very scale, intensity, and speed are calling forth'.

It is at this point that the scale and strength of the Polanyian countermovement become pivotal. Crises of overaccumulation, Arrighi argues, adapting a motif from David Harvey, induce a search for solutions in the form of 'spatio-temporal fixes' that involve,

> a devastation of the human habitat embedded in the obsolescent landscape of capital accumulation. As Karl Polanyi pointed out long

ago, with special reference to the overaccumulation crisis of the late
nineteenth and early twentieth centuries, devastations of this kind
inevitably call forth the 'self-protection of society' in both progressive
and reactionary political form, mobilized by forces seeking to slow
down or reverse the relocation of economic activities and political
power involved in the spatial fix. Polanyi does not speak of spatial
fixes or overaccumulation crises. Nevertheless, his emphasis on the
opposition 'habitation versus improvement' conveys the same idea
of a fundamental contradiction between the tendency of capital to
relentlessly transform geographical landscapes on the one side, and
the tendency of the communities embedded in those landscapes to
resist such transformations on the other.[45]

In borrowing from Harvey, Arrighi signals an important diver-
gence from the standard Polanyian approach. In the latter, the 1970s
crisis was caused by Keynesian (or otherwise social-democratic)
economic regulation generating full employment and wage-fuelled
inflation that inhibited the proper functioning of market forces. It
manifested a clash between regulation and the market, between
'habitation and improvement'. Harvey's thesis, by contrast, roots
the crisis in the laws of motion of capital, and posits a dynamic that
generates overaccumulation crises within regulated and neoliberal
variants of capitalism alike. Unlike banking crises, which are rare
during periods of tougher regulation but have clustered in the neoliberal era, overaccumulation crises are inscribed in capitalism's
DNA. In Harvey's presentation of the case, the long postwar boom
'was in part fuelled through accelerated fictitious capital formation
and increased indebtedness backed by state power', which created
'such a pent-up force for devaluation' that a period of slow growth
interspersed with deep recessions was bound to follow – as occurred
in the 1970s and 1980s.[46]

Where, though, does this leave the Pirennian swing towards
'economic freedom' or the parallel Polanyian swing towards
marketization? It would be difficult to predict its precise duration
but Arrighi has long been forecasting a Polanyian backswing. 'Back
in the 1980s I would say: "If you want to see the future, read *The
Great Transformation.*" '[47] In the 1990s he interpreted that decade's
proliferation of civil wars as evincing 'the self-protection of
society against the disruption of established ways of life under the
impact of intensified market competition' (although with the caveat
that they might generate further violence and chaos rather than a
Polanyian backswing). More recently he identified the 'growing
neoconservative backlash centred on the U.S. South' as exemplify-

ing a reactionary countermovement, and prognosticated that the neoliberal age will last 'only another few years' before the pendulum swings back once again.[48] Whether that moment is upon us now is a question to which I turn below, following a general assessment of 'pendular' approaches to economic regime change.

The Great Oscillation

In *The Great Transformation*, the double movement ceases with the new form of society that it had brought forth, which is, depending upon one's interpretation, either socialist planning or 'an institutional form of capitalism termed "embedded liberalism"'.[49] For those that hold with the latter interpretation, that economies in the postwar era were 'embedded' in non-economic institutions, the demise of those arrangements poses a question over the scope of the double movement. Should it be confined to the period to which it refers in TGT? Or can it be refunctioned as a repeating process, and applied to the rise and expected fall of neoliberalism? Those who apply this perspective have given a new infusion of life to what might be called the 'pendular' tradition in political-economic theory. Celebrated exponents include Pirenne and more recently Albert Hirschman, with his psycho-economic account of the swings modern societies experience between episodes of public-spiritedness and absorption in the private sphere. More recent instances include Harold James' thesis on the cyclical oscillation of rules-based international order (globalization) and force-based autarky,[50] and of course, Polanyian theories of the alternation between nationally embedded and global free market capitalism.[51]

The strength of pendular approaches centres upon their capacity to reveal transformative historical shifts that would otherwise lie buried beneath accumulations of detail. In the Polanyian versions we have discussed above there exists, in addition, an undeniable elegance in the interlacing cycles and pendulums, and in the Newtonesque thesis that the commodifying thrust draws an equal and opposite reaction, yielding a pendular motion of marketization and protection. Their potential weakness consists in the fact that socioeconomic trends are sufficiently complex and multi-layered to enable the criteria according to which they are periodized to be defined all too easily in order to fit an envisaged pattern. Beguilingly neat models can be produced if the messier evidence is overlooked.

Some scholars appear to be so hypnotized by the pendular perspective that they erroneously impute it to Polanyi – as in Zaki Laïdi's assertion that

> Polanyi has shown how capitalism oscillates between phases in which it either tries to free itself from the social institutions that keep it in check or [is] forced to embed itself in social institutions, by reason of the intensity of the disruptions that ensue from the logic of self-regulation.[52]

As this quotation exemplifies, in recent Polanyian theory the four-stage model of the double movement in TGT – marketization, countermovement, disruptive strains, socialist resolution/fascist irruption – has tended to become reduced to a simpler and different perspective centred upon an undulation between regulating and commodifying trends, a perpetual to-and-fro between regimes that disembed and re-embed the market. The analysis is sometimes accompanied by a plea for a reduced-velocity pendulum swing. In the 1950s and 1960s, it is said, regulation and protectionism went too far, leading to excessive wage demands and constrained profits, which threatened 'improvement'; in the 1980s and 1990s, by contrast, marketization went too far, levels of insecurity (or 'precarity') grew, endangering 'habitat'. During those latter decades, with neoliberal triumphalism as the backdrop, it was an analysis that carried a radical edge. Now, though, it is barely distinguishable from mainstream opinion. Here, by way of illustration, is how these matters are viewed from the office of the assistant editor of the *Financial Times*.

> If you look back over history in the last century you see pendulum swings between statism and excessive devotion to free market ideals, and the pendulum swings one way and then swings back the other way. We have clearly swung very strongly in favour of free market extremes in the last 20 or 30 years; now, we are swinging back the other way. I would guess that probably the least bad option is to be somewhere in the middle.[53]

Along similar lines, the business executive Sir Martin Sorrell has offered that:

> Just as the crash was inevitable, so will be the pendulum swinging the other way. The teeth and claws of capitalism will be blunted, and we will see the return of forms of state corporatism familiar to those of us who lived and worked in the 1970s.[54]

There is, of course, a measure of sturdy common sense in the pendulum thesis. On the scale of the world as a whole, and whether the index taken is state regulation of trade, of finance or of the conditions of work, or the degree of trade or financial globalization, or the strength of the ideology of self-regulating markets, it is not far-fetched to discern a wave-like political-economic pattern. During the two world wars the boundary lines between politics and economics were comprehensively redrawn, with the states of the warring nations supervising or taking direct control of the supply of labour-power, raw materials and a wide range of manufactures. The twin peaks of the resulting 'embedded' economy appear clear to the eye: a smaller but sharp one at the time of the First World War followed by a towering massif, with a western wall that climbs steeply during the Great Depression and an eastern flank that begins its more gradual descent some two decades later. As to the valleys, the mid-nineteenth century is the paradigmatic case (even though commodification, marketization and globalization grew apace until 1914 despite an increasingly protectionist policy regime). The 1920s is a second, its creeping corporatism notwithstanding. The third, of course, occupied the final quarter of the twentieth century and beyond; the question of its endpoint is discussed below.

The peaks and troughs can appear superficially as if clearly etched, but a closer look reveals that one assumption that underlies the 'twin peaks' image cannot stand, to wit, that historical periods characterized by market dominance and a pronounced commodification trend coincide with the deregulation of the conditions of labour and a *laissez-faire* approach by states towards economic affairs. There are some obvious cases that do not fit the model. In chapter 5 I discussed the example of Stalin's Russia, in which regimentation of business by the state coincided with an assault upon the rules, customs and institutions that protected labour, while in the 'Keynesian welfare capitalism' of advanced economies during the postwar boom the trend to the commodification of labour, nature and knowledge was powerfully present, and in this respect the advent of neoliberalism did not mark a turnaround. To the degree that the neoliberal era represents a pendular turn, it is primarily with respect to the regulation of labour conditions and not commodification as such.[55] The decisive neoliberal departure – a sharp, pendular swing, if you will – has been the loosening of restrictions upon the institutions and flows of international finance. But patterns in the globalization of trade in manufactures are less straightforward. International trade remains a politically managed process. Although the world economy witnessed a decline of tariff barriers in the postwar epoch, a trend which continued into the neoliberal age, it has been accompanied by a proliferation of non-tariff barriers coupled with continued protection and subsidization of agriculture by the USA, the EU and Japan. In addition, even in the free market 1990s, goods deemed to be of importance to power relations, of which oil is the outstanding example, have not been left to the market. On Wall Street itself, neoliberalism has functioned as ideological gloss; far from being the embodiment of a self-regulating market, the big financial institutions more closely resemble a cartel.[56] In the modern neoliberal order, in short, states and corporations manage trade relations and administer prices; these practices are integral to the global market system and are not its antithesis.

There are, moreover, long-term trends towards the involvement of states in modern market economies that partially negate the pendular pattern. One of these is rooted in secular changes in the nature of production processes. As these become more complex, the provision of physical infrastructure and the equipping and management of the workforce – including education and training, and the supply and security of labour-power – become more costly and essential. In so far as these tasks are managed or supervised by states, their weight grows accordingly. Another trend results from the growth of social movements that have historically striven to widen and politicize the public sphere, pressing states to take on a vigorous role in domestic economic management. A third has developed with the increasing intensity of world-market competition, to which governments have responded by upping their subsidies to business. Talk of free markets notwithstanding, state welfare for the wealthy, in the form of the subsidization of corporations and of executive pay packets, has spiralled upward. (One estimate puts the figure for the USA in 2006 alone at well in excess of $100 billion.[57]) There is, finally, the tendency for states to involve themselves more actively in the management of economic crises. This reflects both their endemic economic involvement and the danger that arises from technical interdependence between big capitals: that bankruptcy in one may gravely destabilize reproduction of the system as a whole.

It seems, then, that while neoliberal governments have indubitably presided over a far-reaching deregulation of international finance, the notion that states have retreated from their role as economic managers *per se* is misleading. In the 1980s and 1990s many did indeed loosen their hold over some areas of economic life, such as the direct ownership of certain industries, yet this coincided with the subjection of others to more intensive regulation. The economic weight of nation states within the world economy (measured by the ratio of government tax revenue to GDP), meanwhile, remained stable,[58] and with the rise of sovereign wealth funds an increasing proportion of the world's largest companies has passed into state ownership. These phenomena are perfectly compatible with Arrighi's 'corporate-national' formal capitalism, in which big government and big business call the shots, but less so with the notion that the neoliberal age can be seen as a repeat of the first phase of Polanyi's double movement.

Reflections on the current predicament

What, then, is to be made of the global economic crisis? It seemed, as I drafted this chapter in early 2009, that the pendulum had reached its point of return. The free market model seemed to have imploded. The neoliberal belief system was visibly cracking asunder. In mainstream discourse it became reasonable to advocate 'big government', nationalization and tax hikes. The abruptness of the shift was striking. 'This crisis has turned the world upside down', as an economic advisor to former Czech president Vaclav Havel put it. Whereas in the 1990s the West would lecture the former Eastern bloc countries about the need to privatize and deregulate, he continued, now the message emanating from Washington is to nationalize bankrupt or defaulting financial institutions, and to re-regulate. 'People here who argue that open markets are the solution to everything are no longer being taken as seriously.'[59] With asset prices and growth rates spiralling downwards, Keynesian deficit spending was rediscovered, in the USA, Europe and most conspicuously China. As banks and businesses topple, state-funded corporate welfare has escalated to dizzying heights, and included temporary and/or partial nationalizations – AIG, GM, RBS and Lloyds–HBOS, to name just the high-profile examples. 'Only nationalization can save the market economy!' was the prevailing motto for a while. Financial deregulation had evidently generated instability, and many of those who supported it in the 1980s and 1990s underwent a change of heart. According to the chief economics commentator of the *Financial Times*, the era of liberalization that he had championed for so long contained the seeds of its own downfall, as witnessed in the excessive growth of the financial sector, frenetic financial innovation, parlous global macroeconomic imbalances, an explosion of debt, and asset price bubbles. Now that this defective model had lost its credibility, he added, 'the legitimacy of the market process itself is damaged', and this 'is particularly true of the free-wheeling "Anglo-Saxon" approach'.[60]

Few readers of this book, one assumes, would deny that the boundary between politics and economics was allowed to shift too far in the age of Reagan, Clinton and Bush, with excessive marketization and insufficient state regulation, and at least for a moment, in early 2009, it seemed that a readjustment had begun to take place, with the disinterring of the Keynesian policy toolbox and a strengthening of institutions that can restrain market forces. The trickier questions concern the trajectory of these developments. Some have predicted – here in the words of the anthropologist Keith Hart – that 'a genuine revival of Keynesian redistributive politics seems to be inevitable', and if the 'pendulum model' is taken as a guide, it would appear to suggest that neoliberalism's decline is indeed clearing the path for a reassertion of social control over the economic sphere, with widespread re-regulation preparing for the re-emergence of a prosperous, equitable and stable capitalism.[61]

But this is too sanguine, on three counts. The first is that it misreads the current policy shift. There is, at the time of writing, little sign of the world's ruling classes blaming capitalism or even neoliberalism – as opposed to an overexuberant financial sector and lax regulation – for the global market meltdown.[62] The free market utopia that ostensibly defines neoliberalism was ideological cover for a drive, pioneered in the USA and adopted widely, to restore corporate profit rates at the expense of workers and welfare recipients. It does not automatically follow that a change of heart by some policy-makers and opinion leaders at the ideological level, even if coupled with a partial strengthening of the regulation of finance, will undermine the wider project. Even if the current étatiste rebound is sustained, it cannot in itself be equated with 'social control' in any meaningful sense of the term.

Given the market-fundamentalist record of so many policy-makers in the advanced industrial countries (of which the notables in Washington include Paul Volcker, Lawrence Summers and Tim Geithner), the prospect at least in the short term is of the continuation of the underlying neoliberal agenda by other means, with continued privatization (despite temporary nationalizations of firms that are 'too big to fail'), with marketization at the micro level even if Keynesian techniques are essayed at the macro, and with continued tendencies to deregulation, even if somewhat tighter regulation of the FIRE (finance, insurance and real estate) sector is envisaged. Even as I write, news reports are flagging a return to the 'bonus culture' in the big financial institutions, and that the government is determined to return recently nationalized banks post-haste to private hands. In several European countries, meanwhile, there are plans afoot to impose further onerous conditions upon welfare recipients, and much talk of the need for more 'flexible' labour markets and decentralized pay bargaining. Along such routes the march of market society appears, for the moment at least, to be continuing unabated. Taxes, it is true, will rise, but in large measure to cover the astronomical losses that states have assumed from bailing out banks and insurance companies. Having extended market freedoms that facilitated the accumulation of profits in corporate hands, their losses during the current crisis have been socialized by states. The chief beneficiary of governmental largesse has been the corporate sector, and the transfer of toxic assets from shareholders to taxpayers will be paid for by bitter austerity for years to come. Meanwhile, on the most important issue facing the human species, anthropogenic climate breakdown, no policy shift away from the neoliberal position – that pricing pollution is the best solution – can be discerned. That approach has been woefully ineffectual. As the Polanyian environmental economist Larry Lohmann has put it, emissions trading encourages businesses

> to treat global warming not as a social and environmental problem to be solved but as a business and public relations problem to be kept out of ordinary people's hands and to be managed at the least possible relative financial and market loss to themselves. . . . Far-sighted companies treat carbon trading as an opportunity to gain *new* property rights, assets and openings for capital accumulation, even if climate change is accelerated in the process.[63]

The second shortcoming of the expectation that an étatiste rebound will yield a prosperous, equitable and stable capitalism is that it misidentifies the causes of the postwar golden age. Just as the current slump is not primarily the product of policy mistakes but of overaccumulation, so too the dimensions and stability of the postwar boom cannot be attributed to Keynesian or other social-democratic policies as much as to the devaluation and destruction wrought by the Great Depression and the Second World War, the unprecedented levels of arms spending that ensued, and the industrialization of previously agricultural regions of Europe and North America. Indeed, Keynesian deficit spending was not implemented systematically until the 1970s, and even then was unable to restore the profit or growth rates of the previous decades. It is not neoliberalism but capitalism that lurches from crisis to crisis, and to think that the replacement of neoliberalism by an étatiste species of capitalism would inaugurate a new golden era is to overestimate the ability of states to engineer prosperity. Re-regulation in the interests of what Polanyi's generation called 'the common man' is a moral/political imperative but it should not be confused with a return to a 'managed capitalism'. The danger of that dream is that it plays to the oscillation of free market and étatiste regimes, an infernal pendulum that leaves what might be called Polanyi's maximum programme – the wholesale decommodification of labour and land – postponed *ad infinitum*.

Thirdly and finally, this expectation overlooks the degree to which changes in the global economy over previous decades contributed to the failure of Keynesian and étatiste techniques in the 1970s. During the long boom, big businesses had tended to view vigorous domestic economic management by states favourably, but an increasing density of cross-border interactions and resource flows, by intensifying competition on the international scale, tended to undermine that support. Globalization, as David Kotz has described,

> transformed big business from a supporter to an opponent of the interventionist state. It has done so partly by producing TNCs whose tie to the domestic markets for goods and labor is limited. More importantly, . . . the process of globalization has sharply increased the degree of competitive pressure faced by large corporations and banks, as competition has become a world-wide relationship. Even if those who run large corporations and financial institutions recognize the need for a strong nation-state in their home base, the new competitive pressure they face shortens their time horizon. It pushes them toward support for any means to reduce their tax burden and lift their regulatory constraints, to free them to compete more effectively with their global rivals.[64]

Linked to and running in tandem with these changes was the financialization of the advanced capitalist economies, which added to the powerful backers of the neoliberal project. I am not suggesting that the amassing of powerful business support behind it guarantees its continuation in perpetuity, but it does suggest that for neoliberalism to meet its demise powerful social movements would be required.[65]

Conclusion

Writing this book in Britain in the first decade of the new century, it is easy to understand the renaissance of interest in the writings of Karl Polanyi. The parallels between the nineteenth-century market society he describes and our own neoliberal age are inescapable. In Britain, market competition has been driven into every sphere of social life, with the institutions of politics, education, health, welfare and science reorganized as businesses oriented to exploiting opportunities for profit without regard to extra-economic costs and benefits. Social Darwinism is the order of the day, as school is pitted against school, hospital against hospital, and employee against employee. Managerial strategies implement programmes of ongoing 'modernization' the ulterior purpose of which is to keep the workforce in a condition of permanent stress. Amongst workers the empowering of management and concomitant weakening of trade unions, combined with the rebasing of individual economic welfare upon debt, generates profound insecurity. At all levels of society, commoditization and commercialization trends have undermined the institutions and social relations upon which solidarity, trust and citizenship had hitherto depended. The citizen is replaced by the consumer, with the previously prevalent sense of social membership becoming effaced by individualist consumerism, but the ostensibly egalitarian ideology of 'consumer choice' is too flimsy to veil the steep rise in inequality and stalling of social mobility. Housing estates have become ghettoes, from which the well-heeled hide in their gated zones girdled with barbed wire and CCTV. And in case this assessment is adjudged to be impressionistic, there are metrics aplenty to back it up. Since Thatcher entered office, Britain has forged an unassailable lead over its European neighbours on a range of indices, including prison population and the incarceration of children, levels of income inequality, child and pensioner poverty, premature births, self-harm, anorexia and depression. Income inequality, Richard Wilkinson has shown in meticulous detail, tends to vary directly with levels of stress, hostility towards fellow citizens, violence and homicide, and inversely with indices of life expectancy, health, trust, and participation in political and community life.[1] Perhaps the most damning piece of evidence was UNICEF's 2007 survey of the wellbeing of children in twenty-one rich countries, which put Britain in tail position, just behind the USA.[2]

At the level of the world economy a similar picture can be seen. The parallels between the age of Clinton and Bush and that of Gladstone and Disraeli are hard to miss. Is not the conflict between the imperatives of a liberal world economy and the promotion of social welfare within nation states as relevant in our day as it was in Polanyi's? Does not the 'Washington consensus' involve the imposition of a similar 'institutional standardization' upon the countries of the world against which Polanyi warned in TGT?[3] Its designers and boosters surely drew from the same 'utopian' well as did their forebears Ricardo and Malthus, and with an equally zealous faith that every corner of society should be colonized by the market, that dismantling the controls upon economic transactions would redound to the benefit of all and, at the extreme, that global integration would render national boundaries redundant. And what of Polanyi's account of the vulnerability of the small and weak peripheral states of Central and East Europe within a monetary regime based on gold? As Kari Polanyi-Levitt has remarked, it reads like a preview of the IMF 'adjustment programmes' of the 1980s and 1990s, in which currency stabilization and the satisfaction of foreign creditors were achieved by means of austerity measures, mass redundancies and wage repression.[4] Finally, Polanyi's concern that the restriction of democratic power to the political sphere leaves the demos ill-equipped to address economic issues on the national stage, let alone globally, has lost none of its relevance today. The realization is dawning, one *Guardian* columnist remarked during the market meltdown of autumn 2008, 'that this is not just a financial or economic crisis, but a democratic crisis – the people and their representatives have little or no control over what affects them directly'.[5]

The renaissance of interest in Polanyi has reawakened debates as to how best to characterize his *Weltanschauung*. In the following pages I shall explore these through an evaluation of recent interventions that present him as a Cold War liberal, a Marxist, and a Romantic, before closing with a summary of the strengths and weaknesses of his work as a whole.

A liberal anti-communist?

If there is one intellectual current to which Polanyi indisputably belonged it is institutionalism, of the 'old' school. Beyond that, the matter is less straightforward. For most, possibly all, of his adult life Polanyi saw himself as a socialist, but as we saw in the introduction and chapter 1, his socialism evolved. A liberal socialist in the 1910s, in the following decade he was close to Austromarxism and especially to Guild Socialism. During the Great Depression he renewed his interest in Marx, became an engaged Christian Socialist and an enthusiast for Stalin's Russia. Yet the best-known statement of his socialist perspective was written some years later, in the final chapter of TGT. The subject of the book, as discussed in chapter 2, was 'the Great Crisis' – the breakdown of liberal civilization. TGT consists largely of economic and political history, interleaved with anthropology; but the three penultimate pages sum up the historical and anthropological findings in a compressed philosophy of history. In that final chapter, 'Freedom in a Complex Society', Polanyi outlines and defends a socialist solution to the crisis, as contrasted with the liberal approach, which denies its existence, the conservative, which wishes to address it by returning to a past age, and the fascist, which seeks to tackle it by sacrificing democracy and individual freedom.[6]

In 'Freedom in a Complex Society' Polanyi's fire is directed at liberalism. Instead of cherishing freedom, the sacrosanct human value bequeathed to them by Christianity, liberals had allowed it to degenerate into mere advocacy of free enterprise, by which term the power of 'giant trusts and princely monopolies' is euphemistically known.[7] Their neglect of the deeper meaning of freedom, combined with their opposition to socialism, gave succour to the fascist cause. (And some liberals, Polanyi notes, gave direct support for 'various brands of fascism' – the allusion may well be to von Mises, who approved of the crushing of the Austrian labour movement in 1934 and served as advisor to Dollfus' 'clerical fascist' regime.) At the philosophical level, liberalism's central flaw is that it defines freedom negatively, as a question of individual rights. Polanyi concedes that in the simple societies of previous centuries there was a progressive element to this view but that no longer holds. In modern conditions, the lives of human beings are so thoroughly interwoven with their social surroundings that the freedom of the individual is an illusion. Worse, this approach encourages a denial of the 'reality of society', and opposition to socioeconomic regulation. And regulation, he insists, is the indispensable means by which freedom in a complex society can be extended; via political intervention, society is brought democratically into the shaping of the economic sphere.

One of the more powerful passages in Polanyi's oeuvre, on the antepenultimate page of TGT, seeks to explain whence comes liberalism's adherence to a negative definition of liberty. The answer lies in the 'market-view of society which equated economics with contractual relationships, and contractual relations with freedom'. If the volition of the contracting individual is established as the highest moral good, and at the same time individuals' economic actions are mystified by the workings of the market system, the great arena of economic life is darkened, and freedom is restricted to a narrow zone around isolated individuals. 'Vision', writes Polanyi, had been constrained by the market-generated fragmentation of life into

> the producers' sector that ended when his product reached the market, and the sector of the consumer for whom all goods sprang from the market. The one derived his income 'freely' from the market, the other spent it 'freely' there. Society as a whole remained invisible. The power of the State was of no account, since the less its power, the smoother the market mechanism would function. Neither voters, nor owners, neither producers, nor consumers could be held responsible for such brutal restrictions of freedom as were involved in the occurrence of unemployment and destitution. Any decent individual could imagine himself free from all responsibility for acts of compulsion on the part of a State which he, personally, rejected; or for economic suffering in society from which he, personally, had not benefited. He was . . . unentangled in the evil of power and economic value. His lack of responsibility for them seemed so evident that he denied their reality in the name of his freedom.

The practice of market capitalism combines with the theory of negative liberty to occlude from view the inescapable participation of individuals in the formation of social structures, including power hierarchies and value relations, which, Polanyi asserts, would be recognized in a regulated society with a socialist conception of liberty. With this, the argument returns to the historical conjuncture in which the book was written. Market society has been discarded, leaving the denizens of mid-twentieth-century modernity face to face with the reality of society – a reality that liberalism denies but both fascism and socialism accept. Lest he be misunderstood, Polanyi makes clear that despite this specific commonality and despite certain superficial economic similarities – by which he presumably refers to corporatism and economic planning – the two movements embody absolutely opposed principles *in moral and religious terms*: socialists uphold and expand freedom while fascists deny it.

If any three pages in Polanyi's oeuvre can be taken as his manifesto it is these. As such, they merit mention in their own right. Yet there is an additional and less satisfying reason why I have chosen to elucidate them at some length. It is that they have been crassly misconstrued. In early treatments this was rarely, if ever, the case. In his *Critique of Karl Polanyi's New Economics* (1949), Morris Sievers summarized the argument accurately:

> The market system, being at bottom anti-social in character, not merely wreaked its own evil effects but also engendered an antithetical movement which ultimately disintegrated the whole social structure, causing great hardship in the process. Fascism was one of the several alternative responses to the collapse of the old system. *We still have it in our power to choose a more desirable alternative, which Polanyi seems to believe is some sort of socialism.*[8]

The same cannot be said of many a recent interpretation – and the culprits are not only Polanyi's critics but his admirers too. For example, the economic journalist Will Hutton interprets TGT as arguing that 'Communism and fascism alike arose as protective, if equally destructive, responses to the potential "annihilation of the human and natural substance of society" that the market imposed',[9] while the historian Heide Gerstenberger appears to read TGT as an anti-socialist tract.[10] These errors are egregious enough, but worse has come from the pen of a political philosopher, Ira Katznelson, in his *Desolation and Enlightenment*. Whereas the actual author of TGT wrote of the absolute antithesis between fascism and socialism, including its communist variants, the dummy Polanyi as ventriloquized by Katznelson speaks of a dividing line that separates liberalism on the one hand from fascism and bolshevism on the other: against the totalitarian duo, liberalism strives to ensure 'freedom and the institutional basis on which it might be upheld'.[11]

A few pages on, Katznelson's Polanyi is presented as a proponent of the case that nineteenth-century liberal civilization was destroyed *not* by the pathological products of its own contradictions but 'by revolutionary fascist and communist regimes',[12] and as the theoretician of the 'remarkable bifurcation' between liberal states that defend freedom and totalitarian ones that assault it.[13] In his conclusion he takes this great traducement to the limit, in championing Polanyi as an adherent of a 'fighting doctrine' of liberalism, one that was defined against 'two clear foes, condensed, despite the differences between bolshevism and fascism, into totalitarianism as a single category'.[14]

What is going on? Do these misunderstandings stem from the ambivalent meaning of liberalism? Certainly, Polanyi tended to use the European variant and this may help to explain Katznelson's misdesignation of TGT as a liberal manifesto, but it cannot explain his retrospective recruitment of Polanyi to the anti-communist crusade. The generous reader may treat the first one or two such slips as perfunctory or accidental, yet they are repeated, in multiple formulations, throughout his book.[15] The misreading must be deliberate, but is it a sign of ignorance or of tendentiousness? Circumstantial evidence suggests it is the latter. Clues can be found in Katznelson's text, for example where he reveals that during the writing process a copy of *The Black Book of Communism: Crimes, Terror, Repression* lay on his desk – a book that bundles communism and Nazism together as totalitarian twins (with the twist that the former is singled out as the worse offender).[16] In our age of liberal hubris, could it be that some scholars are no longer able even to comprehend the longstanding socialist tenet that the recuperation of the liberal values of individuality and tolerance, and to a degree even the freedoms of speech and assembly, necessitates a break with liberal commitments to the market system and private property in the means of production? If one cannot envisage this as a rational position one cannot begin to comprehend Polanyi's work. Pasting *The Great Transformation* into the back catalogue of liberal anti-communism, as Katznelson does, leaves misunderstanding behind and enters the realm of farce.

A Marxist? A Romantic?

'Marxism is today an unfashionable ethic', one rather dyspeptic economic historian has proposed.

Are we therefore to see a flourishing of Marx surrogates? Is this why there is a revival of interest in Polanyi? Do those who now turn to Polanyi seek in him a new socialist figurehead? For them there can only be this clear message: Polanyi is baloney![17]

It is open to doubt whether Marxists are either such a tremulous bunch that they would abandon their beliefs when the going gets tough or so fickle that they would ditch them when the winds of fashion turn. Be that as it may, it is clear that Polanyi, particularly in the inter-war period, was profoundly influenced by the Marxist tradition. The zones of convergence between Polanyi and Marxists cropped up throughout the first half of this book. His fellowship with the Austromarxists and his analysis of alienation and commodity fetishism were discussed in the introduction and chapter 1, while chapter 2 introduced the affinities between the concerns of Marx and Engels and themes in TGT, notably with regard to the degradation of nature and human society under a market regime. Although the 'fictitious commodity' is strictly speaking a Tönniesian–Polanyian concept, in practice Marxists share the belief that labour and nature, food and health, water and education, should not be treated as commodities. There is also Marxist–Polanyian concord on the analysis of neoliberalism: that the widening and deepening of markets have unleashed pernicious tendencies: the yawning gap between rich and poor, financial crises galore, growing pressure on the natural environment, the commodification of increasing areas of life, the ideological naturalization of commodity relations, and the subordination of society to the casino rhythms of finance and the world market.

For many years there has been busy traffic between the Polanyian and Marxist traditions. The 1990s saw the appearance of a welter of such studies, including James O'Connor's 'ecological Marxism'[18] and a series of essays by writers from the 'neo-Gramscian' school of international relations theory.[19] More recently Michael Burawoy has joined the lists; he goes so far as to catalogue Polanyi as one of 'the great Marxist theorists of the twentieth century'.[20] This is an influential thesis, but is it accurate?

In brief, Burawoy's agenda is to construct a synthesis of Polanyian theory with Gramsci's thoughts on hegemony, reinterpreted as an argument for the formation of lasting multi-class coalitions.[21] He dubs the resulting concoction 'Sociological Marxism', in contradistinction to 'classical Marxism' – although, confusingly, Gramsci is placed in the latter bracket. For classical Marxists the pivotal concept in accounting for resistance to capitalism is the relationship of exploitation between the working class and the owners of the means of production. It is a concept that combines issues of social justice and human suffering with those of power and interest: in their exploitation, workers are simultaneously powerful creators and wronged victims. For Marx and Gramsci 'the market is epiphenomenal, obscuring the productive core of capitalism' – the exploitation relation – and it is this that 'spells the demise of the old order and the basis of the new one'.[22] Burawoy's critique of classical Marxism is that the notion of an irreconcilable conflict between capital and labour is outmoded, for it privileges one part of the population as the group with both the power and the interest to resist capitalism.

Against classical Marxism, Polanyi 'supplies a more convincing rationale for counterhegemony', one based on the market rather than the exploitation relation. In this move from 'classical' to 'sociological' Marxism there is a twofold switch in focus: that no one part of society, even if the majority, has the potential to represent universal interests, and that the wellspring of resistance is to be found not in the conjunction of latent power with oppression but in the realm of torment and misery, a realm the universality of which stems from its common source. 'Everyone suffers from the market', writes Burawoy. To workers it appears in the form of unemployment, poverty and sweatshop conditions; to peasants, the loss of land and proletarianization; to landed aristocrats, the 'degradation of space and the importation of cheap food'. For 'capitalists, the anarchy of the market threatens their survival with ever stiffer competition, increasingly of a global character', while for human beings in general the market, 'inasmuch as it is unrestrained', leads to environmental destruction, climate breakdown and 'the colonization of free time'. For Sociological Marxism, then, the global development that generates a constituency with a 'universal interest' is not the formation of a working class but the expansion of the market: it 'touches everyone in multiple ways'. Following Polanyi, and in contrast to Gramsci, Burawoy postulates 'society' as the antithesis of the free market. Mediating between state and economy it provides the ground upon which 'solidarity among all classes' of the population can arise. But on one issue Burawoy parts company with both Polanyi and Gramsci. Whereas they believed the development of capitalism to be preparing the ground for transition to a socialist system, for him 'society' successfully 'contains and absorbs' capitalism's tendencies towards breakdown. The intervention of 'society' into economic life, he enthuses, 'lays the foundation of a new form of capitalism – a capitalism conjoined with society'.[23]

Whether Marx would recognize himself in Burawoy's sociological mirror is open to doubt – but that question lies beyond the scope of this book. As regards Polanyi's recruitment as a Marxist theorist, Burawoy's case relies upon a sleight of hand: he strips Marxism of its core theses and then reconstructs it as an essentially Polanyian research programme, dubbed 'Sociological Marxism'. To catalogue Polanyi as a Marxist is not completely implausible, but it requires the net to be cast widely – so far, indeed, that Tönniesian or Weberian would be equally appropriate labels. A more accurate and useful approach, it seems to me, is to identify the areas of convergence between Polanyi and Marxism while recognizing the considerable differences.

If Polanyi resists assimilation to either liberal or Marxist traditions, perhaps his identifying feature is the 'organic' or 'holistic' tropes in his thought? For Don Robotham his worldview is imbued with 'nostalgia',[24] while according to John Ruggie he anchored his critique, despite his socialist instincts, 'in an organic conception of society that was deeply conservative in the traditionalist sense of the term'.[25] What is the truth in these depictions?

To begin with, let us consider holism. In its weakest sense a holistic approach is one that assumes that phenomena, in their interconnections, create some kind of entity based upon mutual influence between the various elements. Polanyi considered himself a holist in this general sense, and approved of the Aristotelian perspective that the whole comes before the part.[26] Specifically in the social sciences, the term can be used in a similar way to 'functionalism', to signify that the social whole tends necessarily to cohere in a harmonious way. Here too, despite the Marxian and Weberian elements in Polanyi's thought, he did incline to functionalism, at least with regard to non-capitalist societies. In its strongest sense holism posits an essentialized whole as the sole appropriate subject of social-scientific inquiry, denying that individuals and their actions and attitudes are the proper units of social scientific analysis. This was decidedly not Polanyi. In his 'Essence of Fascism' he sharply rebukes philosophies that deny individuality in favour of an organic conception. Society, he proposes, should instead be seen as 'a conscious relationship of persons'.[27] And although, he writes, society is ontologically an interdependent and integrated 'whole', to adopt that as an epistemic and methodological guide would be 'disabling and inaccessible'. For the purpose of analysis it is necessary (even if 'ontologically inaccurate') to differentiate society 'into constituent sub-systems'.[28]

As regards the broader question of Polanyi's alleged Romanticism, we alighted briefly upon it in chapter 3, but it deserves to be addressed in more detail. Is there anything to the suggestion that he was a Romantic? The label is sometimes flung as a polemical dart, as in the phrase 'Polanyi's popularity signals the triumph of yearning and romanticism over science.'[29] When used in this fashion the implicit assumption is that Enlightenment values of tolerance and respect, civil liberties, free markets, individualism, liberalism and democracy form a single package, ergo those who oppose liberalism or free markets cannot coherently support the others. This is not a sustainable case. For one thing, some of the most distinguished members of the liberal pantheon, such as John Stuart Mill, drew inspiration from the German Romantic movement. As for Polanyi, the core principles to which he was committed were democracy, socialism, community and individuality. He espoused the traditional socialist position that Enlightenment values, civil liberties, democracy and individuality can only flourish fully in a socialist society and, conversely, that market fundamentalism fragments and atomizes society, creating conditions inimical to virtuous behaviour and preparing the ground for authoritarianism.

I don't think, however, the terms of debate set by the critics should be accepted and that one should feel obliged to fend off 'accusations' of Romanticism. The question is more fruitfully approached by considering Romanticism in its Lukacsian construal, as a movement of reaction against the way of life of capitalist modernity, one that is bound up with an experience of loss and a quest for the lost object.[30] The most recent systematic work that frames Romanticism in this way, by Robert Sayre and Michael Löwy, distinguishes various subtypes, including 'Marxist' (such as William Morris), 'socialist' (Erich Fromm) and 'resigned' (Tönnies). The last of these is characterized by a tragic conviction that although the reintroduction of *Gemeinschaft* elements can make *Gesellschaft* more hospitable, no return to an authentic *Gemeinschaft* is possible, and social decadence is inevitable.[31] As for socialist Romantics, they

> construct a model for a socialist alternative to bourgeois-industrial civilization, a collectivist utopia, while they refer to certain social paradigms and ethical and/or religious values of the precapitalist type. They present their critique not in the name of a class but in the

name of humanity as a whole, and especially the part of humanity that is suffering.

Socialist Romantics contrast 'the communist principle of humanity with the principle of selfishness, the spirit with Mammon, the socialist community of the future with the selfish and inorganic individual of bourgeois society'.[32] Alongside Fromm, an exemplar is the utopian socialist Charles Fourier (although not Robert Owen: his championing of progress, technology and industry aligns him more closely with Enlightenment humanism).[33]

Within this framework where should Polanyi be situated? Evidently, his work incorporates utopian-socialist and Marxist strands, as well as a less utopian, 'resigned' aspect too, as expressed in his argument that because 'power and value' are universal, every society is 'necessarily imperfect' and none 'can be the realisation of community'.[34] More generally, he alloys Romanticism with Enlightenment rationalism. With the Romantics he shared the acclamation of the value and uniqueness of the individual and a fascination with ancient Greece. His focus upon social integration at the expense of structural social conflicts may also be seen as Romantic. Romanticism is there too in his longing for 'social unity' and in the idea that the market system disrupts this, and in his tendency to depict the reciprocal exchange of small-scale societies as accompanied by attitudes of 'generosity and grace', in contrast to modern market values.[35] And it is there in his view that in pre-modern societies economic processes served social ends, and that in this respect they surpassed market society. But it is going too far to say, as some have done, that he believed that 'there was almost nothing progressive about the rise of market capitalism'.[36] His fierce critique notwithstanding, he held that capitalism was propitious to the development of an ethic of individual responsibility and civic conscience, the rule of law, and political democracy. He searched in the past for ideal instances of non-alienated cultures but, rather than pining for the 'dead old', he was a modernist through and through, aspiring to a society that would be capable of welding the *Gemeinschaft* of the old to the universalism, egalitarianism and democracy of the new. He marvelled at the productivity growth market capitalism facilitated, and even maintained that despite its ruthless methods the British-engineered expansion of 'machine civilisation all over the globe' was, at the time, 'in every accepted sense of the term, a progressive policy'.[37] It is, one should add, absurd to suggest that Polanyi symbolizes 'the triumph of romanticism over science'. His critique of market society may be an affront to its enthusiasts but it was developed in a scientific manner involving the standard repertoire of empirical research and hypothesis formation.

Tribute and critique

As I hope to have shown in this book, many of the charges against Polanyi miss their target. But some do not. These can be arranged under three headings: methodology, pre-modern and redistributive economies, and the modern market system. With regard to the first, Polanyi's adoption of the ideal-type method from German sociology was not without difficulties, as we saw in chapter 3. He fails to argue, rather than assert, why the pattern of 'locational and appropriational movements' is the feature essential to explaining the character of an economy, and his explanation of how economies are 'embedded' in societies consequently lacks precision. His mechanisms of integration describe patterns of goods exchange in empirical societies but function ultimately as formal categories, with wholly dissimilar institutions assembled together under the same heading. The method also generates ambiguity in respect of whether the referent – say, 'pure capitalism' – approximates to actually existing societies. Polanyi tends to use it in the latter sense but not invariably; while for some Polanyians, notably Mario Liverani, its use is purely as a model to assist analysis, a device with which to ask questions of any set of empirical economic relations.[38]

On the second issue area, non-market economies, a number of Polanyi's empirical assertions are untenable, as discussed in chapter 4. To a degree, such errors are the inevitable product of a generalist entering the domain of specialist historians: with his eye trained upon the borderlines that demarcate modern from ancient societies he tended to make sweeping statements about the latter that generalized from the particular periods most conducive to his argument. More importantly, he has been accused of a rose-tinted view of pre-market societies – that, in the words of one economist, he makes them seem 'like a band of idyllic Christian brothers endlessly extending the helping hand, to background choruses of "Kumbaya"'.[39] This is a polemical exaggeration but is not altogether unfounded. Polanyi's extension to ancient and archaic societies of the thesis – extracted and adapted from Thurnwald and Malinowski – that the motive of individual economic gain possessed negligible significance in 'primitive' societies is, at best, bald.[40] And he did tend to overstate the degree to which reciprocal arrangements imply communistic or altruistic attitudes and to understate the competitive or unjust aspects of 'redistributive' societies, from Mesopotamia to Dahomey to the Soviet Union. As Szelényi has remarked, he developed a sophisticated theory of the pathologies of market society but did not ask the same set of questions about redistribution.[41] The underlying reason for this lies in Polanyi's lack of a concept of exploitation in particular and his neglect of conflict, competition and power relations in general. The weight of explanation always falls upon the pattern of economic integration and rarely if ever upon the exercise of control over productive property and the systematic relationships of inclusion and exclusion that flow from it. Thus, he roots the sociocultural corrosion of nineteenth-century capitalism not in exploitation *and* the commodification of labour-power but solely in the latter – even though generalized commodity exchange and large-scale proletarianization were two sides of the same coin. When similar processes of social atomization and cultural deracination were witnessed in the Soviet Union in the 1930s he failed to notice, so bedazzled was he by its GDP growth and the rhetoric of 'planning'.

My third criticism is that Polanyi's theory of market capitalism is ultimately rather thin. It makes a moral distinction between natural and artificial commodities but lacks the sort of developed theory of the commodity form that one encounters in Marx, in which analysis of the contradictions between the commodity's qualitatively different aspects, use and exchange, provides a platform for a theory of capitalism (in essence, generalized commodity production) that includes meticulous examination of price formation as well as the dynamics of competition, centralization, crisis and uneven development, demonstrating in the process that tendencies to monopolization and state interventionism are not contradictory to but generated by the structures of capitalism itself. By comparison, Polanyi's conceptualization of capitalism seems undeveloped. As one sympathetic critic explains, he accepts 'too much of the systemic logic attributed to the capitalist economy by neo-classical economic theory', and this left his case against economic liberalism resting exclusively 'on the basis of a *moral* argument'.[42] Other critics – again, of the sympathetic variety – have suggested that his 'static' conception of capitalism fails to identify the way in which the development of capitalism modifies the forms taken by markets and commodities; that his analysis yielded an inadequate explanation of what guided the pragmatic retreat from the extremes of the market in the mid-twentieth century, with an undue explanatory weight placed upon the contradiction between economics and politics; that he failed to anticipate that state intervention could contribute to the stabilization of market societies; and that he tended to downplay the degree to which étatisme represented a recharged apparatus of control over exploited groups.[43] The anti-capitalist edge in Polanyi's work, at its sharpest in his discussion of the radical novelty of the market economy, is blunted by his belief, most apparent in his postwar writings, that its iniquities can be overcome through institutional reform.

Such are in my view the shortcomings of Karl Polanyi's contribution, but what of the strengths? What cannot but impress is his ability to combine painstaking empirical research with theoretical originality, not to say genius. In his comparative approach to premodern societies, he carefully delineates their *differentia specifica* and in the process denaturalizes, and in so doing contributes to a deeper understanding of, the market economy. He convincingly despatches the assumption found in a good deal of classical and neoclassical economics that the forms of market behaviour witnessed in modern capitalism reflect natural human inclinations. If denizens of market society act as rational, calculating egotists such behaviour is the product of that society, one in which most institutions and the everyday orientation of social actors are brought into line with the operative principles of the market: individualism, competition and self-interest. Historians would be rash to ignore his admonition against projecting the 'market mentality' onto non-market and ancient societies, while economists can learn much from his critique of their discipline's orthodox approach: the charges that it fails to appreciate the historical specificity of the modern market system, that it exaggerates the degree to which its subject matter exists trans-historically, and that it banishes ethics from its purview. The disciplinary-imperialist and de-moralizing instincts of the mainstream economist have been highlighted by this most lapidary of statements in a recent best-seller: 'Morality is the way we'd like the world to work; economics is how it actually does work.'[44] As glib as it is arrogant, in exposing the decrepitude of the discipline it contrasts with the strength and sophistication of Polanyi's alternative. For him, economic behaviour has an irreducibly ethical component and cannot be comprehended unless ethics is at the heart of the analysis.

In addition to the strengths of his holist and historicist method, not to mention his seminal contribution to the *oikos* debate (outlined in chapter 4), a number of Polanyi's theses on the modern market economy also deserve mention. One is his debunking of the myth of the Industrial Revolution as a purely private process supervised by a 'nightwatchman' state. In fact, he reveals, behind the construction of the market system lay a forceful programme of social engineering, steered by states that are far more intrusive and muscular than any pre-modern equivalent. A second consists in his account of the devastating cultural consequences of the imposition of the market system: few other texts come close to such a powerful and evocative account of the disintegration of a society's normative and customary fabric under the impact of marketization as *The Great Transformation*. Its axial concept, the double movement, is, for all the shortcomings discussed in chapters 2 and 6, original and justly famous. Its subplot concerning the 'disembedding' consequences that arise when 'economy' comes to dominate 'society' is particularly compelling, with its depiction of a sorcerer's apprentice world of untrammelled market forces, the constructions of humans but beyond conscious control, a world in which networks of exchange are spun that appear to have enmeshed us all in a web of coercion. The account of the inter-war crisis that Polanyi presents in journalistic articles of the 1930s and in TGT is impressive in its ability to connect together developments in various dimensions of social life and regions of the world. Unlike rival theories that target just one slice of the problem, such as the 'internal contradictions' of capital or the collapse of the international monetary regime, Polanyi's account encompasses the full range of issues, including society's metabolism with nature, the contradictions and synergies of market competition and geopolitical conflict, the clashes of class forces and political programmes, and the crisis-induced restructuring of capital and of policy regimes.

As this last point intimates, the significance of Karl Polanyi's oeuvre, I would argue, results less from any one or other of his specific theses than from the general example it sets. The intellectual tradition from which he came was preoccupied with the meaning of human history and the future of liberal civilization, and his work is geared to questions on that grand scale. Combining a holistic methodology with wide-ranging comparative analysis, his aim was to comprehend the character and trajectory of an entire epoch. Today, whereas research and publications tend to be focused on narrower issues than in Polanyi's time, the challenges facing humanity are greater. I'm thinking less of the global economic recession in itself (which at the time of writing does not appear to be on the scale of the Great Depression) than of the danger that it heightens the likelihood of fascist revival and/or war. But most of all I'm thinking of the prospect of runaway global warming and climate break-down. When Brecht wrote 'What times are these, in which / A conversation about trees is almost a crime / For in doing so we maintain our silence about so much wrongdoing!'[45] he could hardly have imagined that three generations later the meaning of his lines would be reversed, with 'trees' no longer symbolizing escapism or the avoidance of responsibility but repositories of that carbon upon which all eyes should be fixed. If we fail to do enough to mitigate climate change, the Stern Report warned in 2007, the disruptions ahead will be 'on a scale similar to those associated with the great wars and economic depression of the first half of the 20th Century'.[46] Already in the three years that have elapsed since the report was written, the new climatological data have made the predictions on which even that grim conclusion was based seem wildly optimistic, and yet those with power, influence or wealth do little or nothing to resist the expansion of the high-carbon economy, as the emissions graphs all too starkly reveal. While humankind busily builds a funeral pyre for tens of thousands of species, including conceivably itself, it would be faintly ridiculous were the social sciences to be preoccupied with a narrow, business-as-usual agenda. The age calls for vision, for the sort of critically engaged social science of which Karl Polanyi is an outstanding representative.

Notes

Preface

1 Dale, 2009a, 2009b.
2 Dale, forthcoming.
3 Dale, in press, b.
4 Dale, 2008.
5 Dale, in press, a.

Introduction

1 Cole, 1943, p. 165.
2 TGT, p. 53.
3 Soros, 1998.
4 Greider, 1998, p. 53.
5 Munck, 2006.
6 Lindsey, 2001.
7 Stiglitz, 2001, p. vii.
8 TGT, p. 76.
9 Porritt, 2005.
10 Marquand, 1997, pp. 30–2.
11 Bernard, 1997, p. 75.
12 Daly and Cobb, 1994. Other works in political and economic ecology that make extensive use of TGT include Henderson, 1981; Worster, 1993; and Wall, 2005. See also Rogers, 1994.
13 Stiglitz, 2001, p. xiii.
14 E.g. Esping-Andersen, 1990; 1999.
15 Ruggie (1982).
16 Their approach, according to Alain Lipietz (1997), can be seen 'as an enlargement, an *Aufhebung* of Polanyi's work'. On the régulationists' differences with Polanyi see Jessop, 2002.
17 Ágh, 1990, p. 93.
18 Hann, 1992, p. 149.

19   Dale, 2009a, 2009b, in press, a.
20   1-6 (1909) 'The Crisis in Our Ideologies'. Emphasis in original.
21   Hollis, 1977.
22   Baum, 1996, p. 41.
23   In Congdon, 1976, p. 174.
24   Ibid., p. 174.
25   Congdon, 1991, p. 223.
26   19-22, n.d., 'Christianity and Economic Life'.
27   Kari Polanyi-Levitt, telephone conversation with the author, 1 June 2008.
28   21-22, 1937, 'Community and Society'.
29   Polanyi, 2005a, pp. 138, 149.
30   4-9, early 1920s, 'Early Christianity and Communism', trans. Kinga Sata.
31   Polanyi-Levitt and Mendell, 1987, p. 25.
32   Nagy, 1994.
33   Polanyi, 2005b, p. 72.
34   50-3, 1958, Letter to George.
35   Its meanings can also be rendered by 'transparency', 'supervision', 'survey', 'panoramic view' and 'compendium'.
36   Cangiani et al., 2005, p. 35.
37   The global crisis that commenced in 2007 is often attributed to the 'lack of oversight'. See e.g. Jesse Jackson, BBC2 *Newsnight*, 4 November 2008.
38   Polanyi, 2005c, p. 126.
39   Kuhn, 2007, p. 190.
40   Marx, 1992, p. 323.
41   Schmoller, in Peukert, 2001, p. 99.
42   Schmoller, in Nau, 1998, p. 96.
43   Kuhn, 2007.
44   30-1, 1940–84, 'Karl Polanyi: Biographical information'.
45   Telephone interview with Kari, 29 November 2008.
46   TGT, p. 31.
47   Boyer, 1997, pp. 62–67.
48   LOM, p. 124.
49   32-6 (1953–5) 'On Forms of Trade in the Ancient Near East'.
50   Steiner, 2009.

Chapter 1 The economics and ethics of socialism

1   56-13, 1929, Letter to Donald Grant, 7 December.
2   Polanyi, 2005b, p. 109.
3   One prominent Paretian socialist, Jacob Marschak, was a mentee of Polanyi's in-law Emil Lederer and, later, a friend of Polanyi. Marschak

(1924) attacks Mises from a Guild Socialist position but directs some criticisms at Polanyi too.

4 Mises, 1972, p. 81.
5 2-22, 1924–7, 'Pure Economic Theory'.
6 In Sugden, 1986, p. 13.
7 2-22, 1924–7.
8 2-22, 1924–7. Emphasis in original.
9 Polanyi, 2005a, pp. 159–60.
10 Ibid. For a critique of the notion of *Arbeitsleid*, see Hilferding, 1904(?).
11 Polanyi, 1925a, p. 19.
12 Ibid., p. 21.
13 Ibid., p. 23.
14 Carpenter, 1922, pp. 147–8. Emphasis in original.
15 Cole, 1919, p. 141. See also Hirst, 1994, p. 105.
16 Polanyi, 2005b, p. 96.
17 Polanyi, 2005a, pp. 161–3.
18 Polanyi, 2005c, p. 127.
19 29-10, Felix Schaffer (1973–4) 'Karl Polanyi's Life in Vienna'.
20 Polanyi, 2005b, p. 72.
21 3-1, 1919–33, 'Das Uebersichtsproblem'.
22 Polanyi, 2005c, p. 128.
23 Polanyi, 1925b, p. 224.
24 Polanyi, 2005a, p. 163.
25 Ibid., pp. 156–60.
26 Polanyi, 2005b, p. 109.
27 Mises, 1925. See also Mises, 1932, p. 481. In this, Mises anticipates the critique of Cole's Guild Socialism by the fascist legal theorist Carl Schmitt in his *The Concept of the Political*.
28 Weil, 1925.
29 Polanyi, 1925b.
30 Kari Polanyi-Levitt, telephone conversation with the author, 1 June 2008.
31 56-13, 1963, Letter to Irene Grant.
32 Cangiani et al., 2005, p. 34.
33 Polanyi, 2000, p. 317.
34 Polanyi, 2005a, p. 144.
35 Tawney, 1938, pp. 270, 253 and *passim*.
36 45-5 Abraham Rotstein, 1956, 'Notes of Weekend IV with Karl Polanyi', pp. 22, 41.
37 Polanyi, 2005a, p. 146.
38 See Liebersohn, 1988.
39 LOM, p. 49.
40 Liebersohn, 1988, p. 26.
41 Polanyi, 1935, p. 375.

42 Some Marxists are closer to Polanyi on this question than others. Lukacs, for example, contrasts the fragmentation of capitalist society with 'the organic unities of pre-capitalist societies'. See Lukacs, 1971, p. 92.
43 At other times he credits this discovery to Hegel and Owen.
44 3-2, 1927, 'Das Ubersichtsproblem, ein Hauptproblem des Sozialismus'.
45 Marx, 1973, p. 84.
46 Özel, 1997, p. 161.
47 20-12, 1938, 'Notes of a Week's Study on *The Early Writings of Karl Marx* and Summary of Discussions on *British Working Class Consciousness*'.
48 21-22, 1937, 'Community and Society. The Christian Criticism of Our Social Order'.
49 Ibid.
50 Polanyi's arguments on the fragmenting and objectifying effects of capitalist markets, on the domination of ends by means, on how commodity fetishism occludes our ability to recognize objectification, and on the apparent autonomy of the economic sphere in capitalist society evidently resemble those of Lukacs (1971). Polanyi knew Lukacs' book well, but whether it influenced his turn towards Marxist theory is unclear.
51 3-3, 1919–33, 'Ist Sozialismus eine Weltanschauung?'
52 On this question his view is similar to that of Lukacs but antithetical to that of his younger self and of Tönnies, for whom capitalists are the self-driven elements within *Gesellschaft*.
53 19-19, n.d., 'Individualism and Socialism'.
54 Ginzburg, 1994.
55 Polanyi, 2005a, pp. 153–4.
56 Ibid., p. 149.
57 Ibid., p. 142. See also the texts in 20-11, 1936–8, Christian Left Group: *Bulletin*, no. 1, 'Trotzkyism. Earlier Works of Marx' and 'Marx on Self-Estrangement'.
58 Polanyi, 2005a, p. 158.
59 Ibid., p. 151.
60 Ibid., p. 160.
61 Ibid., p. 147.
62 21-7, 1937, 'Lecture'.
63 20-12, 1938; 21-13, 1938.
64 20-11, 1936–8.
65 20-10, 1938, Newsletters of the Auxiliary Christian Left.
66 Kirkpatrick, 2005, p. 157.
67 Macmurray, 1933; Kirkpatrick, 2005, pp. 24, 39.
68 Lind, 1994, p. 158.
69 56-11, 1932–5, Correspondence: Polanyi–Joseph Needham.
70 18-39, n.d., 'The Meaning of Peace'.

71 See also 18-36, n.d., 'Western Socialism: A Tract on Values and Power'.
72 18-39, n.d.
73 Polanyi, 1935, p. 392.
74 Ibid., p. 361.
75 21-2, 1936, 'Xtianity and the new social order'.
76 17-1, 1938–9, 'Canterbury IV'; 20-19, 1934, 'What is Fascism?'
77 21-2, 1936.
78 As paraphrased by Goldfrank, 1990, p. 88.
79 20-14, 1939, 'Russia in the World'.
80 18-21, 1937, *Europe To-Day*, p. 56.
81 TGT, p. 242.

Chapter 2 *The Great Transformation*

1 TGT, p. 32.
2 18-8, n.d., 'The Fascist Virus'.
3 Polanyi-Levitt, 1990, p. 8.
4 Stiglitz, 2001, p. vii.
5 31-10, n.d., 'Lecture 2. The trend towards an integrated society', Columbia University.
6 TGT, p. 3.
7 37-3, 1957, 'Freedom in a Complex Society'.
8 TGT, p. 16.
9 TGT, p. 58.
10 TGT, pp. 45, 72.
11 TGT, pp. 205, 72.
12 McNally, 1993, pp. 94, 107.
13 19-13, n.d., '1820 vs 1920'.
14 15-2, 1937–8, Lecture 2: 'Conflicting Philosophies in Modern Society'. Emphasis in original.
15 TGT, p. 190.
16 TGT, pp. 109, 172, 188; 39-7, 1954, 'Tyranny or Tyrannies'.
17 TGT, pp. 190, 188, 73.
18 15-8, 1943–4, Government and Industry, Lecture 6. Emphases in original.
19 PAME, p. 62.
20 15-8, 1943–4, Lecture 6. Emphases in original.
21 20-7, late 1950s, 'New Frontiers in Economic Thinking'.
22 TGT, pp. 39–40, 79.
23 TGT, pp. 57–8, 73, 106, 225.
24 16-11, 1937–8, English Economics, Lecture 21; Mantoux, 1928, p. 445.
25 TGT, pp. 42–4. Elsewhere, Polanyi contradicts this thesis. When discussing Adam Smith's contention that a developed division of labour depends upon a large market, he claims that 'that does not in any way imply a market-dependence of human society. Merely that

markets for manufacturing articles should be large enough to allow division of labor in manufacturing – this is very very far from the extension of the market principle to labor and land'. 9-1, 1934–46, 'Notes on readings'.

26   Polanyi, 2005d, p. 326.
27   TGT, p. 71.
28   TGT, pp. 116, 45; 38-8, 1956, 'Draft manuscript, *Trade and Market in the Early Empires'*.
29   Ricardo, 1973, p. 52.
30   Ibid., pp. 52, 54–5.
31   Ibid., pp. 61, 63.
32   TGT, ch. 7.
33   35-8, 1947, 'On the Belief in Economic Determinism', *Sociological Review*, 39(1), 99–100.
34   TGT, pp. 81, 86, 129; Polanyi, 2005e, pp. 289, 292.
35   TGT, p. 130.
36   Owen, 1927, p. 69 and *passim*; Block and Somers, 2003.
37   Block and Somers, 2003, p. 30.
38   TGT, pp. 291, 128.
39   8-12, 1934–46, 'Notes on readings'.
40   Ibid.
41   TGT, pp. 107, 90.
42   TGT, pp. 128–9, 131–2, 231.
43   Barker, 1988, p. 17. Emphasis in original.
44   TGT, p. 129.
45   TGT, pp. 141–5, 226.
46   TGT, pp. 145–6, 189.
47   Barker, 1988, p. 4.
48   TGT, pp. 76–7.
49   TGT, p. 202.
50   TGT, pp. 136–8.
51   TGT, pp. 166–7.
52   TGT, pp. 137, 80, 87.
53   TGT, pp. 136, 138, 89.
54   Tönnies, 1974, p. 127.
55   TGT, pp. 192, 200.
56   TGT, pp. 150, 210; 15-2, 1937–8; 16-14, 1939–40, 'Modern European History'. For further detail, see Dale, 2008.
57   TGT, p. 220.
58   Polanyi, 1979, p. 66; 2002d, p. 149; 8-7, 1934–46, 'The Christian and the World Economic Crisis'; 15-2, 1937–8.
59   TGT, p. 223; 31-10, n.d. Emphasis in the original.
60   15-8, 1943–4, Lecture 24.
61   This paragraph draws upon Pilling, n.d., and Block, 2001a.
62   In Pilling, n.d.

63 TGT, p. 26. In respect of Marx and his followers this is an oversimplification: they were sharply critical of the theory deployed to explain and justify the gold standard, in particular the assumption that gold inflows automatically produce an increase in the domestic money supply and price inflation. Lenin, famously, envisaged little use for gold in a communist society other than as material for the construction of public toilets. This side of the demonetized global commonwealth, however, he and Trotsky did indeed share the prevailing belief that the gold standard was irreplaceable, and a lesser evil than the perceived alternative – world market fragmentation accompanied by the 'reactionary and utterly utopian' trend to autarky. See Trotsky, 1934.

64 Eichengreen, 1992; Kindleberger, 1986; Patnaik, 2009.

65 Eichengreen, 1992.

66 45-3 Abraham Rotstein, 1956, 'Notes of Weekend II with Karl Polanyi', pp. 25–6.

67 Keynes, 1930, pp. 302–4.

68 TGT, pp. 201–2.

69 TGT, pp. 207–8.

70 Block, 2001a, p. xxxi.

71 15-4, 1936–40, 'Notes on Free Trade'.

72 TGT, p. 227.

73 15-4, 1936–40, Morley Lecture xix.

74 TGT, p. 234.

75 15-2, 1937–8.

76 Polanyi, 2003, p. 132.

77 LOM, p. l; TGT, p. 29.

78 20-4, 1939–40, 'Common Man's Masterplan'.

79 TGT, pp. 241–3, 228, 252.

80 TGT, p. 257.

81 15-4, 1936–40, Morley Lecture xxiv. Emphasis in original.

82 McRobbie, 2000, p. 86.

83 Marx, 1989, p. 90.

84 See Watson, 2005.

85 For Hayek, see Anderson, 2005.

86 Hayek, 1986, p. 14.

87 Ibid., p. 16.

88 TGT, pp. 71, 258.

89 31-10, n.d.

90 TGT, pp. 202–5.

91 TGT, pp. 155–6.

92 Randles, 2007, p. 145.

93 TGT, p. 40, quoted in McCloskey, 1997.

94 Stiglitz, 2001, p. vii.

95 Chang, 2002; Samuelson, 2009; Arrow 1978, p. 477.

96 Smith, 1993, p. 299. The references are to Thomas More's *Utopia* and to James Harrington's *Oceana*. For drawing my attention to this quotation, my thanks to Alasdair MacIntyre via Richard Poirier.
97 TGT, pp. 153–6, 185.
98 Jones and Novack, 1980, p. 145.
99 Ibid., p. 166.
100 *Today* programme, BBC Radio 4, 4 February 2005.
101 Engels, 1844.
102 Özel, 1997, p. 182.
103 Waller and Jennings, 1991.
104 TGT, p. 77.
105 Nafissi, 2005, p. 168.
106 Offe, 1998, p. 40.
107 Anthony Giddens, paraphrased by Özel, 1997, p. 62.
108 Munck, 2006.
109 Martinelli, 1987, p. 139.
110 Sievers, 1949, pp. 43, 83–4.
111 Stanfield, 1986, pp. 105–6.
112 Tawney, 1938, pp. 155, 180, 267–9, 262, 195. See also Mielants, 2007.
113 Appleby, 1978, pp. 94, 62, 245.
114 Ibid., pp. 168, 177, 41, 244, 242, 97, 192–3, 239.
115 Bayly, 2004, p. 136.
116 15-8, 1943–4, Lecture 5; LOM, p. 86.
117 McNally, 1993, pp. 12–15.
118 Ibid, p. 16. If a broader criterion is applied one finds that as early as the fourteenth century over one third of the population earned most of their living in this way. However, wage labour in the late Middle Ages was rarely 'free' but may be more accurately construed as a monetized form of feudal relations. See e.g. Dyer, 1989.
119 47-12, 1942, Letter to John, 12 September.
120 See e.g. Bruland, 1990.
121 Fleming, 2001.
122 48-1, 1946, Letter G. D. H. Cole to Polanyi, 11 February.
123 19-6 G. D. H. Cole, 1943, 'Notes on *The Great Transformation*'.
124 Ibid.
125 Ibid.
126 TGT, pp. 288–93.
127 TGT, p. 84. Emphasis added.
128 TGT, pp. 291–5. Emphasis added. See also 9-1, 1934–46. On the agricultural employers' interest in perpetuating the Speenhamland system, cf. Thompson, 1991, p. 244.
129 For a more recent exposition of this idea, see Milward, 2005.
130 LOM, p. 1.
131 TGT, p. 105. See also Rieger and Leibfried, 2003, p. 62.
132 Hilferding, 1981, pp. 312, 314.

Chapter 3 The descent of economic man

1 Frazer, 1922, pp. x–xi.
2 Schneider, 1974, p. 224.
3 17-24, 1945, 'Rise and Decline of the Profit Motive'; See also 15-8, 1943–4, Government and Industry, Lectures 5, 6, 24.
4 Quoted by Polanyi in 38-5, 1963, 'Bücher, Karl (1847–1931)'. Emphasis in original.
5 Thurnwald, 1932a.
6 Thurnwald, 1932b, p. 46.
7 Tawney, 1929, p. xv.
8 Ibid., p. xi.
9 10-8, 1934–46, 'Notes on Malinowski'.
10 Polanyi, 1947a, p. 99.
11 In Kuper, 1996, pp. 24–5.
12 Polanyi, 1957a, p. 68.
13 Sahlins, 1965, p. 153.
14 This paragraph draws upon Cohen, 1967, p. 111.
15 Moore, 1980, p. 8.
16 Marx, 1973, pp. 487–8.
17 Maine, 1863, pp. 168–70.
18 Ibid., pp. 310–11.
19 Polanyi, 1957b, p. 69.
20 Lukacs, 1980, p. 8.
21 Whether or not Tönnies was the originator of the 'ideal type' method of sociological argumentation, as some have claimed, he did, late in life, describe *Gemeinschaft* and *Gesellschaft* as Weberian ideal types. Tönnies, 2005, p. 504.
22 Weber, quoted in Rehmann, 1998, p. 187.
23 Schmoller, 1902, p. 2.
24 Polanyi, 1968, pp. 163–4.
25 Schmoller, 1902, p. 61.
26 Schmoller, in Peukert, 2001, p. 104.
27 In Therborn, 1976, p. 242. Cf. also Schmoller, in Peukert, 2001, p. 102.
28 Nau, 1998.
29 Peukert, 2001, p. 104.
30 Clarke, 1982, p. 187.
31 Hodgson, 2001, p. 82.
32 Michie, 1994, p. 398.
33 Menger was one of the first to relate rational action to the scarcity postulate.
34 Schumpeter, 1908.
35 Schumpeter, 1986, p. 887.
36 Clarke, 1982, p. 227.
37 Hodgson, 2001, p. 84.

38 Barber, 1967, pp. 209–10.
39 Mirowski, 2002, p. 21.
40 Nafissi, 2005, p. 127.
41 Oppenheimer, 1910, p. 79.
42 2-22, 1924–7 'Pure Economic Theory'.
43 42-9, 1958, 'KP's remarks on Menger, Brunner & the history of thought about the substantive economy'. These appear to have been taken down by a student.
44 Cangiani et al., 2005, p. 42.
45 Özel, 1997, pp. 54–5. 'Strong evaluator' is borrowed from Charles Taylor.
46 Polanyi, 2005a, p. 156; 51-1, 1959, 'University seminar on the institutionalization of the economic process'; 51-5, 1961, Letter to George Dalton, 27 March.
47 Hodgson, 2001, p. 346.
48 LOM, p. 26.
49 Hodgson, 2001, p. 241; Landa, 1994, p. 181; Murray and Schuler, n.d.; *New Scientist*, 3 January 2008.
50 Frank, 2007.
51 Harford, 2008, p. 232.
52 51-1, 1959, Letter to George Dalton, 16 October.
53 Herskovits, 1968, p. 43.
54 In Halperin, 1994, p. 20.
55 Plattner, 1989, p. 12.
56 Goodfellow, 1968, pp. 64, 58.
57 Herskovits 1968, p. 47 and *passim*; LeClair and Schneider, 1968, p. 9.
58 Burling, 1962, p. 819.
59 PAME, p. 7.
60 31-16/17, 1953, 'Semantics of General Economic History', p. 1; Cangiani and Maucourant, 2008.
61 Somló, 1909.
62 51-4, 1960, Letter to George, 7 November.
63 23-6, 1947–60, 'Fragments'.
64 Weber, 1947, p. 184ff.
65 7-9, 1934–46, 'Origins of Institutions'; 23-6, 1947–60.
66 Menger, 1923, pp. 72–9.
67 Ibid., p. 85.
68 42-9, n.d., 'A Note on the Translation of Menger's "Grundsaetze"'.
69 Polanyi, 1959, pp. 162, 166.
70 Ibid., p. 163.
71 30-18, 1950, 'The Contribution of Institutional Analysis to the Social Sciences'.
72 30-16, 1963, 'Model of a Classical Economist'.

73 51-1, 1960, Letter to George Dalton, 29 January; 50-1, 1957, Letter to Murray, 17 January. Emphasis in the original.
74 Pearson, 1957a, p. 320. More recent analyses have extended the argument, pointing out that choices can occur for reasons other than scarcity – as for example with 'operationally induced choices' that occur in situations where possibilities bifurcate and where alternative options realize similarly valued goals. See Campbell and Elardo, 2001.
75 LOM, p. 28; 49-2, 1953, Letter to Finley, 18 October; PAME, p. 98.
76 Hopkins, 1957, pp. 289–90.
77 23-6, 1947–60.
78 Hopkins, 1957, p. 291.
79 Ibid., p. 291; Neale, 1977, p. xxxi.
80 20-7, late 1950s, 'New Frontiers in Economic Thinking'.
81 Polanyi, 2005d, p. 329.
82 Sahlins, 2004, p. 14.
83 Polanyi, 1959, pp. 163–6.
84 51-1, 1959, 'University seminar'.
85 Since Polanyi's time, non-cooperative game theory has been developed to deal with this criticism, but it too takes for granted the assumption of isolated individual actors and is unable to model the more extensive communication and co-ordination that occur in much non-market economic decision-making. See Campbell and Elardo, 2001.
86 42-9, n.d.; 23-6, 1947–60; 31-16/17, 1953, p. 7.
87 30-18, 1950.
88 23-6, 1947–60. Emphasis added.
89 48-6, 1951, Letter to Pierre Crosson 13 December. It is unfortunate, observes Rhoda Halperin (1994, p. 62), that Polanyi places distribution under the rubric of appropriational movements and production with locational movements. 'By associating production with locational movements, and distribution with appropriational movements, the appropriational (read: institutional or relational) aspects of production and locational (read: spatial, ecological, or technological) aspects of distribution are eliminated from the framework.'
90 22-3, 1947–60.
91 30-18, 1950.
92 PAME, pp. 306–8.
93 PAME, pp. 8–9.
94 31-15, 1948–62, Memorandum No. 1.
95 This formulation borrows from Gregory 1982. For a critique of Gregory, see Hart and Hann, n.d.
96 Neale, 1957b, p. 222.
97 PAME, pp. 10, 87.

98 Ibid., pp. 10–11. For a succinct account of the kula trade, see Hart, 2000, pp. 190–2.
99 Thurnwald, 1932a. In his own copy of Thurnwald's volume, wherever 'distribution' appears Polanyi writes 're-' in the margin.
100 In a letter to George Dalton (50–4, 1959) Polanyi equates the opposition 'administered/market' with '*Tausch-/Verwaltungswirtschaft*'.
101 McNally, 2006.
102 31-16/17, 1953, p. 9; 32-3/4, 1955, 'The Two Meanings of Economic', p. 21.
103 In Donlan, 1982, p. 18.
104 Sally Humphreys (1978, p. 67) misleadingly interprets Polanyi and his collaborators in TMEE as suggesting that the mechanisms of integration necessarily conflict.
105 PAME, p. 309; 31-16/17, 1953, p. 7.
106 32-3/4, 1955, p. 23; 31-15, 1948–62; Cella, 1997.
107 Fried, 1967; Sahlins, 1965; Humphreys, 1978, p. 68.
108 31-15, 1948–62; 32-3/4, 1955, p. 21.
109 Halperin, 1988a, p. 51; 1994, p. 148.
110 Gudeman, 2001, p. 85; Valenis, 1981, p. 7.
111 Clarke, 1982, p. 282.
112 49-1, 1953, Letter to Connie Arensberg, 11 July; Polanyi, 1959, p. 173.
113 15-10, 1944, 'The Study of Human Institutions (Economic and Social)'.
114 LOM, p. 42.
115 PAME, p. 307.
116 32-3/4, 1955, p. 26.
117 Schaniel and Neale, 2000, pp. 89–104.
118 Voss, 1987, p. 130.
119 Lukacs, 1980, pp. 611–12.
120 Allen, 2004, pp. 79–80.
121 Gudeman, 2001, p. 84.
122 32-3/4, 1955, p. 25.
123 Halperin, 1988a, p. 5.
124 57-8, 1943, Letter to Michael.
125 15-10, 1944, 'Notes on primitive economics'. Emphasis in original.
126 PAME, p. 308.
127 Gledhill and Larsen, 1982, p. 199.
128 Jenkins, 1977, pp. 87–8.
129 Nafissi, 2005, p. 165.
130 Cook, 1968, p. 221.
131 Ibid., pp. 209, 213.
132 Isaac, 2005, pp. 20–1.
133 Joy, 1967, p. 32.
134 Burling, 1962, pp. 811–19.
135 Goodfellow, 1968, p. 63.
136 Ibid., p. 61.

137 Ibid., 1968. With this, writes Prattis (1982, p. 207), Goodfellow 'unwittingly supplies the petard upon which to hang the entire formalist argument'.
138 Joy, 1967, p. 41.
139 Burling, 1962, p. 819.
140 Prattis, 1987.
141 North, 1977, p. 715.
142 Landa, 1994. See also Gudeman, 2009; Stodder, 2002, p. 40.
143 Godelier, 1981, p. 68; 1986, p. 207.
144 Godelier, 1978, pp. 52–5.
145 Donham, 1990.
146 Others have made a similar point, viz., that the formalist position that, given adequate information, individuals will maximize their gains by obtaining the highest possible return for any given resources – for instance, that if a woman feeds her kinsmen regardless of any return she is said to be investing in social solidarity – is tautological and without explanatory value. The position simply asserts that individuals do their best, given their preferences and the information available to them. See e.g. Cohen, 1967, pp. 99–106.
147 Donham, 1990, p. 25. Some formalists would cheerfully concede this point. As Robbins Burling put it, 'the maximization principle is an "empty concept" in the sense that it is a definition of behaviour, and an assumption we make, and there is no conceivable behaviour which would contradict it'. 52-4, 1962, Letter Robbins Burling to Harry Pearson, 7 December.
148 Donham, 1990, pp. 35–6.
149 Clarke, 1982, pp. 208–9.
150 Hart, 2000, p. 230.
151 Godelier, 1981; 1986, p. 189.
152 Godelier, 1986, pp. 189, 200–1.
153 Godelier, 1981, p. 67.
154 Ibid, p. 67 and *passim*.
155 Meillassoux, 1972, p. 96.
156 In Krippner, 2004.
157 Godelier, 1981, p. 66.
158 Ibid. On this point the harshest critic of Polanyi – in my view too harsh – is the Korean-American sociologist John Lie (1991).
159 45-12, Abraham Rotstein, 1957, 'Notes of Weekend XVII with Karl Polanyi', p. 38.
160 Hart and Hann, n.d.
161 Frankenberg, 1967, p. 65. Extraordinarily, a debate amongst formalists as to whether Keynesian theory applies to low-surplus economies did in fact arise (see Schneider, 1974, pp. 94–5). For LeClair it does not, because savings and investment decisions are made by the same people. For Schneider it does. Primitive economies experience

positive feedback mechanisms so require dynamic analysis; and in all economies exogenous mechanisms operate to adjust the feedback system, whether that be the Federal Reserve or a severe drought, which, among the Turu of Tanzania, counters economic polarization by reducing the stock of wealthy cattle herders.

162 For examples, see Henrich et al., 2004.
163 Robotham, 2009, p. 272.
164 Wilk, 1996, pp. 11–13.
165 Latham, n.d.
166 For examples, see Meillassoux, 1971.
167 Donham, 1990, p. 13; Prattis, 1982, p. 208.
168 Lapavitsas, 2003.
169 Menard and Shirley, 2005; Ensminger, 1992.
170 Chang, 2002, p. 557. Emphasis in original.
171 Michie, 1994, p. 405.
172 Ibid., p. 398.
173 Gudeman, 2001, p. 2.
174 Ibid., p. 4.
175 For a brief critique of culturalism, see Wilk, 1996, or Hann, 2000.
176 DST, p. xxv.

Chapter 4 Trade, markets and money in archaic societies

1 In Murray, 1997, p. 7.
2 49-2, 1953, Letter to Bill [Bennett], 8 August.
3 LOM, p. 49.
4 42-14, n.d., 'On the primitivist–modernist debate'.
5 In Pearson, 1957b, p. 7.
6 In Meikle, 1979, p. 68.
7 Weber, 1976, p. 51. For discussion, see Love, 1991; Nafissi, 2005.
8 Weber, 1981; 1976, pp. 45, 157, 394.
9 In Wiener, 1982, p. 397.
10 Hasebroek, 1933, pp. vii, 21, 106, 140.
11 Finkelstein, 1935, p. 320. See also Finley, 1973, pp. 26, 116 and *passim*.
12 Finley, 1973, pp. 121–2, 141–2, 144.
13 Meikle, 1995.
14 42-14, n.d.
15 37-2, n.d., 'Methodology – The Methodological Problems Connected with the Question of Capitalism in Antiquity'. Polanyi seems to have been unaware of Marx's *Grundrisse*, which denies that a system of interconnected price-making markets obtained in ancient Greece.
16 42-14, n.d., p. 2.
17 32-3/4, 1955, 'The Two Meanings of Economic', p. 5.

18　56-13, 1963, Letter to Irene Grant, 15 March; 31-16/17, 1953, 'Semantics of General Economic History', p. 2.

19　22-3, 1947–57, 'Notes – economic anthropology'.

20　31-15, 1948–62, Memorandum No. 1.

21　PAME, p. 322.

22　31-16/17, 1953, p. 12.

23　Polanyi, 1959, p. 177. See also 51-4, 1961, Transcript of conversation between professors Tsagolov and Polanyi.

24　Bohannan, 1955, p. 60.

25　PAME, p. 105; LOM, p. 276.

26　Dalton, 1975, p. 104.

27　LOM, p. 85.

28　DST, p. xix.

29　Polanyi, 1960, pp. 334–7.

30　42-1, 1960–3, 'Economy and Society in the Negro Kingdom of Dahomey'.

31　Humphreys, 1978, p. 56. She continues: 'Political power is more effective in collecting these goods than market institutions would be. . . . Polanyi tends to present the port of trade as a restriction on the trader's activities, but it was equally a means of overcoming the formidable difficulties he would have faced had he tried to deal directly with producers.'

32　LOM, p. 95.

33　Niemeyer, 1990, p. 485.

34　LOM, p. 95.

35　Geertz, 1980. Polanyi does not see these characteristics as necessary to the port of trade. In his discussion of ports of trade in medieval Europe, the definition is loose, including sites where buyers are absent but sellers are resident, or where buyers are resident but which sellers visit for varying lengths of time. See Hodges, 1982, p. 24.

36　42-1, 1960–3; Revere, 1957; Polanyi, 1960, pp. 334–7; DST; LOM, p. 95.

37　Revere, 1957, pp. 54, 65. Humphreys (1978, pp. 54–55) criticizes this point. She doubts whether neutrality or distance from the main centres of power is an essential aspect of the economic functioning of the port of trade.

38　32-3/4, 1955, p. 26; 22-10, 1947–60, 'The Role of Market Methods in the Western World up to the High Middle Ages'; LOM, p. 43.

39　Bohannan and Dalton, 1962. This paragraph also draws upon McNally, 1993, and Tandy, 1997, p. 124.

40　Simmel, 1903; Marx, 1973, p. 165.

41　Lapavitsas, 2003, p. 115. Malinowski belongs to the same school. For him, money's key function is as medium of exchange.

42　PAME, p. 303; LOM, p. 119; DST, p. xviii.

43 Lapavitsas, 2003, pp. 119–22.
44 Quiggin, 1949, pp. 4, 321, 7.
45 PAME, p. 178.
46 LOM, p. 109.
47 The latter point is noted by Paul Einzig, in a book that Polanyi read and annotated meticulously: *Primitive Money*, 1949.
48 DST, p. 174.
49 Polanyi, 1957b, p. 16.
50 Weber, 1976, pp. 157, 85, 104–5.
51 Deimel, 1931, esp. p. 72.
52 Finley, 1973, p. 28.
53 Gress, 1998.
54 42-14, n.d.; 49-4, 1955, Letter to John, 5 January; LOM, p. 74.
55 Polanyi, 1957b, pp. 19, 22; 49-4, 1955.
56 PAME, p. 324; LOM pp. 116–17, 141.
57 Polanyi, 1957b, p. 25. Emphasis added.
58 LOM, p. 59; Polanyi, 1957b, p. 16; 31-11, 1955, 'The Institutionalization of the Economic Process', minutes, 10 March; 23-2, 1953, 'Notes on capitalism in antiquity'.
59 Oppenheim, 1964, pp. 85–6.
60 31-11, 1955; 23-2, 1953; Polanyi, 1957b, p. 17. See also Oppenheim, 1957, p. 32.
61 Bossuyt et al., 2001; Ellickson and Thorland, 1995, p. 339; Zagarell, 1986, p. 416; Gledhill and Larsen, 1982, p. 204; Chase-Dunn et al., n.d.
62 Steinkeller, 2002, p. 115. See also Renger, 1994; 2002, pp. 141–3; van de Mieroop, 2002, p. 66; Hudson, 1996a, p. 7; Liverani, 2005, p. 49.
63 Lamberg-Karlovsky, 1976, p. 67; Hudson, 1999, pp. 457–9; 2000b, p. 328.
64 Dandamayev, 1996, p. 197; Liverani, 2005, p. 53; Lamberg-Karlovsky, 1976, pp. 67–8.
65 Lamberg-Karlovsky, 1986, p. 423; 1978, p. 479.
66 Lamberg-Karlovsky, 1975, p. 345.
67 Bossuyt et al., 2001.
68 Aubet, 1993, p. 118.
69 Silver, 1983, p. 795. Emphasis added.
70 Ibid., pp. 810–11.
71 Mayhew et al., 1983, p. 131.
72 Renger, 1994, part 2, section 5.
73 Finley, 1954. My thanks to Daniel Tompkins for supplying me with a copy of this letter.
74 Renger, 1994; Bedford, 2005, p. 62.
75 Hudson, 2000b, p. 318.
76 Hudson, 2002, p. 24.
77 Veenhof, 1977, p. 117; 1995.
78 Aubet, 1993, p. 89.

79 Gledhill and Larsen, 1982, pp. 211–13.
80 Chase-Dunn et al., n.d.
81 Liverani, 2005, p. 53. See also Zaccagnini, 1977.
82 Goldsmith, 1987, pp. 10, 13.
83 Hudson, 2002, p. 16.
84 Hudson, 2004a, p. 99. See also Hudson, 2004b; 2002, p. 15.
85 Foster, 1977.
86 Steinkeller, 2002, p. 113; Hudson, 2002, p. 18.
87 van de Mieroop, 2002, p. 84; Renger, 1994.
88 See also Steinkeller, 2002.
89 Hudson, 2005/6.
90 Polanyi, 1957b, p. 25.
91 Mann, 1986, p. 87. Emphasis added. Mann (p. 165) sees this as exemplifying a historical law: 'In all known long-term periods, the level of state wealth and private wealth and the level of state interest in trade and private merchant trade appear positively correlated.'
92 Hudson, 1996a, pp. 2–3; 1996b, p. 44; 2002, p. 16.
93 Hudson, 1996b, p. 44. For a contrasting neoliberal position – 'the ancient record tends to support the relative efficacy of civil society and the . . . utter unreliability of the state' – see Ellickson and Thorland, 1995, pp. 408–9.
94 Hudson, 1996c, pp. 295–6. A similar point is made in Zagarell, 1986.
95 Hudson, 2000b, p. 317.
96 Ibid.
97 Hudson, 1996a, p. 9.
98 Hudson, 2000a, pp. 7–8.
99 Ibid.; Hudson 1996b, p. 52; 2005/6.
100 23-2, 1953.
101 42-14, n.d.
102 40-2, 1954, 'The economy of the classical polis'. This, incidentally, refutes Nippel's claim (1990, p. 145) that Polanyi applies the concept of redistribution in an undifferentiated way to both aristocratic and polis disbursements.
103 PAME, pp. 321–4.
104 Hudson, n.d.
105 Tandy, 1997, p. 111.
106 41-5, 1954, 'Archaic Greece'.
107 Engen, n.d.
108 LOM, ch. 11. Polanyi consistently elevates the earlier period as gracious and splendid, in partial contrast to Finley (1962, pp. 137, 142), for whom not only was the Homeric world fiercely competitive, but its heroes 'had a streak of the peasant in them, and with it went a peasant's love of possessions, a calculating, almost niggardly hoarding and measuring and counting'.
109 Anderson, 1975, p. 25.

110 Polanyi, in Humphreys, 1978, p. 47.
111 LOM, p. 193; PAME, p. 107; 49-2, n.d., Letter to Bill.
112 51-3, 1960, Letter to Geoffrey de Ste Croix, 6 August.
113 LOM, pp. 198, 214–38.
114 48-6, 1951, Letter to Moses Finley, 17 November.
115 37-11, 1959, 'Aristotle and Galbraith on Affluence'; LOM, p. 166.
116 40-2, 1954; LOM, p. 166.
117 LOM, p. 229; 31-7, n.d., Lecture notes on 'Capitalism in antiquity'.
118 Tandy and Neale, 1994.
119 LOM, p. 229.
120 48-6, 1951, Letter to Moses Finley; LOM, pp. 229, 273.
121 See e.g. Renfrew, 1972; Voutsaki and Killen, 2001.
122 See e.g. Cartledge, 1983, pp. 5–6.
123 Donlan, 1982, p. 28.
124 Ibid., pp. 5, 28.
125 Snodgrass, 1983, p. 26.
126 Finley, 1974, p. 39.
127 Finley, 1975, p. 117, emphasis added.
128 Nafissi, 2005, pp. 182, 261.
129 Meikle, 1995, p. 177.
130 Cohen, 1992, pp. 6–7, 34–5, 9.
131 38-9, Geoffrey de Ste Croix, n.d., Review of TMEE.
132 Nippel, 1990.
133 Figuiera, 1984.
134 Engen, 2001.
135 Ibid., p. 183; n.d. For Finley's case see Finley, 1973, pp. 169–70.
136 Saller, 2005, p. 225; Nippel, 1990, p. 192.
137 Meikle, 1995, p. 179.
138 Millett, 1983; 2002; Meikle, 1991. For a modernist counter-blast, see Cohen, 1992, and for a review of the debate, Morris, 1994.
139 Itoh and Lapavitsas, 1999, p. 75.
140 De Ste Croix, 2004, pp. 353–7.
141 Nafissi, 2005.
142 Goldsmith, 1987, p. 22. This, incidentally, invites scepticism towards the contrast – drawn among others by Finley (1973, pp. 28–9) – between the predominantly public economies of the Near East and the largely private ones of Greece.
143 Schoenberger, 2008.
144 In ibid., p. 669.
145 See e.g. Tandy, 1997; Redfield, 1986.
146 35-11, 1950–5, 'Draft Manuscript – *Livelihood of Man*'.
147 Arnold, 1957a, p. 155.
148 DST, p. xx.
149 42-1, 1960–3.
150 Arnold, 1957a, p. 155.

151 DST, p. 131.
152 PAME, p. 231.
153 DST, p. 33.
154 42-1, 1960–3.
155 DST, p. xxiv.
156 42-1, 1960–3.
157 DST, pp. xxii, 81, 87.
158 DST, p. 90. Polanyi is quoting Herskovits.
159 DST, p. 87; PAME, p. 226.
160 42-1, 1960–3.
161 Ibid.
162 Arnold, 1957b, pp. 177, 181–2.
163 DST, pp. 174–5. Emphasis in original.
164 Polanyi, 1968, p. 281; DST, pp. 175, 192.
165 DST, p. 9.
166 Bohannan, 1955, pp. 62, 67; 1959, pp. 494, 498.
167 Sacks and Brodkin, 1982, p. 232.
168 Sandall, 2001.
169 Law, 1995, p. 55.
170 Curtin, 1975, pp. 166–7, 238–9, 257. The latter charge, however, is based upon a misreading of Polanyi's work. Compare DST, pp. 166ff.
171 Moseley, 1979; Manning, 1982.
172 In Eriksen, 2001, p. 178.
173 Şaul, 2004, p. 80.
174 See e.g. Zelizer, 1994.
175 Latham, 1971.
176 Latham, n.d.
177 Latham, 1971, pp. 603–4.
178 Dorward, 1976.
179 Guyer, 2004, p. 30.
180 Fardon, 1999, p. 30.
181 Douglas, 1967.
182 Polanyi et al., 1957, p. 241.
183 Maurer, 2006.
184 Gregory, 1982, p. 49.
185 Leyshon and Thrift, 1997, p. 6.
186 Chapman, 1957, pp. 115–134. Held up against recent scholarship, Chapman's theses remain fairly resilient. Some historians (e.g. Hirth, ed., 1984) argue forcefully that markets in the Aztec economy were more extensive than she assumed. On the other hand, research by Pedro Carrasco, among others, confirms the 'archaic' character of Aztec society: its basis consisted of largely self-sufficient peasant households, and the maintenance of the ruling class came through payments in labour and kind, and not via markets. Circulation took place primarily in accord with administrative decisions, 'and wealth

was distributed on the basis of status. In the case of the ruling estate, income was received primarily in the form of products from public lands and shares from other forms of revenue. The market mechanism existed to fill the gaps left by the politically defined distribution. It was of secondary importance because it did not enter into the process of production; land and labor were not handled as commodities'. Carrasco, 1982, p. 25.

187 Benet, 1957, pp. 193–4, 210.
188 Neale, 1957b, pp. 226–34.
189 Neale, 1957a, p. 368.
190 Neale, 1957b, p. 227.
191 Ibid. When revisiting the subject some decades later, together with William Schaniel, he adopts a different formulation. Now, the village economy is described as a redistributive process *if viewed from the angle of the threshing-room floor* but reciprocative if viewed *as an arrangement among castes* – 'with members of each caste performing that caste's own speciality for the members of the other castes [in a] complex integrated circuit of obligatory performance without recompense, but in which each was recompensed'. See Schaniel and Neale, 2000, p. 97.
192 One might add that in this he is in distinguished company, alongside the likes of Jonathan Parry (1979) and Louis Dumont (1970, esp. p. 105).
193 Fuller, 1989, pp. 44–5.
194 Bang, 2007.
195 Bloch, 1989, p. 170.
196 LOM, p. 73.
197 33-4, n.d., 'Grant application'.
198 35-7, 1946, 'Marxist Economic Thought', *Journal of Economic History*.
199 'Polanyi provides us with an account of reciprocity and redistributive systems which is inherently changeless', writes Douglass North. 'There is nothing in his framework that explains changes in the mix of the system over time.' North, 1977, p. 715. See also Block and Somers, 1984; Nafissi, 2005; Cartledge, 1983.
200 For an important discussion of how economic categories evolve in interrelation with relations of production, see Banaji, 1977.

Chapter 5 'Disembedded' and 'always embedded' economies

1 35-8, 1947, 'On the Belief in Economic Determinism', *Sociological Review*, 39(1), p. 101
2 51-5, 1961, Annotation to letter from Paul Medow, 22 February.
3 Halperin, 1988a, p. 34; Cangiani et al., 2005, pp. 62–3.
4 Lapavitsas, 2003, p. 37.
5 Barker, 1998, p. 28.

6   Tönnies, 1974, pp. 75, 129–30.
7   Löwy, 2007.
8   Clarke, 1982, pp. 230, 216.
9   Rehmann, 1998.
10   Polanyi, 2002b, p. 239.
11   18-8, n.d., 'The Fascist Virus'.
12   45-2, Abraham Rotstein, 1956, 'Notes of Weekend I with Karl Polanyi', p. 11.
13   Ibid.
14   LOM, p. 52
15   42-2, 1961, 'Dahomey'; see also DST, p. 106.
16   PAME, p. 84.
17   LOM, p. 52.
18   Polanyi, expertly paraphrased in Watson, 2005, p. 97.
19   PAME, p. 70. Emphasis in original.
20   45-3, Abraham Rotstein, 1956, 'Notes of Weekend II with Karl Polanyi', p. 6.
21   See Gemici, 2008.
22   Hopkins, 1957, p. 299. A similar argument has been made with respect to Mao's China by Hann, 2009.
23   Konrád and Szelényi, 1979, p. 54.
24   Keynes, 1936.
25   Lewin, 1985, p. 32.
26   Streeck, 1999, pp. 208–9.
27   Some have claimed that the term is Thurnwald's, but I disagree. See Dale, in press, b.
28   Beckert, 2007.
29   See e.g. Menard and Shirley, 2005.
30   Hart, 2004.
31   Granovetter, 2004.
32   Granovetter, 1985, pp. 481–2.
33   Ibid., pp. 481, 487. Emphasis added.
34   Granovetter, 1985; 1992.
35   Granovetter, 1985, p. 504.
36   Cangiani and Maucourant, 2008. See also Barber, 1995; Randles, 2007, p. 148; and Harvey et al., 2007, pp. 4–5.
37   E.g. Boyer and Hollingsworth, 1999, pp. 444–5.
38   In Krippner, 2004.
39   Ibid.
40   Ibid.
41   In Beckert, 2009, p. 42.
42   Lie, 1991.
43   Gemici, 2008, section seven.
44   Beckert, 2009, p. 50.
45   Block, 2001b. See also Barber, 1995.
46   Block, 1991.

47 Block, 2008.
48 Block, 2001b.
49 Dale, in press, a.
50 Stanfield, 1986, p. 107.
51 McCloskey, 2009.
52 Ibid.
53 Watson, 2005, p. 153.
54 MacIntyre, 2007. See also McMylor, 2003; 1994.
55 Neale, 1957a, p. 364.
56 Cangiani and Maucourant, 2008.
57 Polanyi, 2002a, pp. 96, 103. Emphasis added.
58 Schumpeter, 1954, p. 418.
59 TGT, pp. 185–6, 239, 260.
60 Polanyi, 2002c, p. 259.
61 Polanyi, 2005e, p. 282; TGT, p. 259.
62 Polanyi, 2005d; 1959, p. 162; 49-3, 1954, Letter to Carter, 17 February.
63 45-4, Abraham Rotstein, 1956, 'Notes of Weekend III with Karl Polanyi', pp. 40–4; 20-2, 1938–9, 'Book outline and introduction – *Tame Empires*'.
64 18-33, 1945–6, 'Draft articles'.
65 35-11, 1950–5, 'Draft Manuscript – *Livelihood of Man*'.
66 49-4, Letter Peter Drucker, 1955, to Polanyi, 2 October.

Chapter 6 At the brink of a 'great transformation'? Neoliberalism and the countermovement today

1 Gray, 2002, p. 7
2 Habermas, 2001, p. 85.
3 Boyer and Hollingsworth, 1999, p. 440.
4 Ibid., pp. 60–1 and *passim*.
5 Ibid. p. 437.
6 Ibid.
7 Adaman et al., 2003, p. 358.
8 See e.g. Gray, 2002; Helleiner, 1994; 2000.
9 Davidson, 2010.
10 Devine, 1988; 1992; 2002; Adaman and Devine, 2001. There are also a number of points on which Devine's model differs from Polanyi's, notably the absence of a dyadic structure of Producers' and Consumers' associations and of the distinction between technical and social costs.
11 Glasman, 1996, pp. 56–8.
12 Hann, 1992, p. 156.
13 Ibid., p. 152. As an example of reciprocal behaviour, he mentions families helping one another to build their homes.

14 Hann, 2009. For a critique, see Dale, in press, b.
15 Mendell, 2007.
16 Hettne, 1995, p. 5; 1990.
17 Lomnitz, 2000, p. 247.
18 Buğra, 2002, pp. 392–5.
19 Quijano, 2000, pp. 164, 160.
20 Crichlow, 2000, p. 166.
21 Cockburn, 2006.
22 Altvater and Mahnkopf, 1999.
23 Hettne, 1991, pp. 148–52. To pre-empt misinterpretation, he adds that his case differs from 'the classical Listian argument for a coherent national economy', if only because the Listian model 'is not a viable proposition today'. By 1994 Hettne had come to choose his words more carefully. He now distinguished between a benign West European regionalism and 'the infamous European Fortress – the threat of regional protectionism' that will provoke other regional bloc formations. Hettne, 1994.
24 Cox, 1994.
25 Cox, 1996, p. 533.
26 Mittelman, 1997, p. 3; Chin and Mittelman, 2000, p. 42.
27 Chin and Mittelman, 2000, p. 42.
28 Mittelman, 2000, pp. 227, 233.
29 Adaman et al., 2003, p. 358.
30 Baum, 1996, pp. 57–60.
31 Ringmar, 2005.
32 Van Apeldoorn, 2002.
33 Helleiner, 2000, p. 18.
34 Randles, 2007, p. 265.
35 Kregel, 2000, p. 114.
36 Silver, 2003, pp. 26, 177–8.
37 Stanfield, 1986, p. 119.
38 See e.g. Patten, 2008.
39 See e.g. Stalker, 2000; Harris, 2002; Dale and Cole, 1999.
40 Silver, 2003, pp. 17–20, 106, 167.
41 Arrighi, 1994, pp. 328–9. See also Arrighi and Moore, 2001.
42 See also Arrighi and Silver, 1999.
43 Arrighi, 1994, pp. 75–6, 330–1.
44 Ibid, pp. 328–9.
45 Arrighi, 2005. In fact, Polanyi (1979) did utilize concepts very similar to the spatio-temporal fix in his analysis of the 1930s Depression.
46 Harvey, 2001, p. 324.
47 Arrighi, plenary speech, 10th International Karl Polanyi Conference, Istanbul, October 2005.
48 Arrighi, seminar contribution, 10th International Karl Polanyi Conference, Istanbul, October 2005.

49 Blyth, 2002, p. 2.
50 Hirschman, 1982; James, 2006, Conclusion and *passim*.
51 In addition to others mentioned in this chapter, see Halperin, 2003a and 2003b, p. 44.
52 Laïdi, 2007, p. 17.
53 www.bbc.co.uk/radio4/news/anyquestions.shtml, accessed 5 March 2009.
54 Sorrell, 2009.
55 The economic sociologist Colin Williams (2005) has attempted to rebut the notion that a commodification tendency exists at all. Throughout the high-income world, he argues, recent decades have witnessed a squeeze on state provisioning but this does not equate to a growing dominance of profit-motivated exchange, for the supply of many formerly state-provided goods and services has been trans-ferred to non-profit organizations. Using the ratio of paid to unpaid economic activity as a proxy for the degree of commodification, he finds that most OECD countries have in recent decades become either only marginally more commodified or even slightly less so. Williams makes his case rigorously, but it is not without flaws. In particular, the ratio of paid to unpaid economic activity is at most a very partial measure of commodification. He exaggerates its importance, pays insufficient attention to those 'grey' areas in which economic activity becomes partially privatized and marketized, and ignores the intru-sion of commodity relations into new realms.
56 Gowan, 2009.
57 Monbiot, 2008. Monbiot's sources include reports by the Cato Insti-tute and the US Institute for Policy Studies.
58 See e.g. Harman, 2008, p. 96; Glyn, 2006, p. 17.
59 Tomas Sedlacek, quoted in 'A Crisis is Separating Eastern Europe's Strong from its Weak', www.iht.com/articles/2009/02/24/business, accessed 27 February 2009.
60 Wolf, 2009.
61 Hart, 2009, p. 102
62 See e.g. Žižek, 2008.
63 Lohmann, 2006, p. 89.
64 Kotz, 1999.
65 See Davidson, 2010.

Conclusion

1 Wilkinson and Pickett, 2009; Wilkinson, 2005; 2000.
2 www.unicef-irc.org/publications/pdf/rc7_eng.pdf, accessed 11 June 2008.
3 TGT, p. 261.

4 Polanyi-Levitt, 2000, p. 5.
5 Freedland, 2008.
6 20-8, 1934–5, 'The Fascist Transformation'.
7 TGT, p. 257.
8 Sievers, 1949, pp. 362–3. Emphasis added.
9 Polanyi-Levitt, 1994, p. 133.
10 Gerstenberger, 2000, citing p. 342 in the 1995 German edition of TGT.
11 Katznelson, 2003, p. 44.
12 Ibid., p. 98.
13 Ibid., p. 95.
14 Ibid., p. 160.
15 The error on p. 44, for example, is repeated on pp. 71 and 81.
16 Katznelson, 2003, p. 47.
17 Latham, n.d.
18 O'Connor, 1998.
19 Robert Cox, Stephen Gill, James Mittelman, Vicki Birchfield and Bastiaan van Apeldoorn. There is some irony in the adoption of Polanyi by neo-Gramscians, for, as Burawoy (2003, p. 240) points out, Polanyi 'has little sense of the power of imperialism or the hegemony of world powers that would ground a Gramscian reading of the world order'.
20 Ibid. Others who cast Polanyi as a Marxist include Halperin (1984) and Stroshane (1997).
21 Burawoy, 2003, p. 242.
22 Ibid., p. 231.
23 Ibid., pp. 230–1, 242.
24 Robotham, 2009.
25 Ruggie, 2002, p. 99.
26 45-4, Abraham Rotstein, 1956, 'Notes of Weekend III with Karl Polanyi', p. 33. See also Özel, 1997.
27 Polanyi, 1935.
28 Polanyi, in Randles and Ramlogan, 2007, p. 261.
29 Clark, 2008.
30 Sayre and Löwy, 2001.
31 Ibid., pp. 70–1.
32 Ibid., p. 78.
33 Ibid., p. 79.
34 21-22, 1937, 'Community and Society. The Christian Criticism of Our Social Order'.
35 PAME, pp. 110–11.
36 Nafissi, 2005, p. 128.
37 Polanyi, 1947b, p. 28. A useful article that disputes presentations of Polanyi as a Romantic is Inayatullah and Blaney, 1999.
38 Liverani, 2002.
39 Clark, 2008.

40 PAME, p. 19.
41 Szelényi, 1991, p. 238.
42 Lacher, 1999, p. 326. Emphasis in original.
43 Haynes and Husan, 1998; Block and Somers, 1984.
44 Levitt and Dubner, 2006, pp. 50, 206.
45 'An die Nachgeborenen'.
46 Stern, 2007.

References

1 Documents from the Karl Polanyi Archive

Unless stated otherwise, the following texts are by Karl Polanyi. Numerals in the form '1-11' refer to folder and file numbers respectively.

1-6 (1909) 'The Crisis in Our Ideologies'.
2-22 (1924–7) 'Pure Economic Theory'.
3-1 (1919–33) 'Das Uebersichtsproblem'.
3-2 (1927) 'Das Ubersichtsproblem, ein Hauptproblem des Sozialismus'.
3-3 (1919–33) 'Ist Sozialismus eine Weltanschauung?'.
4-9 (early 1920s) 'Early Christianity and Communism'.
7-9 (1934–46) 'Origins of Institutions'.
8-7 (1934–46) 'The Christian and the World Economic Crisis'.
8-12 (1934–46) 'Notes on readings'.
9-1 (1934–46) 'Notes on readings'.
10-8 (1934–46) 'Notes on Malinowski'.
15-2 (1937–8) Lecture 2: 'Conflicting Philosophies in Modern Society'.
15-4 (1936–40) Morley College Lectures xix, xxiv.
15-4 (1936–40) 'Notes on Free Trade'.
15-8 (1943–4) Government and Industry, Lectures 5, 6, 24.
15-10 (1944) 'Notes on primitive economics'.
15-10 (1944) 'The Study of Human Institutions (Economic and Social)'.
16-11 (1937–8) English Economics, Lecture 21.
16-14 (1939–40) 'Modern European History'.
17-1 (1938–9) 'Canterbury IV'.
17-24 (1945) 'Rise and Decline of the Profit Motive'.
18-8 (n.d.) 'The Fascist Virus'.
18-21 (1937) *Europe To-Day*.

18-33 (1945–6) 'Draft articles'.

18-36 (n.d.) 'Western Socialism: A Tract on Values and Power'.

18-39 (n.d.) 'The Meaning of Peace'.

19-6 G. D. H. Cole (1943) 'Notes on *The Great Transformation*'.

19-13 (n.d.) '1820 vs 1920'.

19-19 (n.d.) 'Individualism and Socialism'.

19-22 (n.d.) 'Christianity and Economic Life'.

20-2 (1938–9) 'Book outline and introduction – *Tame Empires*'.

20-4 (1939–40) 'Common Man's Masterplan'.

20-7 (late 1950s) 'New Frontiers in Economic Thinking'.

20-8 (1934–5) 'The Fascist Transformation'.

20-10 (1938) Newsletters of the Auxiliary Christian Left.

20-11 (1936–8), Christian Left Group: *Bulletin*, 1, 'Trotzkyism. Earlier Works of Marx' and 'Marx on Self-Estrangement'.

20-12 (1938) 'Notes of a Week's Study on *The Early Writings of Karl Marx* and Summary of Discussions on *British Working Class Consciousness*'.

20-14 (1939) 'Russia in the World'.

20-19 (1934) 'What is Fascism?'.

21-2 (1936) 'Xtianity and the new social order'.

21-7 (1937) 'Lecture'.

21-13 (1938) 'Xty and the Present System of Government'.

21-22 (1937) 'Community and Society. The Christian Criticism of Our Social Order'.

22-3 (1947–57) 'Notes – economic anthropology'.

22-10 (1947–60) 'The Role of Market Methods in the Western World up to the High Middle Ages'.

23-2 (1953) 'Notes on capitalism in antiquity'.

23-6 (1947–60) 'Fragments'.

29-10, Felix Schaffer (1973–4) 'Karl Polanyi's Life in Vienna'.

30-1 (1940–84) 'Karl Polanyi: Biographical information'.

30-16 (1963), 'Model of a Classical Economist'.

30-18 (1950) 'The Contribution of Institutional Analysis to the Social Sciences'.

31-7 (n.d.) Lecture notes on 'Capitalism in antiquity'.

31-10 (n.d.) 'Lecture 2. The trend towards an integrated society', Columbia University.

31-11 (1955) 'The Institutionalization of the Economic Process', minutes, 10 March.

31-15 (1948–62) Memorandum No. 1.

31-16 and 31-17 (1953) 'Semantics of General Economic History'.

32-3/4 (1955) 'The Two Meanings of Economic'.

32-6 (1953–5) 'On Forms of Trade in the Ancient Near East'.

33-4 (n.d.) 'Grant application'.

35-7 (1946) 'Marxist Economic Thought', *Journal of Economic History*.

35-8 (1947) 'On the Belief in Economic Determinism', *Sociological Review*, 39(1).

35-11 (1950–5) 'Draft Manuscript – *Livelihood of Man*'.

37-2 (n.d.) 'Methodology – The Methodological Problems Connected with the Question of Capitalism in Antiquity'.

37-3 (1957) 'Freedom in a Complex Society'.

37-11 (1959) 'Aristotle and Galbraith on Affluence'.

38-5 (1963) 'Bücher, Karl (1847–1931)'.

38-8 (1956) 'Draft manuscript, *Trade and Market in the Early Empires*'.

38-9 Geoffrey de Ste Croix (n.d.) Review of TMEE.

39-7 (1954) 'Tyranny or Tyrannies'.

40-2 (1954) 'The economy of the classical polis'.

41-5 (1954) 'Archaic Greece'.

42-1 (1960–3) 'Economy and Society in the Negro Kingdom of Dahomey'.

42-2 (1961) 'Dahomey'.

42-9 (1958) 'KP's remarks on Menger, Brunner & the history of thought about the substantive economy'.

42-9 (n.d.) 'A Note on the Translation of Menger's "Grundsaetze"'.

42-14 (n.d.) 'On the primitivist–modernist debate'.

45-2 Abraham Rotstein (1956) 'Notes of Weekend I with Karl Polanyi'.

45-3 Abraham Rotstein (1956) 'Notes of Weekend II with Karl Polanyi'.

45-4 Abraham Rotstein (1956) 'Notes of Weekend III with Karl Polanyi'.

45-5 Abraham Rotstein (1956) 'Notes of Weekend IV with Karl Polanyi'.

45-12 Abraham Rotstein (1957) 'Notes of Weekend XVII with Karl Polanyi'.

47-12 (1942) Letter to John, 12 September.

48-1 (1946) Letter G. D. H. Cole to Polanyi, 11 February.

48-6 (1951) Letter to Moses Finley, 17 November.

48-6 (1951) Letter to Pierre Crosson, 13 December.

49-1 (1953) Letter to Connie Arensberg, 11 July.

49-2 (1953) Letter to Finley, 18 October.

49-2 (1953) Letter to Bill [Bennett], 8 August.

49-2 (n.d.) Letter to Bill.

49-3 (1954) Letter to Carter, 17 February.

49-4 (1955) Letter to John, 5 January.

49-4 Letter Peter Drucker (1955) to Polanyi, 2 October.

50-1 (1957) Letter to Murray, 17 January.

50-3 (1958) Letter to George [presumably Dalton], 8 October.

50-4 (1959) Letter to George Dalton, 23 April.

51-1 (1959) 'University seminar on the institutionalization of the economic process'.

51-1 (1959) Letter to George Dalton, 16 October.

51-1 (1960) Letter to George Dalton, 29 January,

51-3 (1960) Letter to Geoffrey de Ste Croix, 6 August.

51-4 (1960) Letter to George, 7 November.

51-4 (1961) Transcript of conversation between professors Tsagolov and Polanyi.
51-5 (1961) Annotation to letter from Paul Medow, 22 February.
51-5 (1961) Letter to George Dalton, 27 March.
52-4 (1962) Letter Robbins Burling to Harry Pearson, 7 December.
56-11 (1932–5) Correspondence: Polanyi–Joseph Needham.
56-13 (1963) Letter to Irene Grant, 15 March.
56-13 (1929) Letter to Donald Grant, 7 December.
57-8 (1943) Letter to Michael.

2 Published texts

Fikret Adaman and Pat Devine (2001) 'Participatory Planning as a Deliberative Democratic Process: A Response to Hodgson's Critique', *Economy and Society*, 30(2).

Fikret Adaman, Pat Devine and Begum Ozkaynak (2003) 'Reinstituting the Economic Process: (Re)embedding the Economy in Society and Nature', *International Review of Sociology – Revue Internationale de Sociologie*, 13(2).

Attila Ágh (1990) 'The Hundred Years' Peace: Karl Polanyi on the Dynamics of World Systems', in Kari Polanyi-Levitt, ed., *The Life and Work of Karl Polanyi*, Black Rose.

Kieran Allen (2004) *Max Weber: A Critical Introduction*, Pluto.

Elmar Altvater and Birgit Mahnkopf (1999) *Grenzen der Globalisierung: Ökonomie, Ökologie und Politik in der Weltgesellschaft*, 4th edn, Westfälisches Dampfboot.

Perry Anderson (1975) *Passages from Antiquity to Feudalism*, New Left Books.

—— (2005) *Spectrum*, Verso.

Bastiaan van Apeldoorn (2002) *Transnational Capitalism and the Struggle over European Integration*, Routledge.

Joyce Oldham Appleby (1978) *Economic Thought and Ideology in Seventeenth-Century England*, Princeton University Press.

Rosemary Arnold (1957a) 'A Port of Trade: Whydah on the Guinea Coast', in Karl Polanyi, Conrad M. Arensberg and Harry W. Pearson, eds, *Trade and Market in the Early Empires: Economies in History and Theory*, Free Press.

—— (1957b) 'Separation of Trade and Market: Great Market of Whydah', in Karl Polanyi, Conrad M. Arensberg and Harry W. Pearson, eds, *Trade and Market in the Early Empires: Economies in History and Theory*, Free Press.

Giovanni Arrighi (1994) *The Long Twentieth Century*, Verso.

—— (2005) 'Hegemony Unravelling', *New Left Review*, 32.

Giovanni Arrighi and Jason Moore (2001) 'Capitalist Development in World Historical Perspective', in Robert Albritton, Makoto Itoh, Richard

Westra and Alan Zuege, eds, *Phases of Capitalist Development: Booms, Crises and Globalizations*, Palgrave.

Giovanni Arrighi and Beverly Silver (1999) *Chaos and Governance in the World System*, University of Minnesota Press.

Kenneth Arrow (1978) 'A Cautious Case for Socialism', *Dissent*, 45(Fall).

Maria Aubet (1993) *The Phoenicians and the West: Politics, Colonies and Trade*, Cambridge University Press.

Jairus Banaji (1977) 'Modes of Production in a Materialist Conception of History', *Capital and Class*, 3.

Peter Fibiger Bang (2007) 'Trade and Empire: In Search of Organizing Concepts for the Roman Economy', *Past and Present*, May, 195.

Bernard Barber (1995) 'All Economies are "Embedded": The Career of a Concept and Beyond', *Social Research*, 62(2).

William Barber (1967) *A History of Economic Thought*, Penguin.

Colin Barker (1988) 'State-Building and Poverty: The Poor Law Report of 1834', http://sites.google.com/site/colinbarkersite, accessed 29 August 2009.

———— (1998) 'Industrialism, Capitalism, Value, Force and States', unpublished manuscript. Amended version forthcoming in *Historical Materialism* (2010).

Otto Bauer (1976) *Werkausgabe*, Vol. II, Europa.

Gregory Baum (1996) *Karl Polanyi on Ethics and Economics*, McGill-Queen's University Press.

Christopher Bayly (2004) *The Birth of the Modern World, 1780–1914*, Blackwell.

Jens Beckert (2007) 'The Great Transformation of Embeddedness: Karl Polanyi and the New Economic Sociology', MPIfG Discussion Paper 07/1, Max Planck Institute for the Study of Societies.

———— (2009) 'The Great Transformation of Embeddedness: Karl Polanyi and the New Economic Sociology', in Chris Hann and Keith Hart, eds, *Market and Society: The Great Transformation Today*, Cambridge University Press.

Peter Bedford (2005) 'The Economy of the Near East in the First Millennium BC', in J. G. Manning and Ian Morris, eds, *The Ancient Economy: Evidence and Models*, Stanford University Press.

Francisco Benet (1957) 'Explosive Markets: The Berber Highlands', in Karl Polanyi, Conrad M. Arensberg and Harry W. Pearson, eds, *Trade and Market in the Early Empires: Economies in History and Theory*, Free Press.

Mitchell Bernard (1997) 'Ecology, Political Economy and the Counter-Movement: Karl Polanyi and the Second Great Transformation', in Stephen Gill and James Mittelman, eds, *Innovation and Transformation in International Studies*, Cambridge University Press.

Vicki Birchfield (1999) 'Contesting the Hegemony of Market Ideology: Gramsci's "Good Sense" and Polanyi's "Double Movement"', *Review of International Political Economy*, 6(1).

Maurice Bloch (1989) 'The Symbolism of Money in Imerina', in Maurice Bloch and Jonathan Parry, eds, *Money and the Morality of Exchange*, Cambridge University Press.

Fred Block (1991) 'Contradictions of Self-Regulating Markets', in Marguerite Mendell and Daniel Salée, eds, *The Legacy of Karl Polanyi: Market, State and Society at the End of the Twentieth Century*, Macmillan.

―――― (2001a) 'Introduction', in Karl Polanyi, *The Great Transformation*, Beacon Press.

―――― (2001b) 'Karl Polanyi and the Writing of The Great Transformation', paper presented at the Eighth International Karl Polanyi Conference, Mexico City, November.

―――― (2003) 'Karl Polanyi and the Writing of *The Great Transformation*', *Theory and Society*, 32.

―――― (2008) 'Swimming Against the Current: The Rise of a Hidden Developmental State in the United States', *Politics and Society*, 36(2).

Fred Block and Margaret Somers (1984) 'Beyond the Economistic Fallacy: The Holistic Social Science of Karl Polanyi', in Theda Skocpol, ed., *Vision and Method in Historical Sociology*, Cambridge University Press.

―――― (2003) 'In the Shadow of Speenhamland: Social Policy and the Old Poor Law', *Politics and Society*, 3(2).

Mark Blyth (2002) *Great Transformations: Economic Ideas and Institutional Change in the Twentieth Century*, Cambridge University Press.

Paul Bohannan (1955) 'Some Principles of Exchange and Investment Among the Tiv', *American Anthropologist*, 57.

―――― (1959) 'The Impact of Money on an African Subsistence Economy', *Journal of Economic History*, XIX(4).

Paul Bohannan and George Dalton (1962) 'Introduction', in Paul Bohannan and George Dalton, eds, *Markets in Africa*, Northwestern University Press.

Audrey Bossuyt, Laurence Broze and Victor Ginsburgh (2001) 'On Invisible Trade Relations Between Mesopotamian Cities During the Third Millennium B.C.', *Professional Geographer*, 53(3).

Robert Boyer (1997) 'The Variety and Unequal Performance of Really Existing Markets: Farewell to Doctor Pangloss?', in J. Rogers Hollingsworth and Robert Boyer, eds, *Contemporary Capitalism: The Embeddedness of Institutions*, Cambridge University Press.

Robert Boyer and J. Rogers Hollingsworth (1999) 'Conclusion', in J. Rogers Hollingsworth and Robert Boyer, eds, *Contemporary Capitalism: The Embeddedness of Institutions*, Cambridge University Press.

Kristine Bruland (1990) 'The Transformation of Work in European Industrialization', in Peter Mathias and John Davis, eds, *The First Industrial Revolutions*, Blackwell.

Ayşe Buğra (2002) 'Political and Economic Implications of Reciprocity Networks in Modern Societies', in Fikret Adaman and Pat Devine, eds, *Economy and Society: Money, Capitalism and Transition*, Black Rose.

Michael Burawoy (2003) 'For a Sociological Marxism: The Complementary Convergence of Antonio Gramsci and Karl Polanyi', *Politics and Society*, 31(2).

Robbins Burling (1962) 'Maximization Theories and the Study of Economic Anthropology', *American Anthropologist*, 64(4).

Al Campbell and Justin Elardo (2001) 'Is the Neoclassical Choice Theoretical Model a General Model of Economic Choice? A Formal Presentation of Polanyi's Criticisms', paper presented at the Eighth International Karl Polanyi Conference, Mexico City, November.

Michele Cangiani and Jérôme Maucourant (2008) 'Introduction', in Michele Cangiani and Jérôme Maucourant, eds, *Essais de Karl Polanyi*, Seuil.

Michele Cangiani, Kari Polanyi-Levitt and Claus Thomasberger (2005) 'Die Polarität: Menschliche Freiheit – marktwirtschaftliche Institutionen', in Michele Cangiani, Kari Polanyi-Levitt and Claus Thomasberger, eds, *Chronik der großen Transformation*, Vol. 3, Metropolis.

Niles Carpenter (1922) *Guild Socialism: An Historical and Critical Analysis*, Appleton.

Pedro Carrasco (1982) 'The Political Economy of the Aztec and Inca States', in G. A. Collier, Renato Rosaldo and John Wirth, eds, *The Inca and Aztec States, 1400–1800: Anthropology and History*, Academic Press.

Paul Cartledge (1983) '"Trade and Politics" Revisited; Archaic Greece', in Keith Hopkins, Peter Garnsey and C. R. Whittaker, eds, *Trade in the Ancient Economy*, Chatto and Windus.

Gian Primo Cella (1997) 'Forms of Economic Allocation: Transition and Choice', in Michele Cangiani, ed., *The Milano Papers: Essays in Societal Alternatives*, Black Rose.

Ha-Joon Chang (2002) 'Breaking the Mould: An Institutionalist Political Economy Alternative to the Neo-Liberal Theory of the Market and the State', *Cambridge Journal of Economics*, 26(4).

Anne Chapman (1957) 'Port of Trade Enclaves in Aztec and Maya Civilizations', in Karl Polanyi, Conrad M. Arensberg and Harry W. Pearson, eds, *Trade and Market in the Early Empires: Economies in History and Theory*, Free Press.

Christopher Chase-Dunn, Daniel Pasciuti, Alexis Alvarez and Thomas Hall (n.d.) 'The Ancient Mesopotamian and Egyptian World-Systems', www.irows.ucr.edu/papers/irows14/irows14.htm, accessed 14 March 2008.

Christine Chin and James Mittelman (2000) 'Conceptualizing Resistance to Globalization', in Barry Gills, ed., *Globalization and the Politics of Resistance*, Palgrave.

Gregory Clark (2008) 'Reconsiderations: "The Great Transformation" by Karl Polanyi', www.nysun.com/arts/reconsiderations-the-great-transformation-by-karl/79250, accessed 14 January 2009.

Simon Clarke (1982) *Marx, Marginalism and Modern Sociology: From Adam Smith to Max Weber*, Macmillan.

Alexander Cockburn (2006) 'A Nobel Peace Prize for Neoliberalism? The Myth of Microloans', www.counterpunch.org/cockburn10202006.html, accessed 15 November 2008.

Edward Cohen (1992) *Athenian Economy and Society: A Banking Perspective*, Princeton University Press.

Percy Cohen (1967) 'Economic Analysis and Economic Man', in Raymond Firth, ed., *Themes in Economic Anthropology*, Tavistock.

G. D. H. Cole (1919) *Guild Socialism Re-stated*, Leonard Parsons.

—— (1943) *Fabian Socialism*, George Allen and Unwin.

Lee Congdon (1976) 'Karl Polanyi in Hungary, 1900–19', *Journal of Contemporary History*, 11.

—— (1991) *Exile and Social Thought: Hungarian Intellectuals in Germany and Austria, 1919–1933*, Princeton University Press.

Scott Cook (1968) 'The Obsolete "Anti-Market" Mentality: A Critique of the Substantive Approach to Economic Anthropology', in Edward LeClair and Harold Schneider, eds, *Economic Anthropology: Readings in Theory and Analysis*, Holt, Rinehart and Winston.

Robert Cox (1994) 'The Crisis in World Order and the Challenge to International Organization', *Cooperation and Conflict*, 29(2).

—— (1996) *Approaches to World Order*, Cambridge University Press.

Michaeline Crichlow (2000) 'Conclusion: Under the Shadows of Capital', in Faruk Tabak and Michaeline Crichlow, eds, *Informalization: Process and Structure*, Johns Hopkins University Press.

Philip Curtin (1975) *Economic Change in Precolonial Africa: Senegambia in the Era of the Slave Trade*, University of Wisconsin Press.

Gareth Dale (2008) 'Karl Polanyi's *The Great Transformation*: Perverse Effects, Protectionism, and *Gemeinschaft*', *Economy and Society*, 37(4).

—— (2009) 'Karl Polanyi in Budapest: On His Political and Intellectual Formation', *Archives Européennes de Sociologie/European Journal of Sociology*, 50(1).

—— (2010) 'Karl Polanyi and Oszkar Jászi: Liberal Socialism, the Aster Revolution and the *Tanácsköztársaság*', in Tamás Krausz and Judit Vértes, eds, *A Magyarországi Tanácsköztársaság – 90 éve*, ELTE.

—— (in press, a) 'Social Democracy, Embeddedness, and Decommodification: On the Conceptual Innovations and Intellectual Affiliations of Karl Polanyi', *New Political Economy*, 15(3).

—— (in press, b) 'Polanyian Meditations on Economy and Society: A Review of "Market Society: *The Great Transformation* Today"', *Dialectical Anthropology*.

—— (forthcoming) *Karl Polanyi: An Intellectual Biography* [provisional title], University of Michigan Press.

Gareth Dale and Mike Cole, eds (1999) *The European Union and Migrant Labour*, Berg.

George Dalton (1975) 'Karl Polanyi's Analysis of Long-Distance Trade and His Wider Paradigm', in Jeremy Sabloff and Carl Lamberg-Karlovsky, eds, *Ancient Civilization and Trade*, University of New Mexico Press.

Herman Daly and John Cobb (1994) *For the Common Good: Redirecting the Economy toward Community, the Environment, and a Sustainable Future*, 2nd edn, Beacon Press.

Muhammed Dandamayev (1996) 'An Age of Privatization in Ancient Mesopotamia', in Michael Hudson and Baruch Levine, eds, *Privatization in the Ancient Near East and Classical World*, Peabody Museum of Archaeology and Ethnology.

Neil Davidson (2010) 'Introduction: What Was Neoliberalism?', in Neil Davidson, Patricia McCafferty and David Miller, eds, *Neoliberal Scotland: Class and Society in a Stateless Nation*, Cambridge Scholars Press.

Mike Davis (2001) *Late Victorian Holocausts: El Niño Famines and the Making of the Third World*, Verso.

Anton Deimel (1931) *Sumerische Tempelwirtschaft zur Zeit Urukaginas und seiner Vorgänger*, Analecta Orientalia 2.

Pat Devine (1988) *Democracy and Economic Planning: The Political Economy of a Self-Governing Society*, Polity.

—— (1992) 'Market Socialism or Participatory Planning?', *Review of Radical Political Economics*, 24(3 and 4).

—— (2002) 'Participatory Planning Through Negotiated Coordination', *Science and Society*, 66(1).

Pat Devine, Andrew Pearmain and David Purdy, eds (2009) *Feelbad Britain: How to Make It Better*, Lawrence and Wishart.

Donald Donham (1990) *History, Power, Ideology: Central Issues in Marxism and Anthropology*, Cambridge University Press.

Walter Donlan (1982) 'Reciprocities in Homer', *Classical World*, 75(3).

D. C. Dorward (1976) 'Precolonial Tiv Trade and Cloth Currency', *International Journal of African Historical Studies*, IX(4).

Mary Douglas (1967) 'Primitive Rationing: A Study in Controlled Exchange', in Raymond Firth, ed., *Themes in Economic Anthropology*, Tavistock.

Peter Drucker (1939) *The End of Economic Man: A Study of the New Totalitarianism*, Heinemann.

Gerard Duménil and Dominic Lévy (2004) *Capital Resurgent*, Harvard University Press.

Louis Dumont (1970) *Homo Hierarchicus: The Caste System and its Implications*, Weidenfeld and Nicolson.

Christopher Dyer (1989) *Standards of Living in the Later Middle Ages: Social Change in England c. 1200–1520*, Cambridge University Press.

Barry Eichengreen (1992) *Golden Fetters: The Gold Standard and the Great Depression*, Oxford University Press.

Paul Einzig (1949) *Primitive Money in Its Ethnological, Historical and Economic Aspects*, Eyre and Spottiswoode.

Robert Ellickson and Charles Thorland (1995) 'Ancient Land Law: Mesopotamia, Egypt, Israel', *Chicago-Kent Law Review*, 71.

Friedrich Engels (1844) 'Outlines of a Critique of Political Economy', www.marxists.org/archive/marx/works/1844/df-jahrbucher/outlines.htm, accessed 23 July 2009.

Darel Tai Engen (2001) 'Trade, Traders, and the Economy of Athens in the Fourth Century B.C.E.', in David Tandy, ed., *Prehistory and History: Ethnicity, Class and Political Economy*, Black Rose.

—— (n.d.) 'The Economy of Ancient Greece', http://eh.net/encyclopedia/article/engen.greece, accessed 4 March 2008.

Jean Ensminger (1992) *Making a Market: The Institutional Transformation of an African Society*, Cambridge University Press.

Thomas Hylland Eriksen (2001) *Small Places, Large Issues: An Introduction to Social and Cultural Anthropology*, Pluto.

Gøsta Esping-Andersen (1990) *The Three Worlds of Welfare Capitalism*, Polity.

—— (1999) *Social Foundations of Post-Industrial Economies*, Oxford University Press.

Richard Fardon (1999) *Mary Douglas: An Intellectual Biography*, Routledge.

T. J. Figuiera (1984) 'Karl Polanyi and Ancient Greek Trade', *Ancient World*, 10(1).

Moses Finkelstein (1935) '*Ἔμπορος, Ναύκληρος,* and *Κάπηλος*: A Prolegomena to the Study of Athenian Trade', *Classical Philology*, 30.

Moses Finley (1954) Letter to Polanyi, 7 June. In the possession of the author.

—— (1962 [1954]) *The World of Odysseus*, Penguin.

—— (1973) *The Ancient Economy*, Chatto and Windus.

—— (1974) 'Aristotle and Economic Analysis', in Moses Finley, ed., *Studies in Ancient Society*, Routledge and Kegan Paul.

—— (1975) *The Use and Abuse of History*, Chatto and Windus.

Berkeley Fleming (2001) 'Three Years in Vermont: The Writing of Karl Polanyi's *The Great Transformation*', paper presented at the Eighth International Karl Polanyi Conference', Mexico City, November.

Benjamin Foster (1977) 'Commercial Activity in Sargonic Mesopotamia', in J. D. Hawkins, ed., *Trade in the Ancient Near East: Papers Presented to the XXIII Rencontre Assyriologique Internationale, University of Birmingham*, British School of Archaeology in Iraq.

Robert Frank (2007) *The Economic Naturalist: In Search of Explanations for Everyday Enigmas*, Basic Books.

Ronald Frankenberg (1967) 'Economic Anthropology: One Anthropologist's View', in Raymond Firth, ed., *Themes in Economic Anthropology*, Tavistock.

James Frazer (1922) 'Preface', in Bronislaw Malinowski, *Argonauts of the Western Pacific*, Routledge.

Jonathan Freedland (2008) 'Our Leaders Are Impotent To Tame the Beast: This Crisis Is One of Democracy', *Guardian*, 8 October.

Morton Fried (1967) *The Evolution of Political Society: An Essay in Political Anthropology*, McGraw-Hill Humanities.

Chris Fuller (1989) 'Misconceiving the Grain Heap: A Critique of the Concept of the Indian Jajmani System', in Maurice Bloch and Jonathan Parry, eds, *Money and the Morality of Exchange*, Cambridge University Press.

Clifford Geertz (1980) 'Ports of Trade in Nineteenth-Century Bali', *Research in Economic Anthropology*, 3.

Kurtuluş Gemici (2008) 'Karl Polanyi and the Antinomies of Embeddedness', *Socio-Economic Review*, 6(1).

Heide Gerstenberger (2000) '"Disembedding" and "Re-Embedding"? Oder: Wie aktuell ist Polanyis Analyse "The Great Transformation"', in Rudolf Hickel, Klaus Peter Kisker, Harald Mattfeldt and Axel Troost, eds, *Politik des Kapitals – heute: Festschrift zum 60. Geburtstag von Jörg Huffschmid*, VSA.

Carlo Ginzburg (1994) 'Killing a Chinese Mandarin: The Moral Implications of Distance', *Critical Inquiry*, 21(1).

Maurice Glasman (1996) *Unnecessary Suffering: Managing Market Utopia*, Verso.

S. T. Glass (1966) *The Responsible Society: The Ideas of Guild Socialism*, Longman.

John Gledhill and Mogens Larsen (1982) 'The Polanyi Paradigm and a Dynamic Analysis of Archaic States', in Colin Renfrew, Michael Rowlands and Barbara Abbott Segraves, eds, *Theory and Explanation in Archaeology*, Academic Press.

Andrew Glyn (2006) *Capitalism Unleashed: Finance, Globalization, and Welfare*, Oxford University Press.

Maurice Godelier (1978 [1965]) 'The Object and Method of Economic Anthropology', in David Seddon, ed., *Relations of Production: Marxist Approaches to Economic Anthropology*, Frank Cass.

—— (1981) 'Discussion', *Research in Economic Anthropology*, 4.

—— (1986) *The Mental and the Material: Thought, Economy and Society*, Verso.

Walter Goldfrank (1990) 'Fascism and *The Great Transformation*', in Kari Polanyi-Levitt, ed., *The Life and Work of Karl Polanyi*, Black Rose.

Raymond Goldsmith (1987) *Premodern Financial Systems: A Historical Comparative Study*, Cambridge University Press.

D. M. Goodfellow (1968) 'The Applicability of Economic Theory to So-called Primitive Communities', in Edward LeClair and Harold Schneider, eds, *Economic Anthropology: Readings in Theory and Analysis*, Holt, Rinehart and Winston.

Peter Gowan (2009) 'Crisis in the Heartland', *New Left Review*, 55 (January–February).

Mark Granovetter (1985) 'Economic Action and Social Structure: The Problem of Embeddedness', *American Journal of Sociology*, 91(3).

—————— (1992) 'The Nature of Economic Relations', in Sutti Ortiz, ed., *Understanding Economic Process*, University Press of America.

—————— (2004) 'Opening Remarks on Embeddedness', in Greta Krippner et al., 'Polanyi Symposium: A Conversation on Embeddedness', *Socio-Economic Review*, 2(1).

John Gray (2002) *False Dawn: The Delusions of Global Capitalism*, Granta.

Chris Gregory (1982) *Gifts and Commodities*, Academic Press.

—————— (2009) 'Whatever Happened to Householding', in Chris Hann and Keith Hart, eds, *Market and Society: The Great Transformation Today*, Cambridge University Press.

William Greider (1998) *One World Ready Or Not: The Manic Logic of Global Capitalism*, Simon and Schuster.

David Gress (1998) *From Plato to NATO: The Idea of the West and Its Opponents*, Free Press.

Stephen Gudeman (2001) *The Anthropology of Economy: Community, Market, and Culture*, Blackwell.

—————— (2009) 'Necessity or Contingency: Mutuality and Market', in Chris Hann and Keith Hart, eds, *Market and Society: The Great Transformation Today*, Cambridge University Press.

Jane Guyer (2004) *Marginal Gains: Monetary Transactions in Atlantic Africa*, University of Chicago Press.

Jürgen Habermas (1987) *The Theory of Communicative Action*, Cambridge University Press.

—————— (2001) *The Post-National Constellation*, Polity.

Rhoda Halperin (1984) 'Polanyi, Marx, and the Institutional Paradigm in Economic Anthropology', *Research in Economic Anthropology*, 6.

—————— (1988a) *Economies across Cultures: Towards a Comparative Science of the Economy*, Macmillan.

—————— (1988b) 'The Formalism of Karl Polanyi: Science and Humanism in the Analysis of Economies Across Cultures', paper presented at the Second International Karl Polanyi Conference, Montréal, November.

—————— (1994) *Cultural Economies, Past and Present*, University of Texas Press.

Sandra Halperin (2003a) *War and Social Change in Modern Europe: The Great Transformation Revisited*, Cambridge University Press.

—————— (2003b) 'The Dis-Embedding and Re-Embedding of Capital: Lessons from History', in Sandra Halperin and Gordon Laxer, eds, *Global Civil Society and its Limits*, Palgrave.

Chris Hann (1992) 'Radical Functionalism: The Life and Work of Karl Polanyi', *Dialectical Anthropology*, 17(2).

—————— (2000) *Teach Yourself: Social Anthropology*, Hodder and Stoughton.

—————— (2009) 'Embedded Socialism? Land, Labour, and Money in Eastern Xinjiang', in Chris Hann and Keith Hart, eds, *Market and Society: The Great Transformation Today*, Cambridge University Press.

Tim Harford (2008) *The Logic of Life: Uncovering the New Economics of Everything*, Little, Brown.

Chris Harman (2008) 'Theorising Neoliberalism', *International Socialism*, 117.

Nigel Harris (2002) *Thinking the Unthinkable*, I. B. Tauris.

Gillian Hart (2004) 'The Career of the Concept of Embeddedness', in Greta Krippner et al., 'Polanyi Symposium: A Conversation on Embeddedness', *Socio-Economic Review*, 2(1).

Keith Hart (2000) *Money in an Unequal World: Keith Hart and His Memory Bank*, Texere.

——— (2009) 'Money in the Making of World Society,' in Chris Hann and Keith Hart, eds, *Market and Society: The Great Transformation Today*, Cambridge University Press.

Keith Hart and Chris Hann (n.d.) 'A Short History of Economic Anthropology', http://thememorybank.co.uk/2007/11/09/a-short-history-of-economic-anthropology, accessed 3 January 2009.

David Harvey (2001 [1985]) 'The Geopolitics of Capitalism', in *Spaces of Capital: Towards a Critical Geography*, Edinburgh University Press.

——— (2005) *A Brief History of Neoliberalism*, Oxford University Press.

Mark Harvey, Sally Randles and Ronnie Ramlogan (2007) 'Working With and Beyond Polanyian Perspectives', in Mark Harvey, Sally Randles and Ronnie Ramlogan, eds, *Karl Polanyi: New Perspectives on the Place of the Economy in Society*, Manchester University Press.

Johannes Hasebroek (1933 [1928]) *Trade and Politics in Ancient Greece*, G. Bell and Sons.

F. A. Hayek (1986 [1944]) *The Road to Serfdom*, Routledge.

Mike Haynes and Rumy Husan (1998) 'The State and Market in the Transition Economies: Critical Remarks in the Light of Past History and the Current Experience', *Journal of European Economic History*, 27(3).

Eric Helleiner (1994) *States and the Reemergence of Global Finance*, Cornell University Press.

——— (2000) 'Globalization and *Haute Finance* – *Déjà vu?*,' in Kari Polanyi-Levitt, ed., *Karl Polanyi in Vienna: The Contemporary Significance of The Great Transformation*, Black Rose.

Hazel Henderson (1981) *The Politics of the Solar Age: Alternatives to Economics*, Anchor Press.

Joseph Henrich et al., eds (2004) *Foundations of Human Sociality: Economic Experiments and Ethnographic Evidence from Fifteen Small-Scale Societies*, Oxford University Press.

Melville Herskovits (1968) 'Economizing and Rational Behavior', in Edward LeClair and Harold Schneider, eds, *Economic Anthropology: Readings in Theory and Analysis*, Holt, Rinehart and Winston.

Björn Hettne (1990) 'The Contemporary Crisis: The Rise of Reciprocity', in Kari Polanyi-Levitt, ed., *The Life and Work of Karl Polanyi*, Black Rose.

——— (1991) 'Europe and the Crisis: The Regionalist Scenario Revisited', in Marguerite Mendell and Daniel Salée, eds, *The Legacy of Karl Polanyi: Market, State and Society at the End of the Twentieth Century*, Macmillan.

——— (1994) 'The Regional Factor in the Formation of a New World Order', in Yoshikazu Sakamoto, ed., *Global Transformation: Challenges to the State System*, United Nations University Press.

——— (1995) 'Introduction: The International Political Economy of Transformation', in Robert Cox and Björn Hettne, eds, *International Political Economy: Understanding Global Disorder*, Zed.

Rudolf Hilferding (1904?) 'Böhm-Bawerk's Criticism of Marx', www.marx. org/archive/hilferding/1904/criticism/index.htm, accessed 23 July 2009.

——— (1981 [1909]) *Finance Capital*, Routledge.

Albert Hirschman (1982) *Shifting Involvements: Private Interest and Public Action*, Princeton University Press.

Paul Hirst (1994) *Associative Democracy: New Forms of Economic and Social Governance*, Polity.

Kenneth Hirth, ed. (1984) *Trade and Exchange in Early Mesoamerica*, University of New Mexico Press.

Richard Hodges (1982) *Dark Age Economics: The Origins of Towns and Trade A.D. 600–1000*, Duckworth.

Geoffrey Hodgson (2001) *How Economics Forgot History: The Problem of Historical Specificity in Social Science*, Routledge.

Martin Hollis (1977) *Models of Man: Philosophical Thoughts on Social Action*, Cambridge University Press.

Terence Hopkins (1957) 'Sociology and the Substantive View of the Economy', in Karl Polanyi , Conrad M. Arensberg and Harry W. Pearson, eds, *Trade and Market in the Early Empires: Economies in History and Theory*, Free Press.

Michael Hudson (1996a) 'Introduction', in Michael Hudson and Baruch Levine, eds, *Privatization in the Ancient Near East and Classical World*, Peabody Museum of Archaeology and Ethnology.

——— (1996b) 'The Dynamics of Privatization, From the Bronze Age to the Present', in Michael Hudson and Baruch Levine, eds, *Privatization in the Ancient Near East and Classical World*, Peabody Museum of Archaeology and Ethnology.

——— (1996c) 'Early Privatization and its Consequences', in Michael Hudson and Baruch Levine, eds, *Privatization in the Ancient Near East and Classical World*, Peabody Museum of Archaeology and Ethnology.

——— (1999) 'Methodology Discussion', in Michael Hudson and Baruch Levine, eds, *Urbanization and Land Ownership in the Ancient Near East*, Peabody Museum of Archaeology and Ethnology.

——— (2000a) 'Mesopotamia and Classical Antiquity', *American Journal of Economics and Sociology*, December, 59(5).

——— (2000b) 'Karl Bücher's Role in the Evolution of Economic Anthropology', in Jürgen Backhaus, ed., *Karl Bücher: Theory – History – Anthropology – Non-Market Economies*, Metropolis.

——— (2002) 'Reconstructing the Origins of Interest-Bearing Debt and the Logic of Clean Slates', in Michael Hudson and Marc van de Mieroop, eds, *Debt and Economic Renewal in the Ancient Near East*, CDL Press.

——— (2004a) 'The Archaeology of Money in Light of Mesopotamian Records', in L. Randall Wray, ed., *Credit and State Theories of Money: The Contributions of A. Mitchell Innes*, Edward Elgar.

——— (2004b) 'The Development of Money-of-Account in Sumer's Temples', in Michael Hudson and Cornelia Wunsch, eds, *Creating Economic Order: Record-Keeping, Money and the Development of Accounting in the Ancient Near East*, CDL Press.

——— (2005/6) 'Book Review of Chancier, F., et al., eds, *Autour de Polanyi: vocabularies, théories et modalities des échanges*, and J. G. Manning and Ian Morris, eds, *The Ancient Economy: Evidence and Models*', *Archiv für Orientforschung*, 51.

——— (n.d.) 'Did the Phoenicians Introduce the Idea of Interest to Greece and Italy – and If So, When?', www.michael-hudson.com/articles/debt/9003PhoeniciansInterest.html, accessed 6 June 2009.

Sally Humphreys (1978) *Anthropology and the Greeks*, Routledge.

Naeem Inayatullah and David Blaney (1999) 'Towards an Ethnological IPE: Karl Polanyi's Double Critique of Capitalism', *Millennium*, 28(2).

Barry Isaac (2005) 'Karl Polanyi', in James Carrier, ed., *A Handbook of Economic Anthropology*, Edward Elgar.

Makoto Itoh and Costas Lapavitsas (1999) *Political Economy of Money and Finance*, Macmillan.

Harold James (2006) *The Roman Predicament: How the Rules of International Order Create the Politics of Empire*, Princeton University Press.

Alan Jenkins (1977) '"Substantivism" as a Theory of Economic Forms', in Barry Hindess, ed., *Sociological Theories of the Economy*, Macmillan.

Bob Jessop (2002) 'The Social Embeddedness of the Economy and its Implications for Economic Governance', in Fikret Adaman and Pat Devine, eds, *Economy and Society: Money, Capitalism and Transition*, Black Rose.

Chris Jones and Tony Novack (1980) 'The State and Social Policy', in P. Corrigan, ed., *Capitalism, State Formation and Marxist Theory*, Quartet.

Leonard Joy (1967) 'One Economist's View of the Relationship between Economics and Anthropology', in Raymond Firth, ed., *Themes in Economic Anthropology*, Tavistock.

Ira Katznelson (2003) *Desolation and Enlightenment: Political Knowledge After Total War, Totalitarianism and the Holocaust*, Columbia University Press.

John Maynard Keynes (1930) *A Treatise on Money*, Vol. 2, Macmillan.

——— (1936) *The General Theory of Employment, Interest and Money*, Macmillan.

Charles Kindleberger (1986) *The World in Depression, 1929–1939*, University of California Press.

Frank Kirkpatrick (2005) *John Macmurray: Community Beyond Political Philosophy*, Rowman and Littlefield.

György Konrád and Ivan Szelényi (1979) *The Intellectuals on the Road to Class Power*, Brighton.

David Kotz (1999) 'The State, Globalization, and Phases of Capitalist Development', in Robert Albritton, Makoto Itoh, Richard Westra and Alan Zuege, eds, *Phases of Capitalist Development: Booms, Crises and Globalizations*, Palgrave.

J. A. Kregel (2000) 'On the Economic Implications of (Mis)understanding Markets in Transition Countries', in Kari Polanyi-Levitt, ed., *Karl Polanyi in Vienna: The Contemporary Significance of The Great Transformation*, Black Rose.

Greta Krippner (2004) 'Opening Remarks on Embeddedness', in Greta Krippner et al., 'Polanyi Symposium: A Conversation on Embeddedness', *Socio-Economic Review*, 2(1).

Rick Kuhn (2007) *Henryk Grossman and the Recovery of Marxism*, University of Illinois Press.

Adam Kuper (1996) *Anthropology and Anthropologists: The Modern British School*, 3rd edn, Routledge.

Hannes Lacher (1999) 'The Politics of the Market: Re-reading Karl Polanyi', *Global Society*, 13(3).

Zaki Laïdi (2007) *The Great Disruption*, Polity.

Carl Lamberg-Karlovsky (1975) 'Third Millennium Modes of Exchange and Modes of Production', in Jeremy Sabloff and Carl Lamberg-Karlovsky, eds, *Ancient Civilization and Trade*, University of New Mexico Press.

—— (1976) 'The Economic World of Sumer', in Denise Schmandt-Besserat, ed., *The Legacy of Sumer*, Undena.

—— (1978) 'Comment on Philip Kohl', *Current Anthropology*, 19(3).

—— (1986) 'Comment', *Current Anthropology*, 27(5).

Janet Tai Landa (1994) *Trust, Ethnicity, and Identity: Beyond the New Institutional Economics of Ethnic Trading Networks, Contract Law, and Gift-Exchange*, University of Michigan Press.

Costas Lapavitsas (2003) *Social Foundations of Markets, Money and Credit*, Routledge.

Anthony Latham (1971) 'Currency, Credit and Capitalism on the Cross River in the Pre-Colonial Era', *Journal of African History*, XII(4).

—— (n.d.) 'Karl Polanyi: Some Observations,' www.history.ac.uk/resources/e-seminars/latham-paper, accessed 27 August 2008.

Robin Law (1995) 'Cowries, Gold and Dollars: Exchange Rate Instability and Domestic Price Inflation in Dahomey in the Eighteenth and Nineteenth Centuries', in Jane Guyer, ed., *Money Matters: Instability, Values and Social Payments in the Modern History of West African Communities*, Heinemann.

Edward LeClair and Harold Schneider (1968) 'Introduction', in Edward LeClair and Harold Schneider, eds, *Economic Anthropology: Readings in Theory and Analysis*, Holt, Rinehart and Winston.

Steven Levitt and Stephen Dubner (2006) *Freakonomics*, Penguin.

Moshe Lewin (1985) *The Making of the Soviet System: Essays in the Social History of Interwar Russia*, Methuen.

Andrew Leyshon and Nigel Thrift (1997) *Money/Space: Geographies of Monetary Transformation*, Routledge.

John Lie (1991) 'Embedding Polanyi's Market Society', *Sociological Perspectives*, 34(2).

Harry Liebersohn (1988) *Fate and Utopia in German Sociology, 1870–1923*, MIT Press.

Christopher Lind (1994) 'How Karl Polanyi's Moral Economy Can Help Religious and Other Social Critics', in Kenneth McRobbie, ed., *Humanity, Society and Commitment: On Karl Polanyi*, Black Rose.

Brink Lindsey (2001) 'The Decline and Fall of the First Global Economy: How Nationalism, Protectionism, and Collectivism Spawned a Century of Dictatorship and War', www.thefreelibrary.com, accessed 23 March 2009.

Alain Lipietz (1997) 'The Next Transformation', in Michele Cangiani, ed., *The Milano Papers: Essays in Societal Alternatives*, Black Rose.

Mario Liverani (2002) *International Relations in the Ancient Near East, 1600–1100 BC*, Macmillan.

—— (2005) 'The Near East: The Bronze Age', in J. G. Manning and Ian Morris, eds, *The Ancient Economy: Evidence and Models*, Stanford University Press.

Larry Lohmann (2006) 'Carbon Trading: A Critical Conversation on Climate Change, Privatisation and Power', *Development Dialogue*, 48 (September).

Larissa Lomnitz (2000) 'Reciprocity and the Informal Economy in Latin America', in Kari Polanyi-Levitt, ed., *Karl Polanyi in Vienna: The Contemporary Significance of The Great Transformation*, Black Rose.

John Love (1991) 'Max Weber and the Theory of Ancient Capitalism', in Peter Hamilton, ed., *Max Weber: Critical Assessments*, Vol. 2, Taylor and Francis.

Michael Löwy (2007) 'Marx and Weber: Critics of Capitalism', *New Politics*, 11(2).

Georg Lukacs (1971 [1923]) *History and Class Consciousness: Studies in Marxist Dialectics*, Merlin.

—— (1980 [1962]) *The Destruction of Reason*, Merlin.

Alisdair MacIntyre (2007 [1981]) *After Virtue*, Duckworth.

John Macmurray (1933) *The Philosophy of Communism*, Faber and Faber.

Henry Sumner Maine (1863) *Ancient Law: Its Connection with the Early History of Society, and its Relation to Modern Ideas*, 2nd edn, John Murray.

Bronislaw Malinowski (1922) *Argonauts of the Western Pacific*, Routledge.

Michael Mann (1986) *The Sources of Social Power*, Vol. 1, Cambridge University Press.

Patrick Manning (1982) *Slavery, Colonialism and Economic Growth in Dahomey, 1640–1960*, Cambridge University Press.

Paul Mantoux (1928) *The Industrial Revolution in the Eighteenth Century: An Outline of the Beginnings of the Modern Factory System in England*, Jonathan Cape.

Stephen Marglin (2008) *The Dismal Science: How Thinking Like an Economist Undermines Community*, Harvard University Press.

David Marquand (1997) *The New Reckoning: Capitalism, States and Citizens*, Polity.

Jacob Marschak (1924) '"Wirtschaftsrechnung und Gemeinwirtschaft": Zur Misesschen These von der Unmöglichkeit sozialistischer Gemeinwirtschaft', *Archiv für Sozialwissenschaft und Sozialpolitik*, 51(2).

Alberto Martinelli (1987) 'The Economy as an Institutional Process', *Telos*, 73.

Karl Marx (1989 [1867]) *Das Kapital*, Vol. I, Dietz.

——— (1992 [1863–7]) *Marx Engels Gesammelte Ausgabe*, II 4.2, Dietz.

——— (1973) *Grundrisse*, Penguin.

Bill Maurer (2006) 'The Anthropology of Money', *Annual Review of Anthropology*, 35.

Anne Mayhew, Walter Neale and David Tandy (1983) 'Markets in the Ancient Near East: A Challenge to Silver's Argument and Use of Evidence', *Journal of Economic History*, XLV(1).

Deirdre McCloskey (1997) 'Polanyi Was Right, and Wrong', *Eastern Economic Journal*, Fall, 23(4).

——— (2009) 'Bourgeois Towns: How Capitalism Became Virtuous, 1300–1776', www.deirdremccloskey.org/docs/towns2.doc, accessed 7 February 2009.

Peter McMylor (1994) *Alasdair MacIntyre: Critic of Modernity*, Routledge.

——— (2003) 'Moral Philosophy and Economic Sociology: What MacIntyre Learnt from Polanyi', *International Review of Sociology – Revue Internationale de Sociologie*, 13(2).

David McNally (1993) *Against the Market*, Verso.

——— (2006) *Another World Is Possible: Globalization and Anti-Capitalism*, Arbeiter Ring.

Kenneth McRobbie, ed. (1994) *Humanity, Society and Commitment: On Karl Polanyi*, Black Rose.

——— (2000) 'Vision and Expression: Literature and *The Great Transformation*', in Kari Polanyi-Levitt, ed., *Karl Polanyi in Vienna: The Contemporary Significance of The Great Transformation*, Black Rose.

Scott Meikle (1979) 'Aristotle and the Political Economy of the Polis', *Journal of Hellenic Studies*, XCIX.

────── (1991) 'Aristotle and Exchange Value', in David Keyt and Fred Miller, eds, *A Companion to Aristotle's Politics*, Blackwell.

────── (1995) 'Modernism, Economics, and the Ancient Economy', *Proceedings of the Cambridge Philological Society*, 41.

Claude Meillassoux, ed. (1971) *The Development of Indigenous Trade and Markets in West Africa*, Oxford University Press.

────── (1972) 'From Reproduction to Production: A Marxist Approach to Economic Anthropology', *Economy and Society* 1(1).

Claude Menard and Mary Shirley (2005) 'Introduction', in Claude Menard and Mary Shirley, eds, *Handbook of New Institutional Economics*, Edward Elgar.

Margie Mendell (2007) 'Karl Polanyi and the Instituted Process of Economic Democratisation', in Mark Harvey, Sally Randles and Ronnie Ramlogan, eds, *Karl Polanyi: New Perspectives on the Place of the Economy in Society*, Manchester University Press.

Marguerite Mendell and Daniel Salée, eds (1991) *The Legacy of Karl Polanyi; Market, State and Society at the End of the Twentieth Century*, Macmillan

Carl Menger (1923) *Grundsätze der Volkswirtschaftslehre*, 2nd edn, Hölder-Pichler-Tempsky.

Barry Michie (1994) 'Reevaluating Economic Rationality: Individuals, Information and Institutions', in James Acheson, ed., *Anthropology and Institutional Economics*, University Press of America.

Eric Mielants (2007) *The Origins of Capitalism and the Rise of the West*, Temple University Press.

Marc van de Mieroop (2002) 'A History of Near Eastern Debt?', in Michael Hudson and Marc van de Mieroop, eds, *Debt and Economic Renewal in the Ancient Near East*, CDL Press.

Paul Millett (1983) 'Maritime Loans and the Structure of Credit in Fourth-Century Athens', in Keith Hopkins, Peter Garnsey and C. R. Whittaker, eds, *Trade in the Ancient Economy*, Chatto and Windus.

────── (2002) *Lending and Borrowing in Ancient Athens*, Cambridge University Press.

Alan Milward (2005 [1981]) 'Tariffs as Constitutions', in Kevin O'Rourke, ed., *The International Trading System, Globalization and History*, Vol. I, Edward Elgar.

Philip Mirowski (2002) *Machine Dreams: Economics Becomes a Cyborg Science*, Cambridge University Press.

Ludwig von Mises (1925) 'Neue Beiträge zum Problem der sozialistischen Wirtschaftsrechnung', *Archiv für Sozialwissenschaft und Sozialpolitik*, 51(2).

────── (1932) *Die Gemeinwirtschaft: Untersuchungen über den Sozialismus*, 2nd edn., Gustav Fischer.

———— (1972) 'Economic Calculation in the Socialist Commonwealth', in Alec Nove and D. M. Nuti, eds, *Socialist Economics: Selected Readings*, Penguin.

James Mittelman (1997) 'The Dynamics of Globalization', in James Mittelman, ed., *Globalization: Critical Reflections*, Lynne Rienner.

———— (2000) *The Globalization Syndrome*, Princeton University Press.

George Monbiot (2008) 'The Free Market Preachers Have Long Practised State Welfare for the Rich', *Guardian*, 30 September.

Stanley Moore (1980) *Marx and the Choice Between Socialism and Communism*, Harvard University Press.

Ian Morris (1994) 'The Athenian Economy Twenty Years after *The Ancient Economy*', *Classical Philology*, 89(4).

K. P. Moseley (1979) 'The Political Economy of Dahomey', *Research in Economic Anthropology*, 2.

Ronaldo Munck (2006) 'Globalisation, Labour and the Polanyi Problem', www.theglobalsite.ac.uk/press/402munck.htm, accessed 15 February 2008.

Patrick Murray (1997) 'General Introduction: On Studying Commercial Life', in Patrick Murray, ed., *Reflections on Commercial Life: An Anthology of Classic Texts from Plato to the Present*, Routledge.

Patrick Murray and Jeanne Schuler (n.d.) 'Why Wealth is a Poor Concept', unpublished manuscript.

Mohammad Nafissi (2005) *Ancient Athens and Modern Ideology: Value, Theory and Evidence in Historical Sciences*, Institute of Classical Studies.

Endre Nagy (1994) 'After Brotherhood's Golden Age: Karl and Michael Polanyi', in Kenneth McRobbie, ed., *Humanity, Society and Commitment: On Karl Polanyi*, Black Rose.

Heino Heinrich Nau, ed. (1998) *Gustav Schmoller: Historisch-ethische Nationalökonomie als Kulturwissenschaft. Ausgewaehlte methodologische Schriften*, Metropolis.

Walter Neale (1957a) 'The Market in Theory and History', in Karl Polanyi, Conrad M. Arensberg and Harry W. Pearson, eds, *Trade and Market in the Early Empires: Economies in History and Theory*, Free Press.

———— (1957b) 'Reciprocity and Redistribution in the Indian Village: Sequel to Some Notable Discussions', in Karl Polanyi, Conrad M. Arensberg and Harry W. Pearson, eds, *Trade and Market in the Early Empires: Economies in History and Theory*, Free Press.

———— (1977) 'Editor's Introduction', in Karl Polanyi, *The Livelihood of Man*, Academic Press.

H. G. Niemeyer (1990) 'The Phoenicians in the Mediterranean: A Non-Greek Model for Expansion and Settlement in Antiquity', in Jean-Paul Descoeudres, ed., *Greek Colonists and Native Populations*, Clarendon Press.

Wilfried Nippel (1990) *Griechen, Barbaren und 'Wilde': Alte Geschichte und Sozialanthropologie*, Fischer.

Douglass North (1977) 'Markets and Other Allocation Systems in History: The Challenge of Karl Polanyi', *Journal of European Economic History*, 6.

James O'Connor (1998) *Natural Causes: Essays in Ecological Marxism*, Guilford.

Claus Offe (1998) 'Fifty Years After the "Great Transformation": Reflections on Social Order and Political Agency', in Takashi Inoguchi, Edward Newman and John Keane, eds, *The Changing Nature of Democracy*, United Nations University Press.

Leo Oppenheim (1957) 'A Bird's-Eye View of Mesopotamian Economic History', in Karl Polanyi, Conrad M. Arensberg and Harry W. Pearson, eds, *Trade and Market in the Early Empires: Economies in History and Theory*, Free Press.

——— (1964) *Ancient Mesopotamia: Portrait of a Dead Civilization*, University of Chicago Press.

Franz Oppenheimer (1910) *Theorie der reinen und politischen Ökonomie: Ein Lehr- und Lesebuch für Studierende und Gebildete*, Georg Reimer.

Robert Owen (1927 [1813–20]) *A New View of Society and Other Writings*, J. M. Dent.

Hüseyin Özel (1997) 'Reclaiming Humanity: The Social Theory of Karl Polanyi', PhD dissertation, University of Utah.

Jonathan Parry (1979) *Caste and Kinship in Kangra*, Routledge and Kegan Paul.

Prabhat Patnaik (2009) *The Value of Money*, Columbia University Press.

Chris Patten (2008) *What Next? Surviving the Twenty-First Century*, Allen Lane.

Harry Pearson (1957a) 'The Economy Has No Surplus: Critique of a Theory of Development', in Karl Polanyi, Conrad M. Arensberg and Harry W. Pearson, eds, *Trade and Market in the Early Empires: Economies in History and Theory*, Free Press.

——— (1957b) 'The Secular Debate on Economic Primitivism', in Karl Polanyi, Conrad M. Arensberg and Harry W. Pearson, eds, *Trade and Market in the Early Empires: Economies in History and Theory*, Free Press.

Helge Peukert (2001) 'Bridging Old and New Institutional Economics: Gustav Schmoller and Douglass C. North, Seen with Oldinstitutionalists' Eyes', *European Journal of Law and Economics*, 11(2).

Geoffrey Pilling (1972) 'The Law of Value in Ricardo and Marx', *Economy and Society*, 1(3).

——— (n.d.) *The Crisis of Keynesian Economics*, www.marxists.org/archive/pilling, accessed 3 March 2009.

Stuart Plattner (1989) 'Introduction', in Stuart Plattner, *Economic Anthropology*, Stanford University Press.

Karl Polanyi (1925a) 'Neue Erwägungen zu unserer Theorie und Praxis', *Der Kampf*, (January).

—— (1925b) 'Die funktionelle Theorie der Gesellschaft und das Problem der sozialistischen Rechnungslegung', *Archiv für Sozialwissenschaft und Sozialpolitik*, 52.

—— (1935) 'The Essence of Fascism', in Karl Polanyi and Donald Kitchin, eds, *Christianity and the Social Revolution*, Gollancz.

—— (1947a) 'On the Belief in Economic Determinism', *Sociological Review*, 39(1).

—— (1947b) *The Citizen and Foreign Policy*, Workers' Educational Association.

—— (1947c) 'Our Obsolete Market Mentality', *Commentary*, 3(2).

—— (1957a) 'Aristotle Discovers the Economy', in Karl Polanyi, Conrad M. Arensberg and Harry W. Pearson, eds, *Trade and Market in the Early Empires: Economies in History and Theory*, Free Press.

—— (1957b) 'Marketless Trading in Hammurabi's Time', in Karl Polanyi, Conrad M. Arensberg and Harry W. Pearson, eds, *Trade and Market in the Early Empires: Economies in History and Theory*, Free Press.

—— (1959) 'Anthropology and Economic Theory', in Morton Fried, ed., *Readings in Anthropology*, Vol. II, Thomas Crowell.

—— (1960) 'The Early Development of Trade, Money and Market Institutions', *Year Book of the American Philosophical Society*.

—— (1968) 'Karl Bücher', in David Sills, ed., *International Encyclopedia of the Social Sciences*, Vol. 2, Macmillan.

—— (1971) 'Carl Menger's Two Meanings of "Economic"', in George Dalton, ed., *Studies in Economic Anthropology*, American Anthropological Association.

—— (1979) 'Der Mechanismus der Weltwirtschaftskrise', in S. C. Humphreys, ed., *Oekonomie und Gesellschaft*, Suhrkamp.

—— (2000) 'Letter to a Friend, 1925', in Kari Polanyi-Levitt, ed., *Karl Polanyi in Vienna: The Contemporary Significance of The Great Transformation*, Black Rose.

—— (2002a [1928]) 'Liberale Sozialreformer in England', in Michele Cangiani and Claus Thomasberger, eds, *Chronik der großen Transformation*, Vol. 1, Metropolis.

—— (2002b [1934]) 'Lancashire als Menschheitsfrage', in Michele Cangiani and Claus Thomasberger, eds, *Chronik der großen Transformation*, Vol. 1, Metropolis.

—— (2002c [1934]) 'Tory Planwirtschafter', in Michele Cangiani and Claus Thomasberger, eds, *Chronik der großen Transformation*, Vol. 1, Metropolis.

—— (2002d [1934]) 'Wirtschaft und Demokratie', in Michele Cangiani and Claus Thomasberger, eds, *Chronik der großen Transformation*, Vol. 1, Metropolis.

—— (2003) 'Neue Schutzzollwelle', in Michele Cangiani and Claus Thomasberger, eds, *Chronik der großen Transformation*, Vol. 2, Metropolis.

—— (2005a) 'Über die Freiheit', in Michele Cangiani, Kari Polanyi-Levitt and Claus Thomasberger, eds, *Chronik der großen Transformation*, Vol. 3, Metropolis.

—— (2005b) 'Sozialistische Rechnungslegung', in Michele Cangiani, Kari Polanyi-Levitt and Claus Thomasberger, eds, *Chronik der großen Transformation*, Vol. 3, Metropolis.

—— (2005c) 'Zur Sozialisierungsfrage', in Michele Cangiani, Kari Polanyi-Levitt and Claus Thomasberger, eds, *Chronik der großen Transformation*, Vol. 3, Metropolis.

—— (2005d) 'Über den Glauben an den ökonomischen Determinismus', in Michele Cangiani, Kari Polanyi-Levitt and Claus Thomasberger, eds, *Chronik der großen Transformation*, Vol. 3, Metropolis.

—— (2005e) 'Der faschistische Virus', in Michele Cangiani, Kari Polanyi-Levitt and Claus Thomasberger, eds, *Chronik der großen Transformation*, Vol. 3, Metropolis.

Karl Polanyi, Conrad M. Arensberg and Harry W. Pearson (1957) 'The Place of Economies in Societies', in Karl Polanyi, Conrad M. Arensberg and Harry W. Pearson, eds, *Trade and Market in the Early Empires: Economies in History and Theory*, Free Press.

Kari Polanyi-Levitt (1990) 'Introduction', in Kari Polanyi-Levitt, ed., *The Life and Work of Karl Polanyi*, Black Rose.

—— (1994) 'Karl Polanyi as Socialist', in Kenneth McRobbie, ed., *Humanity, Society and Commitment: On Karl Polanyi*, Black Rose.

—— (2000) '*The Great Transformation*: From 1920 to 1990', in Kari Polanyi-Levitt, ed., *Karl Polanyi in Vienna: The Contemporary Significance of The Great Transformation*, Black Rose.

Kari Polanyi-Levitt and Margie Mendell (1987) '*Karl Polanyi*: His Life and Times', *Studies in Political Economy*, Spring, 27.

Jonathon Porritt (2005) *Capitalism as if the Earth Matters*, Earthscan.

J. I. Prattis (1982) 'Synthesis, or a New Problematic in Economic Anthropology', *Theory and Society*, 11.

—— (1987) 'Alternative Views of Economy in Economic Anthropology', in John Clammer, ed., *Beyond the New Economic Anthropology*, St Martin's Press.

Alison Quiggin (1949) *A Survey of Primitive Money: The Beginnings of Currency*, Methuen.

Aníbal Quijano (2000) 'The Growing Significance of Reciprocity from Below: Marginality and Informality in Debate', in Faruk Tabak and Michaeline Crichlow, eds, *Informalization: Process and Structure*, Johns Hopkins University Press.

Sally Randles (2007) 'Issues for a Neo-Polanyian Research Agenda in Economic Sociology', in Mark Harvey, Sally Randles and Ronnie Ramlogan, eds, *Karl Polanyi: New Perspectives on the Place of the Economy in Society*, Manchester University Press.

Sally Randles and Ronnie Ramlogan (2007) 'Corporate Merger as Dialectical Double Movement and Instituted Process', in Mark Harvey, Sally Randles and Ronnie Ramlogan, eds, *Karl Polanyi: New Perspectives on the Place of the Economy in Society*, Manchester University Press.

James Redfield (1986) 'The Development of the Market in Archaic Greece', in B. L. Anderson and A. J. H. Latham, eds, *The Market in History*, Croom Helm.

Jan Rehmann (1998) *Max Weber: Modernisierung als passive Revolution. Kontextstudien zu Politik, Philosophie und Religion im Übergang zum Fordismus*, Argument.

Colin Renfrew (1972) *The Emergence of Civilization: The Cyclades and the Aegean in the Third Millennium B.C.*, Methuen.

Johannes Renger (1994) 'On Economic Structures in Ancient Mesopotamia', *Orientalia*, 63.

———— (2002) 'Royal Edicts of the Old Babylonian Period: Structural Background', in Michael Hudson and Marc van de Mieroop, eds, *Debt and Economic Renewal in the Ancient Near East*, CDL Press.

Robert Revere (1957) '"No Man's Coast": Ports of Trade in the Eastern Mediterranean', in Karl Polanyi, Conrad M. Arensberg and Harry W. Pearson, eds, *Trade and Market in the Early Empires: Economies in History and Theory*, Free Press.

David Ricardo (1973) *The Principles of Political Economy and Taxation*, J. M. Dent.

Elmar Rieger and Stephan Leibfried (2003) *Limits to Globalization: Welfare States and the World Economy*, Polity.

Erik Ringmar (2005) *Surviving Capitalism: How We Learned To Live With the Market and Remained Almost Human*, Anthem Press.

Don Robotham (2009) 'Afterword: Learning From Polanyi 2', in Chris Hann and Keith Hart, *Market and Society: The Great Transformation Today*, Cambridge University Press.

Raymond Rogers (1994) *Nature and the Crisis of Modernity: A Critique of Contemporary Discourse on Managing the Earth*, Black Rose.

John Ruggie (1982) 'International Regimes, Transactions, and Change: Embedded Liberalism in the Postwar Economic Order', *International Organization*, 36(2).

———— (2002) 'At Home Abroad, Abroad at Home: International Liberalization and Domestic Stability in the New World Economy', in Eivind Hovden and Edward Keene, eds, *The Globalization of Liberalism*, Palgrave.

Bertrand Russell (1918) *Roads to Freedom: Socialism, Anarchism and Syndicalism*, Cornwall Press.

Karen Sacks and Karen Brodkin (1982) *Sisters and Wives: The Past and Future of Sexual Equality*, University of Illinois Press.

Marshall Sahlins (1965) 'On the Sociology of Primitive Exchange', in Association of Social Anthropologists of the Commonwealth, *The Relevance of Models for Social Anthropology*, Tavistock.

―――― (2004) *Stone Age Economics*, new edn, Aldine Transaction.

Richard Saller (2005) 'Framing the Debate Over Growth in the Ancient Economy', in J. G. Manning and Ian Morris, eds, *The Ancient Economy: Evidence and Models*, Stanford University Press.

Paul Samuelson (2009) 'On Economics, Obama Would Be Wise To Steer a Middle Course', *Independent*, 19 January.

Roger Sandall (2001) 'The Culture Cult', www.rogersandall.com/Archive_Anthropological-Farce_Amazing-Dahomey.php, accessed 17 February 2009.

Mahir Şaul (2004) 'Money in Colonial Transition: Cowries and Francs in West Africa', *American Anthropologist*, 106(1).

Robert Sayre and Michael Löwy (2001) *Romanticism Against the Tide of Modernity*, Duke University Press.

William Schaniel and Walter Neale (2000) 'Karl Polanyi's Forms of Integration as Ways of Mapping', *Journal of Economic Issues*, 34(1).

Carl Schmitt (1996) *The Concept of the Political*, University of Chicago Press.

Gustav Schmoller (1902) *The Mercantile System and its Historical Significance*, Macmillan.

Harold Schneider (1974) *Economic Man: The Anthropology of Economics*, Free Press.

Erica Schoenberger (2008) 'The Origins of the Market Economy: State Power, Territorial Control, and Modes of War Fighting', *Comparative Studies in Society and History*, 50(3).

Joseph Schumpeter (1908) *Das Wesen und der Hauptinhalt der theoretischen Nationalökonomie*, Duncker and Humblot.

―――― (1951 [1919]) 'The Sociology of Imperialism,' in Joseph Schumpeter, *Imperialism and Social Classes*, Meridian Books.

―――― (1954) *Capitalism, Socialism, Democracy*, Unwin University Books.

―――― (1986) *History of Economic Analysis*, Allen and Unwin.

Alan Scott (2000) 'The Privatization of the State: The British Experience', in Kari Polanyi-Levitt, ed., *Karl Polanyi in Vienna: The Contemporary Significance of The Great Transformation*, Black Rose.

Allen Morris Sievers (1949) *Has Market Capitalism Collapsed? A Critique of Karl Polanyi's New Economics*, Columbia University Press.

Beverly Silver (2003) *Forces of Labor: Workers' Movements and Globalization since 1870*, Cambridge University Press.

Morris Silver (1983) 'Karl Polanyi and Markets in the Ancient Near East: The Challenge of the Evidence', *Journal of Economic History*, XLIII(4).

Georg Simmel (1903) 'The Metropolis and Mental Life', www.gsz.hu-berlin.de/dokumente/georg_simmel-the_metropolis_and_mental_life.pdf, accessed 29 August 2009.

Adam Smith (1993) *An Inquiry Into the Nature and Causes of the Wealth of Nations*, Oxford University Press.

A. M. Snodgrass (1983) 'Heavy Freight in Archaic Greece', in Keith Hopkins, Peter Garnsey and C. R. Whittaker, eds, *Trade in the Ancient Economy*, Chatto and Windus.

Bódog [Felix] Somló (1909) *Der Güterverkehr in der Urgesellschaft*, Misch and Thron.

George Soros (1998) *The Crisis of Global Capitalism: Open Society Endangered*, Little, Brown.

Martin Sorrell (2009) 'The Pendulum Will Swing Back', www.ft.com/cms, accessed 18 April 2009.

Peter Stalker (2000) *Workers Without Frontiers: The Impact of Globalization on International Migration*, Lynne Riener.

Ron Stanfield (1986) *The Economic Thought of Karl Polanyi: Lives and Livelihood*, Palgrave.

G. E. M. de Ste Croix (2004) *Athenian Democratic Origins, and Other Essays*, Oxford University Press.

Philippe Steiner (2009) 'Who is Right about the Modern Economy: Polanyi, Zelizer, or Both?', *Theory and Society*, 38.

Piotr Steinkeller (2002) 'Money-Lending Practices in Ur III Babylonia: The Issue of Economic Motivation', in Michael Hudson and Marc van de Mieroop, eds, *Debt and Economic Renewal in the Ancient Near East*, CDL Press.

Nicholas Stern (2007) *The Economics of Climate Change*, Cambridge University Press.

Joseph Stiglitz (2001) 'Foreword', in Karl Polanyi, *The Great Transformation*, Beacon Press.

James Stodder (2002) 'Human Computability and the Institutions of Exchange: Polanyi's Models', in Fikret Adaman and Pat Devine, eds, *Economy and Society: Money, Capitalism and Transition*, Black Rose.

Wolfgang Streeck (1999) 'Beneficial Constraints: On the Economic Limits of Rational Voluntarism', in J. Rogers Hollingsworth and Robert Boyer, eds, *Contemporary Capitalism: The Embeddedness of Institutions*, Cambridge University Press.

Tim Stroshane (1997) 'The Second Contradiction of Capitalism and Karl Polanyi's *The Great Transformation*', *Capitalism, Nature, Socialism*, 8(3).

Robert Sugden (1986) 'Labour, Property and the Morality of Markets', in B. L. Anderson and A. J. H. Latham, eds, *The Market in History*, Croom Helm.

Ivan Szelényi (1991) 'Karl Polanyi and the Theory of a Socialist Mixed Economy', in Marguerite Mendell and Daniel Salée, eds, *The Legacy of Karl Polanyi: Market, State and Society at the End of the Twentieth Century*, Macmillan.

David Tandy (1997) *Warriors into Traders: The Power of the Market in Early Greece*, University of California Press.

David Tandy and Walter Neale (1994) 'Karl Polanyi's Distinctive Approach to Social Analysis and the Case of Ancient Greece', in Colin Duncan and David Tandy, eds, *From Political Economy to Anthropology: Situating Economic Life in Past Societies*, Black Rose.

Richard Tawney (1929) 'Preface', in Raymond Firth, *Primitive Economics of the New Zealand Maori*, Routledge.

—— (1938 [1922]) *Religion and the Rise of Capitalism*, Penguin.

Göran Therborn (1976) *Science, Class and Society: On the Formation of Sociology and Historical Materialism*, New Left Books.

Edward Thompson (1991 [1963]) *The Making of the English Working Class*, Penguin.

Richard Thurnwald (1932a) *Economics in Primitive Communities*, Oxford University Press.

—— (1932b) *Die menschliche Gesellschaft*, Vol. 3: *Werden, Wandel und Gestaltung der Wirtschaft*, Walter de Gruyter.

Ferdinand Tönnies (1974 [1921]) *Karl Marx: His Life and Teaching*, Michigan State University Press.

—— (2005 [1934–5]) 'Vorrede zur achten Auflage', in Brigitte Zander-Lüllwitz and Jürgen Zander, eds, *Nachgelassene Schriften 1919–1936*, Walter de Gruyter.

Leon Trotsky (1934) *Nationalism and Economic Life*, www.marxists.org/archive/trotsky/1934/xx/nationalism.htm, accessed 7 May 2009.

Lucette Valenis (1981) 'Economic Anthropology and History: The Work of Karl Polanyi', *Research in Economic Anthropology*, 4.

Klaas Veenhof (1977) 'Some Social Effects of Old Assyrian Trade', in J. D. Hawkins, ed., *Trade in the Ancient Near East: Papers Presented to the XXIII Rencontre Assyriologique Internationale, University of Birmingham*, British School of Archaeology in Iraq.

—— (1995) 'Kanesh: An Assyrian Colony in Anatolia', in Jack Sasson, ed., *Civilizations of the Ancient Near East*, Hendrickson.

Joachim Voss (1987) 'The Politics of Pork and the Rituals of Rice', in John Clammer, ed., *Beyond the New Economic Anthropology*, St Martin's Press.

Sofia Voutsaki and John Killen, eds (2001) *Economy and Politics in the Mycenaean Palace States*, Supplementary Volume No. 27, Cambridge Philological Society.

Derek Wall (2005) *Babylon and Beyond: The Economics of Anti-Capitalist, Anti-Globalist and Radical Green Movements*, Pluto.

William Waller and Ann Jennings (1991) 'A Feminist Institutionalist Reconsideration of Karl Polanyi', *Journal of Economic Issues*, 25.

Matthew Watson (2005) *Foundations of International Political Economy*, Palgrave.

Max Weber (1947) *The Theory of Social and Economic Organization*, Free Press.

—— (1976 [1896/1909]) *The Agrarian Sociology of Ancient Civilizations*, New Left Books.

—— (1981 [1923]) *General Economic History*, Transaction.

Felix Weil (1925) 'Gildensozialistische Rechnungslegung: Kritische Bemerkungen zu Karl Polanyi's "Sozialistischer Rechnungslegung"', *Archiv für Sozialwissenschaft und Sozialpolitik*, 52(1).

Jonathan Wiener (1982) 'Max Weber's Marxism: Theory and Method in the *Agrarian Sociology of Ancient Civilizations*', *Theory and Society*, 11(3).

Richard Wilk (1996) *Economies and Cultures: Foundations of Economic Anthropology*, Westview Press.

Richard Wilkinson (2000) *Mind the Gap: Hierarchies, Health and Human Evolution*, Weidenfeld and Nicolson.

—— (2005) *The Impact of Inequality: How To Make Sick Societies Healthier*, Routledge.

Richard Wilkinson and Kate Pickett (2009) *The Spirit Level: Why More Equal Societies Almost Always Do Better*, Allen Lane.

Colin Williams (2005) *A Commodified World? Mapping the Limits of Capitalism*, Zed.

Martin Wolf (2009) 'Seeds of its Own Destruction', *Financial Times*, 8 March.

Donald Worster (1993) *The Wealth of Nature: Environmental History and the Ecological Imagination*, Oxford University Press.

Carlo Zaccagnini (1977) 'The Merchant at Nuzi', in J. D. Hawkins, ed., *Trade in the Ancient Near East: Papers Presented to the XXIII Rencontre Assyriologique Internationale, University of Birmingham*, British School of Archaeology in Iraq.

Allen Zagarell (1986) 'Trade, Women, Class, and Society in Ancient Western Asia', *Current Anthropology*, 27(5).

Viviana Zelizer (1994) *The Social Meaning of Money*, Basic Books.

Slavoj Žižek (2008) 'Use Your Illusions', *London Review of Books*, 14 November.

Index